ATTITUDES AND ATTITUDE CHANGE

Attitudes have been a central topic in social psychology from its early beginnings. But what exactly are attitudes, where do they come from and how can they be modified? The overall aim of *Attitudes and Attitude Change* is to provide students with a comprehensive and accessible introduction to these basic issues in the psychological study of attitudes.

This completely revised and updated second edition covers many recent developments and reports cutting-edge research while also addressing the classic findings and theories that advanced the field. In four parts, readers learn about how attitudes can be measured, how attitudes are shaped in the course of life, how they are changed by other people, and finally, how attitudes in turn affect our thoughts and behaviour. In addition to integrating the new topics emerged from the rise of implicit attitude measures, this edition also adds chapters on social influence and resistance to persuasion.

This comprehensive and user-friendly book carefully balances theoretical underpinnings and empirical findings with applied examples to enable readers to use the insights of attitude research for practical applications. Critical discussions also instigate readers to develop their own thinking on key topics.

Tobias Vogel is a psychologist primarily interested in the questions of what, how and why. His research focuses on social cognition with an emphasis on judgement, decision making and evaluation. After his dissertation on persuasion, he studied and taught social and consumer psychology in Germany and Switzerland. He currently works as a research fellow at the University of Mannheim, Germany, and blogs about psychological phenomena of public interest.

Michaela Wänke has interests in various fields of social cognition and the intersections of social cognition and consumer and political psychology. Her research areas include persuasion, fluency, social judgement and attitude measuring, among many other topics. She held a chair for social psychology at the University of Basel, Switzerland, from 2002 to 2011 and currently holds a chair for consumer and economic psychology at the University of Mannheim, Germany.

ATTITUDES AND ATTITUDE CHANGE

Second edition

TOBIAS VOGEL AND
MICHAELA WÄNKE

Routledge
Taylor & Francis Group

LONDON AND NEW YORK

Second edition published 2016
by Routledge
2 Park Square, Milton Park, Abingdon, Oxon OX14 4RN

and by Routledge
711 Third Avenue, New York, NY 10017

Routledge is an imprint of the Taylor & Francis Group, an informa business

First edition published by Psychology Press 2002

British Library Cataloguing in Publication Data
A catalogue record for this book is available from the British Library

Library of Congress Cataloging in Publication Data
Names: Vogel, Tobias K., author. | Wänke, Michaela, author. | Bohner, Gerd,
1959– Attitudes and attitude change.
Title: Attitudes and attitude change / by Tobias Vogel and Michaela Wèanke.
Description: 2nd Edition. | New York : Routledge, 2016. | Revised edition of
Attitudes and attitude change, 2002. | Includes bibliographical references
and index.
Identifiers: LCCN 2015040378| ISBN 9781841696737 (hb : alk. paper) |
ISBN 9781841696744 (pb : alk. paper) | ISBN 9781315754185 (ebk)
Subjects: LCSH: Attitude (Psychology) | Attitude change.
Classification: LCC BF327 .V64 2016 | DDC 152.4—dc23
LC record available at http://lccn.loc.gov/2015040378

ISBN: 978-1-84169-673-7 (hbk)
ISBN: 978-1-84169-674-4 (pbk)
ISBN: 978-1-315-75418-5 (ebk)

Typeset in Giovanni Book, Bookman and Helvetica Neue
by Florence Production Ltd, Stoodleigh, Devon, UK
Printed in Great Britain by
Ashford Colour Press Ltd, Gosport, Hants

MIX
Paper from
responsible sources
FSC
www.fsc.org   FSC® C011748

Contents

PROLOGUE

The history of this book dates back to the mid-1990s when Gerd Bohner and Michaela Wänke committed themselves to the first edition. It took a while but ultimately, in 2002, this book's predecessor came to light. The first years of the new millennium, however, were particularly productive for attitude research and soon an update seemed in order. By the time this project was seriously tackled, a host of new perspectives, methods, models and studies had accumulated and although we critically discarded and condensed previous material, the book inevitably increased in volume.

Perhaps the most striking development in attitude research has been triggered by the advance of indirect measurement techniques, in particular the so-called implicit measures. Whereas in the previous edition these measures took up only a paragraph in the measurement chapter, a whole new chapter is now devoted to these methodological issues. But more importantly, these measures substantially changed how we conceive of attitudes and this is reflected throughout the book. We cover new models that were built on the distinction of implicit and explicit attitudes and related properties, and also considerably extended the chapter on the relation of attitudes and behaviour. In fact, what was formerly one chapter is now two.

We also substantially extended the review on evaluative conditioning, which has become a major topic in attitude research in recent years. Furthermore, the new edition features two entirely new chapters, one on social influence and one on resistance to persuasion. Although what these chapters cover is not necessarily new, we realised that these topics had been missing previously.

Needless to say, the format and the space did not allow, nor did we want to incorporate each and every aspect of attitude research. Our aim was to provide an up-to-date and accessible textbook for an advanced under-graduate course on attitudes that can also be used for background reading – complemented with selected reading assignments – for a course at the master's level. To this end, we tried to cover all major aspects, as well as historical developments, current debates and applied implications. We strived to back up the conceptual issues by describing the relevant studies in detail as we believe that a more concrete and vivid representation helps learning and understanding. Although we made a considerable effort to include most recent developments, we also remained faithful to a feature of the previous book by striking a balance between describing cutting- edge research while ensuring there was still room for the classic studies. To know where something is coming from should not only help to see the bigger picture but also lay the groundwork for students to develop their own ideas. We deliberately refrained from 'selling' a particular perspective – at least intentionally – but strived for a fair description of different positions and to give each of them attention. We tried to hold back our personal opinions and merely point out critical issues, and leave it to the readers to build their own opinion. Hopefully, this will allow for class projects to discuss, refute or extend the respective research and contribute to educating a new generation of critical researchers as well as consumers of research.

Of course, this project would not have been possible without helping hands. Fortunately, the process was supported by many colleagues who provided valuable comments. We are particularly indebted to Pablo Briñol, Bill Crano, Malte Friese, Bertram Gawronski, Jan de Houwer and Mandy Hütter. We would also like to thank Michael Strang, Katharina Adam, Tamsyn Hopkins, Caroline Tremble and Moritz Ingendahl for editing and critical proofreading. Finally, and most prominently, we gratefully acknowledge Gerd Bohner's contribution to the first edition upon which we could build.

We hope that readers will profit from this book and come to understand the psychology of attitudes. Moreover, we hope that readers will even go on to form or strengthen a positive attitude towards this fascinating area of research.

Chapter 1

WHAT IS AN ATTITUDE AND WHY IS IT IMPORTANT?

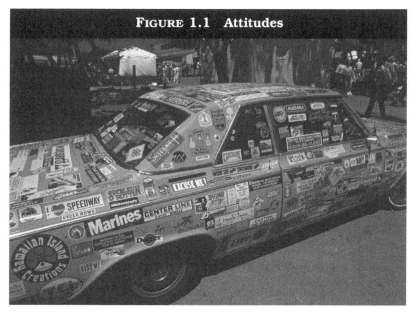

FIGURE 1.1   Attitudes

Note: We not only have attitudes, but we express them. They are a central part of individuality and identity. (Joseph Sohm/Shuttercock.com)

Throughout history, people have fought for freedom of belief, freedom of thought, and freedom of speech. Many examples can be found of people ready to die for their convictions. On the dark side, even today people kill, persecute and inflict suffering because of misguided attitudes based on nationalism, racism or religious fanaticism.

People love and hate, like and dislike, favour and oppose. They agree, disagree, argue, persuade and sometimes even convince each other. Every day, each of us is exposed to countless attempts to change or reinforce our attitudes via personal communication or the mass media. Every day, social scientists and market researchers conduct studies and polls. They report that about three-quarters of EU citizens are in favour of putting pictorial health warnings on cigarette packages (Special Eurobarometer 385, 2012), that more than 70 per cent of people are usually satisfied with their work (Furnham, 1997), that more Americans express that they like rather than dislike blacks (Associated Press, 2012), or that young singles living in urban areas value health aspects and gourmet appeal in convenience food. Such findings in turn provide input for political, organisational or marketing decisions. Moreover, when individual attitudes turn into public opinion, these attitudes determine the social, political and cultural climate in a society, which in turn affects the individual lives of the people in that society. In the 1950s, in an era of more conservative sexual attitudes, unmarried student couples would have faced a very different experience from today had they moved in together. Before the new millennium, homosexual couples were virtually non-existent on TV, because producers shied away from such 'controversial' issues. If you are not convinced yet that attitudes might be an important concept, we have more – and hopefully more convincing – arguments below.

In any case, you may come up with many questions. For example, you may wonder how one can possibly know the views of the average European regarding cigarette on-package warnings. How is it that people have different attitudes? How was it possible that attitudes towards homosexuals changed so dramatically within a relatively short period? Can one really influence attitudes, and if so, how? What are attitudes good for? Will a person who opposes animal testing also act upon her attitude and boycott products involving animal testing? Social psychology has a lot to say about such issues – in fact, much more than we can cover in this book. In our attempt to answer some of these questions we will first provide you with a more formal definition of what attitudes are.

WHAT IS AN ATTITUDE?

We have already provided some examples of attitudes. Sexism, liberalism, love for chocolate or the belief that the Rolling Stones are the greatest rock band ever represent other examples. As different as these are, they all represent an evaluative response towards an object – and this basic statement is a common denominator that emerges from many different definitions in the literature of attitudes. Accordingly, we define an **attitude** as 'a summary evaluation of an object of thought'.

An attitude object can be anything a person discriminates or holds in mind. Attitude objects may be concrete (e.g. pizza) or abstract (e.g. freedom of speech). They may be inanimate things (e.g. sports cars), persons (e.g. your teacher, oneself) or groups (e.g. conservative politicians, foreigners). Attitudes can encompass affective, behavioural and cognitive responses, as

Attitude: Summary evaluation of an object of thought.

Attitude object: This can be anything a person discriminates or holds in mind – e.g. things, persons, groups or abstract ideas.

summarized in the **Tripartite model** of attitudes (Allport, 1935). For example, an environmentalist might strongly believe that air pollution destroys the ozone layer, which increases the risk of cancer (cognitive); she might get angry or sad about the extinction of endangered species (affective); and she might use public transportation rather than a car, and participate in recycling (behavioural). Because it is difficult to separate the different classes of response from each other, and because it is not essential for all three classes to be represented, we have adopted a one-dimensional definition of attitude as a summary evaluation.

Our definition corresponds with the perspective taken by most attitude researchers (cf. Albarracín *et al.*, 2005). One source of debate regarding attitude conceptualisations is whether evaluations have to be stable over a longer time period and have to be stored in the long-term memory to qualify as an attitude. Some definitions characterise attitudes as enduring concepts which are stored in the memory and can be retrieved accordingly (e.g. Allport, 1935; Eagly & Chaiken, 2007, for a classic and a more recent reference). This perspective was termed the **'file-drawer model'** because it perceives attitudes as mental files which individuals consult for the evaluation of the object in question (Wilson *et al.*, 1990). In contrast, other researchers have proposed that attitudes are temporary constructions; according to this **attitudes-as-constructions perspective**, people do not retrieve any previously stored attitude from memory, but instead generate an evaluative judgement at the time it is needed, based on the information that comes to mind in the situation (for reviews, see Schwarz & Bohner, 2001; Wilson & Hodges, 1992).

Both perspectives can draw upon supporting evidence. On one hand, some attitudes – for example, political attitudes (e.g. Marwell *et al.*, 1987; Sears & Funk, 1999) – have been shown to be relatively stable over time. On the other hand, numerous studies have shown that people have different attitudes depending on the context – for example, when they experience different mood states (e.g. Schwarz & Clore, 1983), or when the situation brings different contents to mind (e.g. Tourangeau & Rasinski, 1988), or when faced with different interviewers (e.g. Schuman & Converse, 1971). We will extend this discussion in Chapter 6.

Although the defining variable of attitudes is valence, attitudes may differ in other respects too. Most prominently, attitudes differ regarding their strength (e.g. Abelson, 1988; Bassili, 2008; Petty & Krosnick, 1995). For instance, think of an attitude towards energy conservation in a lay-person and an expert. Both may hold a somewhat positive attitude towards renewable energies. However, the expert's attitude will be based on much more information, and because the attitude is confronted more frequently, it will also spring to mind more quickly. Also, the expert might have a clearer conception about what his or her attitude is. As we will see later (Chapters 10 and 13), **attitude strength** is a meaningful construct that, if taken into account, enables more specific predictions than merely attitude valence (cf. Table 1.1).

Tripartite model: The assumption that affective, cognitive and behavioural responses are independent elements of an attitude.

File-drawer model: A theoretical perspective that characterises attitudes as enduring concepts which are stored in the memory and retrieved when needed for object evaluation.

Attitudes-as-constructions perspective: A theoretical orientation positing that individuals construct evaluative judgements on the basis of chronically and temporally accessible information.

Attitude strength: Reflects the intensity of an individual's feelings or beliefs as manifested in attitude extremity, accessibility, certainty and other indicators.

TABLE 1.1 Indicators of attitude strength	

Indicator of attitude strength	Key question
Accessibility	Upon encounter, how fast does the evaluation of an object come to your mind?
Ambivalence	Do you have both positive and negative thoughts or feelings about the object?
Certainty	Are you sure about how to evaluate the object, or do you have doubts?
Ego-involvement	Is the attitude an important part of your personality?
Extremity	Are you a big fan of the object or do you just like somewhat?
Issue-involvement	Is the topic important to you?
Knowledge base	Is your evaluation based on much knowledge about the object, or just a little?

Note: Summary evaluations of an object are not all alike, but may differ regarding their strength. The table lists some indicators summarised under the umbrella of attitude strength and the key questions to illustrate their meaning. Stronger attitudes are more accessible, extreme, held with higher certainty and less ambivalence. Note that the indicators are correlated, but constitute distinct, separable constructs (e.g. Pomerantz *et al.*, 1995; Raden, 1985). For an illustration, consider different persons, a political scientist and a partisan, both holding strong attitudes towards communism. Both may have highly accessible attitudes held with great certainty. A partisan of the communist party, however, may hold a more extreme attitude and identify with communism (i.e. high ego-involvement). However, the political scientist may hold a less extreme attitude towards communism, but politics is considered an important issue (i.e. high issue-involvement) and there is substantial objective topic knowledge. Further indicators refer to the attitude formation process and an attitude's consequences, and therefore will be dealt with later in this book

Accessibility: The ease with which information (e.g. an attitude) comes to mind.

A particular indicator of attitude strength that has received more attention lately is attitude **accessibility**. It has been proposed that some attitude objects are linked so strongly to an evaluation that the object activates the respective attitude 'automatically'[1] – that is, without effortful or voluntary control (e.g. Fazio, 1990, 2007). Such automatic evaluations typically determine the initial response to an attitude object. However, conflicting thoughts, beliefs and attitudes may override the initial response. For example, your initial reaction to a piece of rich chocolate cake may be 'yummy' (positive), but when you think of the high fat and sugar content your overall evaluation will turn more negative. With such discrepant tendencies, the interesting question is which process – automatic or deliberative – will surface under which conditions and will affect the summary evaluation, as well as further information processing and behaviour. Given that such automatic responses may easily be overridden once deliberate reasoning kicks in, measuring the automatic evaluative responses has proved a challenge. With the advance of such measures (often referred to as implicit attitude measures), which we review in Chapter 3, attitude research entered a new era with the beginning of the millennium. The interplay of spontaneous responses and more deliberative processes in attitude change and implications for attitude-behaviour correspondence are addressed further in Chapters 6, 7 and 13.

WHY DO PEOPLE HAVE ATTITUDES?

Over the years social psychologists have suggested different classes of psychological needs or goals which may be served by holding attitudes. The assumption guiding initial thoughts and research was that in order to change a particular attitude, one needs to know which function it serves. Consequently, researchers who were concerned with prejudice focused on functions possibly underlying prejudice. Other researchers looked at functions relevant to consumer behaviour. Although each theoretical analysis needs to be understood within the specific context in which it evolved, most taxonomies overlap to some extent. We suggest here two main **attitude functions** that can be seen as the essence of different theoretical approaches:

Attitude function:
The purpose that holding an attitude serves for an individual.

a)   serving knowledge organisation and guiding approach and avoidance;
b)   serving higher psychological needs.

Organisation of knowledge, and regulating approach and avoidance

Without an attitude towards an object, a person would be condemned upon each encounter with the object to 'the energy-consuming and sometimes painful process of figuring out de novo how he shall relate himself to it' (Smith *et al.*, 1956, p. 41). Identifying good and bad or categorising the environment into friendly and hostile seems to be the most obvious and essential function, and, not surprisingly, it is part of all analyses of attitude functions. Attitudes provide a simple structure for organising and handling an otherwise complex and ambiguous environment (i.e. **knowledge function**; Katz, 1960). In this sense, attitudes represent **cognitive schemata** (see Bless *et al.*, 2004 for a review of the schema concept in social cognition; see also Chapter 11). Clearly, knowing whether something is good or bad is quite useful when it comes to regulating approach or avoidance. Many researchers proposed a function that serves achieving rewards and avoiding punishments; this function is often referred to as '**utilitarian**'.

Knowledge function:
An attitude's function of providing structure for organising and handling an otherwise complex and ambiguous environment.

Cognitive schema:
A cognitive structure representing an individual's knowledge (including evaluative beliefs) about an object, person, group, situation or event. Schemata are abstractions containing attributes and relationships among attributes of the object.

Utilitarian function:
An attitude's function of maximising rewards and minimising punishment.

Several studies support the notion of attitudes as energy-saving devices. In a choice situation in which people were lacking the opportunity and the motivation to process detailed information about various options, they tended to rely more on their overall attitudes towards the objects (Sanbonmatsu & Fazio, 1990). Moreover, physiological measures show that having accessible attitudes towards two choice options reduces the effort spent on choosing. In one study, (Blascovich *et al.*, 1993), research participants were presented with pairs of abstract paintings and had to indicate within 2.5 seconds which of the two paintings they liked better. In a previous phase, participants in two experimental conditions had already been exposed four times to each of the 30 paintings. In 120 trials, participants of one group had to report how much they liked each painting, in order to render their attitudes more accessible. Participants of another group, who were also exposed four times to each of the paintings, merely had to name the predominant colour. A third group had previously not been exposed to the paintings. The main dependent variables were changes in three measures of autonomic arousal – skin conductance response, pulse transit time and heart rate – during the pairwise preference task compared to a baseline period. Finally, all participants were given ample time to rank-order all 30 paintings from the one they personally liked best to the one they liked least. All three physiological measures indicated lower stress reactions during decision in the attitude-rehearsal condition than in both the colour-naming and the no-task condition, while the latter two conditions did not differ from each other. For example, heart rate did not increase at all compared to baseline for participants who had repeatedly expressed their attitudes, whereas it did increase by about 5 beats per minute for participants in each of the control conditions. Furthermore, for participants in the attitude-rehearsal condition the pairwise preferences were more in line with their final rankings than for participants in each of the control conditions. Taken together, these results indicate that accessible attitudes both facilitate efficient decision-making and reduce the stress experienced during decision-making.

These laboratory findings are complemented by the results of a longitudinal field study (Fazio & Powell, 1997). The participants, first-year college students, completed self-report questionnaires on negative life-events and mental and physical health at two points in time: during their first two weeks on campus (time 1) and again two months later (time 2). At time 1, the accessibility of the students' attitudes towards various academic issues was also assessed; the target issues included specific courses, possible majors, types of classes and academic activities (e.g. studying in the library, talking to a professor after class). The finding was that stressors experienced during the period decreased health status. Importantly, formerly healthy students were less affected by the stressors if their attitudes towards academic matters were highly accessible. Apparently, it is not only quite convenient and effort-saving to have clear knowledge of good and bad, and to have one's attitudes help one deal with the environment, it may also even have health benefits. Presumably, when students had highly accessible attitudes, they could rely on them when making academic decisions, and thereby save energy and avoid stressful mental conflicts. In this respect, accessible attitudes served as a stress buffer. Apparently, 'knowing one's likes and dislikes' (Fazio & Powell, 1997) provides both short-term and long-term benefits. One may speculate, however, that accessible attitudes not only facilitated decisions, but also helped buffering against identity threat – an interpretation that would be in line with attitudes fulfilling higher psychological needs.

Higher psychological needs

As most attitude objects may generally be classified as pleasant or unpleasant, thus representing rewards and punishments, one might suppose that most attitudes would serve a utilitarian function. Yet, a positive attitude towards homosexuality does not necessarily serve for spontaneously approaching homosexual people. Nor is it the function of a positive attitude towards a space programme to join a trip to Mars. Instead, holding or expressing an attitude may also serve an expressive or **symbolic function**.

Some symbolic functions have been labelled 'social identity functions' (Shavitt, 1989). First, some attitudes may be central to a person's self-concept, and by expressing or activating this attitude a person affirms his or her central values (value-expressive function). With this in mind, Prentice and Carlsmith (2000) have likened attitudes to other valued possessions of a person. Second, attitudes may also serve the maintenance of social relationships and allegiance to highly valued social groups – for example, holding or expressing attitudes that are viewed favourably by one's peers (social-adjustive function). Wearing a badge to express your attitude (see also Figure 1.1) or clicking the like-button on Facebook nicely illustrate both of these attitude functions.

Another example for a symbolic function is the maintenance of self-esteem. For example, college students were more likely to wear the varsity colours on campus (presumably presenting themselves as fans) when on the previous weekend their university's sports team had won than they had lost (Cialdini *et al.*, 1976). By identifying with a successful or otherwise attractive target, people aspire to some share of that attractiveness. Such behaviour has been referred to as **basking in reflected glory (BIRG)**. The reverse strategy – i.e. downgrading other persons or groups to boost one's own self-esteem – is also observed. In its early times attitude research was largely inspired by research on prejudice (the usually negative attitude towards a social group); the reduction of fear or inner conflict and the coping with threats to the self were all proposed as a function for prejudice (Katz, 1960). In recent years these ideas have been reinvigorated when looking at a particularly existential threat to the self: death. According to **terror management theory** (Greenberg *et al.*, 1997), knowing about one's mortality has the potential of creating fear or terror in humans. One strategy to cope with this fear is to focus on and enhance those aspects of the self that will remain, such as one's social group or culture. Therefore, positive attitudes towards the in-group and one's cultural values and negative attitudes towards the out-group and other cultures will serve as self-protective for the individual. Indeed, many studies show in-group enhancement and out-group degradation after mortality salience (for a review, see Solomon *et al.*, 2004). However, mortality salience also fosters adherence to cultural values and the culture at large. For example, shortly

Symbolic function: Class of attitude functions that are related to the hedonic consequences of expressing a particular attitude.

Basking in reflected glory (BIRG): Identification with successful others, serving a positive self-evaluation.

Terror management theory: An approach whose central claim is that humans' knowing about their mortality has the potential of creating fear or terror, which people cope with by emphasising their being part of a greater 'immortal' cultural group. Among other things, this may result in prejudice against members of other groups.

before the introduction of the new European currency, the euro, German participants reported generally more positive attitudes towards the mark, their old national currency, than towards the euro, but this difference was much more pronounced when they were interviewed near a cemetery, which presumably had prompted thoughts about mortality (Jonas *et al.*, 2005).

Inter-individual differences and multiple functions

Although some particular classes of attitude objects may correspond more with one particular function than others – for example, political attitudes seem to correspond more to symbolic functions than to utilitarian self-interest (for a review, see Sears & Funk, 1990) – identical attitudes may serve different functions for different people. For example, some women may oppose gender discrimination in job promotions because it decreases their chances of a successful career (utilitarian), whereas other women feel that such practices violate their sense of social justice and equal opportunities (value-expressive). Still others may speak out in order to align themselves with their feminist peers (social-adjustive). People may be prejudiced against a social group because by degrading others they may elevate their own self-esteem (e.g. Tajfel, 1981), they may conform to the norm of their social group, or they may justify existing power differentials within a society (e.g. Jost *et al.*, 2004). And the same attitude may serve different functions for the same person at different times.

Moreover, the same person may hold different attitudes pertaining to different functions at different times. But most likely, all of the functions in our example may play a role, implying that attitudes may be multi-functional. A positive attitude towards classical music, for instance, may facilitate behaviour towards the attitude object, such as attending classical music concerts, but also connecting with people who share the same music preferences. In a similar vein, an **ambivalent attitude** may result from conflicting attitude functions: you may appreciate discussions about organ donation because they express your altruistic values, but dislike these discussions as they are inconvenient and cost time (cf. Wang, 2011, 2012).

Ambivalence: Holding conflicting feelings or beliefs towards one object.

Research applying attitude functions

As mentioned above, research on attitude functions was guided by the assumption that in order to change attitudes a persuasive appeal must be tailored to match the underlying attitude functions (**functional matching hypothesis**). According to this perspective, any attempt to improve the plight of victims of prejudice and extinguish prejudice itself would have to take into account what function being prejudiced fulfils for those who hold the negative views in question. Most data on the functional matching hypothesis have been collected in advertising research. Figure 1.2 provides a real world example of how advertisers may appeal to different attitude functions.

Functional matching hypothesis: Persuasive attempts are considered more effective if they adjust to the prime attitude function of the object and/or the target person.

FIGURE 1.2   Adverts appealing to different attitude functions

FIGURE 1.2A

We built it quartz-accurate to seconds a month. We added a feature never seen before. Then, we made it sing. The Citizen Quartz Analogue Alarm.

Some Citizen designers thought it a pity that even the most elegant analogue alarm watches must have an alarm indicator. Some of our engineers solved the problem. They eliminated the pointer by making the two hands do the work. Having created the world's first indicator-less analogue alarm, they decided the sound of the alarm, too, should be unique. So, instead of a beep, buzz, or inane little tune, the new watch plays a harmonized melody.

The un-disconcerting Alarm.
You're at a place where the sudden sound of a wrist alarm is a minor annoyance: a meeting, say, or a theater. Citizen Quartz Analogue Alarm will remind you of that promised phone call with a melody, soft and harmonious as a clear summer evening.

The point-less pointer.
Pull your watch's crown out one notch. The hands quickly move to

Citizen watches are available the world over.

another setting: the time you last set your alarm. You reset for the new reminder, push the crown back in, and the hands slide right back to show you the present time—with not a second lost. To reset the time, you just pull out the crown another notch.

It doesn't look it.
Citizen Quartz Analogue Alarm flaunts no futuristic shape to tell of

its uniqueness. Citizen quartz technology shows up somewhat in this complex timepiece's extraordinary slenderness. It is simply a fine-looking watch.   And the first.

 **CITIZEN**

Note: These two adverts represent different advertising strategies, which seem to appeal to different functions underlying the recipient s attitude towards watches. The advert in Figure 1.2A appeals to a utilitarian function, the advert in Figure 1.2B appeals to a symbolic function. (© Jeff Morgan 14/Alamy Stock Photo)

FIGURE 1.2B

If you want to wear
the watch that has been worn
by people at the top
since 1904*
wear a Cartier

Box 1.1   Individual differences in attitude functions: the case of self-monitoring

High self-monitors are mainly concerned with fitting well into a social situation, whereas low self-monitors are concerned with their behaviour reflecting their own values. Snyder and DeBono (1985) assumed that for high self-monitors attitudes fulfil a social-adjustive function but not so for low self-monitors. These researchers therefore hypothesised different reactions of these two groups to advertising strategies. They presented both groups with adverts for different products that focused either on the image conveyed by the product or on product quality. For example, a print advert displayed a bottle of whisky resting on a set of house blueprints. In the image version the copy in the whisky advert read 'you're not just moving in, you're moving up'. In the quality version the copy read 'When it comes to great taste everyone draws the same conclusion'. Snyder and DeBono found that high self-monitors were more responsive to adverts that appealed to the images supported by product use than to adverts that focused on the inherent quality of the product. The reverse relationship was found for low self-monitors (cf. Figure 1.3).

FIGURE 1.3   Self-monitoring and attitude functions

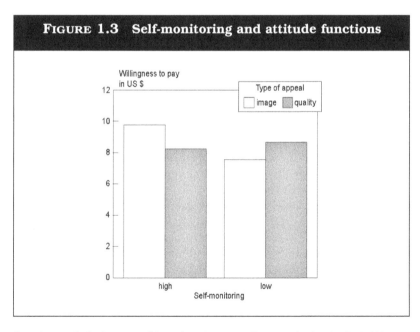

Note: Amount of US dollars that recipients of an advert were willing to pay for the advertised whisky as a function of the advertising strategy and recipients' level of self-monitoring (data from Snyder & DeBono, 1985)

These two adverts represent different advertising strategies, which seem to appeal to different functions underlying the recipient's attitude towards watches.

Although advertising and consumer behaviour prove a prominent field of application, it should also be pointed out that in much of this research it is not always so clear whether it is really the attitude towards an advertised product, or actually having or using the product that fulfils a particular function. Theoretically and empirically the two may be difficult to disentangle and therefore are often treated as the same. If we grant this lack of precision, the matching hypothesis was supported by many studies (for a review, see Maio & Olson, 2000). Some studies used the individual difference measure of **self-monitoring** as an operationalisation for different functions (for a review, see DeBono, 2000); we have described one of these studies in Box 1.1.

Self-monitoring:
An individual difference variable. High self-monitors adjust their behaviour to fit situational cues and the expectations of others, whereas low self-monitors act more in accordance with their internal states and dispositions.

Other studies manipulated the underlying attitude function (Julka & Marsh, 2005; Shavitt, 1990; Shavitt *et al.*, 1994). Julka and Marsh (2005), for example, had their participants either think about their values or made participants feel that they lacked information, before participants received either a value-based or a knowledge-based persuasive message to increase organ donation. Matching appeals were more persuasive and elicited more relevant behaviours (e.g. taking a donor card) than did mismatching appeals.

WHY STUDY ATTITUDES?

No introduction to the psychology of attitudes will fail to include the quote that 'attitudes are probably the most distinctive and indispensable concept in contemporary social psychology' (Allport, 1935, p. 798). Despite some fluctuations in popularity, the attitude construct is still considered as 'probably one of the most important concepts in psychology' (Gawronski & Bodenhausen, 2007, p. 687), and research around it has continuously featured prominently in social psychology throughout the decades. Few texts however explain *why* attitudes are so important (for an exception, see Greenwald, 1989). Why indeed?

Students typically reply that attitudes influence behaviour. Although the relationship between attitudes and behaviour is complex (see Chapters 12 and 13) and not always straightforward, it is most certainly the case that a person's attitude towards a particular attitude object may influence his or her behaviour towards that object. If you like pizza, you will be more likely to order it than a person who is disgusted by the mere thought of pizza.

Attitudes do not only influence behaviour, they also determine how we process information regarding the attitude object (for a review, see Pratkanis, 1989). As we will discuss in more detail in Chapter 11, individuals often search for and select information that confirms their beliefs and attitudes rather than information that may disconfirm them. Moreover, when exposed to information that cannot be avoided, people tend to interpret it in line with their attitudes. In a classic study, Hastorf and Cantril (1954) asked students from two rival universities, Princeton and Dartmouth, to view a film of the Princeton vs. Dartmouth football match and to report the fouls of each team. Although they watched the same film, Princeton students reported more fouls of the Dartmouth team than the Dartmouth students.

That attitudes may influence behaviour and further information processing makes them a prime subject of psychological research. But from a broader perspective the main reason why the concept of attitudes has been central to social psychology since the 1930s is that attitudes play a major role in many things social psychologists study. For example, researchers of person perception are interested in what causes liking, researchers of intergroup relations focus on the topic of prejudice, and researchers of the self rarely fail to include measures of self-esteem (an evaluation of oneself). In addition, findings from attitude research are applied in many different fields such as advertising, politics, health, education and others.

We argue that the concept of attitudes is so pervasive in all areas of social psychology because attitudes are central to our social lives. Imagine yourself during your first week at university. You don't know anybody but bravely strike up a conversation with a fellow classmate. Think of the topics you would address. We bet that soon your conversation will turn to such topics as what kind of music (or films or books, etc.) you like or what you think of university so far. In other words, you will try to find out something about your new acquaintance's attitudes while trying to express yours. As a consequence you will develop an attitude towards that person which may lead you to continue, intensify or discontinue your relationship. People approach and like others whose attitudes are similar to their own (e.g. Byrne, 1971) but they avoid and dislike people who hold different attitudes (e.g. Rosenbaum, 1986). We categorise people according to their attitudes (e.g. as 'conservatives' or 'feminists'; see Hymes, 1986) and infer other attitudes they may hold. For example, we expect conservative people to oppose a woman's right of abortion whereas we expect feminists to endorse it. In turn, by expressing our own attitudes we reaffirm our own identity. And, as we explained above, attitudes may serve other important psychological functions.

In summary, the construct of attitudes seems to be an important mediating link between the social information we perceive in our environment and how we respond to it. Attitudes may determine to a large extent how we react to social stimuli including ourselves, and how we feel, think and act relative to them. The importance of attitudes becomes apparent at various levels of analysis, which are all the subject of social psychological and social research:

- At the *individual level*, attitudes influence perception, thinking, other attitudes and behaviour. Accordingly, attitudes contribute heavily to a person's psychological make-up.

- At the *interpersonal level*, information about attitudes is routinely requested and communicated. If we know others' attitudes, the world becomes a more predictable place. Our own thought and behaviour may be shaped by this knowledge, and we may try to control others' behaviour by changing their attitudes. Moreover, attitudes towards one's own groups and other groups are at the core of intergroup cooperation and conflict. A negative out-group attitude or prejudice (e.g. towards disabled people) can cause discrimination (e.g. refusing to employ them or even direct aggression).
- At the *societal level*, individuals' attitudes contribute to public opinion and shape the values and climate within a society.

In sum, attitudes are a central concept in many topics that social psychologists study. And, perhaps more importantly, by shaping the social world for individuals, groups and societies at large, attitudes are most relevant for everybody's daily life. So read on.

OVERVIEW OF THE BOOK

This volume is supposed to give you an overview of classic and contemporary issues in attitude research, but we will refer you to further reading if you want a more detailed and exhaustive perspective. We divided the topics into four parts: in Part I we will deal with how researchers gain access to attitudes: if we think of attitudes as different degrees of evaluation it becomes obvious that one of the basic topics in attitude research is the measurement of attitudes. Chapter 2 will show you how to measure attitudes via various techniques exploiting self-reports. Given that the role of automaticity has gathered much attention since the last edition of this book (Bohner & Wänke, 2002), in Chapter 3 we will turn to indirect measures, including measures developed to assess the more automatic evaluations.

Part II will deal with the origins of attitudes. Would you guess that attitudes differ depending on whether you are in a good or a bad mood? As you will see in Chapter 4, our attitudes are influenced by our everyday experiences, let them be as small as some incidental affect or body movements such as mimics and gestures. In Chapter 5, we will extend the report on how attitudes are formed by experiences. After reviewing the classic principles of learning, we will phase in the cognitive processes involved in the conditioning of attitudes.

Some theorists view attitudes not as enduring concepts which are stored in memory but as malleable. Accordingly, the information at hand in a given situation will influence the formation of attitudes, an issue we will discuss in Chapter 6. We will outline how context provides the building blocks of evaluative judgements and determines their valence. If you wonder how the building blocks of an attitude are integrated to form a sound attitude, Chapter 7 will provide you with some answers. Logical reasoning is part of human nature, and as a consequence, humans shape their attitudes in order to hold logically consistent attitude structures. Of course, individuals do not always shape their attitudes on their own. Social agents – mass media, parents or friends – have an interest in manipulating what you like and dislike. Similarly, you are often interested in changing other' attitudes, too. Part III of this book will deal with this fascinating topic, termed 'persuasion'. We will review several classic approaches to persuasion in Chapter 8, then in Chapter 9 turn to how attitudes are affected by the attitudes held by our peers. In Chapter 10, we then focus on forces that work against being persuaded – that is, when and why individuals are resistant to attitude change.

In Part IV we will address the influence of attitudes on how people interact with their environment: how they process information about the social world (Chapter 11) and, last but not least, how they behave (Chapters 12 and 13). You will see, among other issues, that the specific information about an object that people attend to, and how they interpret it and how they further process it, is all substantially influenced by their attitudes towards that object. Finally, researchers and practitioners alike have been interested in the extent to which people's attitudes guide their overt behaviour. Can we change what people do by changing how they think and feel about an issue? The relationship between attitudes and behaviour is quite complex, and we will discuss some of its boundary conditions.

CHAPTER SUMMARY

1   An attitude represents a summary evaluation of an attitude object. Components of this summary evaluation may be affective, cognitive or behavioural, and may encompass any type of information which holds evaluative implication.

2   Some researchers have conceptualised attitudes as relatively stable and enduring concepts, which are retrieved from memory upon encounter with the attitude object. Alternatively, others conceive of attitudes as being constructed in the respective situation and influenced by information that comes to mind in this particular situation.

3   Attitudes may be automatically elicited evaluative responses or may result from a more effortful integration of information one has about the attitude object.

4   Common to all attitudes is the function of organising and categorising a complex environment. Attitudes may be utilitarian insofar as people hold positive attitudes towards objects that promise benefits or rewards and negative attitudes towards objects that are associated with costs or punishment. Attitudes may serve higher psychological needs such as the expression of values, social adjustment, the reduction of threat to the self or the reduction of inner conflict.

5   The same attitude may serve different functions for different people. The same attitude may serve different functions for the same person at different times. And, of course, the same person may hold different

attitudes pertaining to different functions at different times. Most attitudes serve multiple functions.

6   Attitudes are central in social psychology because they influence behaviour (their own and others'; see Chapters 12 and 13), they influence information processing (see Chapter 11), they influence social encounters and they form part of a person's self-concept.

7   Different forms of attitudes are the topic of central research areas in the social sciences and in social psychology – e.g. prejudice and stereotyping, values, self-esteem.

Exercises

1   Make a list of as many attitudes of yours you can think of. Can you find some order? Are some related, are some part of a hierarchy, etc.? Are there some you hold with more certainty or conviction than others? Are some more important to you than others?

2   Try to think of how you got those attitudes. This is a preparation for Part II of this volume.

3   List behaviours of yours that are consistent and those that are inconsistent with the attitudes you described in the previous exercise. Identify reasons why your behaviours are sometimes incongruent with your attitudes. This will lead you to Chapter 7.

4   Think of some examples of how you are affected by other people's (e.g. your parents', friends') attitudes.

5   Think of different attitudes of yours and try to analyse their main function.

6   Thumb through a magazine and try to explain which attitudinal function(s) various adverts address. Which ones seem most appealing to you and why?

Further reading

Definition of the attitude concept:

Eagly, A. H. & Chaiken, S. (1993). *The Psychology of Attitudes*. Fort Worth, TX: Harcourt Brace Jovanovich (Chapter 1).

Why study attitudes:

Greenwald, A. (1989). Why are attitudes important? In A. R. Pratkanis, S. J. Breckler & A. G. Greenwald (eds), *Attitude Structure and Function* (pp. 429–440). Hillsdale, NJ: Erlbaum.

Attitude functions:

Maio, G. R. & Olson, J. M. (eds) (2000). *Why We Evaluate*. Mahwah, NJ: Erlbaum.

Shavitt, S. & Nelson, M. (2001). The role of attitude functions in persuasion and social judgment. In J. P. Dillard & M. Pfau (eds), *The Persuasion Handbook: Theory and Practice* (pp. 137–153). Thousand Oaks, CA: Sage.

Solomon, S., Greenberg, J. & Pyszczynski, T. (2004). The cultural animal: 20 years of terror management research. In Greenberg, J., Koole, S. L. & Pyszczynski, T. (eds), *Handbook of Experimental Existential Psychology* (pp. 13–34). New York: Guilford.

Note

1   Social psychologists use the term 'automatic' for cognitive processes that occur without intention, are efficient in the sense that they do not take up much cognitive capacity, often occur outside of awareness and are difficult to control for the individual (e.g. Bargh, 1994). Central to the concept of automatic attitudes as proposed by Fazio (1995, 2007), an evaluative response is inevitably elicited upon encounter of the attitude object.

Part *I*

Gateways to our attitudes

Many different techniques have been developed in order to assess attitudes. Some are widely used, while others apply only for special purposes, but they all have their strengths and weaknesses. Probably the easiest way is to simply ask a person directly. Not surprisingly, such **direct measuring techniques** are most commonly used in both academic and applied research. You may have experienced this yourself when answering a questionnaire on consumer satisfaction or evaluating your university courses. As easy as this may seem, there are many issues involved in this kind of measurement. In Chapter 2, we therefore introduce the fundamental concepts of measurement that guide the construction and use of attitude measures.

As an alternative to direct questions, attitudes may be inferred indirectly from other cues. In such cases, the person does not have to retrieve or construct the attitude and then report it, but it is assumed that the attitude influences the person's verbal or behavioural response and can therefore be inferred from that response. One advantage of **indirect measurement** is that the person may not even be aware that her attitudes are under assessment, so even those attitudes that a person is not willing to reveal honestly can be assessed. A second advantage is that indirect measurement is suitable for assessing more spontaneous and less elaborated attitudes. Recent years have seen a boost of indirect attitude measures, mostly in the context of so called *implicit attitude measures*. We will introduce several techniques and discuss the advantages and problems of indirect measures in Chapter 3. We will also discuss the concept of implicit attitude measures and how they relate to indirect measures.

Direct measuring techniques:
Respondents are asked to evaluate the attitude object. It is assumed that attitudes can be retrieved via introspection.

Indirect measuring techniques:
Measurements exploiting that attitudes can be inferred from behaviours other than the evaluation of the attitude object.

Chapter **2**

ASKING FOR ATTITUDES: NOT THAT SIMPLE AFTER ALL

THE CONCEPT OF MEASUREMENT

When we speak of 'measurement', we mean the assignment of numbers to objects according to rules (Stevens, 1946) in such a way that properties of the numbers reflect certain relations of the objects to each other. There are several levels of measurement, which are characterised by different amounts of information about the relation between objects that are reflected in the numbers assigned (see Table 2.1). At the lowest level are *nominal scales*; their numbers reflect only equality versus difference with respect to the property being measured.

Of course, we would not usually be content with simply knowing if two individuals' attitudes are the same or different. We might also want to know how people compare along a continuum of evaluation: whose attitude is more favourable and whose is less favourable? This is achieved by an *ordinal scale*, where the numbers assigned also reflect the ordering of objects with respect to the property being measured. However, these numbers alone would not tell us whether the differences between the ranks are large or small. The representation of the amount of difference is achieved by the next level of measurement: an *interval scale*. Here, in addition to the properties of an ordinal scale, the relative differences between scores represent the relative differences between the objects measured with respect to the measured property. The highest level of measurement is a *ratio scale*. It has all the properties of an interval scale and in addition it has a meaningful zero point. As a consequence, it allows for the representation of ratios between the scores themselves. Attitude measures rarely achieve this scale level. It just does not make much sense to say that Person A's attitude is several times as positive as Person B's attitude. Whereas we can say that Peter attended twice as many Manchester United matches as Tom, we can hardly say that Peter's attitude towards the club is twice as positive.

TABLE 2.1   Levels of measurement

Scale level	Examples with regard to attitudes	Relations represented		Permissible scale transformations[a]
Nominal	Soccer club fans: ManU = 1; Arsenal = 2; Chelsea = 3	= ≠Objects sharing the same number share their soccer club Objects with different numbers are fans of different soccer clubs	Peter = 1 (is a ManU fan) Sarah = 2 (is an Arsenal fan)	Any that leave equality and inequality of scores intact
Ordinal	Pro-abortion = 3, indifferent = 2, anti-abortion = 1	= ≠ < > Objects with lower numbers are favouring abortion less than objects with higher numbers	Saskia = 2; Claire = 3; Ellen = 1. Saskia favours abortion less than Claire does, but more than Ellen does	Any that leave order of scores intact
Interval	Favouring abortion (1 = not at all; 11 = highly)	As ordinal, plus:ratio between differences among scores; higher differences between numbers represent larger differences in attitudes	Saskia = 6; Claire = 5; Ellen = 3. The difference between Claire's and Ellen's attitudes is twice as large as the difference between Saskia's and Claire's	Any positive linear transformation: $y' = by + a$
Ratio	Frequency of target behaviour	As interval, plus: ratio between scores	Peter goes to twice as many Man U matches as Tom	Any positive multiplicative transformation[a]: $y' = by$

Note: a y' = new scale value; y = old scale value; b = any positive real number; a = any real number

Indeed, attitude researchers are usually content with scales that approximate the interval level of measurement – i.e. scales that have reasonably equal intervals between adjacent scale points but typically lack a meaningful zero point. These allow for the computation of arithmetic means and correlations and most of the statistical operations psychologists use in analysing data (for a more extensive discussion, see Himmelfarb, 1993).

HOW DO WE KNOW IF THE MEASUREMENT IS GOOD?

Independent of whether attitudes are measured directly or indirectly, a good instrument should be reliable and valid. By **reliability** we mean that it should measure consistently whatever it measures, and by **validity** we mean that it should measure the attitude it is designed to measure, rather than something else. Before we turn to particular measures, let us start with a closer look at the general logic underlying the concept of measurement and the criteria of good measures.

> **Reliability:** The extent to which a measure assesses a construct consistently.

Whichever scale we use, like any measured variable, an attitude score is influenced not only by the construct of interest, but also by other factors (see Himmelfarb, 1993). On one hand, there are influences known as **random error**, which can be thought of as chance fluctuations in measurement. Sources of random error include participants' misreading or misinterpretation of questions, measurement at different times of day, coding errors in the process of entering data into a computer file, and many others.

> **Validity:** The extent to which a measure assesses the construct it is supposed to assess.

> **Random error:** Chance variations in measurement; a threat to reliability.

On the other hand, the attitude score may be influenced by other constructs that are not part of the attitude construct to be measured. As this type of influence can systematically increase or decrease the attitude score, it is called **systematic error**. For example, if respondents assume that the experimenter expects positive evaluations from them and then answer attitude items accordingly to please the experimenter, their attitude scores partly reflect the respondents' motivation to comply, rather than their attitude.

> **Systematic error:** The extent to which a measurement is consistently influenced by constructs other than the one that is intended to be measured; a threat to construct validity.

Two criteria for good measurement are related to the degree to which these two sources of error are avoided. The reliability of an attitude measure is high to the extent that attitude measurement is free from random error; in other words, a reliable scale measures consistently whatever it measures. Construct validity is said to be high when measurement is free from both random and systematic error; in other words, a construct valid procedure measures consistently the attitude it is designed to measure (and not something else). The association of random and systematic error with an attitude measure's reliability and construct validity is illustrated in Figure 2.1.

Reliability

One way of assessing a scale's reliability is by computing its *test–retest reliability*, which is the extent to which scores assessed at two different points in time correlate with each other. But with regard to attitudes, low test–retest correlations can sometimes reflect a change in the attitude rather than a problem of the measurement scale. For these reasons, more popular indices of reliability are based on a scale's *internal consistency*. Internal consistency is the degree to which the items of a scale correlate with each other and thus reflect the attitude construct of interest rather than random error. It can be assessed by correlating the score on one half of a scale's items

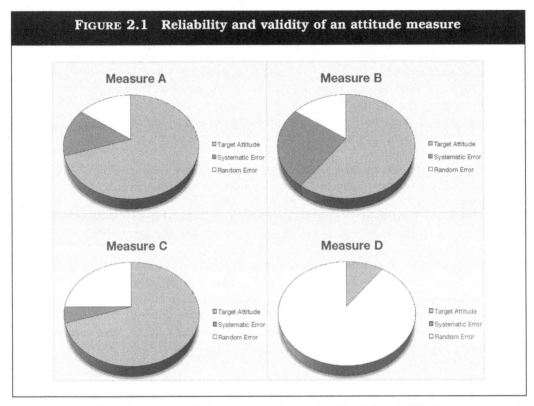

FIGURE 2.1   Reliability and validity of an attitude measure

Note: The constructs affecting the score on an attitude measure and their association with reliability and validity: the grey area represents the reliable proportion, but the white area represents the random error. Measures A and B have a small random error. The reliable proportion, however, is further split up into a valid part (i.e. the target attitude) and some systematic error. Though reliability is high in both cases, measure B is less construct valid due to higher systematic error. Measure C has smaller reliability than A and B, yet it is as construct valid as is Measure A because systematic error is small. Finally, as measure D is not very reliable, it cannot be very valid, even if there is no systematic error. This shows that validity cannot be higher than the reliability

Cronbach's alpha:
A popular coefficient of reliability based on the intercorrelations of items.

with the score on the other half, the resulting coefficient being known as the *split-half reliability*. As any scale can be split into halves in different ways, split-half reliability varies somewhat according to the particular split being made. This problem is avoided by the most widely used index of internal consistency, **Cronbach's alpha**, which can be thought of as the mean of all possible split-half coefficients (Cronbach, 1951). All else being equal, reliability can be enhanced by using a sufficiently large number of items to measure an attitude.

Validity

Obviously, an instrument that fluctuates in precision is not very useful. Imagine your watch being fast on some days and slow on others: you would have difficulty ever being on time. Now imagine you own a highly reliable precision watch but because you have set it incorrectly, it still does not show the correct time. Although its measurement is highly reliable, it is not valid. Thus, reliability is a prerequisite of validity but not vice versa (see Figure 2.1). Once high reliability is established, a researcher should therefore be concerned with optimising construct validity. Again, there are various ways of assessing and improving this criterion. Two facets of construct validity are *convergent* and *discriminant validity*. These are high to the extent that attitude scores are closely related to scores from other scales designed to measure the same attitude and are unrelated to measures designed to assess different constructs. So far this sounds easy. The problem is, however, that there are many ways to interpret low correlations between different measures. For example, in a study on attitudes towards minority group members, you might have administered two scales: in addition to some straightforward prejudice items, another scale may have asked for prejudice in a more subtle manner (e.g. Pettigrew & Meertens, 1995). Weak correlations between the two instruments could be seen as an indicator for poor validity of the subtle measure, if one assumes that the blatant prejudice scale is valid. Alternatively, the subtle prejudice scale could be interpreted as the unbiased attitude whereas the blatant prejudice scale may reflect some distortion. Third, one may conceive of attitudes as multidimensional constructs of which every measure only reflects a part, therefore not correlating strongly (Cook & Selltiz, 1964). If so, a multimethod approach is required to fully capture an attitude. Finally, it has been suggested that multiple attitudes towards the same target may exist and therefore low correlations of different measures are not surprising (e.g. Wilson *et al.*, 2000). We will return to this complexity when we discuss indirect measures in Chapter 3.

Often, validity is assessed with respect to an external criterion thought to be theoretically related to the construct of interest. For example, if a theory posits that attitudes guide behaviour, then measures of attitude should be good predictors of behavioural measures (see Chapters 12 and 13), which would reflect their *predictive* or *criterion validity*.

One particular threat to validity stems from the measuring process itself and is called **reactivity**. First, individuals may intentionally distort their responses when they are aware that their attitude is being measured. Second, even in the absence of motivational distortions, the impact of certain stimuli (e.g. questions) or the social interaction with the interviewer could affect a person's behaviour or verbal statements (see Chapter 5 on how responses of the interviewer, in turn, may affect attitudes).

Reactivity: A change in response (e.g. a reported attitude) brought about by the mere fact that a measurement is taken.

DIRECT MEASUREMENT

Borrowing from a classic taxonomy (Cook & Selltiz, 1964), we define direct measures as self-reports of beliefs, feelings or behaviour towards the attitude object. The main advantage is that asking someone directly for his or her attitude is pretty simple. Most likely, one will get an answer. But how good – or, in technical terms, how valid – is that answer? To what extent does it reflect the person's attitude? The validity of direct measures can be best under-stood within a theoretical framework of the cognitive and communicative processes involved in answering attitude questions. Researchers who were interested in improving survey techniques and data quality have investigated extensively what happens between the question and answer (for a review, see Sudman *et al.*, 1996). These processes apply whenever respondents are faced with attitude questions, whether measurement consists of only one question or of multiple items.

The question–answering processes

What happens when people are asked for their attitude? For example, when a person is asked for an evaluative reaction to strawberries, Barack Obama or educational contributions? Most people will know what strawberries are, and most people will know Obama, but even so, you might wonder whether to react to his politics or to him as a person. And what exactly is an educational contribution? These examples demonstrate that, as a first step, respondents have to interpret the question and decide what they are being asked to report. In the case of strawberries this may not require much thought but a concept will spring to mind automatically from a person's world knowledge. Respondents may further make sense of the meaning of a question by using the context in which it is embedded, even if they have no knowledge whatsoever about the attitude object. Strack *et al.* (1991) asked German students to indicate their attitude towards a (fictitious) 'educational contribution' in two different contexts: in one condition, the preceding question referred to the average tuition fees that US students have to pay; in another condition, the preceding question concerned financial support that the Swedish government pays every student. Strack and his colleagues found that participants' attitudes towards the ominous 'educational contribution' were more favourable in the 'Swedish' than in the 'US' context. Apparently, respondents were more likely to interpret the educational contribution as something students receive (rather than as a fee they have to pay) when the question about financial support for students, rather than the question about tuition fees, preceded it. Such con-textual cues may guide interpretation automatically or because respond-ents deliberately look for them.

Once respondents have identified the attitude object, they will retrieve their attitude towards it provided they had previously formed one and stored it in memory. Or, if they had not 'filed' an evaluation or cannot find it in their mental 'file drawer', they will need to build one on the spot. To do so, they will use the information that comes to mind in the specific situation. Extensive research has shown how such situational information can influ-ence judgements (see Chapter 6), which presents a particular problem for surveys because the specific context created by the measurement may influ-ence the measurement itself. Possible influences can come from the response alternatives or scales provided, the interviewer (if present) or the purpose of the survey, its introduction and literally all other survey elements. The most prominent and best researched influences are those of question order (see Box 2.1).

From the retrieved information respondents will 'compute' a judgement, but the answering process does not end there. Respondents may be unwilling to report these privately computed attitudes and may wish to adjust them – for example, to conform to the social norms they infer in the situation or because of other motives (DeMaio, 1984). Finally, respondents report their judgement, which usually involves accommodating it to certain response alternatives or translating it into a scale value. We present examples of such standardised response formats in the following section. A flowchart of the question–answering process is provided in Figure 2.2 (see also Sudman *et al.*, 1996).

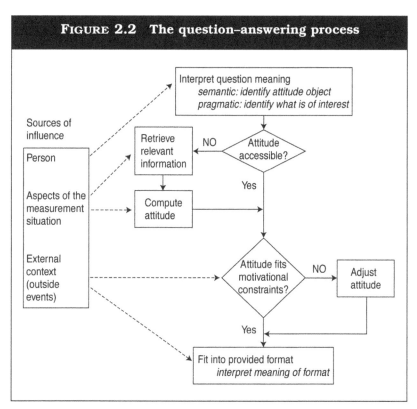

FIGURE 2.2   The question–answering process

Note: Being asked how much you like soccer, you may consider your attitude towards 'playing soccer yourself' or 'watching soccer in TV' (semantic level). The latter would become more likely if the preceding questions asked for your evaluation of different TV shows (pragmatic level). Even if you cannot retrieve an attitude from memory, you may compute an ad hoc evaluation based on external events. You may say that you dislike soccer, if the TV coverage of the world championship replaced your favourite TV show. Or you might be motivated to answer in a certain direction: Knowing that the interviewer loves soccer, you may provide a rather favourable response in order to match with her attitude (also see Chapter 6)

To summarise, the attitudes reported in direct assessments are subject to a number of influences, some of which originate from the measurement process itself. However, a crucial distinction needs to be made. Some effects of measurement reflect motivational distortions of the attitude report, and below and in the next chapter we will address how to deal with this particular aspect of reactivity. The other types of effect, which we discussed in this section, are not errors but reflect processes inherent in the construction of the attitude in question. Depending on the prime goal of the investigation, the researchers may actually be interested in the evaluation of an attitude object within a certain context. When interpreting empirical findings, it is therefore always a good idea to take contextual factors into consideration and to look closely at the methods that were used to measure an attitude (e.g. Schwarz & Bohner, 2001; Schwarz & Sudman, 1992; Wänke, 1997).

Box 2.1   Question order effects in attitude surveys

Research on **question order effects** dates back to the 1930s when Janet Sayre systematically investigated attitudes towards radio advertising (1939) and found that responses to an attitude question differed systematically depending on what question had preceded it. Since then survey researchers have documented a wide range of question order effects (for reviews, see Schuman & Presser, 1981; Schwarz & Sudman, 1992; Tourangeau & Rasinski, 1988). Of course, question order is merely a technical variable and its effects may be due to different psychological processes – namely, how respondents make sense of the question, which information they retrieve for this response, how they interpret the response alternatives or scale values, or what they think is appropriate to report in the situation (for a review, see Wänke & Schwarz, 1997). The following example illustrates how previous questions may affect the information retrieval for constructing the attitude under scrutiny.

In a telephone survey, Tourangeau *et al.* (1989) asked 1,056 Chicago residents about their opinions on increased welfare spending. For about half of the respondents, this question was preceded by four items related to the liberal side of the target issue, which is concerned with government responsibility for the poor – for example, 'Do you agree or disagree: Some people in America really need help from the government'. For the other half of the respondents, the target question was preceded by four questions linked to the conservative side of the issue, which could be labelled 'economic individualism' – for example, 'Do you agree or disagree: In America, any person who is willing to work hard has a good chance of succeeding'.

The context items were selected because they all showed a high ratio of agreement in the population. They were supposed to affect how respondents thought about welfare by rendering specific related beliefs about welfare more accessible (e.g. 'there are many people in need' versus 'people in need are just too lazy to work'). Later, the target question was asked: 'Do you favour or oppose increased spending for welfare programs?' Tourangeau and his colleagues found that the context had a profound influence on responses. In the liberal context, a majority of respondents (61.7 per cent) favoured increased welfare spending, whereas in the conservative context, this was true only of 46.2 per cent.

Question order effect: The response to a question is influenced by the questions asked previously if they bring to mind relevant information that would not have been accessible otherwise.

Instruments for direct attitude measurement

The simplest way to assess a person's attitude is to ask a single question about her general evaluation of the attitude object and to have her mark a response alternative along a numeric response scale. Although multi-item scales are often superior in reliability (e.g. Himmelfarb, 1993; see previous section), **single-item measures** are, in fact, most common in survey research (see above) and are also employed in experimental studies. For instance, Bargh *et al.* (1992) used single items to assess attitudes towards each of a large number of objects. Respondents were instructed to give their personal evaluation of each object listed, for example:

Single-item measure: An attitude measure consisting of a single question or statement.

strawberries

extremely bad –5 –4 –3 –2 –1 0 +1 +2 +3 +4 +5 extremely good.

An obvious advantage of single-item measures is that they are highly economical. The major disadvantage of single-item measures is that their reliability may be low (or at least difficult to assess). Any item score not only reflects the attitude under consideration, but also chance variations in measurement, known as random error. In multi-item scales, greater reliability can be achieved because the final score is computed as the sum or mean of all items, which compensates for random error in any single item. Furthermore, in the construction phase of a multi-item scale, inappropriate items that do not meet certain measurement criteria are eliminated (see next section for detail). Moreover, with complex attitude objects such as euthanasia or prostitution, a single item may not be sufficiently differentiated to cover all the various facets of an attitude. Therefore, it is often preferable to assess attitudes with multi-item scales.

The most widely used multi-item attitude scales are the **semantic differential** (Osgood *et al.*, 1957) and the **Likert Scale** (Likert, 1932). We briefly describe the central properties of these scales (for a more comprehensive treatment of these and other scale types, see Himmelfarb, 1993); some item examples for each scale type are given in Table 2.2.

The semantic differential consists of a list of bipolar adjective scales, usually divided into seven response categories. Respondents rate an attitude object by marking one of the seven categories for each of the bipolar adjective pairs. These ratings are later scored –3 to +3, with positive numbers attached to the positive adjective in each pair. A total attitude score is computed for each respondent by summing or averaging scores across the bipolar scales (see Table 2.2). The original work of Osgood *et al.* (1957) with the semantic differential was aimed at studying the meaning of concepts. In a large number of studies using long lists of adjective pairs and a multitude of concepts, these researchers found that mainly three underlying dimensions or factors accounted for the interrelations of the scales; these were labeled *evaluation* (e.g. 'good–bad'), *potency* (e.g. 'strong–weak')

Semantic differential: A multi-item attitude measure consisting of several bipolar adjective scales.

Likert Scale: A multi-item attitude scale that consists of several evaluative statements about an object or issue. Respondents are asked to express their degree of agreement with each statement along a numerical response scale.

TABLE 2.2   Attitude scales: item examples for common self-report measures

(a) *Semantic differential* on attitudes towards Germans (numbers for scoring are given in parentheses; these are not normally presented to respondents).

Germans

lazy :_____:_____:_____:_____:_____:_____:_____: industrious

(−3)   (−2)   (−1)   (0)   (+1)   (+2)   (+3)

friendly :_____:_____:_____:_____:_____:_____:_____: unfriendly

(+3)   (+2)   (+1)   (0)   (−1)   (−2)   (−3)

(b) *Likert Scale* items assessing sexist attitudes towards women (from the Neosexism Scale; Tougas *et al.*, 1995). Each item is presented with a scale from 1 to 7, with 1 indicating total disagreement and 7 indicating total agreement; items with an asterisk are later reverse-scored.

Discrimination against women in the labour force is no longer a problem in Canada.

I consider the present employment system to be unfair to women.*

It is difficult to work for a female boss.

In order not to appear sexist, many men are inclined to overcompensate women.

In a fair employment system, men and women would be considered equal.*

and *activity* (e.g. 'fast–slow'). The evaluation factor usually explained the largest proportion of variability.[1] Semantic differentials designed to measure attitude (rather than meaning in general) are made up exclusively of items that load on the evaluation dimension (as those items shown in Table 2.2).

Another highly popular scaling technique was developed earlier by Likert (1932). In his method of summated ratings (better known simply as the Likert Scale), respondents indicate the extent of their agreement, usually on a five-point or seven-point scale, with each of several statements pertaining to an attitude object. These have been preselected from a larger pool of statements so that agreement with each item unambiguously implies either a favourable or an unfavourable attitude. Usually, the statements can be characterised as beliefs about the attitude object, but it is also possible to use statements about affective reactions or behaviours towards the attitude object (e.g. Kothandapani, 1971). As with the semantic differential, an attitude score on a Likert Scale is defined as the sum or mean across all items, after reverse-scoring those items on which agreement implies an unfavourable attitude (e.g. items marked with an asterisk in Table 2.2).

Both semantic differentials and Likert Scales are constructed in such a way that each of their items represents an unambiguous evaluation of the attitude object. It is thus usually possible to achieve high internal consistency by summing or averaging scores across all items to derive an overall attitude score. Semantic differentials provide the benefit that identical item sets can be used with different attitude objects, allowing for comparisons between objects (e.g. attitudes towards public transportation may be compared directly with attitudes towards individual traffic). By contrast, Likert Scales need to be constructed specifically for each attitude object or valence and generally require more extensive pilot work. Both types of multi-item scales we discussed have comparable levels of reliability and validity,[2] and accordingly tend to be highly correlated with each other when applied to the same attitude object (e.g. Jaccard *et al.*, 1975; Kothandapani, 1971).

Motivated response distortions and how to deal with them

The structure of an attitude questionnaire, the context of a study, or subtle cues in the experimenter's behaviour might all signal to participants that certain hypotheses are being tested. Participants may then choose to respond to these **demand characteristics** (Orne, 1962) in a fashion that either confirms or disconfirms these hypotheses. They may also engage in **impression management** (Tedeschi, 1981), trying to present themselves favourably or giving a response that seems to meet with social approval (Crowne & Marlowe, 1964) rather than responding truthfully. To reduce such motivated biases, researchers have proposed strategies that range from temporarily misinforming participants about the purpose of a study to asking for their cooperation by emphasising the importance of truthful responses (Aronson *et al.*, 1990; Rosenthal & Rosnow, 1991).

Demand characteristics: Cues in a research setting that participants may use to infer how they are expected to respond or behave.

One strategy of controlling for distortions is to administer other self-report scales that measure tendencies of socially desirable responding (e.g. Crowne & Marlowe, 1964; Paulhus, 1998). These scales contain positive statements that are true of hardly anyone and negative statements that are likely to be true for virtually everyone (e.g. 'I have never felt joy over someone else's failure'). Endorsement of the positive statements and rejection of the negative statements are thus interpreted as self-enhancement, a tendency to appear in a favourable light.

Impression management: Actions aiming at being positively viewed by others (e.g. by acting consistent with one's attitudes; by uttering desirable attitudes).

In principle, social desirability scales allow for reducing biases for various enhancement-tendencies, including impression management (i.e. the tendency to present oneself in a favourable manner to others) as well as self-deception (i.e. the denial of negative characteristics that threaten a positive self-view). By correlating an attitude measure with one of these control scales, the extent of response bias can be estimated and controlled for.

The problem with such measures, however, is that the underlying assumptions are not necessarily met. For one thing, the measure has to take for granted that there is common ground about what the normative behaviour actually is. Consider an item asking respondents whether they sometimes broke speed limits. As breaking speed limits is illegal, a person denying that she does so should be regarded as biased. By contrast, assuming that experimenters also break speed limits, the norm during the interview can be a different one. Thus, an adapted respondent might be especially prone to admit the illegal action. Furthermore, the assumption that there is no true variation in the behaviour described is problematic. A person might deny breaking speed limits simply because she does so to a lesser degree than her peers or even does not break speed limits at all. Thus, items might sometimes measure actual traits rather than a response style (e.g. Paulhus, 2001). Assuming that we found a positive correlation between an impression management scale and pro-environmentalist attitudes, it would be wrong to conclude that pro-environmentalist attitude judgements are corrupted by response biases. Instead, pro-environmentalist judgements might be unbiased but reflect the respondents' true conscientiousness.

Bogus pipeline technique: A procedure designed to reduce motivated response distortions in direct attitude measurement. The respondent is hooked up to fake psychophysiological machinery, which purportedly gives the experimenter access to the respondent's true attitudes.

A method aimed at reducing response distortions is the **bogus pipeline technique** (Jones & Sigall, 1971). Participants are asked to report their attitudes while being hooked up to an impressive-looking apparatus. They are made to believe that the apparatus works like a lie detector and are thereby discouraged to distort their attitudes. Although the procedure has been shown to increase the validity of attitude self-reports (see Roese & Jamieson, 1993), it is rarely used because of the complex set-up and cover story it requires.

CONCLUDING COMMENT: IF THE BEST SELF-REPORT IS NOT GOOD ENOUGH

In this chapter, we reported various ideas guiding the constructing of self-report measures. Thus, thoughtful scale construction can pave the way to assessing attitudes in a reliable and valid manner. We have also described various techniques to avoid motivated distortions. Nonetheless, self-reports will still sometimes emerge as biased indicators of the attitudes researchers want to find out. Another way to avoid the problem of motivational distortions is to rely not on self-reports but on indirect measures. We will deal with the fascinating but tricky nature of indirect measures in Chapter 3.

CHAPTER SUMMARY

1   Direct attitude measures may consist of a single item accompanied by a numeric response scale, or of a series of such items.
2   When responding to a direct measurement, the respondent must complete a sequence of steps: interpreting the meaning of the question, retrieving or constructing an evaluation, and translating it into the answer format provided. Prior to reporting, the privately formed judgement may be edited, e.g. to make a favourable impression.

The context of the measurement can influence all steps of the question–answering process and thus can affect the response.

3   Scores on an attitude scale are a function of the attitude studied, but also contain random error (chance fluctuations of measurement) and systematic error (influences by constructs other than the attitude being measured). A scale is reliable to the extent that it is free from random error, and valid to the extent that it is free from both random and systematic error.

4   Common multi-item scales are the semantic differential and the Likert Scale. They are generally higher in reliability than single-item measures, but their construction involves considerable effort. Researchers therefore often resort to measuring attitudes with one or a few items compiled ad hoc.

Exercises

1   Find examples for nominal, ordinal, interval and ratio scales we use in everyday life. Why would you aim for an attitude measure having at least interval scale level?

2   Which of the following statements are true?

   a)   If reliability increases, then construct validity increases.
   b)   If reliability decreases, then construct validity decreases.
   c)   A measure can be reliable without being valid.
   d)   A measure can be valid without being reliable.

3   Think of context effects that might affect a person's evaluation of his/her job. Specifically, what preceding questions might elevate (or lower) responses to a question on work satisfaction?

4   Generate items that could be included in a Likert scale measuring attitudes toward genetically modified food.

5   What external criteria would you use to construct-validate the scale you generated in exercise 4?

Further reading

Technical aspects of measurement, reliability, validity:

Himmelfarb, S. (1993). The measurement of attitudes. In A. H. Eagly & S. Chaiken, *The Psychology of Attitudes* (pp. 23–87). Fort Worth, TX: Harcourt Brace Jovanovich.

Psychological aspects of the question-answering process:

Sudman, S., Bradburn, N. M. & Schwarz, N. (1996). *Thinking About Answers: The Application of Cognitive Processes to Survey Methodology.* San Francisco, CA: Jossey-Bass.

Notes

1   With respect to the definition of an attitude provided in Chapter 1, the first dimension can be considered the attitude.

2   Besides their equality with regard to measuring the *summary* evaluation, semantic differentials make stronger assumptions about the dimensionality of the underlying construct. This may result in information loss. When we ask for an evaluation on a one-dimensional differential from negative to positive, for instance, we would obtain the same response for a person who is indifferent or a person who holds both positive and negative thoughts (i.e. a person who is ambivalent).

Chapter 3

BEYOND ASKING FOR ATTITUDES: FROM INDIRECT MEASURES TO IMPLICIT ATTITUDES

Some attitudes are taboo. A good member of society is neither sexist, nor racist, nor culturally insensitive (e.g. van Boven, 2000). But even so, would anyone imagine that politically incorrect attitudes do not exist at all? For reasons of self-presentation, respondents may not want to admit to attitudes that deviate from what they believe to be the social norm. Perhaps they might even deny them to themselves if these attitudes were likely to threaten their self-image. To avoid problems like this that compromise the validity of self-reports, researchers have devised a plethora of alternative attitude measures hoping to get closer to their respondents' 'real' attitudes. Broadly speaking, the construction of measures avoiding distortions is guided by two principles: a) keeping respondents unaware that their attitudes are being assessed,[1] and b) minimising the respondents' ability to voluntarily influence the measurement outcome. Measures trying to address the first principle are typically based on the non-trivial assumption that respondents who do not realise that their attitudes are being assessed will not be motivated to distort their evaluations. Based on this assumption, researchers have come up with measures which cannot be identified as attitude measures – at least, not intuitively. This is achieved by using indirect measures. In short, we define indirect measurement techniques as any technique that does not involve a self-report of an evaluative response towards the attitude object.

However, what if the researcher was unable to mask the measure's intent and the respondent becomes suspicious that her attitude is being assessed? A second notion guiding the construction of alternative measures, therefore, is to reduce the respondent's ability to voluntarily alter their evaluative response. The idea is to create conditions under which people – even while they are aware that their attitudes are being assessed – cannot fake their attitudinal expression. For instance, participants are sometimes asked to evaluate an object within a very small time window, so it becomes almost impossible for them to align their answer with the social norm that might apply to the situation. The advantage of such measures is that they tap into the less elaborated and more spontaneously accessible attitudes, which is an important requirement for predicting certain behaviours (see Chapter 13).

Either strategy – undermining motivation or undermining capacity for distortions – would be sufficient to avoid desirable responding. Respondents are unlikely to modify their evaluation of an attitude object if they lack the motivation to do so. And of course, they will not modify their response if they lack the knowledge or skills to do so. Often, however, measures are constructed to meet both requirements (a detailed treatise of the requirements for these measures can be found in De Houwer *et al.*, 2009). We will start this chapter by reviewing some classic unobtrusive measures, before turning to some more sophisticated, standardised measures. In the first part of that section, we will deal with measures building on the idea that respondents are unaware that their attitudes are being assessed. We will then turn to measures which (additionally) exploit the fact that some behavioural reactions towards attitude objects are hard to modify.

ASSESSING EVALUATION WITHOUT ASKING FOR IT

For more than half a century, researchers were intrigued by the idea of assessing attitudes without asking for them directly. In the 1960s, various measures emerged, building on the notion that attitudes are evident in many other behaviours besides direct evaluations in an attitudinal survey (Cook & Selltiz, 1964). The majority of these indirect measures exploit the fact that respondents are unaware of what the behaviour that is being recorded reveals about their attitudes. In extreme cases, however, the respondent is unaware that his or her behaviour is recorded at all, an issue we will deal with next.

Attitudes expressed in everyday behaviour

Lost-letter technique: A behavioural measure of attitude that involves leaving addressed letters in public places as if they had been lost, and then recording the return rate and condition of the returned letters. The attitude object studied is reflected in the address printed on the letter.

A truly unreactive method is to infer attitudes from observed real-life behaviour. For example, one might infer a person's prejudice against skinheads by the distance the person chooses to sit apart from a skinhead (Macrae *et al.*, 1994). Many behaviours are related to attitudes and are open to unobtrusive observation – for example, donating money to Amnesty International or throwing away a Greenpeace leaflet may be reasonably interpreted as reflecting attitudes towards these organisations and what they stand for. One of the best known non-reactive behavioural measures of attitude is the **lost-letter technique**. In a classic demonstration of this technique, Milgram and his colleagues (Milgram *et al.*, 1965) dispersed 400 sealed, stamped and addressed envelopes in various public places (shops, pavements, etc.) in a US town. One hundred letters were assigned to each of the following addresses: 'Friends of the Communist Party', 'Friends of the Nazi Party', 'Medical Research Associates' and 'Mr Walter Carnap'. The researchers expected that the prevailing negative attitudes towards extremist political organisations would lead to a reduced return rate for the letters addressed to either the Communist or the Nazi organisation. Their results supported this hypothesis.

An impressive collection of such '**unobtrusive**' techniques of data gathering was presented by Webb *et al.* (1981) in a book that is both scholarly and entertaining. Their compilation includes techniques of un-obtrusive behavioural observation in natural settings, the study of *physical traces* of behaviour and *archival records*. As an example for a physical trace measure, the wear on floor tiles in front of museum exhibits can indicate the exhibits' popularity (Webb *et al.*, 1981, p. 7). Archival records can also yield indicators of attitude: to examine potential preferences for male offspring in families of high socioeconomic status, Winston (1932) obtained from official birth records the sex and birth order of each child. He hypothesised that, in families estimated to be complete, a preference for sons over daughters would be reflected in a larger boy-to-girl ratio among the children born last, compared to the boy-to-girl ratio among all children of these families. Winston's hypothesis was strongly supported.

Undoubtedly, these behavioural measures are highly creative. And as mentioned above, one advantage of behavioural measures is that the person may not even be aware that the behaviour is observed, so these measures are truly non-reactive. However, using real-life behaviours as instances of an attitude, the attitude measure may come very close to the behaviour one actually wants to predict. As long as researchers are not primarily interested in what their respondents like or dislike, but with predicting the specific behaviour (e.g. helping others by posting a lost letter), it might even be unnecessary to infer the attitude at all (see De Houwer *et al.*, 2013).[2] Moreover, the observation of real-life behaviour is often very cumbersome. Spontaneous behaviours are rare – only a few invitees may actually click on a link provided in an e-mail – thus large samples are required. Also, observations often only yield aggregate data. These allow for computing effects at the group level, but it is mostly impossible to calculate effects at the individual level. Finally, outside of the laboratory, potential confounding variables are likely to arise.

Unobtrusive technique: Measure of an attitudinal response whereby the 'respondent' is unaware that the attitudinal response is being recorded.

Attitudes expressed in non-attitudinal judgements

Many of the problems that arise in the study of real-life behaviour can be avoided when using more standardised indirect measures, as is typically the case in laboratory studies. Obviously, the use of standardised measures means that the respondents become aware that their behaviour is being recorded. However, as anticipated above, respondents still do not often have any idea a) that the study is about attitudes or b) which is the particular attitude object under study.

For instance, some tasks are presented initially as an objective performance task. In Hammond's (1948) **error-choice method**, respondents receive forced-choice questions that ostensibly measure knowledge. However, none of the provided response alternatives is factually correct; instead, they deviate from the correct answer in opposite directions. Let's assume that Ford ranked number seven in the current car breakdown statistics for your country. An error-choice item assessing respondents' attitudes towards Ford might read:

Error-choice method: A disguised attitude measure based on forced-choice questions that ostensibly measure knowledge but are in fact designed to infer respondents' attitudes.

In the current car breakdown statistics, Ford ranks . . . (*tick one*):

___ a) position 5

___ b) position 9.

People with positive attitudes towards Ford are expected to over-estimate the car's quality and thus to choose the better alternative, whereas respondents with negative attitudes would be more likely to choose the worse alternative. Note, however, that attitudes towards Ford are just one of a number of factors that might plausibly influence estimates, so that the construct validity of this type of measure may not be particularly high.

That people's attitudes can be inferred from logical reasoning errors was first proposed by Thistlethwaite (1950). He showed that people are more likely to judge logically incorrect reasoning structures to be correct if their content corresponds to their attitudes. This insight was used in constructing an indirect measure of racial attitudes, the Racial Argument Scale, by Saucier and Miller (2003). When presented with a series of arguments that supported positive and negative statements about black people, individuals' racist attitudes were reflected by the extent to which they rated negative arguments towards blacks as supportive of the negative conclusion and by the extent to which they rated positive arguments towards blacks as less supportive of the positive conclusion.

As you may have noted, the preceding methods did not require participants to report an attitude at all. It seems plausible, therefore, that participants in those studies did not come to think that the researchers were interested in their attitudes. However, even measures asking for attitudes can still be indirect as long as they do not require participants to evaluate the attitude object itself (De Houwer *et al.*, 2009). Instead, they involve self-reports of responses towards *other objects* but with the assumption that these responses reflect an attitude towards the target object. When asked to evaluate letters of the alphabet, people tend to prefer those letters that are part of their own name over other letters (Nuttin, 1985). Nuttin suggested that this pattern of preference reflects positive attitudes towards the self, although respondents may not be aware of the name-letter connection.

As noted by De Houwer and colleagues, reporting a liking for one's initial is a direct measure of one's attitude towards the letter but an indirect measure of self-esteem. Yet, and pertinent to avoiding motivational distortions, respondents may not have any clue what attitude object the researcher is interested in. Conceiving the measure as some trivial measure of preferences towards letters, the respondent will see no need to shape the response in a certain manner. Generally speaking, whenever there is a social norm involved in how to evaluate the attitude object (e.g. the respondent might consider it appropriate to express a rather favourable self-evaluation), motivated distortions can be circumvented by asking for an alternative, but somehow related, object for which there is no social norm.

The rationale behind these techniques is that the respondents' feelings and opinions about the target object will be projected on to the object asked for, which is why they are called **projective techniques** (Cook & Selltiz, 1964). Projective techniques usually involve the presentation of unstructured or ambiguous material and the assessment of how individuals interpret these stimuli (Prohansky, 1943). One classic instance of projective attitude assessment is the *shopping list* procedure. In the original study (Haire, 1950), two shopping lists were prepared that were identical but for one item; they contained either 'Maxwell House drip ground coffee' or 'Nescafe instant coffee'. Each list was given to 50 housewives, who were asked to describe what they thought of the woman who had put together that shopping list. Nearly half of the respondents described the Nescafe buyer as lazy and unorganised, whereas only a small minority reported similar thoughts about the woman who bought standard coffee. Haire concluded that these responses revealed negative attitudes towards instant coffee, a novelty at that time.

Often such techniques are cumbersome and their analysis relies on subjective interpretations (e.g. of free associations or descriptions), but that is not necessarily so. Imagine being presented with word fragments and being asked to fill in the missing letter – for example, _INISTER or LO_AL. All fragments can be completed creating either a neutral word (minister, local) or a valenced word (sinister, loyal). With each word a black or a white face is presented. More negative completions for words paired with black faces than with white faces were interpreted as a racial prejudice (Dovidio *et al.*, 1997). Another easily applicable projective technique is to rate another person's behaviour with regard to his or her attitude. Presumably, people's judgement on what these behaviours indicate should be influenced by their own attitude. For example, Mary is described by a number of religious (praying occasionally, watching religious programmes) and non-religious (skipping church for years) behaviours (Vargas *et al.*, 2004). Very religious people will probably see Mary as not so religious because she does not go to church, whereas very non-religious people will see her as religious because of her religious behaviours.

Independent of whether they are easy or cumbersome to conduct, early techniques were frowned upon in academic research because of their

Projective techniques: Family of indirect measures of attitude (and other constructs) that involve the presentation of unstructured or ambiguous material and an assessment of how individuals interpret this material.

allegedly poor psychometric properties (Lemon, 1973). More recently, however, projective techniques have been reinvigorated. Advances at the analytical level promise better psychometric properties (Schnabel & Asendorpf, 2013) and advances at the assessment level even allow for an economic application. In particular, one specific procedure seems to overcome the various shortcomings of previous projective techniques. The *Affect Misattribution Procedure* (AMP; Payne *et al.*, 2005) exploits the finding that current affective states often serve as an indicator of whether we like or dislike what we see (Schwarz & Clore, 1983; see also Chapter 4). In each trial, an attitude object is displayed supraliminally for a short time (e.g. 75 ms) but no response is required. Then, after a small interval (e.g. 125 ms), participants are briefly presented with some affectively neutral Chinese pictograph (e.g. 100 ms) and asked to evaluate it. It is assumed that the target object evokes an affective response which then projects on to the subsequent stimulus. Thus, ratings for the neutral pictographs serve as an indicator of one's attitude towards the object. Due to its good psychometric properties (Payne *et al.*, 2005; Payne *et al.*, 2008), the AMP has become a prominent technique in attitude research. Still, it is not so clear to what extent people are really unaware of the intention behind the AMP. Indeed, many participants say that they intentionally used the prime for evaluating the ambiguous stimuli, and it is for this subsample that the AMP shows the best psychometric properties (Bar-Anan & Nosek, 2012). This suggests that the AMP is sensitive to motivated distortions and that participants motivated to make a certain impression would be able to do so (for a discussion, see Bar-Anan & Nosek, 2013; Payne *et al.*, 2013; Payne & Lundberg, 2014).

Attitudes expressed in involuntary behaviours

Finally, in a research setting, respondents may sense that their attitudes towards the targets are being assessed, or at least are relevant to the research question. Thus, when dealing with sensitive materials (i.e. issues where there is a strict social norm), people in the lab may spontaneously try to avoid giving an undesirable impression. For example, experimental participants presented with materials symbolising religious groups may try to avoid appearing prejudiced towards any religious group, even though the procedure did not ask them to respond to – let alone evaluate – the symbols. Working on an AMP, a participant could become suspicious when evaluating a Chinese ideograph right after having seen pictures of a hijab or a kippah. The participant might then refrain from using his affective response as an input for the evaluation of the subsequent stimulus.

What respondents typically do not know is that evaluations are accompanied by spontaneous – sometimes even involuntary – behavioural expressions. Thus, researchers may profit from not only recording what is said about the object (i.e. the evaluation itself), but also from looking at other dimensions characterising the behaviour – that is, in addition to observing merely whether or not a behaviour occurred, various aspects of behaviour can also be observed, such as frequency, speed, duration or intensity (Aronson *et al.*, 1990). One could observe, for example, whether, how long and how intensively people smile or frown upon encountering the attitude object (see also EMG measures below). Modern computer software can recognise and measure such facial expressions even at very low intensity. Another prominent example is the measurement of viewing times. The basic idea behind this paradigm is that people tend to look longer at stimuli that hold some attraction for them compared to stimuli that do not. For example, the viewing duration of photographs increases with the attractiveness of the person shown in the photo (e.g. Laws & Gress, 2004). Another application showed that relative viewing times for pictures of nude adults and children differed between child-molesters and a control sample (Banse *et al.*, 2010; Harris *et al.*, 1996). Viewing times provide a non-strenuous measure of attitudes, even in a sample that is unable to express likes and dislikes. Newborns as young as three days old already look longer at faces that adults had rated as attractive compared to faces rated as unattractive (Slater *et al.*, 2000).

Assessing viewing times is easy to do and does not require sophisticated technical equipment. However, the validity of viewing times as measures of attitudes has been debated. Viewing times have been shown to depend on the nature of the respondents' task (e.g. Imhoff *et al.*, 2012). If respondents are not concerned with attractiveness, viewing times may reflect the fact that observers are trying to form an accurate impression of a target. For example, if a respondent was trying to judge the targets regarding their trustworthiness or similarity, rather than their attractiveness, longer viewing times will be biased attitude indicators. Other methods assessing viewing behaviour (e.g., eye-tracking) are more precise because in addition to duration they also track changes in viewing direction. They do not necessarily increase validity, however. For example, eye gaze is directed towards dangerous stimuli as well as attractive stimuli (Quigley *et al.*, 2012). In comparison to recording viewing times, gaze tracking is also rather uneconomical, as the technical requirements and analysis effort involved are all high.

Gaze duration and direction are not the only by-products of evaluation processes. Similar considerations pertain to the analysis of verbal reports: as an alternative to analysing what a person said, researchers can have a closer look at how it has been said. Although wisdom has it that 'God has given us language to hide our thoughts' (attributed to the French statesman Talleyrand), a person's attitude may reveal itself in his or her use of language. It has been shown that people tend to use more abstract language to describe stereotype-consistent behaviour and more concrete language to describe stereotype-inconsistent behaviour (**linguistic intergroup bias**; Maass *et al.*, 1996; see also Linguistic Category Model, Semin & Fiedler, 1988). Relevant for its applicability as an attitude measure, empirical

Linguistic intergroup bias: Speakers tend to use more abstract than concrete terms to describe negative behaviour of an out-group and positive behaviour of the ingroup, and vice versa. In this sense, language abstractness can be used as an indicator of attitudes towards groups.

evidence suggests that people are unaware of producing linguistic intergroup biases. Franco and Maass (1996) studied the extent of out-group devaluation in basketball fans. One group of fans widely accepted aggressive behaviours, but the other group advocated a more peaceful social norm. Whereas the former group devalued the out-group in direct attitude measures, the latter did not. Nevertheless, both groups showed out-group devaluation as evident from a linguistic intergroup bias. Based on the bias, von Hippel and colleagues (1997) employed the extent to which descriptions of Afro-American targets contained abstract versus concrete language for positive and negative behaviours as a measure of racial prejudice. Language is an elegant tool for assessing attitudes.

At present, it is not very clear if people are fully unaware of how their language expresses attitude. As demonstrated in studies by Douglas and Sutton (2006), laypeople consider those who use abstract language as holding more biased attitudes than others who use concrete language. It therefore appears that laypeople have some tacit knowledge about the relation between attitudes and abstractness. In other words, people committing the bias themselves realise perhaps that their language reflects some evaluation, but they may have difficulty in actually changing their language from concrete to abstract and vice versa. It could well be, therefore, that language analysis already taps into those automatic processes that are, to some extent at least, beyond respondents' voluntary control.

Attitudes expressed in physiological reactions

Physiological measures, which also include neuroimaging techniques, can hardly be recorded unobtrusively, but unlike many other behavioural measures, they are largely outside participants' voluntary control. Among the physiological measures that have been used as indicators of attitude are the *galvanic skin response* and *pupillary dilatation versus constriction*. Similar to some of the behavioural correlates (e.g. gaze), they are ill-suited, however, because they only reflect the intensity of affective responses and the attentiveness to stimuli respectively, rather than the evaluative direction (favourable versus unfavourable) of these responses. The measurement of

Electromyography:
A technique recording the contraction of facial muscles. Activity of the zygomatic muscles is considered an indicator of a positive evaluation; activity of the corrugator muscles is considered an indicator of a negative evaluation.

subtle changes in individuals' facial muscular activity via **electromyography (EMG)** fares better in this regard. EMG goes a step further than human or computerised visual observation of smiling and frowning. Here, electrodes are applied to the face in order to measure even those muscular responses that are visually unobservable. For example, Cacioppo *et al.* (1986) found that participants showed greater EMG activity in their zygomatic (smiling) muscles when exposed to positive stimuli, but greater activity in their corrugator (frowning) muscles when exposed to negative stimuli. These electromyographic responses reflected not only the stimuli's valence but also their intensity. As cumbersome as the method is, its main advantage is its ability to measure subtle responses even towards stimuli that are only very briefly processed. Winkielman and Cacioppo (2001) could even show affective responses to subliminally presented stimuli (i.e. stimuli that were presented so briefly they could not be detected consciously).

Early research on brain activity used **electroencephalography (EEG)**, the recording of small electric signals of brain activity through electrodes placed on the scalp. As with electrodermal activity, however, this procedure does not allow for a direct assessment of positive or negative responses. Instead, it exploits the observation that unexpected stimuli elicit brain wave activity that differs from the activity elicited by expected stimuli. Therefore, one may infer the evaluation of a target object by embedding its presentation in a series of other objects whose evaluation is known and invariable. The brain activity that the target object elicits will then indicate if its evaluation is consistent or inconsistent with the evaluation of the other objects. Ito *et al.* (2004) presented white participants with pictures of faces of blacks and whites either in the context of positive or negative pictures. In the context of positive pictures, black faces elicited larger activity indicating an evaluative inconsistency to the positive stimuli. In the context of negative pictures, the white faces elicited a larger activity, again indicating an evaluative inconsistency. In sum, the results were interpreted as a racial bias even though the participants self-reported liking of the black and white faces did not differ.

More recently, attitude research has started using **functional magnetic resonance imaging (fMRI)** procedures. In contrast to the EEG, the fMRI exploits the fact that brain activity requires oxygen. Crucial to the measurement is the fact that oxygen-rich and oxygen-poor blood have different magnetic properties. This allows us to visualise oxygen levels in different cerebral areas, which is then taken as an indicator of brain activity in the respective regions. Though changes in cerebral blood flow occur more slowly than electric activity, the advantage is that they can be localised more precisely.

As such, fMRI studies have the potential to reveal neural correlates in very distinct neural areas. For example, activity in the insular cortex is observed during the processing of valenced stimuli. Although evidence suggests that the insula is a key player for the intensity of evaluative judgement (e.g. Berntson *et al.*, 2011), insula activity does not tell us whether participants like or dislike a stimulus. Activity is observed for stimuli of both positive and negative valence. The most studied brain area in attitude research, the *amygdala*, is more valence-specific (cf. Stanley *et al.*, 2008). The amygdala is part of the lymbic system, and is assumed to play a pivotal role in the processing of *negatively* valenced information (Berntson *et al.*, 2007). This is supported by research on fear conditioning (Phelps & LeDoux, 2005) and other studies: assuming a more favourable attitude towards in-group than out-group members, Phelps and colleagues (Phelps *et al.*, 2000) proposed and found higher amygdala activity in white participants when they were presented with pictures of unknown black people than when they were presented with pictures of similarly unknown white people. Complementing the findings, this was not the case for favoured black public figures, such as Michael Jordan or Martin Luther King.

Electroencephalogra phy (EEG): A technique recording fluctuations in electric activity on the scalp. Fluctuations occur if respondents observe an object that differs in valence from previously shown objects.

Functional magnetic resonance imaging (fMRI): Technique to visualise activity in different brain areas. Certain areas (e.g. the amygdala) are involved when processing valenced information.

Although important for the reactivity of the measure, evaluative task goals do not appear to be a necessary condition for amygdala activity – that is, negatively valenced information also evokes amygdala activity when respondents are not asked to form an impression (Cunningham *et al.*, 2004). Amygdala activation has been observed even for stimuli presented outside of conscious awareness (Cunningham *et al.*, 2004; Hoffmann *et al.*, 2012). Crucially, Cunningham *et al.* (2004) found that negative stimuli evoked even higher activity when they were presented **subliminally** rather than supraliminally.

Subliminal exposure: Very brief exposure below the threshold necessary for consciously encoding a stimulus, which may nonetheless affect subsequent responses.

It is the latter difference, however, that also raises questions about what the amygdala actually reflects. It is not clear why amygdala activity should become weaker merely because people are aware of the stimulus. Possibly, other neural structures such as the dorsolateral praefrontal cortex may control amygdala activity (Cunningham *et al.*, 2004; Knutson *et al.*, 2007). If so, amygdala activity as such is not a pure measure of an attitude. More intriguingly, recent findings suggest that people can be trained to voluntarily control amygdala activity. In an experiment (Zotev *et al.*, 2011), in one condition participants were informed about their ongoing amygdala activity during stimulus presentation, but a control group was not. Participants were then asked to counter the activity by thinking of positive memories. In a later test phase, participants in the experimental group were still able to control amygdala activity even without being informed about their current amygdala response. Apparently, they learned to notice their activity, and to react upon it. Finally, it should be noted that the absence of amygdala activity is not necessarily an indication of the absence of negative affect. Affective experiences as severe as panic can occur even in participants with amygdala lesion (Feinstein *et al.*, 2013).

All things considered, fMRI has opened up an interesting research field which might bridge the gap between biological and psychological processes. Viewed in that light, neuroimaging studies in attitude research are interesting on their own. Despite some intriguing findings, however, caution is in order: 'what precisely amygdala activation reflects is not clear yet. . . . (it) cannot be taken as prima facie evidence that a stimulus is evaluated more negatively' (Ito & Cacioppo, 2007, pp. 132–133). Thus, neural substrates, if anything, are only vague proxies for our attitudes. Furthermore, when you consider the substantial technical and economic demands involved in these techniques, it's clear that at present they do not constitute a viable alternative for measuring attitudes.

ATTITUDES IN TIME: REACTION TIME MEASURES

In the preceding paragraphs, we reviewed various indirect attitude measurements. It appears that all of them have their advantages, but they also have certain disadvantages too: some of them appeared rather cumbersome and uneconomic, some very imprecise, while others can be easily detected as an attitude measure, and therefore suffer from the same motivational distortions as the direct survey measures. For this reason perhaps, direct survey measures clearly prevailed at the time of this book's last edition (Bohner & Wänke, 2002). Today, survey measures still predominate for applied research, due to the ease with which they can be applied, but the picture has changed dramatically in fundamental research where indirect measures of attitudes are very popular. This is arguably due to one specific class of indirect measures – namely, those that are based on reaction time measurement. These measures typically combine the different guiding principles proposed in this chapter (for an overview, see Teige-Mocigemba *et al.*, 2010). Their most prominent representatives are indirect and exploit the principles of projection as well as objective tasks. In view of the prominence of reaction time measures in attitude research, it is worth considering them in a separate paragraph.

The most widely used methods are the **implicit association test** (IAT; Greenwald *et al.*, 1998) and methods based on sequential **priming** (e.g. Fazio & Williams, 1986; Fazio *et al.*, 1995), in particular **evaluative priming**.

In the evaluative priming paradigm, the presentation of evaluatively uncontroversial target words (e.g. 'horrible') on a computer screen is immediately preceded by the presentation of attitude objects (e.g. pictures of black or white people) that serve as primes. The respondents' task is to categorise the target word as quickly as possible by pressing a 'good' or a 'bad' response key (see Figure 3.1). If the evaluations of prime and target match, responses to the target are faster than if the two evaluations mismatch. In our example, respondents with negative racial attitudes towards blacks would be faster categorising a negative target word after a black prime than after a white prime, and vice versa for categorising a positive target word. It has been suggested that the magnitude of relative facilitation (i.e. reduction in response time to matching versus nonmatching targets) caused by a given attitude-object prime may be used as an indicator of a person's attitude towards that prime (Fazio & Williams, 1986). This procedure is largely non-reactive, as participants are never asked to consider their attitude towards the primes; the rationale they are given for the primes appearing is that a recognition test will follow. Even less prone to reactivity are variants in which the participants are not asked to evaluate anything, but are asked for a non-evaluative response – for example, naming the target as soon as possible. In such tasks, the valence congruency between prime and target also speeds up responses (e.g. Bargh *et al.*, 1996; Spruyt *et al.*, 2007; for a review of sequential priming measures, see Herring *et al.*, 2013).

The most popular current technique of indirect attitude measurement, the IAT measures the differential association of two target concepts (e.g. 'flower' versus 'insect') with positive versus negative evaluations (e.g. 'pleasant words' versus 'unpleasant words') (Greenwald *et al.*, 1998). As a participant in an IAT, you learn to use two keys, one on the left and one on the right, to quickly respond to stimuli on the screen. For example, you might first learn to press the left-hand key each time a flower name appears,

Implicit association test (IAT): A response-time based method designed to assess attitudes. It measures the differential association of two target concepts (e.g. 'blacks' versus 'whites') with positive versus negative evaluations (e.g. 'pleasant words' versus 'unpleasant words').

Priming: Increasing the accessibility of a particular concept by activating it prior to a processing task or judgement.

Evaluative priming: An attitude measure exploiting priming logic. An attitude object will facilitate the evaluation of stimuli that share the same valence, but slow down the evaluation of stimuli with a different valence.

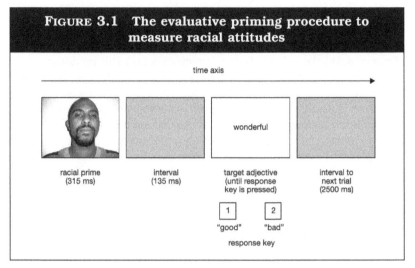

FIGURE 3.1   The evaluative priming procedure to measure racial attitudes

Note: Stimulus sequence of one trial in an evaluative priming paradigm, as introduced by Fazio *et al.* (1995)

and the right-hand key each time an insect name appears. Then you learn to respond with the same two keys to pleasant words (left-hand key) and to unpleasant words (right-hand key). Later, both target stimuli and evaluation words are presented in a random sequence, and you are still asked to perform the responses previously learned. This combined task is performed more rapidly when highly associated categories (flower and pleasant) share the same key than when less associated categories (insect and pleasant) do so. This performance difference is proposed to represent the differences in the evaluation of the two target concepts. Figure 3.2 shows an IAT designed to measure implicit attitudes towards fruit versus candy.

How good are reaction time measures?

Before considering this question, let us recall what the principal requirements are for a good measure. In the previous chapter, we introduced the psychometric properties of reliability and validity, and these must also, of course, be satisfied by reaction time measures. However, it is important to understand that techniques per se do not have fixed psychometric properties. We cannot say that *the* IAT has a certain reliability and validity because each IAT has its specific properties. Given the large number of studies that have used the IAT, however, we can look at the range of reliability and validity coefficients across studies and examine the conditions that may determine their magnitude. On average, split-half and Cronbach's alpha coefficients vary around .8, indicating that the internal consistency tends to be quite high (Hofmann *et al.*, 2005; Nosek *et al.*, 2007), but their test–retest reliability is considerably lower, ranging from .25 to .69 (Lane *et al.*, 2007). Few studies have so far addressed the reliability of priming measures.

Studying priming measures of stereotyping, Kawakami and Dovidio (2001) found modest test–retest reliability coefficients of about .5 over a period of up to 15 days. In a study comparing the stabilities of both IAT and priming measures, the priming measure tended to be slightly more stable even than the IAT (Cunningham *et al.*, 2001). Acceptable test–retest correlations have also been obtained in studies using subliminal face primes when measures were about two months apart (Dannlowski & Suslow, 2006). Other evaluative priming paradigms with subliminal primes, however, revealed poor reliability estimates (e.g. Banse, 1999).

Estimating the validity of reaction time measures is trickier. What is often done to assess the validity of an attitude measure is to correlate it with other attitude measures. Indeed, correlations between reaction time measures and self-reports are often substantial, pointing to the fact that in various cases they both reveal scores of some summary evaluation. However, this is not always the case (e.g. Hofmann *et al.*, 2005) and there may be good reasons for low correlations besides low validity.

Remember that we introduced this chapter by pointing to the fact that direct measures are prone to demand effects. In the case of such motivated distortions in self-reports, we would not expect those self-reports to correlate highly with indirect – and therefore less distorted – measures. Supporting this notion, there is evidence that the discriminant validity of indirect measures (i.e. the extent to which they measure something different than direct measures) is more evident in domains in which socially desirable responding is more likely. Racial attitudes as measured by the priming procedure were positively correlated with a direct self-report measure of racial attitude only for those respondents whose motivation to control their prejudice was low (Fazio *et al.*, 1995). Presumably, students who were motivated to appear non-prejudiced managed to do so on the explicit self-report measure but could not conceal their more automatic responses in the priming procedure. A more systematic study of the relationship between the IAT and self-reports corroborates this finding. A meta-analysis of 126 studies found that correlations between IATs and self-reported attitudes towards an attitude object differed according to topic (Hofmann *et al.*, 2005). They were higher for consumer attitudes than for stereotypes, which may reflect the fact that preference for chocolate over fruit is more likely to be admitted than stereotypes. However, across all domains under study, social desirability was not a significant, independent moderator of the implicit–explicit correlation.

So what is it that distinguishes the IAT from self-reports? In its early days, the IAT was often presented as not being subject to context effects, that it cannot be influenced voluntarily, that the attitudes it measured were the 'true' attitudes, and that unlike questionnaires, which are sensitive to question wording, question order and so on, it is insensitive to the nature of the stimuli. All of these claims turned out to be overstated. In some respects, the IAT may actually suffer from the same problems as self-report measures. For example, great care should be taken in selecting the stimuli and attributes for the categorisation task as the stimuli used in the IAT can fundamentally affect its outcome (see Box 3.1).

FIGURE 3.2   Implicit Association Test for fruits vs. candy (adapted from Friese et al., 2008)

Sequence	1	2	3	4	5
Task description	Initial target-concept discrimination	Associated attribute discrimination	Initial combined task	Reversed target-concept discrimination	Reversed combined task
Example of a trial representing task × stimulus combination	Candy Fruit	Positive Negative joyful	Candy Fruit or or positive negative	Fruit Candy	Fruit Candy or or positive positive
Task instructions	←CANDY FRUIT→	←POSITIVE NEGATIVE→	←CANDY ←POSITIVE FRUIT→ NEGATIVE→	←FRUIT CANDY→	←FRUIT ←POSITIVE CANDY→ NEGATIVE→
Stimuli	Stimuli representing the two target categories, here pictures of fruit and candies	Stimuli representing positive and negative valence, here positive and negative adjectives	Stimuli representing either the two target categories OR positive and negative valence, here pictures of fruit and candies, and positive and negative adjectives	Stimuli representing the two target categories, here pictures of fruit and candies	Stimuli representing either the two target categories OR positive and negative valence, here pictures of fruit and candies, and positive and negative adjectives

Note. Participants perform a series of five discrimination tasks (columns 1 to 5). In this example, a pair of target concepts ('candy' and 'fruit') and an attribute dimension ('positive – negative') are presented in the first two steps. The arrows in the third row indicate that discriminations are assigned to a left–right response. Both discrimination tasks are combined in the third step and later recombined in the fifth step, after response assignments for the target-concept discrimination have been reversed in the fourth step. Using this IAT, Friese et al. (2009) found weak–positive correlations with self-reported preferences. Despite some overlap, the measure seems to capture a unique construct.

Note that the classic IAT only assesses relative attitudes towards two target categories (e.g. candies are preferred to fruit or vice versa) but does not allow conclusions about the attitudes towards each category individually. In our example, the candy could be preferred to the fruit but both categories could be liked. To overcome this drawback, single category IATs (SC-IAT) have been developed (Karpinski & Steinman, 2006), in which positive and negative attributes, but only stimuli of one target category, have to be sorted in a given block of trials. The latency difference between combining a category with a positive attribute and combining it with a negative attribute then indicates the positivity of a given category. This can also be done for multiple categories, thereby making it possible to measure attitudes towards different objects within a single experiment, a clear advantage whenever more than two objects are potentially relevant, as, for example, in political election studies when more than two parties are involved (e.g. Bluemke & Friese, 2008; Friese et al., 2007)

Box 3.1   Selecting stimuli for an IAT

In principle, the IAT is supposed to measure the association between the category (e.g. East Germany vs. West Germany) and an evaluative concept (e.g. good vs. bad). If so, the stimuli used to represent the category or the evaluation should have no influence. This is not the case, however. Attitudes towards East Germany vs. West Germany were measured by seven different IATs (Bluemke & Friese, 2006; for related results, see Nevid & McClelland, 2010). The IATs differed to the extent the stimuli meant to represent East or West Germany and the stimuli meant to represent a positive or a negative evaluation overlapped. For example, in the IAT which rendered the score depicted in the far left in Figure 3.3 the examples for East Germany were rather positive (Baltic Sea) and for West Germany rather negative (materialism). In addition, the examples for the positive stimuli were stereotypical for East Germany (modest) and the negative stimuli stereotypical for West Germany (arrogant). This combination facilitates the responses when East Germany and 'positive' (West Germany and 'negative') are co-assigned to the same response key. Indeed, the result indicates a preference of East over West Germany. However, the bar on the right depicts the results for an IAT in which East Germany was represented by negative stimuli (communism) and West Germany by positive ones (democracy) and moreover, negative attributes were stereotypical for East Germany (xenophobic) and positive ones were stereotypical for West Germany (self-confident). Here, the result reflects a more positive attitude towards West than East Germany. Thus, just like the wording of a question, the scale which is provided or the question order can influence results in self-report measures, the selection of the stimuli in an IAT may influence the outcome.

Also, it was premature to conclude that the IAT is free from socially desirable responding. Although respondents who lack experience or knowledge about the IAT are mostly unable to fake its outcome (e.g. Asendorpf *et al.*, 2002; Egloff & Schmukle, 2002), respondents who are familiar with the procedure or have been taught how the IAT could be faked, actually, can voluntarily influence the outcome (Fiedler & Bluemke, 2005; Steffens, 2004). Moreover, the IAT suffers from some specific problems arising from its task structure (Mierke & Klauer, 2001, 2003). Technically speaking, the IAT measures response latencies caused by a shift from one task to another (i.e. from the compatible block to the incompatible block). Problematically, the ability to switch between tasks is not only caused by respondents' attitudes towards the categories. The order of the different blocks can influence

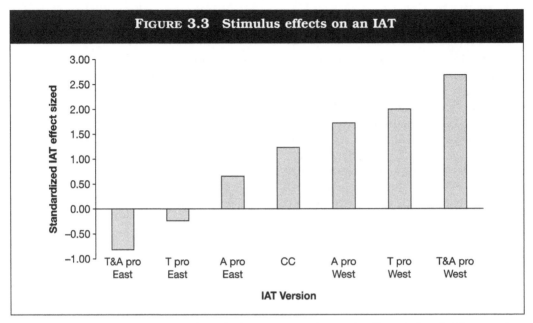

FIGURE 3.3   Stimulus effects on an IAT

Note: IAT-scores depend on the (T)arget and (A)ttribute stimuli used to represent the categories of interest – here, East Germans and West Germans (Bluemke & Friese, 2006)

the results (Klauer & Mierke, 2005; Messner & Vosgerau, 2010). Further-more, switching from the compatible to the incompatible block requires working memory capacity (Schmitz *et al.*, 2013), thus IAT scores also reflect individual differences in intellectual capacity (Klauer *et al.*, 2010). Taken together, constructing an IAT is not a trivial matter and should not be undertaken lightly. Given the criticism mentioned above, reaction time measures cannot be regarded the silver bullet of attitude measures. Nevertheless, it would be too pessimistic to view the glass half empty rather than half full. Although it is not impossible to exert control over IAT outcomes, it appears that the IAT is less prone to motivated distortions than are self-reports, which can be influenced without sophisticated methodological knowledge (Steffens, 2004). One variable that actually emerged as a significant moderator of the IAT self-report correlation in the meta-analysis is spontaneity (Hofmann *et al.*, 2005) – that is, explicit ratings and IAT scores correlate more highly if explicit ratings are given in a spontaneous way. Thus, it appears that the IAT could reveal something like one's gut feelings. With this being said, the main reason for its popularity is not so much a methodological advantage. Rather, the issue of indirect measures has shifted from a purely methodological to a theoretical one and has given rise to a new outlook on attitudes (e.g. Nosek *et al.*, 2011). Arguably for this reason, some prominent attitude researchers consider these measures one of the most influential developments of the last decade of attitude research (cf. Briñol & Petty, 2012).

FROM DIFFERENT MEASURES TO DIFFERENT CONSTRUCTS – AND BACK

The divergent findings obtained by self-reports and reaction time measures led to a new conceptualisation of attitude measures – namely, a distinction between what are now known as explicit and implicit attitude measures. Importantly, explicit and implicit attitude measures do not merely represent different methods of assessing an attitude but are meant to represent different constructs.

So what are implicit attitude measures and what do we gain from them? Greenwald and Banaji (1995) proposed that implicit and explicit attitude measures reveal distinct attitudes, namely – and straightforwardly – implicit and explicit attitudes. Their central claim was that implicit attitudes differ from explicit ones in that they cannot be consciously retrieved – that is, they are inaccessible via introspection. In support of the concept of two independent attitudes, implicit and explicit measures yield outcomes that sometimes converge and sometimes diverge. This conception has been criticised for different reasons. First, many empirical findings suggest that attitudes as revealed by these measures are accessible via introspection (Gawronski *et al.*, 2006). For instance, if participants are led to believe that faking in direct measures can be detected, the correspondence between explicit and implicit measures towards blacks increases (Nier, 2005). Apparently, respondents then chose to explicitly report the attitude they knew they had, but did not want to reveal to the experimenter. Furthermore, a series of studies revealed that respondents are actually able to predict their outcome in implicit measures – clear evidence that they at least can become aware of them (Hahn *et al.*, 2014). Second, the dual attitude conception has been criticised because it suggests that different attitudes are based on independent, separable memory representations (e.g. Fazio & Olson, 2003; but see Nosek & Smyth, 2007 for a discussion). Third, and perhaps most pivotal, the conception does not allow for predictions regarding the conditions under which implicit and explicit measures will yield the same or different responses. As an alternative, many authors departed from a dual attitude perspective, but suggested different processes revealed by implicit as opposed to explicit measures (Fazio, 2007; Fazio & Olson, 2003; Gawronski & Bodenhausen, 2006; Petty *et al.*, 2007). Fazio and Olson (2003), for example, argue that only a single attitude does exist towards any given object. Taking a file-drawer perspective, they propose that attitudes are stored in the memory. Confronted with an object, the attitude will cause an unintended evaluation. It is via implicit measures that this unintended evaluation is represented most accurately. If respondents were neither motivated nor capable of changing the overt response, the same memory-based evaluation would be evident in the explicit measures (cf. Chapters 6 and 13). Another theoretical perspective has been proposed (Gawronski & Bodenhausen, 2006, Chapter 7), which assumes that implicit measures may reflect a spontaneous affective response towards an object, one which the respondent may actually dismiss upon reflection. For instance, a person may have some initial negative affect towards an ugly person and therefore show some negative response in an implicit measure. Integrating further knowledge (e.g. the target person is friendly and smart), however, the respondent might negate the initial, false response and conclude: 'I like this guy'. Nonetheless, the evaluation that is personally considered as true cannot be revealed by the implicit measure because the negation of the initial response requires a time-consuming logical process (Deutsch, 2004; Deutsch *et al.*, 2006). From this perspective, the implicit measure often would not reveal the response that is actually endorsed.

In sum, all the models make some valuable points, but none of them can solve all the problems raised by another conception. However, the common denominator in all these theoretical conceptions is that implicit measures reveal automatic, spontaneous, unintended evaluations (Fazio & Olson, 2003; Gawronski & Bodenhausen, 2006; Strack & Deutsch, 2004). Of course, further evidence is needed to test this assumption (cf. DeHouwer *et al.*, 2009) but it appears that these measures fulfil at least some criteria of automaticity (e.g. Teige-Mocigemba *et al.*, 2010). Derived from these conceptions, we define an implicit measure as *a measure that reveals an object evaluation unaffected by deliberative evaluation of the object.* Note that this definition does not presume that the measure must be indirect. Indeed, some authors have proposed that a direct, but speeded evaluation of an attitude

Implicit Attitude Measure: A measure that reveals an object evaluation unaffected by deliberative evaluation of the object.

object can also be referred to as an **implicit attitude measure** (Vargas *et al.*, 2004, 2007). Further, with the definition in mind, an implicit measure does not necessarily have to be based on reaction times. In fact, other techniques, such as the AMP are widely considered an implicit measure. Ultimately, the definition suggests that whether or not an attitude measure is an implicit measure, again, becomes an empirical one – that is, empirical investigations are typically required to explore whether a measure is free from deliberative processes (cf. De Houwer *et al.*, 2009).

Although there remains some confusion about the exact nature of what an implicit attitude actually is, we would also like to point out the pragmatic surplus of the implicit–explicit taxonomy. A shift from indirect measures to implicit measures connotes a shift from a method to an outcome, the implicit attitude. Rather than suggest that one is the real attitude but the other is an artefact, the terminology suggests that they both reveal what we like or dislike (e.g. Nosek *et al.*, 2011). As we will see later in this book, this emancipated view of explicit and implicit attitude measures has led to novel insights regarding the processes underlying evaluations (Chapters 6 and 7) and behaviour prediction (Chapter 13).

CONCLUDING COMMENT: CHOOSING THE APPROPRIATE MEASURE

In sum, disguised and non-reactive attitude measures can provide important insights into sensitive areas. The decision to use any of these measures, however, should not be arbitrary, but instead researchers must weigh the pros and cons with regard to valid, ethical and economic concerns. When deciding for an appropriate measurement, therefore, one should not feel tempted merely to use the solution that is technically most progressive. Often, simpler measures may not only be more economical, but also yield higher construct validity. Furthermore, indirect measures can often conflict with ethical standards. Unobtrusiveness may clash with the principle of obtaining research participants' informed consent (see Chapter 5 of Webb *et al.*, 1981) as, for example, in the lost letter paradigm. Sometimes the question also arises as to whether or not the research question really necessitates strenuous procedures, or cover stories deceiving participants about the measures' true intent. After all, there is no single gold standard, but rather all methods have their merits and pitfalls. One should consider carefully whether the device in question offers valuable incremental insights compared to simpler attitude measures. In areas where attitude self-reports are likely to be reshaped during the question and answering process, as is typically the case with more sensitive topics, the measures reviewed in this chapter may often constitute a viable alternative, allowing for behaviour predictions beyond attitudes measured via self-reports.

CHAPTER SUMMARY

1   To avoid reactivity effects (i.e. a change in the target attitude due to the measurement), indirect measures have been used. These exploit that attitudes are expressed in other activities than evaluative judgements about the object. The activities include everyday behaviour, judgements other than evaluation, involuntary behaviours accompanying evaluation and physiological activity.

2   Indirect measures often do not correspond with direct ones, but this does not necessarily indicate a lack of validity. Instead, divergence is intended, because indirect measures are meant to capture unique aspects of an attitude.

3   A special class of measurement techniques, including priming measures and the implicit association test, is used to assess the more spontaneous evaluations. The suggestion is that these so-called implicit measures reveal attitudes that respondents do not want to admit or that are free from higher-order validation processes.

Exercises

1   Go to a friend or relative and show him or her pictures that they might like. Can you observe changes in their facial expressions?

2   Consider attitudes towards the following groups, objects and behaviours: immigrants, political parties, beef, the United Nations, pornography, using condoms, working overtime. Which of these

attitudes might show a discrepancy between explicit and implicit measures and what might be the reason in each case?

3   Think of stimuli that might be used in an IAT for measuring implicit self-esteem.

Further reading

Non-reactive measures:

Webb, E. J., Campbell, D. T., Schwartz, R. D., Sechrest, L. & Grove, J. B. (1981). *Nonreactive Measures in the Social Sciences* (2nd edn). Boston, MA: Houghton Mifflin.

Implicit measures:

Teige-Mocigemba, S., Klauer, K. C. & Sherman, J. W. (2010). A practical guide to implicit association tests and related tasks. In Gawronski, B. & Payne, K. B. (eds), *Handbook of Implicit Social Cognition: Measurement, Theory and Applications* (pp. 117–139). New York: Guilford Press.

Examples of IAT measures designed by Greenwald and his colleagues that can be self-administered are available at: www.yale.edu/implicit/

Notes

1   One option of minimising impression management motives is by guaranteeing absolute anonymity. This might be taken for granted as ethical guidelines solicit anonymous data handling, as well as informing participants that data cannot be retraced to the specific respondents. Nevertheless, research participants may sometimes doubt anonymity, which causes biased self-reports, especially for very sensitive topics. Some methods therefore have been proposed that not only increase objective, but also subjective anonymity. In particular, the randomised response technique (RRT; Warner, 1965) asks respondents to provide the true answer depending on a certain condition that the researcher cannot know. For example, a participant is asked to covertly role a dice. Then she is asked a sensitive question, but to answer truly only if the eyes counted three or four. However, she would have to answer 'yes' if the eyes counted one or two, but to answer 'no' if the eyes counted five or six. Given that the sample is large enough, the researcher could then estimate the number of true 'yes' responses, given that one-third of the 'yes' and the 'no' responses had been forced by the procedure. The RRT, however, requires large samples and only allows for assessing attitudes at the group level. Finally, it has received little attention in attitude research and therefore is not discussed in detail.

2   Whether a certain behaviour (e.g. marking a point on an attitude scale, offending a person) is a good proxy for an attitude finally depends on

the current research question and the theoretical models it is built upon. Without any prior assumptions, it is arbitrary whether a certain evaluative behaviour is considered a proxy to an attitude, or the to-be-predicted behaviour, independent of whether the measure is direct or indirect, or whether the behaviour is studied inside or outside of the lab. As a practical guide, however, we recommend that a certain behaviour is a better representative of an attitude; the fewer external variables can be identified influencing the behavioural expression upon encounter of the object (see Chapter 6).

Part *II*

The origins of our attitudes

The two girls were hanging out at their favourite club. As usual, Hannah was having a ginger beer and Zoe was sipping a beer – no ginger! Hannah was the first to notice the dark-haired man passing by. Clearly, she found him attractive and said so to her friend. Zoe raised her eyebrows: 'That peacock? No way! Granted he is good-looking, but the suit is more than embarrassing.'

Obviously, Zoe and Hannah share some attitudes. They like the same club and they both appreciate the man's looks. However, when it comes to drinks or men's fashion their attitudes diverge. That attitudes differ from person to person does not come as a surprise. Philosophers – from Aristotle to Locke – have pointed out that people differ due to different experiences. The essence of this thought is expressed in the metaphor 'tabula rasa' (Aristotle, fourth century BC) which is meant to propose that the new-born is a blank slate, and this slate gets inscribed by experiences. In a similar vein, psychologists proposed that we learn what we like and dislike – and it merely depends on our personal experience, whether we find it more desirable to become an astronaut or a boxer. There is no doubt that our experiences influence our attitudes and as we will see throughout Part II of this book, experiences play a pivotal role in attitude formation processes. Drinking beer, Zoe might have had the party of her life, while Hannah ended up feeling sick. Zoe might have initially copied her older sister drinking beer, feeling very grown-up and good about herself in the process. Hannah may associate beer with drunken hooligans. Explaining attitudes via personal experience with the attitude object is not only intuitive but also viable. Yet, there are also several formation processes that explain why you may like a certain club, without ever having been there. Though one might say that all these processes involve experiences to some extent, many of these are impersonal or they are detached from the attitude object. However, we do not start from scratch, but the experiences of our ancestors paved the way for our attitudes we hold today. We will address the ontogenetic basis of our attitudes in Box II.1.

Chapter 4 will address how cognitive, affective and bodily sensations that are experienced in the presence of an attitude object can influence its

---

Box II.1   Genetic influence

When psychologists explore the origins of a particular psychological phenomenon like a behaviour, trait or ability, they typically investigate to what extent the phenomenon is related to genes and to what extent it is acquired via environmental or social influences. Surprisingly, this nature–nurture debate has not played a prominent role in attitude research at all. It is usually taken for granted that attitudes are acquired and socially formed. In recent decades, however, some researchers propagated the notion that some attitudes may be inherited (for a review, see Bouchard & McGue, 2003; Tesser, 1993) or otherwise biologically based.

Evolutionary psychology explains human behaviour (including personality, preferences etc.) as mechanisms that evolved through natural selection (e.g. Tooby & Cosmides, 2005). According to this perspective, modern humans inherited the behaviour (or more precisely the genes for the behaviour) that increased early humans' inclusive fitness (i.e. enabled them and their kin to survive and reproduce). For example, a dislike of bitter taste helped people avoid toxic substances. Given that this aversion is linked to a gene, it is likely that the offspring inherited the gene. Over several generations, the gene for a bitterness aversion will have successfully multiplied while a gene for bitterness preference would have fared less well as its carriers were less likely to survive and reproduce. In the long run, dislike for bitter taste would have been widespread in the human population. The same reasoning holds for the evolution of liking what is adaptive. A preference for sweet and fatty food helped prehistoric humans to survive, and consequently individuals with such a preference will have produced more offspring than individuals who disliked such high-calorie food. It is worth noting that this preference would persist even though in affluent societies it does not provide a selective advantage any more.

Evolutionary psychologists have suggested quite a number of preferences which may reflect such functional adaptations, including which landscape people prefer and find beautiful: in general, humans prefer lush vegetation to deserts, and trees to built features or grassy expanses (for a review, see Orians & Heerwagen, 1992). The best investigated area, however, are mating preferences (see Buss, 2007; Buss & Schmitt, 1993). For both sexes, attraction to features indicative of a high-quality mate would indicate an adaptation for choosing a high-quality mate. According to this view, what individuals evaluate as attractive is not a culturally shaped standard but the product of biological evolution. Humans consider those physical features as attractive that indicate fertility. In females those features are youthful looks, as women reach their peak fertility in their mid 20s and female fertility is constrained by age. Youthful looks are less important in male attractiveness as male fertility is less constrained by age, but health cues are important. An important empirical criterion for this adaptionist perspective on beauty is cross-cultural consensus about what is rated as attractive. For example, large eyes, a small nose and full lips are considered both as indicating youth and as being attractive in women across different cultures (for a review, see Cunningham *et al.*, 2002).

Evolutionary psychology: Approach that conceives of human behaviour as adapted mechanisms which improve – or at one point in evolution improved – selective fitness.

Although evolutionary theory appears difficult to test, it can be said to have inspired many demonstrations of universal, genetically grounded attitudes. Whereas evolutionary psychology would explain universality in preferences, as there seems to exist in taste (sweet over bitter) and aesthetics (landscape, human faces and bodies), the diversity of attitudes, however, is not easily predicted from evolution theory (with the exception of systematic gender differences). But this is not to say that individual differences may not also have a genetic component. Some are not so surprising. Food preferences, for example, covary with specific enzymes. Lacking crucial enzymes, it is unlikely that a liking for milk or for alcohol will emerge. Genetic variants in olfactory receptors contribute to the detection of a soapy smell in coriander (cilantro) and therefore cause a dislike for the taste (Eriksson *et al.*, 2012, but note that the genetic variant only explains some of the variance in coriander preference). For individual differences in attitudes other than food preferences, a genetic component may be more surprising, yet research has suggested genetic influences for a variety of individual attitudes.

Most of the respective evidence comes from twin studies, which allow researchers to link variance in attitudes to variance in genes. The rationale behind this approach is that monozygotic twins share 100 per cent of their genes, but dizygotic twins share only 50 per cent of their genes. If one assumes that the similarity of environmental influences within each pair of twins does not differ systematically between monozygotic and dizygotic twins (equal environmental similarity assumption – an assumption which has been debated) one can interpret differences between MZ and DZ twins as reflecting genetic differences. The extent to which attitudes are more similar among mono- as compared to dizygotic twins then serves as an indicator of genetic influence. Adoption studies that compare monozygotic twins raised apart (different environments – although, again, it has been debated how different these environments really are) with those raised together (presumably similar environments) also allow for the separation of environmental and genetic influences.

In such studies researchers found **heritability factors** of up to .6 for some attitudes, which means that 60 per cent of the variance in this attitude between individuals of a population may be attributed to genetic variance in this population (for reviews, see Bouchard & McGue, 2003; Tesser, 1993). Although there may be some doubt regarding the exact value of the heritability estimates (separating the variance attributed to genetic factors from the variance attributed to environmental factors involves various methodological problems) and some estimates are considerably lower, the data support the notion that some differences in attitudes between people may be partly due to genetic differences. Attitudes for which such a relationship have been reported are work (for a review, see Ilies *et al.*, 2006), religiousness and sociopolitical attitudes such as authoritarianism and conservatism (for a review of the latter examples, see Bouchard & McGue, 2003). Single items measuring, for example, liking of jazz, royalty, censorship or the death penalty showed heritability factors over .40 (Martin *et al.*, 1986). Also, attitudes towards taking economic risks as revealed by decisions in gambling tasks can be traced back to some genetic variation (Cesarini *et al.*, 2009; Zhong *et al.*, 2009; Zyphur *et al.*, 2009).

Are we supposed to believe that there is a gene for becoming religious, for liking jazz or accepting risky hedge funds? Certainly not, and one should keep in mind that genes are multifaceted. Although individual genes can be associated with specific attitudes there is

Heritability factor: Expresses which proportion of the variance of a phenotype in a population is due to genetic variance in the population.

no specific gene for a political attitude. A more plausible explanation lies in the assumption of mediating variables, which are partly determined by genes and in turn influence attitudes. People form attitudes that are compatible with their dispositions, such as personalities and abilities. To the extent that these have a genetic component one would also observe a genetic component in the related attitudes. Examples for potential mediators (for a detailed discussion, see Tesser, 1993; Olson *et al.*, 2001) may be genetic differences in sensory structures (e.g. taste, hearing etc.), body chemistry, intelligence, temperament and activity level, and conditionability, which is the ease with which one can be conditioned (see Chapter 5). For example, it is reasonable to assume that individuals with naturally good coordination and strength would be more successful at sports than less athletically inclined individuals, with the result that the former individuals developed more favourable attitudes towards sports than the latter. Accordingly, attitudes towards athletics (playing organised sports, exercising, etc.) have been found to have a heritable component. Moreover, they correlate strongly with self-reported athletic ability, which itself is highly heritable (Olson *et al.*, 2001). Likewise, many studies found correlations between political attitudes and personality traits (e.g. Carney *et al.*, 2008; Verhulst *et al.*, 2010). In some cases both the specific attitude and the correlated personality trait show heritability as, for example, conservatism and psychoticism, or liberal out-group attitudes and neuroticism (Verhulst *et al.*, 2010). Such a correlation does not necessarily imply a causal relationship so that the specific trait promotes the formation of the respective attitudes. More likely the observed covariation is an expression of the same underlying genetic factors (Verhulst *et al.*, 2012).

Because the issue of heritability and genetic influences is highly sensitive and often leads to misunderstandings, we would like to explicitly point out a few caveats. First, the heritability factor applies to the variance of an attribute in populations but does not apply to individuals and does not express the extent to which a particular attribute is produced by a particular gene. One could not say, for example, 'I owe 50 per cent of my religiousness to my genes'. Second, given that the genetic influence on attitudes is not only imperfect but also indirect, it should be clear that people are not slaves to their genes when it comes to attitude formation. Even if genes influence an attitude, their influence is neither exclusive nor irreversible nor impervious to modification by other factors. To quote Richard Dawkins, one of the most prominent proponents of modern evolution theory: 'It is a fallacy . . . to suppose that genetically inherited traits are by definition fixed and unmodifiable. . . . Among animals, man is uniquely dominated by culture, by influences learned and handed down' (Dawkins, 1989, p. 3).

evaluation. Next we elaborate on the basics of the ontogenetic influences, showing how attitudes can take on the valence of other co-occurring objects (Chapter 5). Equipped with the basics, in Chapters 6 and 7 you will learn more about the processes involved in attitude formation, how people integrate the information at hand in a given context and how they shape their attitudes by reflecting about them.

Chapter 4

FROM INCIDENTAL SENSATIONS AND NEEDS TO ATTITUDES

Whenever we evaluate something we are subject to a host of sensations and experiences. Some are elicited by the attitude object. In addition, cognitive, affective and bodily sensations and states that are present during the evaluation of an object can shape such evaluations.

An attitude object may stimulate an affective response based on the feelings which arise due to its processing – namely, the ease or fluency with which it is processed. People tend to like things that are perceived easily and dislike things that cause more processing effort. Here it is not the object as such that directly elicits the evaluative response but its processing. Even more removed from the attitude object, its evaluation may also be influenced by co-occurring experiences and sensations that originate from other sources unrelated to the attitude object. Numerous studies found that people evaluate things differently when they already are in a happy or a sad mood. We will first review some effects of perceptual fluency before we turn to the influence of incidental affective states. Then we will address one specific source of incidentally occurring evaluative responses: the body. While an observer appraises the target object, she is also inevitably experiencing sensations caused by her own body. Just as incidental affective states can be used as a base for evaluating an object, so can such bodily reactions. Finally, we will look at a class of incidental influences different from sensations and show how currently activated goals affect evaluative responses.

PROCESSING FLUENCY

You walk into a shop to look for a present for your aunt. A vase may be a good idea. And any other colour than white won't do. You look at an array of white vases and immediately like some. But some are just ugly. Where does this response come from?

One possible reason for liking some vases (or forms, cars, paintings, etc.) more than others may be that they are easier to encode and process, something Jacoby and colleagues termed 'perceptual fluency' (Jacoby *et al.*,

1989). Fluency, or *subjectively experienced ease at processing*, in turn feels good or, as Winkielman and Cacioppo (2001) put it, 'mind at ease puts a smile on your face'. In their study they showed participants pictures of everyday objects, which were each preceded by a subliminally presented contour prime (see Figure 4.1). The contour prime either matched the contours of the target picture, thereby facilitating identification, or mismatched the target picture, thereby hampering identification. Electromyography (see Chapter 3) during picture presentation as well as self-reports revealed that easy-to-process pictures elicited a positive affective response.

Several other studies show that high fluency goes together with more positive evaluations (for a review, see Reber *et al.*, 2004; Unkelbach & Greifeneder, 2013). For example, geometric forms with high figure-ground contrast were judged as prettier than forms with low figure-ground contrast, and similar results have been shown for clarity and symmetry. Another feature that facilitates perceptual processing is prototypicality (Winkielman *et al.*, 2006) – that is, the closeness of a stimulus to its category's central tendency. From geometric patterns to birds or wristwatches, more prototypical exemplars are liked better (Halberstadt, 2006; for an example, see Figure 4.2), an effect that is also referred to as the beauty-in-average effect. It also extends to human faces where blends (morphs) are judged as particularly attractive. Hannah and Zoe, the girls in our introductory example, arguably did not admire the passer-by because his facial features were so exceptional, but because his face looked like the prototypical male face.

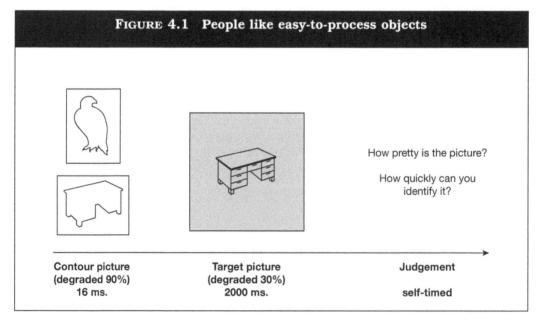

FIGURE 4.1   People like easy-to-process objects

How pretty is the picture?

How quickly can you identify it?

Contour picture
(degraded 90%)
16 ms.

Target picture
(degraded 30%)
2000 ms.

Judgement

self-timed

Note: Paradigm by Winkelman & Cacioppo (2001). Participants were presented with contour primes, a mask and a target stimulus; target stimuli were evaluated more favourably if the contour prime facilitated their identification

FIGURE 4.2   Prototype preferences

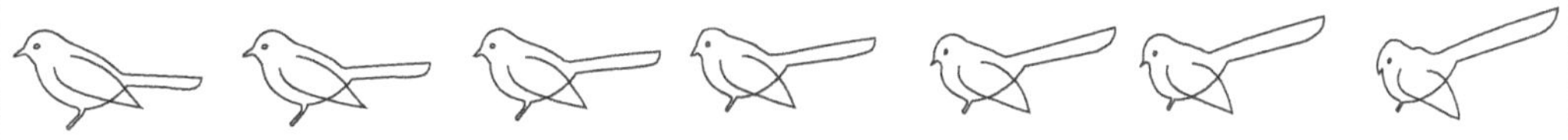

Note: After exposure to different category exemplars, people tend to judge the category average (i.e. the prototype) as most attractive. Here, the bird in the middle is more fluent and liked better than the atypical exemplars (stimuli from Halberstadt and Rhodes, 2003)

Beyond laboratory experiments, the power of fluency is also attested by actual car sales. The prototypicality of a car design may be used as an indicator of the fluency with which it is perceived. Do cars with a prototypical design have an advantage in the market? They do, but only when the design is both fluent (prototypical) and complex (Landwehr *et al.*, 2011). Fluency in case of complexity is more surprising and considered diagnostic whereas fluency in case of simplicity may be expected and discounted (for a review, see Wänke & Hansen, 2015).

The concept of perceptual fluency also explains why liking of a stimulus increases with exposure (Bornstein & D'Agostino, 1994; Zajonc, 1968). Repeated exposure facilitates processing. Of course, we may like a new acquaintance better after we get to know her better but, in fact, a prolonged interaction in which we acquire more information about her is not necessary. Moreland and Beach (1992; see also Saegert *et al.*, 1973) had confederates attend classes posing as students. Four women of equal attractiveness (an independent sample had rated their photographs) were selected. One of the women never attended class, the others 5, 10 or 15 times respectively. Great care was taken that these women did not interact (verbally or non-verbally) with the other students. They merely sat in class. At the end of the semester the other students rated the pictures of the four women. There was a strong effect that the rated attractiveness increased with the number of class visits. Because simple exposure to stimuli is sufficient to increase their perceived favourability, this effect is known as the **mere exposure effect** (Zajonc, 1968). Many studies have documented this phenomenon. Bornstein (1989) reviewed 200 studies with quite different stimulus materials (e.g. nonsense words, ideographs, geometric forms, photographs) and concluded from this evidence that overall, increased exposure to a stimulus increases liking for that stimulus. But as you may have guessed, the mere exposure effect also has its limitations. The increase in liking is strongest at a moderate level of repetition and levels off at higher levels of exposure, as shown in Figure 4.3.

Mere exposure effect: Increase in liking for an object caused by merely being exposed (repeatedly) to that object.

Recent research also showed that the effect is much stronger when the repeated stimuli are intermixed with new stimuli (Dechêne *et al.*, 2009). Presumably, the fluency experience elicited by the repeated stimuli is more diagnostic in the context of other less fluently processed stimuli (Wänke & Hansen, 2015). In fact, when only old stimuli were presented, no increase in liking could be observed.

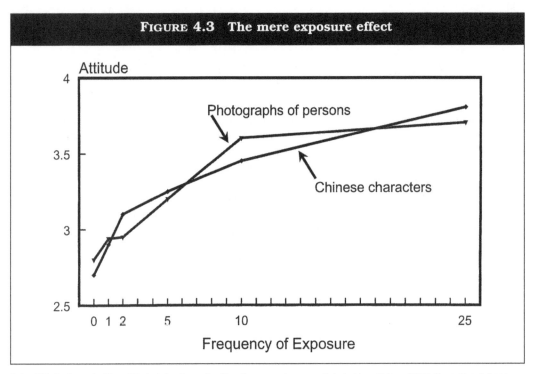

FIGURE 4.3   The mere exposure effect

Note: Attitudes towards different kind of stimuli as a function of exposure frequency (adapted from Zajonc, 1968, Figure 2, p. 14 and Figure 5, p. 18)

Furthermore, Bornstein's (1989) meta-analysis showed that the effect is stronger for more complex stimuli which is compatible with the assumption that fluency is more diagnostic for complex stimuli (see above). The effect is also stronger for shorter exposure times including subliminal exposure, for longer delays between exposure and evaluation, and for exposure sequences in which many other stimuli are presented as well. Finally, it is not necessary for participants to recognise the stimulus as having been presented earlier – in fact, conscious recognition seems to weaken the effect. Even when participants had no conscious recognition but were told that they had seen stimuli in a previous phase of an experiment the effects attenuated (Bornstein & D'Agostino, 1994). Apparently, when the stimulus is believed to be old, the fluency experience is correctly attributed to facilitation due to its previous presentation and not to the stimulus itself.

The fact that mere exposure effects are particularly strong when recognition of the stimuli fails or when the stimuli are presented subliminally (e.g. Bornstein & D'Agostino, 1992) suggests that mere exposure effects depend on unconscious rather than conscious memory. Separating unconscious and conscious memory indeed showed that liking for stimuli only correlated with unconscious but not with conscious memory (Hansen & Wänke, 2009).[1]

The principle of processing fluency as an underlying explanatory mechanism is not restricted to the domain of visual processing. The ease or fluency with which a name can be pronounced also has startling consequences. Fluent (easy to pronounce) names were found to be liked better (independent of their unusualness) and political candidates with more easily pronounced names had more appeal compared to more disfluent names (Laham *et al.*, 2012). Two findings are especially noteworthy as they again highlight the real world impact of pronunciation fluency. Among lawyers, surname fluency predicts higher positions in the firm hierarchy (Laham *et al.*, 2012). This relation also holds if one considers only lawyers with Anglo-American names (or lawyers with foreign names), ruling out any suggestion that the effect reflects some nationalistic bias in personnel selection. Another study showed that easy-to-pronounce stocks perform better at the stock market (Alter & Oppenheimer, 2006).

AFFECTIVE STATES

It does not take a degree in psychology to suspect that our current mood state influences how we evaluate things. Folk wisdom refers to rose-tinted glasses when happiness paints our evaluations in a more favourable hue than would usually be the case. When psychologists explored this phenomenon more systematically, they accumulated abundant evidence showing that attitude objects are indeed evaluated more favourably in a happy mood than in a less happy mood. For example, people who were given a small unexpected gift, which put them in a happy mood, subsequently reported higher satisfaction with a range of products they owned compared to other people who had not received a gift (Isen *et al.*, 1978). Job applicants received higher ratings when the interviewer was in a good mood (Baron, 1993), and mood also affected judgments about political candidates (Ottati & Isbell, 1996). Psychologists also provided explanations of why this phenomenon occurs and examined its boundary conditions (for reviews, see Clore *et al.*, 1994; Forgas, 2006; Pham, 2008).

Originally, it had been suggested that mood would prime evaluatively similar contents (Bower, 1981; see also Box 5.2 in Chapter 5 for the semantic memory model). If people remember the happy times of their lives in a good mood and subsequently rely on those memories for their overall evaluation of life, people would be more likely to report higher life satisfaction in a good mood than in a bad mood. Indeed, in several studies participants were more likely to recall happy memories when they were happy rather than sad and vice versa (for a review, see Blaney, 1986). One problem with the mood-priming explanation was that the evidence for mood-congruent recall is not as strong as one might expect (for reviews, see Bless & Fiedler, 2006; Schwarz & Clore, 2007).

Schwarz and Clore (1983) proposed a different explanation why good mood makes us evaluate things more favourably. According to these authors, a simple strategy of making an evaluative judgement is to rely directly on the feelings provoked by the presence of the attitude object. After all, things we like tend to evoke positive feelings, and things we dislike cause us to feel bad, so why not use these affective responses as a shortcut to an evaluative judgement? When we laugh at a joke, we probably find it funny; when the mere thought of a person elicits tense feelings we probably don't like that person. Interestingly, however, it is not always easy to discriminate between feelings elicited by the attitude object and the feelings one happens to experience at the time of judgement, but for irrelevant reasons. Unless we are aware of the origin of our feelings or at least aware that they have nothing to do with the attitude object, we may misattribute them to the attitude object. When you think about how satisfied you are with your life and ask yourself: 'How do I feel about it?', you may read your present good mood as indicating that life is just great, although in reality your positive feelings may have been caused by an exceptionally sunny day.

Schwarz and Clore (1983) examined this **mood-as-information hypothesis** or 'How do I feel about it?' **heuristic** in a field experiment. People were picked at random from the telephone directory and some were called on a sunny day, whereas others were called on a rainy day. The interviewers explained that they were conducting a study on life satisfaction and asked respondents how satisfied they were with their lives. Furthermore, the interviewers pretended to be calling from another town and, within each weather condition, initially drew the attention of some respondents to the current weather by simply asking 'By the way, how is the weather down there?' The pattern of interviewees' responses to the life satisfaction question, which is presented in Figure 4.4, calls into question Bower's priming hypothesis that positive or negative thoughts and memories about one's life, elicited by one's mood, are at the core of mood effects on judgement. Why is this the case? And why do the results instead support the mood-as-information hypothesis? Before reading the answer, take a look at Figure 4.3 and try to explain the observed pattern in terms of mood-congruent recall.

It can be seen that the results in one half of the study, where respondents' attention was *not* drawn to the weather as a plausible cause of their current mood, are compatible with either view. People reported higher life satisfaction when the weather was sunny rather than rainy. In fact, this result alone would be rather trivial and may have other explanations as well. However, if fine weather elicits good mood which in turn automatically primes positive life events, then these life events should also be recalled in the other half of the study, where people were made aware of the cause of their mood. Irrespective of whether good mood is elicited by the weather (or receiving a cookie or other sources), good mood would make happy life events more accessible. Thus, according to this perspective we would not expect different results whether or not people were made aware of the true cause of their mood. On the other hand, if we assume that people misattribute their happy moods to their (presumably happy) lives, then

Mood-as-information hypothesis: When evaluating an attitude object, a person's current mood informs them on how they feel about it. This information is used for the attitude, unless people are aware of the real mood source.

Heuristic: Simple rule that is used to form an (attitude) judgement with little cognitive effort (e.g. 'the majority is right' or 'experts' statements are valid').

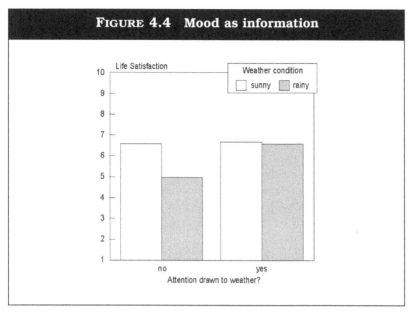

FIGURE 4.4   Mood as information

Note: Mood as information in judgements of life satisfaction as a function of the weather and whether respondents' attention was drawn to the weather or not (data from Schwarz & Clore, 1983)

being made aware of the weather as the source of mood should undermine this process. In turn, we would not expect higher life satisfaction in a happy mood than in a sad mood, which is exactly what Schwarz and Clore's (1983) data show.

There are other moderators of whether feelings are used for a judgement (for a comprehensive review, see Greifeneder *et al.*, 2011). If we assume that mood operates as information, its impact should depend on how much other information is available. Accordingly, consumers showed mood effects in their evaluation of unfamiliar products but not of familiar ones (Srull, 1984), candidate evaluations reflected mood effects mainly for individuals with little political knowledge (Ottati & Isbell, 1996), and mood was shown to influence ratings of ill-defined, complex targets, such as satisfaction with one's life in general, more than ratings of well-defined and specific targets, such as satisfaction with one's income (Schwarz *et al.*, 1987). In a similar vein, novices are more likely to use mood as information than experts, since the latter can build on more knowledge (Forgas & Tehani, 2005). How much other information we have also depends on the motivation and ability to retrieve more information from memory, a point we will elaborate later in this book. Indeed, more pronounced mood effects on judgements of life satisfaction were observed when individuals had less mental capacity available for making their judgement because they were distracted or under time pressure (Siemer & Reisenzein, 1998). Moreover, there are interindividual differences regarding the use of mood as information. For example, people differ in how much they attend to their feelings and accordingly mood effects are more or less pronounced (Gasper & Clore, 2000; Harber, 2005).

Mood is not the only affective experience that has an influence on our evaluative judgements. Incidental disgust, for example, seems to reduce liking if we take the price people were willing to pay for an object or willing to accept when selling an object as an indicator (Lerner *et al.*, 2004). However, the crucial question is to what extent the experienced emotion can be misattributed to the attitude object. Specific emotions are often directed towards a certain target. Anger, for instance, is usually evoked by some specific situation or person, and individuals tend to know what or whom they are angry about. Thus, specific emotions are less likely to transfer to evaluative judgements about things other than their true cause, and therefore they are less likely to serve as a basis for evaluative judgements (Schwarz, 1990, 2002).

Mood's informational value: a question of expectations

The mood-as-information account implies that mood represents relevant information. The impact of mood on judgement may depend on the informative implications of the mood state in the respective situation. When you laugh about a comedian, this indicates that you are amused. Probably you think the comedian is quite good. But when you laugh while watching a performance of *Romeo and Juliet*, this probably indicates that the particular performance was rather poor if it leaves you unmoved at the sight of Romeo's tragic and unnecessary death. Similarly, Martin *et al.* (1997) asked participants to grade happy and sad stories while in a happy or sad mood. Happy participants evaluated happy stories more favourably as compared to sad participants, but sad stories received higher ratings in a sad mood. Apparently, participants reasoned that a supposedly sad story which fails to induce sad mood is not a good story. Thus, participants again inferred their evaluation from their mood. However, they took the circumstances into account in interpreting what their mood indicated.

In a similar vein, one may argue that the affective feelings presumably evoked by the attitude object may be more relevant for some attitude objects but less relevant for others. When the pleasure one derives from an attitude object is central to one's attitude towards it, the current mood provides diagnostic information. For example, your good mood at a party may indicate that you are enjoying yourself and therefore it is a good party, but the same feeling at a seminar does not necessarily indicate that it is a good seminar, in the way that it prepares you well for the exam. Likewise, mood has been shown to have more impact when evaluating hedonic consumer products than utilitarian ones (Yueng & Wyer, 2004) or when the consumption goal was hedonic rather than instrumental (Pham, 1998). For example, when you try out a bike a happy mood is more likely to bias your evaluation in a favourable way if the bike is intended for pleasure rather than weight loss. Actually, if you think that weight loss is strenuous, effortful and torture, a happy mood might indicate that this bike may be ineffective for the purpose.

BODILY STATES

Please do us a favour and read the following paragraph smiling. Research suggests that you will like this paragraph better if you do. People smile when they like something and frown when they dislike something, and we have seen in Chapter 3 that recordings of minute movements of the smiling and frowning muscles can serve as measures of attitude. Apparently, the relationship between facial muscle contraction and evaluation also works the other way. Several studies suggest that the contraction of specific facial muscles produces corresponding affective reactions. James Laird (1974) told research participants that he was interested in measuring facial muscle activity and, apparently for this purpose, attached electrodes between participants' eyebrows, at the corners of their mouth and on their jaws. As part of the cover story, participants were instructed to contract different muscles at different times. With this instruction Laird could induce participants to smile or frown without mentioning a specific emotion. While 'smiling' or 'frowning', participants also rated cartoons according to their funniness. As it turned out, they rated those cartoons as funnier that they had viewed while 'smiling' as opposed to 'frowning'.

There are several explanations for this *facial feedback effect*. One is that people are aware that they are smiling or frowning and consciously interpret this reaction ('If I smile I must like it'). Indeed, many of these studies were criticised for the fact that participants knew that their facial muscle contractions represented a smile or a frown despite the fact that no emotion was mentioned in Laird's study. Thus, one cannot decide whether the effect on evaluative judgements is caused by a) automatic bodily feedback from the muscle contraction per se, b) people's knowledge that they are smiling and its attribution to the target of evaluation, or c) demand effects – i.e. participants knowing and complying with how they think they were expected to behave.

Strack *et al.* (1988) set out to clarify matters by manipulating the contraction of the zygomaticus (smiling) muscles in a truly unobtrusive fashion, thereby disguising the notion of smiling. Students were asked to rate cartoons according to their funniness. To manipulate facial muscles, participants were asked to hold the pen with which they indicated their ratings in their mouths. This was done under the pretext of testing the usability of answering scales for disabled persons who had lost the ability of using their hands. Some of the participants were asked to hold the pen between their teeth, without the lips touching it. Others were asked to hold the pen between their lips but not with their teeth (see Figure 4.5). You may try both conditions to get a feeling for what participants in the study experienced. You may notice that the teeth condition facilitates a smile whereas the lips condition prevents a smile. However, would you have been aware of this as a participant in Strack and colleagues' study, given the elaborate cover story? Probably not. Nevertheless, participants in the original study rated the cartoons as funnier when they held the pen between their teeth than when they held it with their lips. Similarly, in another study, participants rated phonemes more positively whose pronunciation facilitated (e.g. the vowel 'ee') rather than inhibited smiling (the German vowel 'ü') (Zajonc et al., 1989). Moreover, it has also been shown that reading times for sentences describing pleasant events were faster when readers held a pen with their teeth than with their lips and vice versa for sentences describing unpleasant events (Havas et al., 2007). Presumably, the congruent facial expression facilitated the encoding of the sentence.

These findings rule out the possibility that the effect of facial muscle contractions on evaluative responses is a demand effect or even requires conscious interpretation of one's facial expression – e.g. as a smile. They are more compatible with the assumption of a direct, non-conscious path from muscle contractions to evaluative responses.

Influences of muscle contractions on attitudes have also been observed for other body parts. Some researchers proposed that particular body movements may become closely associated with specific affective reactions. For example, when we reach out to grasp a desirable apple, arm flexion is more closely coupled in time with the object's consumption than is arm extension. In the pain-flexor reflex, arm extension is temporarily coupled with the onset of an aversive stimulus whereas flexion is associated with its offset. As a consequence, one may expect that flexion is associated with approach reactions and extension with avoidance reactions. To test this assumption, Cacioppo et al. (1993) presented research participants with characters of Chinese writing (ideographs), which were originally neutral. While the stimuli were presented, participants either pressed their lower arm down on a table (extension) or up against the underside of a table (flexion). Later participants indicated how much they liked each ideograph. The results indicate that arm flexion while viewing increased liking compared to arm extension while viewing.

Arm movement may also affect the evaluation of a priori valenced stimuli. This was, however, only the case when the affective reactions to the stimulus and the feedback elicited by the bodily movement were congruent (positive stimuli and arm flexion; negative stimuli and arm extension) but not when they were incongruent (Förster, 1998, 2004). Förster suggested a motor compatibility account according to which incompatible motor actions are more likely to be discounted as irrelevant information, whereas in the case of compatible responses the two influences are hard to distinguish and the evaluative responses combine rather unintentionally.

Intriguing results also come from studies on other movements' effects on later evaluations. Participants listened to a persuasive communication

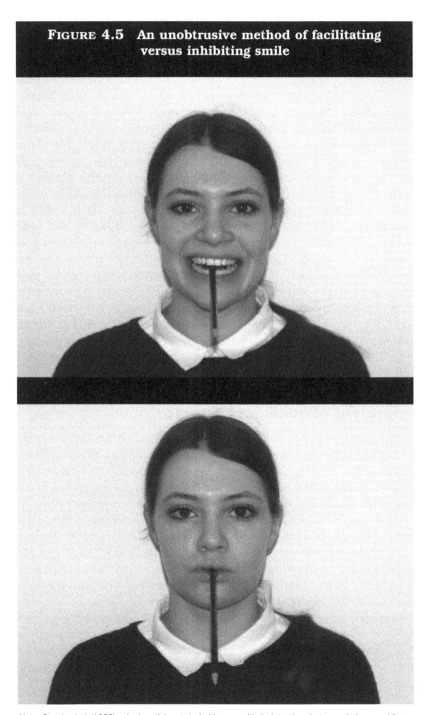

FIGURE 4.5   An unobtrusive method of facilitating versus inhibiting smile

Note: Strack *et al.* (1988) asked participants to hold a pen with their teeth or between their pursed lips, thereby facilitating vs. inhibiting smile. (Copyright Daschek/Scholtz)

(either supporting or contradicting participants' prior attitudes) presented via headphones (Wells & Petty, 1980; see also Briñol & Petty, 2003; Chapter 10, Box 10.2). Under the pretext of testing the functionality of these headphones when walking or dancing, some participants were told to move their heads horizontally (shake), others vertically (nod) while listening to the tape. When participants were later asked about their attitudes, those who had nodded while listening to the message reported attitudes more in line with the message content than those who had been shaking their heads.

Corrugator and zygomaticus activation represent types of muscular stimulation for which it is easy to see why they are associated with affective reactions. To some extent this is also true of arm flexion and arm extension if we consider these movements as representing approach or avoidance behaviour (but see below). The influence of head nodding and head shaking, however, suggests that the evaluative meaning of movements may also be acquired, in this example by adapting cultural conventions. Affective motor information may also be shaped individually. When skilled typists evaluated letter combinations, their evaluations differed systematically from those of non-typists. Compared to non-typists, typists showed less liking for combinations of letters that would be typed with the same finger (van den Bergh *et al.*, 1990) presumably because the letters unconsciously activated incompatible motor responses, which in turn elicited negative affect.

Appraisal of bodily sensations

All the studies described so far are consistent with a fixed link between body perception and evaluative implications. Usually, nodding symbolises agreement and headshaking disagreement. There is, however, also evidence that such expressive cues do not have invariant effects but are interpreted in the respective context and thereby change their implications respectively.

This was already suggested by a research programme conducted in the 1960s (Valins, 1966). Male research participants were allegedly hearing 'biofeedback' of their heartbeat while watching pictures of women. For some pictures, the alleged heartbeat was, however, manipulated by the researchers. It was either accelerated or slowed down. Those women whose pictures were shown with such an accelerated heartbeat were rated as more attractive than those presented with the baseline heartbeat. Likewise, in the other condition those women whose pictures were shown with the slower heartbeat were rated as more attractive. Apparently, the research participants had interpreted the change in heartbeat as information of their physical arousal, suggesting that physiological reactions may be subject to a subjective appraisal that lends meaning to them.

The meaning of real body sensations, such as head shaking and nodding, also depend on their respective contexts. In a social context, for instance, nodding is more often a reaction than an action. We want to agree with someone who has already expressed his opinion. Or we express our admiration for someone's achievement during or after its occurrence. In line with this idea, it has been shown that nodding leads to more positive evaluations if it occurs after the presentation of a neutral stimulus. Nodding before the neutral stimulus occurs, however, had no effect on stimulus evaluations (Wennekers *et al.*, 2012).

The context dependence of head nodding and shaking is particularly well illustrated in the following study (Tamir *et al.*, 2004; also see Laham *et al.*, 2014). Participants were made to nod or shake their head while seeing a video in which either a heroin addict describes the hardships of her life or an ex-convict who 30 years ago tortured and killed a girl, and complains about harassment by his neighbours when he now deserves to live in peace. Note that both videos were somewhat emotionally ambiguous and that nodding or shaking one's head may express different reactions depending on the video clip. Shaking one's head to the misery of the drug addict may be a sign of sympathy whereas shaking one's head to the murderer's story may be less a sign of sympathy but more of dismay and rejection. Although the participants later rated how personally responsible the target person was, the heroin addict was judged as less responsible for her situation by participants who had been induced to shake their head rather than nod. Vice versa, the murderer was attributed more personal responsibility by those who had been made to shake their heads rather than nod. Although the influence of the expressive cues was quite likely unconscious, these unconscious processes apparently took the meaning of this movement in the given context into account.

In sum, there is a host of evidence showing that not only do attitudes influence physical reactions but that the reverse is also true: **proprioceptive feedback** from both facial and body muscles may influence attitudes. The influence described here is often unconscious or at least unintended. Yet the path does not have to be direct – avoidance postures, mimics and gestures signal liking or disliking of the attitude object – but appraisals may determine the way in which bodily states influence how we evaluate things.

Proprioceptive feedback: Information that stems from an individual's perception of her own movements, muscle contractions or body posture.

GOALS AND NEEDS

Imagine Mark. Mark's company is considering abandoning meat and only serving vegetarian dishes in the cafeteria. Mark believes that the meat industry imposes cruelty on animals and in that respect he welcomes the change because he thinks of himself as a kind and moral person. He also believes that vegetarian food is healthy, but healthiness is not high on his agenda. Moreover, he also believes that vegetarian food is rather bland. In that respect the planned change is not conducive to his goal of deriving pleasure from eating tasty dishes. If Mark, however, had the goal of living a healthy life, his belief that vegetarian food is healthy would have more impact on his attitude. If part of his goal was to lose weight he might consider that less tasty food would help him to eat less and may actually be a good thing. Most stimuli are hardly inherently good or bad, favourable or unfavourable, but acquire their evaluative meaning by how they relate to a person's current goals and needs. A piece of apple pie is more attractive when being hungry (see the section on attitude functions in Chapter 1) (Lewin, 1935). Whatever fulfils our needs (and thereby induces pleasure) and brings us closer to our goals is clearly desirable, and whatever obstructs goal attainment is clearly undesirable. The emphasis here is on currently *activated* goals. People usually have quite a number of goals they would eventually like to reach, but these are not all equally relevant or accessible in different situations. When revising for an exam, you may be less concerned about meeting a potential dating partner as compared to when you are at a party. Because different goals may be activated at different times, the evaluation of an attitude object may vary over time, depending on how it advances currently salient goals. For example, a sweet stimulus was evaluated as more pleasing by fasting participants than by participants who had previously consumed sugar (Cabanac, 1971). As folk wisdom knows, hunger makes the best sauce.

Another, more sophisticated research example shows that when trying to change people's attitudes (see Chapter 8), information that is goal-relevant is more effective (Shavitt *et al.*, 1994). Participants either rated a list of behaviours according to whether they would make a good or bad impression on others, or they rated different tastes and smells according to their pleasantness. This procedure had been shown to activate either the goal of making a good impression or to find hedonic pleasure (Shavitt & Fazio, 1991). Afterwards, participants were shown an ad for a restaurant that showed rather unattractive guests endorsing the restaurant. Going to a restaurant that is frequented by rather dull and boring people may be seen as detrimental to one's image, but how strongly this affects one's evaluation of the restaurant and intention to visit the restaurant should depend on how salient the goal is of making a good impression on others. As expected, participants evaluated the restaurant less favourably when impression concerns had been activated rather than concerns about the taste of the food.

Interestingly, there is not only evidence that a currently activated goal increases the evaluation of a goal-relevant object but also that it decreases the evaluation of goal-irrelevant objects. People whose need to eat was experimentally increased rated non-food products as less attractive than people whose current need to eat was low (Brendl *et al.*, 2003). Both tendencies can prove quite adaptive by helping individuals to focus on goal-fulfilment and to dislodge from goal-irrelevant stimuli.

Unfortunately, things may be a bit more complex as people may have conflicting goals, and, moreover, what advances one goal may obstruct another. Accordingly, people may experience ambivalent attitudes towards an attitude object (Kaplan, 1972). Mark has to ponder whether eating tasty food is more important to him than sparing animals cruelty.

Having proposed a relationship between an object's goal relevance and its evaluation two things should be kept in mind. First, progress towards goals is seen as relative (Carver *et al.*, 1996). Even though individuals may progress, they may still experience negative affect if the progress is not as fast as they had anticipated. And vice versa: things that make a person progress faster than anticipated will be associated with positive affect. Second, an evaluation not only depends on the amount of progress towards a goal but also on the importance of the goal. For example, if avoiding cruelty to animals were more important to Mark, he would also evaluate a vegetarian meal more positively than someone for whom being kind to animals was not an important goal, even if both agree that vegetarian nutrition decreases cruelty to animals.

Whatever facilitates a goal is evaluated positively and whatever impedes goal progress is evaluated negatively. But, as seen above, the same attitude object may have implications for different goals, sometimes even contra-dictory implications. We will turn to this issue in Chapters 6 and 7 when we discuss the integration of different evaluative responses. Here, it suffices to say that integrating these different implications is made easier by the fact that not all goals are equally important. More important goals weigh more heavily in the summary evaluation than less important goals. Moreover, not all possible goals are necessarily activated simultaneously.

CONCLUDING COMMENT: SENSATION AND ADAPTATION

At the beginning of this part, we tried to show that how we evaluate stimuli may, to some extent, be hard-wired but is largely flexible and dependent on appraisal and attribution processes. We may be biologically programmed to prefer trees to utility poles, or chocolate to hemlock. Or, more generally, we may be predisposed to like what makes us feel good. After all, pleasure is more conducive to survival than pain, and therefore seeking pleasure and avoiding displeasure seems quite adaptive. In that sense, it is not surprising that experiencing pleasure (even the pleasure of easy processing) becomes a source of liking. Nevertheless, what makes this principle so widely adaptable is the fact that the experienced pleasure (or displeasure) does not need to stem from the attitude object. Incidentally, experienced affect may be misattributed to the object causing liking or disliking. Likewise, motor reactions that are associated with approach (arm flexion) or experiencing pleasure (smile) are read as an indicator of liking and those associated with avoidance (arm extension) or experiencing displeasure (frown) are read as an indicator of disliking. Perhaps the most fascinating aspect about the links between incidental affective states, experienced processing fluency and motor reactions to evaluations is their pliability. Although these processes occur largely outside awareness, they are sensitive to the situational context. It is probably this property that makes them highly adaptive as evaluation sources.

Having introduced the idea that the experience that guides the evaluation of a stimulus in a given situation does not have to come from the target stimulus itself, we will extend this further in the next chapter. You will see how the evaluation elicited by one object may become linked to another object, thereby forming attitude structures in memory.

CHAPTER SUMMARY

1   The ease with which stimuli can be processed (fluency) increases their liking. Fluency can be increased by visual features (e.g. contrast, clarity, Gestalt aspects), priming, repeated presentation, language aspects (e.g. pronuncability) and others.

2   The phenomenon that repeated exposure to a stimulus increases liking for that stimulus is called the mere exposure effect. Mere exposure effects are stronger for more complex stimuli, for shorter exposure times including subliminal exposure, for longer delays between exposure and evaluation, and for exposure sequences in which new stimuli are presented as well. It is not necessary for the effect to occur that participants recognise the stimuli.

3   People may infer their attitude towards an object from their current mood state if they misattribute their current mood as caused by the attitude object (mood-as-information). This account requires that people are unaware of the real source of the mood.

4   Mood is more likely to influence attitudinal judgements the less diagnostic information is available and the more diagnostic mood is deemed for the judgement.

5   Muscular activity may evoke specific affective responses.

6   The implications of fluency, mood and bodily states are not necessarily fixed but each may have different meaning in different contexts and depends on the respective interpretation.

Exercises

1   A car manufacturer has completely redesigned its models. In market research tests, consumers are shown the new designs. In direct as in indirect comparisons the old models fare much better. Can you encourage the designers or is the new line really a disaster? How could one improve the test to take into account mere exposure effects?

2   Think of body movements involved in everyday behaviour, including interactions with other people, machines/computers and consumption goods. Do you find arm flexion, arm tension or both? What movements or gestures signalling approach versus avoidance other than those mentioned in the text can you come up with?

3   Ask your co-students to what extent they like pasta. Do you think it will make a difference if you ask them before or after lunch?

Further reading

Fluency and affect-as-information:

Greifeneder, R., Bless, H. & Pham, M. (2010). When do people rely on affective and cognitive feelings in judgment? *Personality and Social Psychological Review*, 1–35.

Schwarz, N. & Clore, G. (2007). Feelings and phenomenal experiences. In A. Kruglanski & E. T. Higgins (eds), *Social Psychology: Handbook of Basic Principles* (pp. 385–407). New York: Guilford Press.

Embodiment:

Niedenthal, P. (2007). Embodying emotion. *Science 316*(5827). 1002–1005.

Goals:

Ferguson, M. & Porter, S. (2009). Goals and (implicit) attitudes. In G. Moskowitz & H. Grant (eds), *The Psychology of Goals* (pp. 447–479). New York: Guilford Press.

Note

1   Even though many articles have claimed that mere exposure effects are established without participants' awareness of the stimulus presentations, this claim is not entirely uncontested and counter-evidence has been presented as well (de Zilva *et al.*, 2013; Newell & Shanks, 2007). Some of the methodological challenges involved in demonstrating mere exposure effects without awareness are analogous to the challenges in the evaluative conditioning literature which will be reviewed in the next chapter. One example is the fact that awareness tests are often administered *after*, rather than during, the presentation stage, which turns them effectively into tests of long-term memory rather than tests of awareness during learning (de Zilva *et al.*, 2013).

Chapter 5

ATTITUDE CONDITIONING: HOW OBJECTS BECOME LINKED WITH VALENCE

When explaining others' attitudes, we tend to refer to learning processes: 'He must have had some really bad experiences with lawyers to hate them so much'. Likewise, people may list their negative experiences with a social group in order to justify their negative attitudes towards the group. Not only is it highly intuitive that attitudes are formed because attitude objects are accompanied by positive or negative consequences. Crucially, as anticipated in the previous chapter, it is not even necessary that an object *causes* a positive or negative experience. Instead, attitudes towards an object can result if an object merely co-occurs with some other, positive or negative attitude object. With that being said, a large body of scientific evidence demonstrates that attitudes can indeed be conditioned. There are various ways by which an attitude object could become linked with the valence of some co-occurring object. And as you will see, these processes make different predictions of whether, when and how we evaluate the attitude object.

ATTITUDES MAY BE CONDITIONED: THE CLASSIC APPROACHES

Classical conditioning: If the presence of a conditioned stimulus (e.g. a bell) covaries with the presence of an unconditioned stimulus (e.g. food), the presence of the conditioned stimulus alone will be sufficient to elicit the unconditioned response (e.g. salivation).

Most readers will be familiar with the **classical conditioning** experiment by the physiologist Pavlov (1927). After some exposures to the ring of a bell before feeding, Pavlov's dog then began to salivate upon the mere ringing of the bell, regardless of the presence or absence of food. In more general terms, after repeated pairing with an unconditioned stimulus (US; here food), a conditioned stimulus (CS; here the bell) will elicit the same physiological reactions as does the US. If we accept physiological and behavioural measures as indicators of attitudes (see Chapter 3), we might say that this first documented case of conditioning is also a demonstration of attitude acquisition: the bell becomes liked, as evident from autonomous reactions. And presumably, if one could ask the dog it would say that the bell sounds awesome!

A similarly prominent construct in the learning literature is operant conditioning. The basic idea behind *operant conditioning* is that behaviours followed by reinforcement become more frequent. By contrast, behaviours followed by negative consequences become less likely in the future. Thus, if a teenager feels appreciated by his peers after having expressed a positive attitude towards Islam, it will become more likely that he will express such an attitude in the future, again. The notion of conditioning verbal behaviours (Skinner, 1957) inspired many applications of reinforcement learning to attitudes. Typical studies on operant conditioning of attitudes involve an experimenter who interviews a participant about his or her attitudes. Unlike well-trained interviewers in professional attitude surveys, this experimenter signals agreement or disagreement by nodding, frowning or some verbal cues (e.g. 'good'). Participants are later – in some studies much later – again asked to report their opinions. In one study (Insko, 1965), students at the University of Hawaii were interviewed over the telephone about their opinions on initiating an 'Aloha Springtime Festival'. Several questions were asked, and half of the students were reinforced by the interviewer saying 'good' every time they responded favourably, whereas the other half were similarly reinforced for unfavourable responses. When the students were again asked about their attitudes towards the festival one week later in a rather different setting, this time using a paper-and-pencil survey, an effect of the conditioning could still be detected: the students who had been reinforced for unfavourable statements still reported a less positive attitude than those students who had been reinforced for favourable statements. Such findings have also profound applied implications. In opinion polls or market research, interviewers should be carefully trained to remain neutral and to avoid any verbal or non-verbal responses that may positively or negatively influence the interviewees' responses.

One might wonder if repeated expressions merely reflect some normative social influence, and respondents simply want to get along with the interviewer, or whether they reflect a more profound attitude shift. Theoretical considerations and empirical findings contradict the former and suggest the latter. First, reinforcement may also represent informational social influence. In other words, reinforcement can reassure individuals that they hold correct attitudes and may consequently strengthen these attitudes (cf. Chapters 9 and 10). Second, research showed that our behaviours – such as expressing attitudes – strongly affect our internal positions (see Chapter 7). In this sense, reinforcement might have a direct effect on the expression, but as an indirect effect attitudes towards the attitude object will follow. Note that it is not necessary that people experience reinforcement themselves. At an early age, children already learn by observing real and even fictitious social role models.

Learning does not guarantee correct attitudes

In the first chapter, we pointed out that attitudes fulfil the function of organising knowledge as well as regulating approach and avoidance behaviour. In this sense, the human ability to learn from the co-occurrence of attitude objects and situational stimuli constitutes one of the most intriguing capacities of the human mind (Crocker, 1981), enabling us to hold 'correct' attitudes, meaning they are adapted to environmental demands (see knowledge function, Chapter 1). Yet, it is noteworthy that learning from co-occurrence does not guarantee that one holds correct attitudes.

For one thing, the informational basis on which attitudes are formed is often not representative of the real world, but provides us with systematically biased samples. For instance, media such as TV presents us with a highly selective sample of information (Gerbner, 1969; Gerbner & Gross, 1976). Whereas, for most of us, violence is an exceptional experience in real life, it is omnipresent in television programmes (Gerbner *et al.*, 1986). Although our experience with objects, ideas or behaviours is indirect – we are not attacked ourselves, nor do we attack others – conditioning can take place, just because we learn from social role models. In TV programmes, from James Bond to *Game of Thrones*, protagonists show a wide range of aggressive behaviours with high frequency. The common denominator of these contents is that desired outcomes, such as peace or freedom, are reached through violent behaviours. Furthermore, the role model is not only reinforced, but it is also liked, which is an optimal precondition for vicarious learning to take place (Bandura, 1962). As a consequence, positive attitudes towards aggression would become very likely.

Second, people's representations of the observed co-occurrence are often biased in a systematic fashion. For example, a plethora of studies on stereotype formation suggests incorrect prejudice may follow from insufficient covariation learning (e.g. Hamilton & Gifford, 1976; Mullen & Johnson, 1990). In their original demonstration of the so-called illusory correlation phenomenon, Hamilton and Gifford (1976) provided participants with information about individuals belonging to one of two social groups, and displaying either positive or negative behaviour. An important characteristic of the experimental material was that one group occurred more often than the other (thus constituted the numerical majority), and positive behaviour was displayed more often than negative behaviour. Specifically, 18 out of the 26 majority members were described as having behaved in a desirable way. For the minority group, the number of positive behaviours was set to 9 out of 13. Although the proportions of positive to negative behaviours were equal within both social groups, members of the majority were judged more favourably than minority members. In a condition in which negative behaviours were more frequent than positive ones, the effect reversed, yielding less positive trait assignments towards majority than minority members. Illusory correlations have been replicated in numerous studies (Mullen & Johnson, 1990), even in experiments in which participants were reinforced for making accurate judgements about the social groups (Kutzner *et al.*, 2011). Since occasions for learning about different categories (e.g. different ethnic groups) vary in their frequency, learners have problems integrating experiences into correct attitudes. Hence, a person justifying a negative attitude towards a minority group, because one personally experienced them as aggressive, may just have fallen prey to illusory correlation, which links rare groups with rare behaviours (for other frequency-based illusory correlations, see Fiedler *et al.*, 2013; Vogel *et al.*, 2013; Vogel *et al.*, 2014).

To wrap up, various classic conditioning and learning accounts serve as plausible explanations for attitude formation based on experience. Together, they suggest that attitudes are a mirror of our past experience with the object, direct or indirect, but this mirror may sometimes be biased. However, it must be added that little of the research on these approaches directly addressed the formation of attitudes. In the next paragraphs, we will deal with research that directly addressed the conditioning of attitudes.

EVALUATIVE CONDITIONING

To start with, consider an everyday object, such as a pen. Which colour would you prefer, light blue or beige? Would the background music in an advertisement change this preference? This is what is suggested by the following experiment (Gorn, 1982): participants were shown an advert featuring a pen, which was either beige or light blue. The music played was either from *Grease*, an up-beat musical, or a piece of classical East Indian music played at half-speed. According to pilot studies, *Grease* generally produced a positive emotional response whereas the East Indian music elicited a negative response. Thus, four conditions were run, with each of the two colours being paired with either liked or disliked music. After having rated the advert and the music, participants were told that they could select a pen as reward for their participation. Two colours were available: light blue and beige. The results showed that when the liked music was played, the advertised colour was chosen in 79 per cent of the cases. This might merely reflect that the advertisement in general, fostered some positive attitudes. Crucially, however, among participants who had been exposed to the disliked music, only 30 per cent chose the advertised colour, but 70 per cent decided for the non-advertised colour. As such, the experiment nicely illustrates evaluative conditioning as well its viability for applied purposes. However, it also shows that practitioners have to take care when choosing the US. In Gorn's study the music was carefully pretested for eliciting positive versus negative responses. Outside of the lab it may well be possible that the music chosen to appeal to a particular target group serves as a negative US for other recipients. Not surprisingly, commercials featuring country music caused negative product evaluations among recipients who dislike country music (Redker & Gibson, 2009).

By now – more than a hundred years after Pavlov's seminal work – the conditioning of attitudes, better known as **evaluative conditioning (EC)**

Evaluative conditioning: Attitude change towards an object due to paired exposure with a valenced stimulus.

established a distinct research field in social and cognitive psychology. Simply defined, EC refers to the change in *liking* of a stimulus after pairing with some valenced stimulus. In contrast, Pavlovian conditioning refers to a change in *behaviour* which results from the pairing of stimuli (de Houwer, 2007; Hofmann *et al.*, 2010).[1]

Early evidence of EC was already obtained in empirical investigations by Staats and Staats (1957, 1958). In one of the authors' studies (Staats & Staats, 1958), participants were asked to learn words presented in different modalities. Nationalities (e.g. 'French') appeared on a screen, and an experimenter subsequently read a word. For all nationalities, the spoken word was neutral (e.g. chair), except for 'Dutch' and 'Swedish'. In one condition, 'Dutch' was followed by positive (e.g. sacred), but 'Swedish' was followed by negative words (e.g. ugly), but in the other condition it was the other way round. When asked to indicate how they felt about the words, participants rated either 'Swedish' or 'Dutch' as more pleasant, depending on which nationality had been followed by the positive word. Other illustrations of evaluative conditioning exploiting trial-by-trial learning procedures, such as the picture–picture paradigm (Levey & Martin, 1975), corroborate the idea that mere pairing is sufficient for EC effects to occur. In a first phase, participants are asked to rate a series of pictures. In a second phase, participants see pairs of pictures: pictures they had previously rated as neutral are presented together with a picture rated previously as either positive or negative. The prominent finding is that, in a third phase, formerly neutral pictures get more favourable ratings than before, if they had been paired with positive stimuli. In a similar vein, evaluations become worse for those pictures that had been paired with the negative stimuli.

By now, many studies showed that the liking for an object depends on whether it had been paired with positive or negative stimuli, testifying to the importance of the evaluative conditioning approach in explaining attitude formation (for a review, see Hofmann *et al.*, 2010; Walther *et al.*, 2011). However, for EC to become a theoretically meaningful construct, one might think that it requires more than just taking 100 years of classical Pavlonian conditioning and changing the dependent measure from autonomous behaviour to liking. In the following section we will address some specific characteristics of EC, proposed as setting it apart from Pavlonian conditioning (e.g. Baeyens *et al.*, 1993; Walther, 2002) and all of which have high practical relevance for influencing attitude formation.

EC vs. Pavlovian conditioning

Since the very beginning of evaluative conditioning research, different researchers have postulated specific characteristics that distinguish EC from other forms of learning (particularly Pavlovian conditioning) but not all of them withstood empirical tests (for a review, see Hofmann *et al.*, 2010). In the following we will review the major findings.

First of all, evaluative conditioning differs from Pavlonian conditioning in so far as mere co-occurrence of the CS and the US is sufficient (Baeyens *et al.*, 1988; Baeyens *et al.*, 1989). Pavlonian conditioning is sensitive to the statistical contingency between the presence and absence of the CS and the presence and absence of the US. If one is present, the other should be present as well. Learning effects become less likely the more often either CS or US appear without the other. EC effects, however, do not follow this principle. Imagine an advertisement in which George Clooney (a positive US) was paired with a coffee brand (a rather neutral CS). Every time one encounters the ad, a joint observation of George Clooney and the coffee brand occurs. But given the prominence of the actor and depending on the popularity of the coffee brand, one may likely encounter each separately. George Clooney stars in many movies – not advertising coffee; the coffee brand is found in many households, offices and stores – without George Clooney being around. By the laws of Pavlonian conditioning, these separate observations should undermine the formation of an association between George Clooney and coffee, and dilute the extent to which the positive evaluation of George Clooney is transferred to the coffee brand. EC is, however, only dependent on spatial and temporal contiguity (i.e. cases in which both CS and US are present independent of their separate occurrence), and will occur despite isolated observations. From this point of view, evaluative conditioning is an auspicious concept for applied purposes. Marketers do not have to fear dilution effects just because a celebrity endorser or a piece of music is omnipresent.

The insensitivity to isolated US or CS encounters may suggest another crucial consequence: whereas Pavlonian conditioning effects decrease after a while when the paired observations are not repeated and the separate observations prevail, evaluative conditioning effects have been assumed to be immune to extinction (Baeyens *et al.*, 1988). Considering the wide range of studies, however, the claim of resistance to extinction appears too strong. Effects become weaker if paired observations are not repeated but the CS is repeatedly encountered without the US after the acquisition phase (Hofmann *et al.*, 2010).

Another difference from Pavlonian conditioning is that the pairing of the CS and the US does not result in the expectation that the US will follow after the CS appears. When encountering the coffee brand – say, in the supermarket – your attitude towards the coffee should be relatively positive. But this is not because you expect George Clooney to appear in the next aisle (at least, we think you don't). As obvious as this might seem, this fact is not trivial, but points to an important question:[2] what exactly did the celebrity actor change in ad recipients' attitude towards the coffee? How is the new representation of the coffee different from its representation before the paired observation?

In the next paragraph, let us have a look at the **attitude structure** resulting from evaluative conditioning.

Attitude structure:
Representation and organisation of different attitudes or of components belonging to one attitude in memory.

Underlying mental processes

Some authors argued that people form holistic representations (Martin & Levey, 1994): Once the CS was paired with the US, aspects of the US fuse with the representation of the CS. This entails that valence becomes part of the new CS representation, and upon future encounter the CS will yield the evaluative response. Later approaches, however, gave up the idea of a fused representation, but assume that the CS remains a separable concept. Instead, it is assumed that the CS becomes linked with the US, but different approaches suggest different processes.

According to the *referential account* (Baeyens *et al.*, 1992), the two stimuli become associatively linked. This association holds that the CS and the US get interconnected so that the recurrence of the CS leads to an automatic activation of the US. Upon future encounter, therefore, the coffee brand will activate the actor. In turn, the positive valence associated with the actor will become activated, too. Notably, this means that individuals do not store a direct association between the CS and the evaluative response. This is also why EC can be considered a form of stimulus–stimulus learning (see Wickens, 1959).

Some evidence that the CS (e.g. coffee) becomes linked with the stimulus (e.g. the actor), but not with the evaluative response (e.g. 'Awesome!'), stems from so-called US revaluation experiments (Baeyens *et al.*, 1992; Sweldens *et al.*, 2010; Walther *et al.*, 2009). In one study (Walther *et al.*, 2009), participants first learned about ostensible colleagues, half of whom were described by positive attributes, the other half by negative attributes. In the next phase, these colleagues served as USs and each picture was paired with a picture of an ostensibly novel colleague (CS). For these novel colleagues no person information was given. In the third phase, participants were given additional information about the 'old' colleagues. In the revaluation condition, colleagues previously described with positive attributes were now described with negative ones, but colleagues formerly described with negative attributes were newly described with positive ones. In a control condition, participants also received additional information. However, this information was neutral, thus not changing the US valence manipulated in the first phase. At the end of the experiment, an evaluative priming task (cf. Chapter 3) served to indicate the attitude towards all stimuli, CS and US. Results not only showed that the manipulation was effective, as evident from the fact that originally negative US became less negative, but originally positive US became less positive in the revaluation than in the control group. The important finding was that the interaction of valence by revaluation condition was also evident in the CS evaluations. As such, the outcome indicates that the individuals learn a connection between CS and US, not the unconditioned response. Once the US changes its valence, the liking for the CS associated with the US may also change. Thus, whenever you encounter the coffee brand, George Clooney will pop up in your mind. The evaluative response towards George will then reflect the evaluative response towards him *at the time of retrieval.* The advertising effects evoked by pairing an actor with a coffee brand might reverse, once the actor loses his appeal, as might be the case if he were involved in a scandal or was cast in bad films.

The referential approach, however, is not the only approach to suggest that EC reflects stimulus–stimulus learning. This is also suggested by the *propositional account* (e.g. De Houwer, 2009a, b; Mitchell *et al.*, 2009). However, as an alternative to associative links as presumed in the referential account, it is maintained that in addition to the US valence, evaluative conditioning effects depend on the perceived relations between the CS and the US (cf. Box 5.1). A positive attitude towards the coffee brand then would reflect that people also stored a positive relation between the CS and the US. They might remember that the coffee has been drunk, liked or endorsed by the actor: 'This coffee is great because it's the coffee of my star!' Interestingly, the approach specifies conditions under which the pairing of a CS with some positive US will lead to disliking – namely, if a negative relation between both is perceived. If, for example, a popular celebrity rejects the offered coffee, the coffee should become more negative. In contrast, a mere associative account would predict a more positive evaluation by the pairing with a positive US irrespective of the relationship between US and CS.

In line with a propositional approach to evaluative conditioning, it has been shown that relations between CS and US moderate the effects of the pairing. In one experiment, neutral and valenced faces were paired as usual, but in addition, participants assumed that the depicted persons were either friends or enemies. In the case of friends, the standard EC effects emerged, but in the case of enemies they reversed (Fiedler & Unkelbach, 2011). Likewise, persons were evaluated more positively when they were shown with positive animals (e.g. a kitten) rather than negative animals (e.g. a pit bull) if they were explicitly described as liking the respective animal, but the effect reversed when they were described as disliking the animal (Förderer & Unkelbach, 2012).

Evaluative conditioning, however, does not necessarily have to result from stimulus–stimulus learning (see also Chapter 7). This is suggested by Jones and colleagues (Jones *et al.*, 2009) who proposed affect misattribution as a process underlying EC effects. From Chapter 3, you may remember the measurement technique of the affect misattribution procedure (AMP; Payne *et al.*, 2005). This measure actually exploits the idea that a valenced stimulus will elicit some affect, which is then misattributed to an ambiguous target. Whereas measures based on affect misattribution are concerned with revealing the attitude towards the valenced stimulus, the research question could actually focus on what happens to the valence of the target stimulus. Thus, affect misattributed to the target can also be considered an instance of attitude formation, an idea we dealt with in Chapter 4. Taking this idea one step further, one might consider affect misattribution as a source

Box 5.1   Attitudes in memory

Attitudes can be understood as a form of representation in a semantic network (e.g. Anderson, 1983; Collins & Quillian, 1969). Semantic
network models assume that concepts and features are stored in the
form of nodes. These nodes are connected with each other via links.
If one node was activated, this activation is assumed to spread.
Spreading activation then may activate related nodes. The higher the
associative strength, the more likely related nodes become activated.
This already suggests that some concepts might be more or less
strongly linked with positive or negative features. This idea is articulated more clearly in Bower's model (Bower, 1981). Here, it is explicitly noted that some nodes represent affective states (e.g. a happiness
node). Pertinent to the formation of such networks (e.g. by conditioning), simultaneous activation of two concepts is assumed to
strengthen the links. Thus, it is predicted that the co-occurrence
of a CS with a US causes that future activation of the CS spreads to
the US, or its features, such as valence (cf. Figure 5.1).

Importantly, several ideas have been articulated about the nature
of the links connecting the nodes. Anderson and Bower (1972) first
proposed **associative links** which were assumed to connect similar
concepts. For instance, if we activated the concept tiger, concepts
sharing the same features, such as lions or pumas, therefore are likely
to become activated, too (e.g. Collins & Loftus, 1975). In a later
conception, they proposed links as **propositional** in nature (Anderson
& Bower, 1974; Bower, 1981): concepts are interconnected via some
abstract relations that can be probed as *true or false*, suggesting that
co-occurrence can lead to connections between dissimilar concepts.
For instance, soup and a spoon do not have much in common. Yet,
there is a clear link because soup is usually eaten with a spoon. Thus,
thinking of a soup might easily activate the concept of a spoon.

In attitude psychology, the differentiation between association
and proposition has taken a central role. Propositional processes are
often opposed to associative processes to refer to different
mechanisms behind learning (Mitchell *et al.*, 2009) or the formation
of evaluative judgements (Gawronski & Bodenhausen, 2006, 2007,
2011; cf. Chapter 7). Whereas associative processes are assumed to
depend on mere co-occurrence and follow the principle of simple
activation, propositional reasoning is assumed to consider relations
as well as their truth value. In the case of a news anchor, a strong link
may exist to the concept of war. Hence, upon encounter an associative
process would yield that the concept of war, and in turn negative
valence, became activated. However, the relation that the anchor
'reports on' war would exclude the negative valence associated with
war. A negative relation such as the anchor 'does not like' war might

Associative link: Type
of link between concepts in
a semantic network. The
activation of one concept
(e.g. news anchor)
facilitates the activation of
another (e.g. war),
depending on how strong
the associative link is.

Propositional link:
Type of link between
concepts in a semantic
network. Propositional links
consist of how a concept is
semantically related to
another and can be probed
for their truth.

even cause a more positive evaluation of the anchor. Despite some theories assuming either associative or propositional processes (e.g. Mitchell *et al.*, 2009), some theories state their co-existence. In these dual-process models, propositional processes are conceived as a higher-order cognitive process, which may serve for correcting false evaluations triggered by the associative process (Gawronski & Bodenhausen, 2006; also see Strack & Deutsch, 2004).

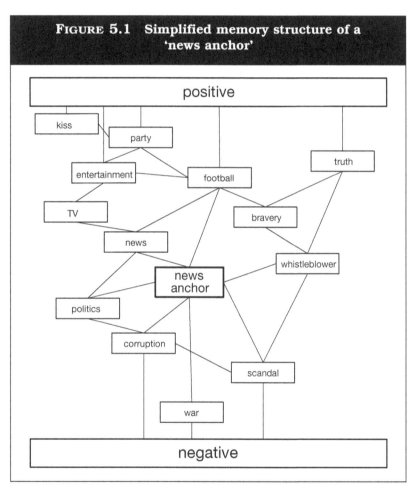

FIGURE 5.1   Simplified memory structure of a 'news anchor'

Note: Some of the concepts (e.g. 'football') are directly related to an evaluative response. Due to repeated co-occurrence with the concept of 'football', a strong connection between these concepts (as illustrated by shorter links) has been built. In semantic network models, it is further assumed that each concept is characterised by specific features. A news anchor might have the features 'serious' and 'smart', which distinguishes him from an overarching concept (e.g. prominent TV person). For the sake of parsimony, these hierarchical relations are not depicted here

of evaluative conditioning. According to this perspective, individuals may consider affect as an indicator of their liking for a conditioned stimulus, even though the affect was evoked by the unconditioned stimulus.

Whereas the classical mood-as-information account implies that currently experienced affect has an impact on evaluative judgements, Jones and colleagues propose that such misattributed affect may be more firmly linked to the CS. If true, stronger evaluative conditioning effects should be observed when source confusion is very likely, as was the case when individuals' attention switched between the stimuli. Eye-gaze recordings during the presentation of CS–US pairings were used to measure such attention shifts. In line with the prediction participants who frequently switched attention between the CS and the US showed stronger conditioning effects. Misattribution to the conditioned stimulus should also be more likely the more salient the conditioned stimulus is compared to the unconditioned stimulus. Accordingly, larger conditioned stimuli also resulted in stronger effects. Finally, a moderately valenced US had more impact than an extremely valenced US. Presumably, strongly evocative stimuli are more likely to be identified as the source of affect, but mildly evocative stimuli leave space for some misattribution.

Note that a misattribution account assumes that the US changes the valence of the CS, but does not become part of its representation. Hence, EC effects would result from stimulus-response learning: the association is not formed between the two stimuli, but between the CS and the evaluative response elicited by the stimulus (for a detailed discussion of the theoretical accounts, see Walther *et al.*, 2011). Importantly, provided that EC occurred due to S-R learning (Figure 5.2), the CS should consequently remain unaffected by a subsequent change in the US' valence. Hence, whereas this model can account for the findings obtained by Jones *et al.* (2009), it cannot account for the revaluation phenomenon described above.

Unaware EC

The different accounts not only differ in how valence is attached to the CS, but another critical feature is whether EC is considered an automatic form of learning that happens without awareness, or whether awareness is required. Although this question has been addressed in many studies, the evidence for either idea, to date, is only indirect. One finding suggesting that stimuli awareness is required is that EC effects are unlikely if stimuli are presented in a subliminal way (e.g. Hofmann *et al.*, 2010). It therefore seems that EC does not occur if people are completely unaware of the stimuli. A more prominent debate on the awareness issue in EC does not focus on stimuli awareness, but on contingency awareness: do individuals know that the CS has been paired with a certain US?

The propositional account assumes that individuals are aware of the specific stimuli that have been paired with each other and of the relation between the two stimuli. According to this perspective, the coffee ad of our

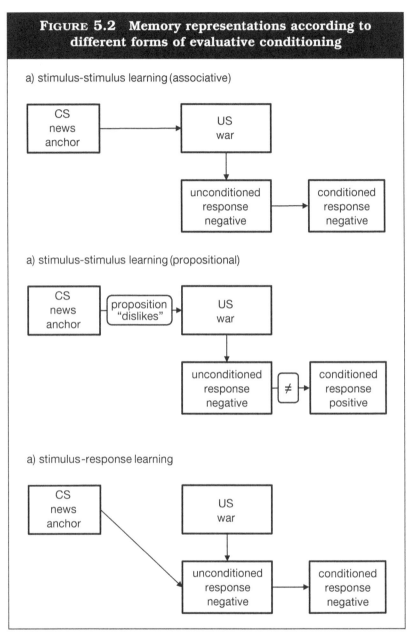

FIGURE 5.2 Memory representations according to different forms of evaluative conditioning

a) stimulus-stimulus learning (associative)

a) stimulus-stimulus learning (propositional)

a) stimulus-response learning

Note: According to associative stimulus–stimulus learning, the concept of the CS becomes linked with the concept of the US, but no direct link forms between the CS and the evaluative response (Figure 5.2a). The same holds for the propositional account. Yet, here the link contains the relation between the concepts. A negative relation between CS and US reverses the response associated with the US (Figure 5.2b). The conditioned response then is positive. Stimulus–response learning refers to the formation of a direct link between the CS and the unconditioned response (Figure 5.2c)

previous example should prove ineffective in increasing brand liking if consumers do not remember that George Clooney loves the coffee. This is likely to happen if during ad exposure recipients do not notice the brand but are completely mesmerised by the celebrity endorser, the funny story, the stunning visual effects or other elements.

The implicit misattribution account actually predicts the opposite and proposes that evaluative conditioning actually profits from a lack of contingency awareness (cf. Jones *et al.*, 2009). The less one remembers the source of the affect the more likely the affect will be misattributed and therefore transferred to the CS. At the experimental level, contingency awareness is typically tested for by assessing participants' ability to recollect the CS–US pairings.

The empirical evidence regarding the contingency awareness issue is mixed. Some authors reported that evaluative conditioning effects occur without awareness for the CS–US pairing (Bayens *et al.*, 1990; Dickinson & Brown, 2007; Walther & Nagengast, 2006), others showed conditioning effects depended on memory for the CS–US combination (Pleyers *et al.*, 2007; Stahl *et al.*, 2009). Also a meta-analysis (Hofmann *et al.*, 2010) finds much stronger EC effects for pairings that participants can recollect. On the other hand, some authors have argued that methodologies that are used to assess contingency awareness may be biased in favour of concluding awareness because participants may infer CS–US pairings from the attitudes they had formed (Hütter *et al.*, 2012; Hütter & Sweldens, 2013). Indeed, using a more sensitive procedure, Hütter and colleagues found compelling evidence for both contingency-aware and contingency-unaware EC within the same paradigm.

Finally, evidence for contingency-awareness is only indirect because awareness is assessed at the time of evaluation and not at the time of presentation: people who note the pairing at the time of exposure but have forgotten it on a later encounter with the CS would be classified as contingency-unaware. Therefore, some effects may erroneously have been interpreted as contingency-unaware EC because participants could have realised the pairing during acquisition, but failed to remember it when expressing their attitudes (for a detailed discussion, see Sweldens *et al.*, 2014).

How to skin the EC cat?

We used the role of contingency awareness to illustrate different predictions by different theoretical accounts. Similar analyses could be done with other procedural conditions with similar results. First, different theoretical accounts are compatible with some of the procedural moderators, but not with others, and none is compatible with all moderators. Second, because of the many contradictory findings it is difficult to establish reliable conclusions about the moderators to begin with. Against this background one may conclude that there is more than one way to skin a cat. EC may not be tied to one particular underlying process but different processes may cause the CS to acquire the valence of the US. Thus, researchers recently started to look for the boundary conditions determining which of the processes will cause EC (Hütter & Sweldens, 2013; Peters & Gawronski, 2011; Sweldens *et al.*, 2010; Zanon *et al.*, 2014). For instance, Sweldens and colleagues (Sweldens *et al.*, 2010) observed US revaluation effects only if the CS is always paired with the same identical US, rather than with several USs of the same valence. Apparently, individuals can store the relation between two specific stimuli, but storing the relation between a CS and multiple USs becomes overwhelming. However, they may still know whether the overall valence associated with the CS was positive or negative. Thus, EC effects obtained when Clooney exclusively advertises the coffee brand may reflect S–S (stimulus–stimulus) learning, as is proposed in the referential and the propositional account. In contrast, EC effects observed after several celebrities had endorsed a party in an election campaign may be explained by accounts presuming forms of S–R (stimulus–response) learning. Furthermore, it appears that the temporal contiguity moderates which processes take place. For instance, research by Hütter and Sweldens (2013) suggests that contingency unaware EC as implied by the affect misattribution approach only takes place if US and CS occur at the same time. In addition to such empirical findings, contemporary dual-process models such as the Associative-Propositional Evaluation Model (APE) (Gawronski & Bodenhausen, 2006; see Chapter 7), suggest that CS and US may become linked in an associative or propositional manner, depending on how much logical reasoning is involved during acquisition.

Despite some controversy regarding the underlying processes, evaluative conditioning has proved a robust phenomenon (Hofmann *et al.*, 2010; Walther *et al.*, 2011). A meta-analysis of more than 200 studies reports moderate effect sizes. As a key module in attitude acquisition, therefore, it has great impact on attitude research. Also, practitioners in marketing as well as psychotherapy can largely profit from evaluative conditioning as a tool, although the application can be tricky.

CONCLUDING COMMENT: FROM NATURE TO NURTURE

We started this part of the book by a demonstration of evolutionary based preferences, such as a newborn's preference for sweetness. Also in support of the 'nature' part in attitudes, we summarised some findings relating to individual differences based on genetic variability. On the other hand, a long history of research suggests that attitudes are acquired. The principles of covariation learning and classical, operant and evaluative conditioning, all offer insights in how our attitudes are shaped by experiences. But in the end, is nurture more important than nature? Different genotypes develop different attitudes because they make different experiences. This can be the case because they come with different talents and are reinforced differently for creative, athletic, intellectual or other performance, thereby leading to different attitudes. In this way, one cannot easily understand the nature influence without taking account of nurture. On the other hand, how could we learn if we started from scratch? At an early age in particular, reinforcers are biologically determined. Children may possibly never develop a positive attitude towards Halloween without having a grounded preference for sweets. Thus, rather than deciding pro or contra nature, the most comprehensive understanding lies in a consideration of the joint influence of nature and nurture on our attitudes.

Together, a picture emerges whereupon our attitudes are shaped in the history of mankind (i.e. the phylogenetic level), and the history of our personal lives (i.e. the ontogenetic level). Whether we like or dislike an object largely depends on the valence of past experiences with the object itself or experiences while it has been encountered. In the course of life, attitudes develop and become entrenched in memory. However, as demonstrated in the previous chapter, attitudes are not necessarily stable, but react to situational states. Even evaluations that are established in memory appear dynamic and may vary across situations. It is the context-dependent malleability of our attitudes that we will address in the next chapter.

CHAPTER SUMMARY

1   Evaluative responses may be conditioned by reinforcement (operant conditioning). To some extent, reinforcement is successful because it represents social information about the validity of one's attitude. Alternatively, reinforcement may represent social norms with which one wishes to comply. It is not necessary that an individual personally experiences reinforcement; the observation of other people's attitude being reinforced may suffice.

2   Evaluative conditioning refers to the change in liking for a stimulus after it has been paired with a valenced stimulus. Different from Pavlonian conditioning, the conditioned stimulus does not signal the occurrence of an event. Also, EC has been shown to be less dependent on the statistical CS-US contingency, but mere co-occurrence is a sufficient condition for EC effects to be obtained.

3   Theoretical accounts differ with regard to some key variables: the role of contingency-awareness, whether it reflects stimulus-stimulus vs. stimulus-response learning, and the nature of links between CS and US.

4   Despite evidence for contingency-aware EC, EC also occurs when people are unaware that the CS had been paired with the US.

5   When EC reflects stimulus-stimulus learning, EC effects are affected if the US valence changes after the CS and the US had been paired.

Exercises

1 Think of your attitudes towards candy, cars and communism. To what extent do you expect these attitudes to be shaped by evolution or in the course of your life? Think of direct and indirect paths.

2 In a TV commercial promoting pesticides, the brand is shown together with spooky bugs. Can evaluative conditioning explain that such advertisements have the intended effect of creating positive attitudes towards the brand? How does the answer depend on the theoretical approach to evaluative conditioning?

3 Few sportsmen earned as much money from advertising than Tiger Woods. Major labels, from Nike to Gatorade, paid the golfer up to a billion dollars to promote their brands. And as would be predicted by all EC accounts, the golfer's great success helped to advance the attitudes towards the brands. Around his career's climax, however, headlines about Tiger Woods turned from sports to sex and transgression scandals. Would EC accounts predict that the brands become less favourable, once that Tiger Woods' image suffered? According to EC, would it make a difference if sponsors terminate the contract?

Further reading

Evaluative conditioning:

Walther, E., Weil, R. & Langer, T. (2011). Why do we like the iPhone? The role of evaluative conditioning in attitude formation. *Social and Personality Psychology Compass, 5,* 473–486.

Notes

1 In a strict sense, the distinction is critical because every assessment of liking somehow involves observing behaviours, autonomic or not. This becomes most obvious if one considers participants' behaviours in indirect measures such as the IAT (cf. Chapter 3). At the operational level, therefore, a paradigm is suitable to capture EC to the extent to which the dependent measure is accepted as revealing the liking. Given the divergent findings for typical attitude measures as opposed to behaviours, however, we consider the definition as useful. Nevertheless, it is noteworthy that EC and Pavlonian conditioning paradigms are not differentiated in terms of the acquisition procedures. Thus, so-termed Pavlonian conditioning and EC can occur in the same paradigm, but stimuli show different effects on measures of liking than on other behavioural measures.

2   Finally, it remains a methodological question whether people do not
    expect Clooney to co-appear with the brand. The threshold for saying
    that one expects a US might be very high in many paradigms. Paradigms
    in which there is a lower threshold for expressing US expectations might
    actually reveal the expectation: holding a packet of coffee in your hand,
    whose actor's portrait would you expect to be on the reverse?

Chapter 6

MALLEABLE ATTITUDES: BETWEEN STORED REPRESENTATIONS AND CONTEXT-DEPENDENT CONSTRUCTIONS

As discussed in Chapter 1, sometimes you just know what your attitude is. The attitude object evokes an immediate evaluative response, a phenomenon referred to as automatic attitudes (more precisely, automatically accessible attitudes). Simply thinking of anchovies elicits a 'yuck' response (or 'yummy' for other people). For other stimuli this may not be the case, but instead an attitude is constructed in the respective situation. You may not immediately know how you feel about skiing, but you might ponder about it for a while. What comes to mind when you think about skiing can be thought of as the building blocks from which you construct your attitude. In a most general way, one may think of attitudes as the result of integrating information relevant to the attitude object, where each piece of information holds evaluative implications. As we have described in Chapter 4, your evaluation of skiing may be influenced by the feelings you are currently experiencing. You may interpret your good mood when thinking about skiing as evidence that thinking of skiing makes you feel happy and that therefore you must like skiing. The present chapter will extend the idea that current situations may determine one's attitudes by bringing relevant aspects to mind from which the attitude is constructed. Attitudes depend on which information is considered and how this information is evaluated, and how it is ultimately integrated.

In our skiing example, you may retrieve some instances when you went skiing (it was cold, the scenery was beautiful, it was expensive, you felt sore for days, you had fun meeting people on the slope, etc.). Your final attitude will depend on how positive and how negative each piece of information is for you, and how you weigh the different implications. Even if attitudes come to mind, they may be the result of an earlier construal that was stored in memory, or perhaps a very fast and efficient construal. This chapter will take a look at some aspects of the construal process: *information retrieval* and *information integration*.

As we review each of these processes it will become obvious that situational influences operate at each step, a point we also saw in Chapter 4. Consequently, attitudinal responses may vary across situations, a fact that caused Tesser and Martin (1996) to remark that 'the three most important influences on evaluation are context, context, and context' (p. 421). That context influences attitude reports has already been shown in Chapter 2: respondents in an opinion survey favoured or opposed welfare spending depending on the directly preceding question in the survey. There again, such context effects do not necessarily reflect measurement errors. They might also indicate that attitudes differ depending on the situation. We like our jobs better when we think about the friendly ambience in the office rather than the long hours we work or when we compare it to being unemployed rather than to our dream job. We also evaluate a slice of apple pie quite differently when we are hungry than we do after having just finished a sumptuous meal.

Because attitude reports are highly context-sensitive, some scholars have proposed that attitudes are constructed on the spot based on the information currently at hand (for reviews, see Lord & Lepper, 1999; Schwarz, 2007; Wilson & Hodges, 1992) rather than stored entities that are merely retrieved from memory or stable personal dispositions. We will discuss the respective evidence for each position at the end of the chapter.

INFORMATION RETRIEVAL FOR ATTITUDE CONSTRUCTION: WHAT COMES TO MIND

Let's return to the skiing example. It illustrates that relevant information can consist of a belief that the attitude object possesses a certain attribute (e.g. skiing is expensive). For some attitude objects, such as (social) categories (e.g. dictators, fast food restaurants), the relevant information may also consist of exemplars of these categories (e.g. Stalin, your favourite fast food restaurant).

When constructing a judgement, people rarely retrieve all potentially relevant information; instead, they are likely to base their judgement on a subset of that information (e.g. Bodenhausen & Wyer, 1987; Wyer & Srull, 1989). Whether a particular piece of information will be retrieved and used depends on how accessible it is in memory – that is, how easily it comes to mind. Accessibility in turn is influenced by a number of different factors (see Higgins, 2012, for a review). Some pieces of information may be more memorable than others because of their inherent qualities. Events or facts that stood out, were unexpected or had vivid qualities are more likely to be remembered than banal, ordinary and pallid information. For example, when asked for their satisfaction with their telephone provider, customers tended to spontaneously recall instances causing dissatisfaction rather than satisfactory experiences (Schul & Schiff, 1993). For products and services people expect adequate performance and smooth experiences will go unnoticed. Failures, however, cause emotional upset and will more likely be remembered.

Accessibility of information also depends on how frequently it is accessed and how it is organised in memory. Again, the conceptualisation of memory as a semantic network (cf. Chapter 5) serves to illustrate this. As shown in Figure 5.1, semantic nodes are connected via some links, along which activation can spread between nodes (e.g. Anderson & Bower, 1973; Bower 1981). In such models, information is being retrieved when the activation of its node exceeds a certain threshold. The closer the activation level is to the threshold, the more likely it is that any additional activation will cross the threshold and bring this information to mind. The activation level of each node slowly decays over time if it does not receive input from activation spreading through the network. The activation level of a given node thus depends on the *recency* of its last activation.

At any given time, frequently activated information is generally close to the threshold and more likely to cross it (i.e. it is more accessible) than information that is activated rarely, all else being equal. Information that is well connected to many other nodes in memory is generally more likely to be activated than relatively isolated information. These factors – inherent salience, frequency of activation, and connectedness, etc. – contribute to the accessibility of information independent of the particular situation (**chronic accessibility**). Representations of attitude objects and in turn attitudes depend to some extent on chronically accessible information. Linda, who defines herself as a liberal, may think of the need to strive for social equality whenever she thinks about welfare. This is because she frequently discusses social justice and equality, and as these values are very important to her, they are linked to many different concepts in her memory.

But to some degree attitudes depend on information that is accessible only in the specific situation (**temporary accessibility**; for reviews, see Bless & Schwarz, 2010; Lord & Lepper, 1999; Tesser, 1978; Tourangeau & Rasinski, 1988; Wilson & Hodges, 1992). The temporary accessibility of information is mainly determined by the length of time since the information was last activated (i.e. its recency; Wyer & Srull, 1989). At any given time, people's attitudes are likely to reflect specific information that was activated recently, in addition to chronically accessible information. In Chapter 2, we reported how such recently activated information may stem from the preceding questions in an attitude survey. In a survey where preceding questions had activated liberal beliefs, respondents favoured increased welfare spending more than in a survey where the preceding question had activated conservative beliefs (Tourangeau *et al.*, 1989).

Of course, the origin of temporarily accessible information is not limited to the preceding questions in a survey. Experimental research has used different techniques to activate information prior to attitude assessment and has overwhelmingly shown that attitudes reflect the situationally accessible information. For example, students considered discrimination as a more

Chronic versus temporary accessibility: The ease with which information comes to mind due to situational factors (temporary) or factors independent of the specific situation (chronic).

pressing problem in society when a well-liked minority exemplar (e.g. the athlete Michael Jordan) had been activated in a previous 'unrelated' experiment (Bodenhausen *et al.*, 1995). Outside of the laboratory, people are primarily concerned with issues that get coverage in the media, and frequently or recently covered issues have a large impact on how people evaluate politicians (for a review, see Iyengar & Kinder, 2010). Imagine, for example, a public opinion poll on attitudes towards using trains rather than private cars. You are one of the people asked. When assessing your attitude towards taking the train, you immediately think that trains are inconvenient and expensive. Consequently, you will arrive at a quite unfavourable opinion. Imagine, however, that just the day before you had watched a TV programme on carbon-dioxide emission and global warming. Because this information was acquired quite recently you can still remember it and with this piece of information your evaluation of train use becomes a little more favourable. Had the programme been broadcast a month ago, you may not have recalled this information, at least not immediately without expending some effort thinking about the issue (see also Figure 6.1).

FIGURES 6.1A AND 6.1B   Attitudes depend on what comes to mind

Note: People's attitudes towards eating meat may differ depending whether they think of a sizzling mouth-watering steak or the cruelty of slaughterhouses ((a) © blickwinkel/Alamy Stock Photo; (b) B. and E. Dudzinscy/Shutterstock.com)

This example also demonstrates that the more you think about an issue, the more information you will generate. Assuming that the evaluative implications of the information vary, different judgements will result at different points of the thought process. That is why 'mere thought' – that is, simply thinking about an issue without receiving any external information – may instigate attitude change. Attitudes may become more extreme (polarisation) if the thoughts are evaluatively consistent (Tesser, 1978; see also Chapter 8), or they may become less extreme if the thoughts are inconsistent (Chaiken & Yates, 1985).

Taken together, these findings whereupon thinking about an attitude object may change its evaluation also indicate that judgements may be constructed based on current thoughts rather than simply being retrieved. Because the temporary accessibility of thoughts about the attitude object will vary over situations, attitudinal judgements are also likely to vary. It should be noted, however, that so far we have treated the evaluation of each piece of information as given. In our train example, we presupposed that reducing carbon dioxide in the atmosphere is a good thing. Whether a piece of information has positive or negative evaluative implications is influenced by the processes covered in Chapters 4, 5, 8 and 9.

WEIGHTING

When more than one piece of information is accessible, the resulting attitude may not reflect all in equal proportion. Some may be more important than others. Clearly, many factors influence the weighting of attributes of the attitude object. Individually shaped preferences as well as contextual factors such as currently activated goals determine what people consider important or less important and thereby contribute to the variety in attitudes. There are nevertheless also systematic influences here; we only discuss one such aspect – namely, the psychological distance to the attitude object.

Imagine you want to buy a radio to listen to music in your kitchen. The radio you buy also has a clock. As it turns out, the only place in your kitchen where you can put the radio is in a corner where the reception is good but you cannot see the clock. Alternatively, consider that the only available place has bad reception but offers a good view of the clock. Not surprisingly, participants in that study (Trope & Liberman, 2000) thought they would be more satisfied when reception was good rather than bad. After all, the goal of the purchase was to listen to music and that was clearly more fulfilled by the radio with the good reception. However, the evaluation also depended on the time frame. When the purchase was believed to be tomorrow, the clock was more important than if the purchase was considered in a year from now. Apparently, people put a little more weight on the clock in the near future rather than in a more distant time (see Figure 6.2).

According to **Construal Level Theory** (Trope & Liberman, 2003, 2010), people construct different representations of the same information

Construal Level Theory: A theory stating that mental representations become more abstract with increasing psychological distance.

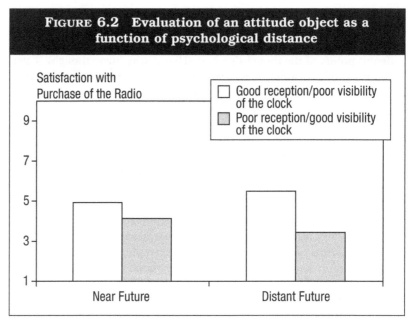

FIGURE 6.2   Evaluation of an attitude object as a function of psychological distance

Note: Essential features have more impact on evaluation if the attitude object is perceived from a distance (Data from Trope & Liberman, 2000, Exp. 3)

depending on the psychological distance, be that temporal distance, spatial distance, social distance or involving hypotheticality (e.g. the likelihood of an event actually occurring). With increasing distance, representations become more abstract and consist mainly of general, superordinate and essential features (high-level construals). In contrast, low-level construals tend to be more concrete and include subordinate, contextual and incidental features. Thus, the impact of a low-level detail (clock in a radio) will be higher relative to a high-level essential feature (reception) when considered from a close distance rather than a large distance. With regard to goals, one might say that from a larger distance attributes are evaluated in terms of advancing the essential goals related to the attitude object (listening to music), whereas from a short distance non-essential goals (reading the time) become relatively more important.

HOW THE JUDGEMENT IS PUT TOGETHER

From everything in this chapter you may have inferred that whether or not a piece of information is used in a judgement merely depends on whether it comes to mind at the time of judgement. If so, it is integrated in an additive or averaging manner (for a detailed treatise, see Anderson, 1971). But things are more complicated. The impact of a particular piece of information depends on *how* it is used (for a review, see Bless & Schwarz, 2010). Not all information that comes to mind is necessarily included in the mental representation of the attitude object. A second factor to consider in the construal of attitudes, in addition to what information is used for the mental representation of the attitude object, is what is used as a standard of comparison. How satisfied you are with a vacation at a three-star hotel depends whether you compare it to a five-star hotel or to a youth hostel. Finally, another factor to consider is the amount of effort spent in information integration and the construal of attitudes.

Beyond accessibility: the appropriateness of information may moderate its impact on judgement

Not every piece of information that comes to mind in a situation is necessarily considered as diagnostic, appropriate or really belonging to the attitude object. For example, when rating a restaurant what may come to mind is the slow service experienced on that day. You may, however, also recall that the staff was reduced to half its size due to a flu epidemic, so you are inclined to ignore the slow service. But what happens when information is deemed inappropriate? Do people simply disregard such information and ignore its implications? The data suggests otherwise. In a study on viewers' satisfaction with television (Bless & Wänke, 2000) participants were given a list of television shows and were asked to pick either two 'typical' high-quality shows or two 'typical' low-quality shows. The list contained a few good shows, a few bad shows and several shows that had been judged as neither good nor bad in pilot testing. Not too surprisingly, individuals who were asked to indicate good shows reported higher satisfaction with TV than those who had been asked to indicate poor shows. This merely reflects that different shows were temporarily accessible in the different conditions. However, in two additional conditions participants were asked to indicate 'exceptionally good' or 'exceptionally bad' shows. As it turned out, they indicated exactly the same good or bad shows, no matter if the instruction asked for 'typical' or 'exceptional' shows – after all, they could only choose from the same list in either condition. But when asked later about their satisfaction with what is broadcast on TV, responses were quite different, as Figure 6.3 reveals.

Assimilation: Evaluation of a stimulus is shifted towards the valence of a context stimulus.

This example demonstrates that identical information can lead to either **assimilation** effects, which means that the judgement reflects the evaluative implications of the information, or **contrast** effects, which means that the judgement reflects a shift in the opposite direction. In the study just described, the information was seen as inappropriate to use for the judgement when it had been categorised as exceptional rather than typical. Typicality is one aspect of appropriateness. Various other factors may indicate that the information is inappropriate to use (for a review, see Bless & Schwarz, 2010).

Contrast: Evaluation of a stimulus is shifted in a direction opposite to the valence of a context stimulus.

Different models have suggested different processes for how people deal with inappropriate information and why it elicits contrast. First, people may

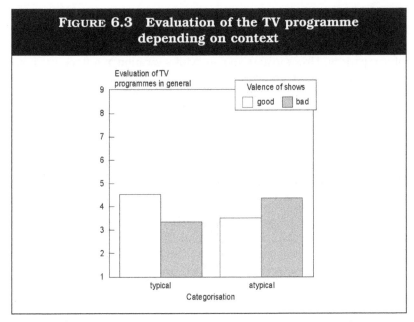

FIGURE 6.3   Evaluation of the TV programme depending on context

Note: Appropriateness of information affects evaluations: evaluation of the TV programme in general depended on whether participants had previously indicated in a list of TV shows which shows were typical and good, typical and bad, exceptional and good or exceptional and bad. Importantly, within each condition of valence participants had picked the same shows as typical or exceptional (data from Bless & Wänke, 2000)

correct for any influence of inappropriate information, provided that they are motivated to judge accurately and have a subjective theory about how the information would influence their judgement (Strack, 1992; Wegener & Petty, 1997). For example, they may be aware that selecting rather good TV shows may have unduly biased their overall evaluation. In order to eliminate the bias they may 'correct' their judgement and make it less positive. If they were accurate in their assessment of a potential inappropriate influence, then any effects of the accessible but inappropriate information should be wiped out. But often people overcorrect; then, contrast rather than no effect occurs.

Second, information deemed inappropriate may be used as a standard of comparison. Respondents may think that compared to those exceptionally good shows the programme overall does not seem so appealing (for a more detailed account, see Bless & Schwarz, 2010). This brings us to a central factor in evaluation.

Standards of comparison

All evaluations are relative. One main reason for this relativity is that we evaluate stimuli with regard to a particular standard. Change the standard and you change the evaluation. This phenomenon is documented in a wide range of studies. For example, being exposed to highly attractive women decreased men's attractiveness ratings of other women, including their own wives (Kenrick *et al.*, 1989). Men and women rate themselves as less attractive after viewing a highly attractive person of the same sex (Brown *et al.*, 1992). Participants in one study rated themselves as more satisfied with their lives when they had previously heard a person suffering from kidney malfunction talk about his problems (Strack *et al.*, 1990).

This demonstrates that the standard of comparison induces a contrast effect. Similar to Gulliver, who appeared as a giant among the diminutive inhabitants of Lilliput but as a midget among the huge people of Brobdingnag,[1] a moderate stimulus will be evaluated more favourably against a negative rather than positive standard. In other words, the standard induces a shift in the target evaluation away from the standard. Depending on the valence of the standard of comparison used, our evaluations of a stimulus will vary. Needless to say, the standard we use depends on which information is (chronically and temporarily) accessible. In the above studies on attractiveness, participants were deliberately exposed to highly attractive standards. While you may have certain people with whom you usually compare your attractiveness – say, your best friend or your classmates – thumbing through a fashion magazine may activate professional models as a standard of comparison, and you are likely to come away feeling fat and ugly (Grabe *et al.*, 2008). A glance around you at the supermarket or the bus may prove helpful in this situation by introducing less extreme standards of comparison.

Note that we consider a standard of comparison a stimulus against which the target stimulus is evaluated. In this role a standard of comparison will most likely elicit contrast, as explained above. But a context stimulus may also elicit a comparison process that highlights possible similarities between the context and the target, and thereby elicit assimilation (e.g. Brunner & Wänke, 2006; Mussweiler, 2003). A context stimulus may thus have two ways to influence the evaluation of the target: a) by influencing its mental representation and b) by functioning as a standard against which the target is evaluated. Both processes are not mutually exclusive but may operate in an additive fashion. For example, a product may benefit from the flagship model of the brand by emphasising the shared parent brand, but at the same time the flagship model will be used as a standard of comparison next to which the other products pale (Wänke *et al.*, 2001). Both influences may cancel each other, and this is one explanation why sometimes context influences do not have an observable impact on the evaluation of the target.

Constructing attitudes or constructing judgements?

So far, we have shown that attitude reports depend on many situational influences. In light of such evidence some researchers suggested that attitudes do not represent stable structures in memory but are constructed in the respective situation based on the currently activated information (e.g. Schwarz, 2007). This perspective, however, has not gone unchallenged.

With the progression of implicit measures (cf. Chapter 3), researchers equipped themselves with tools allowing for closer inspections of situational influences during the evaluation process. The divergent findings obtained from implicit versus explicit measures inspired much theory development, but also relaunched the debate on what an attitude actually is. Defining attitudes as summary evaluations, some theorists proposed models that explain situation-dependent variations as an outcome of variable attitudes (e.g. the Meta-Cognitive Model: Petty *et al.*, 2007; the constructivist model: Bohner & Schwarz, 2001; Schwarz, 2007). Others suggested that attitudes are stable, but their judgemental and behavioural consequences differed across situations (e.g. the Motivation and Opportunity as DEterminants Model (MODE): Fazio, 1990, 2007; Fazio & Towles-Schwenn, 1999; see below). Given the difficulty of measuring an attitude independent of observable judgements, some models instead abandoned the attitude construct but focused on the observable judgements (e.g. the Associative-Propositional Evaluation Model (APE), see Chapter 7, Gawronski & Bodenhausen, 2006, 2007, 2011; the Iterative Reprocessing Model: Cunningham & Zelazo, 2007; Van Bavel *et al.*, 2012). To provide the reader with a parsimonious explanation for context-dependent evaluative judgements without giving up a file-drawer perspective (see Chapter 1), let us consider context influence on evaluation against the backdrop of the MODE model.

The Motivation and Opportunity as DEterminants Model (MODE)

MODE model: Model on attitude-behaviour relations. It states that automatic attitudes guide behaviour as long as people want and can behave different from the attitudinal implication.

Fazio's **MODE model** (1990) suggests that attitudes are stored in the form of object-evaluation links. Just as people store non-evaluative knowledge about objects, they may have stored an evaluation about the object. Such links – which do not necessarily exist for all objects – may vary in strength (see Converse, 1975). The stronger the link, the more automatically – inevitably and effortlessly – the object will yield the evaluative response upon encounter.

Conceiving attitudes as stable memory representations, the model is compatible with the file-drawer perspective (cf. Wilson *et al.*, 1990). Therefore, attitude change would require some change in memory, rather than some situational influence. But how does the model accommodate the findings demonstrating varying attitudinal responses as a function of different goals and contexts?

The answer is very simple. The MODE model does not regard such responses as attitudes but merely as proxies for the underlying attitude. Originally conceived as a model for describing attitude–behaviour relations (cf. Chapter 13), the MODE model only considers the inter-temporarily stable object-evaluation link as an attitude. Any observable evaluative responses – including a verbal response, a marking on a scale or a key stroke in an IAT – are understood as behavioural responses which are triggered by the stored evaluative link, the attitude proper, but which are not equal to the attitude. Thus, by denying that the attitudinal responses that measure attitudes stand for the actual attitude, the model can uphold that 'true' stable attitudes exist despite situationally variable responses.

The evaluative responses may differ from the stored attitude for various reasons. First, if the evaluation is not very strongly linked to the object it may fail to get activated in a particular situation. But even in case of automatic attitudes (those always activated) the evaluative response may diverge. As is suggested by the acronym, whether the overt behaviour (the evaluative response) follows from the activated evaluation (attitude) depends on an individual's motivation and opportunity to adjust the behavioural response. For example, surrounded by some smart co-students, fans of gangster rap music may not want to admit their admiration for the music, but may instead say that it was trashy. The mere motivation to engage in a counter-attitudinal behaviour (response) is not sufficient on its own, however: one must also have the opportunity to alter the response. On the dance floor, perhaps after a few glasses of gin & juice, real fans of gangster rap may have problems glossing over their automatic attitude. In sum, the MODE model does not consider attitudes as constructed, but construction processes occur between the activated attitude and some observable evaluative judgement (or behaviour).

The model implies that attitudes (the stored evaluative links) are more accurately captured by implicit than by explicit measures. Due to the indirect nature of the implicit measures – respondents do not know that their attitudes are being probed – responses are less likely to reflect motivational distortions. Moreover, since the most widely used implicit measures (i.e. the IAT and the priming procedures, cf. Chapter 3) are characterised by respondents having to respond as fast as possible, it is usually taken for granted that they lack the opportunity to change their response, thus revealing the automatically accessible attitude. The finding that explicit ratings were more affected by impression management goals than implicit measures therefore supports the model's predictions (cf. Dunton & Fazio, 1997). But what about situational influence on implicit measures (cf. Chapter 3)?

Implicit measures are not immune to situational influences. They are affected by the used instrument and also by situational variables. Let's first look at measurement issues. As described in Chapter 3, many studies found systematic influences on IAT scores depending on the stimuli used to represent the attitude object (as well as the attributes used to represent valence – e.g. Bluemke & Friese, 2008; Nevid & McClelland, 2010). For example, IAT scores regarding US President Barack Obama differed among conservative participants depending on whether in the pictures of Obama used in the IAT the President's skin colour was artificially manipulated (Nevid & McClelland, 2010). When Obama's skin colour was made to appear lighter, conservatives showed more favourable IAT scores compared to the IAT version with darker skin colour. This result raises the question of to what extent the IAT score reflects the attitude towards Obama. Various answers are possible. First, of course, no measure, not even if implicit, is perfect. Situational variations may simply reflect measurement error (Fazio & Olson, 2003). Note, however, that in the present example the error is systematic (as it depends on condition). Yet, there may be undetected confounds explaining why measurement error produces this result. Second, the material makes different aspects of Obama salient that themselves are linked to evaluations. This would imply that there is not necessarily one (stored) attitude towards Obama but depending on the situation different evaluative links get activated and guide the evaluative response. For this it is not necessary for the aspect to have been previously associated with Obama. Such an assumption would allow for situational construed implicit responses. Third, the different scores may indeed reflect different attitudes as there are different *stored* representations of Obama with the respective stored evaluative links – that is, conservatives have a stored positive evaluative link for a light Obama and a more negative link for a darker Obama. Given that in the present example the stimuli were artificially produced, it is doubtful that an evaluative link could have been pre-established, but in other examples such a possibility may exist. Again, this would, however, imply that there is not one attitude towards Obama but many, depending on what comes to mind. In this vein Fazio (2007) argues that variations in implicit measures are not due to the attitude's instability, but that across situations the target of evaluation changes. Across situations people are likely to retrieve attitudes for different objects (positive African Americans vs. negative African Americans).

The two latter assumptions (i.e. either the context may cause different representations to be construed or different representations of an attitude object exist) also explain why even the same implicit measure may yield different results depending on the situation. For example, compared to a baseline, IAT scores regarding African Americans were more favourable when a film clip had activated positive rather than negative stereotypes about African Americans (Wittenbrink *et al.*, 2001). In another study, non-thirsty participants showed less favourable responses towards thirst-relevant objects (e.g. water) on an evaluative priming measure than participants who had not drunk anything before the experiment, but were asked to eat salty pretzels instead (Experiment 2, Ferguson & Bargh, 2004; for related findings, see Seibt *et al.*, 2007). To be sure, none of this rules out the possibility that stable evaluative links unaffected by situational variables exist in memory. However, such findings demonstrate that even implicit measures do not seem to capture them.

To sum up, whereas the constructivist perspective suggests that people construct different attitudes towards the same object across situations, Fazio suggests that people retrieve their attitude towards different objects across situations (Figure 6.4).

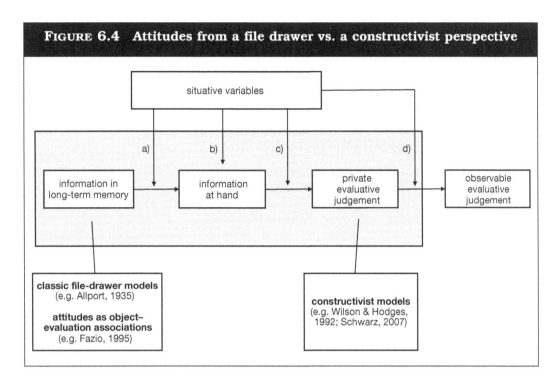

FIGURE 6.4   Attitudes from a file drawer vs. a constructivist perspective

Note: Situative variables determine which information is at hand when making an evaluation, by a) moderating what is retrieved from long-term memory, or b) by providing novel relevant information. Situative variables also moderate c) how the information is integrated into an internal evaluation, and they may further moderate d) how this evaluation is revealed in observable judgements. Whereas both perspectives agree on the moderating function of situational factors on observable behaviours, they disagree which part in the unobservable "black box" (shaded area) constitutes the attitude. From a file-drawer perspective, the attitude represents the stable representation in long-term memory (left part of the shaded area); from a constructivst perspective, it is the outcome of the integration process (right part of the shaded area)

Yet, these diverging theoretical perspectives about what an attitude is and how it is represented make very similar predictions regarding the observable response upon encounter of the stimulus. It seems doubtful, therefore, that this debate can be resolved by empirical evidence. Therefore, some researchers warned of making strong assumptions about what an attitude is (De Houwer *et al.*, 2013). But perhaps it may be attributed to the pragmatic appeal of the attitude construct itself that even proponents of a more parsimonious use of the term attitude presume that there is something to be called attitude that acts between external stimuli and evaluation behaviour, without explicating its nature in the evaluation process.

Unfortunately, it is very difficult, if not impossible, to arrive at definite conclusions regarding the exact nature of mental representations (Wyer, 2007). [. . . But . . .] we can assume that there must be some kind of attitude toward a given stimulus if the presence of that stimulus causes an evaluative response. However, the mere occurrence of evaluation does not allow one to draw strong conclusions about *how* the attitude is represented (Greenwald & Nosek, 2009).

(De Houwer *et al.*, 2014, p. 13)

CONCLUDING COMMENT: TEMPORARY CONSTRUCTION VERSUS STABLE REPRESENTATION

The constructivist perspective mainly rests on attitudes' context sensitivity. Despite their malleability, though, there is also evidence suggesting the stability of attitudes. For example, social and political attitudes tend to be rather stable after young adulthood for the rest of the life-cycle (Alwin *et al.*, 1991; Krosnick & Alwin, 1989). How can a constructivist perspective explain stability over time? Related to this matter, recall that the information that is accessible in any given situation only depends on temporary factors to some degree. Some information is chronically accessible and will come to mind independent of the situation. To the extent that attitudes are based on the part of the information that is chronically accessible, they will reflect stability. To the extent that they are based on temporarily accessible information they will reflect instability as long as the information accessible at time 1 and time 2 also has different evaluative implications (see Schwarz, 2007 for a more detailed discussion).

Accordingly, if the proportion of chronically accessible information is large compared to the proportion of temporarily accessible information, stability of attitude will ensue. This is likely to be the case for well-rehearsed attitudes. In fact, it does not make sense to assume that some information may be chronically accessible through frequency of activation and then exclude attitudes from this process. Moreover, one may expect that similar contexts activate similar information. So even temporarily accessible information may not vary much over time as long as the context in which the attitude is constructed does not change much. When people do not simply rely on what comes to mind easily but instead exhaust their memory, they are likely to come up with more similar information each time. Unless they learn new information, this may also contribute to the stability of attitudes.

Evidence comes from studies in which people reported their attitudes towards several social groups (e.g. politicians, homosexuals, etc.) and named one group exemplar on two occasions one month apart. Among people who named the same group exemplar on the two occasions, the attitudes were more stable than among those who recalled different exemplars (Sia *et al.*, 1997). Moreover, in another study, individuals who retrieved the same exemplars across five weekly assessments were more resistant to attitude change following a counter-attitudinal message than individuals who named different exemplars (Lord *et al.*, 2004). These data suggest that attitude stability is a function of the congruency of the information that comes to mind.

So the constructivist perspective can account for situational variations as well as stability. We have already seen that some models propagating a file-drawer perspective, such as the MODE model, can also accommodate findings showing that evaluation varies across contexts. Different from the constructivist perspective, however, its proponents would deny that the attitude varied across situations, but only the evaluation behaviour. In this account, it is only the stored evaluation that is considered the attitude. With that being said, it appears a matter of preference if one considers the attitude as malleable or not. Independent of your personal preference for either perspective, the interplay of chronically accessible, stable context and temporarily accessible information is pretty important from a functional perspective.

As in Chapter 1 already addressed, it is reasonable to assume that summary evaluations function to simplify the environment and to regulate approach-avoidance. If people were to construct their attitudes anew each time they confront an attitude object, but could not profit from their past experience, this would hardly serve the goal of simplifying the environment. On the other hand, not taking the respective situations into account may also prove dysfunctional. Approaching a glass of water irrespective of the current thirst level may be a waste of time and energy. It seems reasonable to assume that for some objects evaluations may be stored in memory and, depending on their accessibility, these evaluations will come to mind in the situation. But this does not rule out that other accessible information may also come to mind and play a role. After all, outside of experimental studies, what is made accessible by the context is not a random arbitrary selection. Quite often, what is activated in the specific situation is particularly relevant for an adequate judgement and behaviour in that situation. If *liking is for doing* (see Ferguson & Bargh, 2004), then it seems reasonable to assume a highly flexible framework adaptive to the current needs and the present context, but at the same time effort-saving and not unduly wasteful of resources.

CHAPTER SUMMARY

1   When attitudes are constructed they are based on the currently accessible information. This includes chronically accessible information and temporarily accessible information. As a consequence of the latter, attitudes – as a means of summary evaluations – are subject to contextual influences.

2   The accessibility of information depends on its inherent qualities, its organisation in memory, the frequency of its activation and the recency of its activation. As the recency of activation varies between situations, different information may be retrieved for attitude construction at different times. Accordingly, attitudes vary depending on the temporarily accessible information.

3   The context may not only influence which information comes to mind, but may also influence evaluations directly: evaluations are relative insofar as any evaluation depends on the comparison standard used.

4   Attributes of an attitude object (beliefs about the attitude object) are evaluated depending on their relevance to the progress of current goals and these evaluations are weighted according to the importance of the goals. Besides, many personal and contextual factors' psychological distance is an important variable that affects the weighting of information. With decreasing distance less central goals become more relevant.

5   Accessible information is not always used in the same manner. Accessible information that seems appropriate to use will elicit assimilation. When information is deemed inappropriate, contrast may occur.

6   Attitudes based more on chronically accessible information than on temporarily accessible information will be more stable across contexts than attitudes that are primarily made up of temporarily accessible information. However, even attitudes primarily based on temporarily accessible information may reflect stability over time if the context remains stable over time.

7   Whether attitudes are merely situative construals or are stored representations in memory is an open debate. This debate is not necessarily an empirical one, but depends on whether the term attitude is used to refer to an underlying memory representation or some later state in the evaluation process. In any case, assuming a functionality of attitudes as signposts for behaviour regulation would favour the possibility of existing memory representations. Yet such representations would hardly be adaptive if they are not flexible to situational demands.

Exercises

1   Attitude reports are highly dependent upon temporarily accessible information. What does this imply for attitude measurement – for example, opinion polls etc.?

2   Suppose we knew all the information accessible to a person in a given situation. Could we exactly predict that person's attitude?

3   If people were asked repeatedly for their attitude about something that happened in the distant future or in the near future, for which scenario would you expect more attitude stability?

4   In a study (Steffens & Buchner, 2003), participants completed a 'gay –heterosexual men' IAT. Also, they were administered a survey to assess their explicit attitudes towards gay men. One week later, the same participants took the same tests, again. The finding was that the implicit scores were more stable than the explicit scores. However, even the correlation between the IATs was not higher than $r = .5$, suggesting situational influence on the implicit attitude scores. How could you explain the results from a MODE model perspective? How could the constructivist model accommodate these findings?

Further reading

For the debate regarding the construction perspective:

Special issue *Social Cognition* (2007), *25*(5).

For a model on assimilation and contrast:

Bless, H. & Schwarz, N. (2010). Mental construal and the emergence of assimilation and contrast effects: The inclusion/exclusion model. *Advances in Experimental Social Psychology, 42,* 319–373.

Note

1   We borrowed the Gulliver analogy from Brown *et al.* (1992).

Chapter 7

ATTITUDES: A QUESTION OF GOOD BALANCE

Delicious, freshly made and oh-so-mouth-watering. That's what the fast-food chain says about their burgers. Perhaps thinking of their cheeseburgers may make you feel craving and salivate: 'Yummy. Burgers are great!' However, what about your attitudes towards mass meat production and its consequences, ranging from cruelty to animals to air pollution? In the previous chapter we have seen that attitude objects are usually characterised by different attributes, all of which may have implications for the object's summary evaluation. A burger is tasty, but it involves killing animals. Sometimes, our attitudes generate inner conflicts. Liking burgers may not be entirely compatible with advancing humane husbandry and condemning the conditions of meat production. We will see throughout this chapter that individuals often feel torn how they (should) feel or think about an object. But as we will also see, people facing these problems also try to solve them. Thus, triggered by some imbalance, people shape their attitudes in order to form a more coherent attitude structure. This is the essence of a class of theories, summarised under the term consistency theories. We will begin this chapter by reviewing classic consistency theories, formulated in the last century. We will then turn to some novel theories providing a closer inspection of the cognitive processes at work when solving the conflict.

ATTITUDE CONSISTENCY

Early in the history of attitude psychology, the Gestalt psychologist Heider analysed how attitudes towards people and attitudes towards issues are related to each other in a perceiver's mind (Heider, 1946). He proposed that attitudes can be conceived as positive or negative relationships between a social perceiver (p), and some other person (o) or some impersonal issue (x). A positive relationship might be characterised by relational units such as 'loves', 'likes' or 'esteems', and negative relations by their opposites. For instance, Zoe loves her boyfriend Jim and likes the left-wing party. So far, so good. The central point in Heider's work is that a third relational unit between Jim and the left-wing party may cause a state of imbalance.

This would be the case if Jim actually detested the left-wing party (i.e. there was a negative relationship between o and x).

According to Heider's notion, there are eight possible triads between perceiver, other person and some impersonal issue. As is depicted in Figure 7.1, four of these are balanced, four imbalanced. If the product of signs of all three relational units is positive, the triad is in balance.

Thus, there would also be balance if Zoe liked the left-wing party, but her abhorred teacher, Ms Right, would not. However, whenever the product of the signs is negative, the triad is imbalanced. Heider proposed that some forces would then cause a change in one relational unit, so the end state would be balanced. More specifically, the state of balance would be generated by a change of the weakest relation. If we assume that Zoe's love for her boyfriend is stronger than her appreciation of the political party, in the present example the most likely outcome would be that Zoe changes her mind about the left-wing party, and becomes more critical and distant.

It is noteworthy that Heider's conception known as **balance theory** (1946, 1958) already considered affective states. Though not central to his theory, Heider already pointed out that imbalance evokes unpleasant feelings. More precisely, he suggested that whenever people cannot generate a balanced state (e.g. because they are unable to change their attitudes), they would feel tension. The role of unpleasant arousal received more attention in the theory of cognitive dissonance where it is not the outcome of some insolvable imbalance but actually the driving force causing the change.

Balance theory:
A cognitive consistency theory proposed by Heider, according to which individuals strive for consistency among the relations between cognitive elements (representations of self, others and objects).

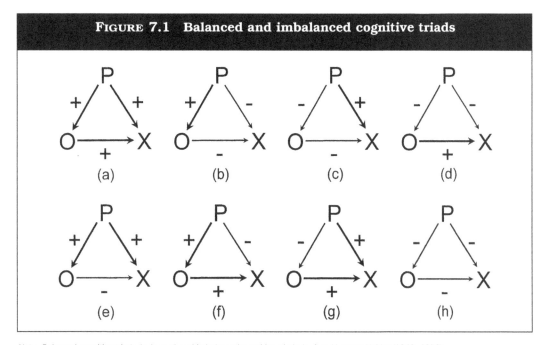

FIGURE 7.1   Balanced and imbalanced cognitive triads

Note: Balanced cognitive triads (a, b, c, d) and imbalanced cognitive triads (e, f, g, h) sensu Heider (1946, 1958)

THEORY OF COGNITIVE DISSONANCE

Theory of cognitive dissonance: A cognitive consistency theory proposed by Festinger (1957). It posits that people who hold incongruent cognitions experience dissonance (= unpleasant arousal) and subsequently strive to reduce dissonance. This is done by changing one or more cognitions – for example, attitudes.

As proposed in the **theory of cognitive dissonance** (Festinger, 1957, 1962), one of the most influential psychological theories in the 1960s and 70s, an individual's 'cognitions' (i.e. thoughts, but also beliefs and attitudes) may be consonant, dissonant or irrelevant. Cognitive dissonance is assumed to create an unpleasant state of arousal and this state motivates the individual to reduce the dissonance. Dissonance can be reduced by *adding, subtracting* or *substituting* cognitions. Thus, thinking about one's behaviour, 'I smoke' is dissonant with the cognition of 'Smoking will kill me'. Cognitive dissonance might be reduced by subtracting the latter cognition – for instance, by denying its truth – by adding a cognition to solve dissonance (e.g. 'I exercise regularly to keep healthy'), or by substituting a dissonant cognition with a consonant one (e.g. 'Smoking helps me lose weight'). One way or the other, the person might persuade him- or herself that smoking is not that bad, rendering the attitude compatible with the behaviour of smoking.

Induced compliance: A research paradigm used in testing cognitive dissonance theory. Research participants are subtly induced to perform a counterattitudinal behaviour in order to create dissonant cognitions.

It is noteworthy that attitude-discrepant behaviours do not necessarily create dissonance. If there is sufficient justification for showing the attitude-discrepant behaviour, dissonance will not be aroused. Festinger and Carlsmith (1959) tested this hypothesis in an **induced compliance** paradigm. In a first phase of this classic experiment, participants performed an extremely dull motor task – namely, turning a series of pegs a quarter turn clockwise. It was assumed that after one hour of the boring task, participants had built a negative attitude towards the experiment. Participants in the experimental conditions were then asked to stand in for the indisposed experimenter and recruit further participants. Most participants decided to help and recruit participants, which involved telling other persons that the experiment was fun – thus, an attitude-discrepant behaviour. In one of these groups, participants were promised $1 for their help, but $20 were promised in the other. Participants in a control group had not been asked to step in for the experimenter. Later on, participants were asked to evaluate the experiment. Those who had had little justification for saying that the experiment was fun (i.e. $1 condition) rated the experiment more positively than participants in the control condition, but also more positively than participants in the high justification (i.e. $20) condition. Therefore, the finding supports the idea that a *voluntary* attitude-discrepant behaviour which cannot be attributed to external factors evokes dissonance, and this dissonance can be reduced by aligning the attitude with the behaviour. To further demonstrate that being personally responsible for the behaviour is a necessary condition for dissonance-induced attitude change, Linder *et al.* (1967) manipulated participants' perception of free choice: participants were either asked or required to write a convincing essay in favour of an unpopular law that restricted freedom of speech. Further, for doing so, they received either a low or a high reward. Students in the no-choice condition did not change their attitudes when the reward was low and tended to change in the direction of the essay when the reward was high. Apparently, the higher monetary reward worked as the stronger reinforcement for the position they had expressed (see Chapter 5; also see Rosenberg, 1965). Crucially, students in the free-choice conditions showed an opposite pattern. These participants changed their attitudes towards the position taken in the essay if they received a low reward but not if the reward was high. Participants in that condition must have thought something like 'I supported the law against freedom of speech without being forced to or rewarded for it. How could I say that this law is bad?'

The reported findings are compatible with dissonance theory. However, they cannot rule out alternative explanations. In Chapter 4, we saw that our behaviour can have an informative value. This idea is central to the most prominent critique raised by Bem (1972). As is articulated in **self-perception theory** (Bem, 1972), individuals often are uncertain about their attitudes, and therefore use their behaviours to infer their attitudes.[1] In this vein, persons who smoke a packet of cigarettes a day would infer that they must love smoking – why else should they smoke if they did not like it? This inference should become especially likely if they do not feel forced to smoke, but consider smoking a behaviour which is internally caused or caused by their attitude. In Festinger and Carlsmith's study, therefore, participants may not have felt any dissonance, but realised that they advertised the study and therefore inferred that their attitude towards the study cannot be too bad. Notably, the latter explanation is more parsimonious than the explanation offered by dissonance theory because it does not have to assume the *experience of some negative arousal*. So should we give up the idea of cognitive dissonance in favour of an explanation in terms of self-perception? To answer this question, let us consider research on this specific additional assumption made by cognitive dissonance theory, one that is not made by self-perception theory – namely, the idea that attitude-discrepant behaviour causes persons to feel an unpleasant arousal.

For a more critical test of dissonance theory, researchers assessed physiological indicators of arousal (e.g. skin conductance responses) and showed that voluntarily engaging in attitude-discrepant behaviour indeed increases an individual's arousal (e.g. Croyle & Cooper, 1983; Elkin & Leippe, 1986; Losch & Cacioppo, 1990). Also, participants who engaged in attitude-discrepant behaviour showed more activity in the anterior cingulate cortex, an area associated with the experience of conflict. Moreover, this activity predicted subsequent attitude change (Van Veen *et al.*, 2009).

Other experiments focused more on the subjective experience of arousal. Some of these studies built on the hypothesis that attitude change only occurs if persons realise that dissonance is due to the attitude-discrepant behaviour (for a review, see Fazio & Cooper, 1983). In a famous study by Zanna and Cooper (1974), participants wrote a counter-attitudinal essay under high- and low-choice conditions. Furthermore, they were informed about the alleged side effects of a (placebo) pill they had taken in an earlier study. Depending on the experimental condition, they were led to believe

Self-perception theory: Theory whose core assumption is that individuals infer their own attitudes by observing their own behaviour in context, just as they would do with other people.

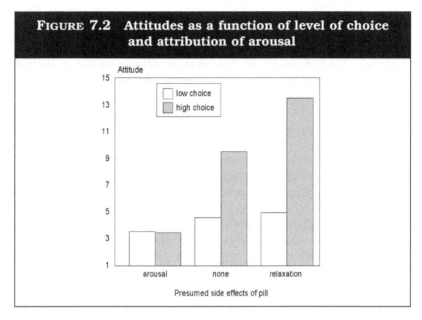

FIGURE 7.2   Attitudes as a function of level of choice and attribution of arousal

Note: In an induced-compliance situation, dissonance effects on attitudes are observed. However, they vanish if arousal can be attributed to an external source (data from Zanna & Cooper, 1974)

that the pill would make them feel tense, or that it would make them feel relaxed, or that it would not have any side effects. The results of this study are shown in Figure 7.2.

Control participants showed the classic dissonance effect, changing their attitudes towards the counter-attitudinal position they had advocated more under high choice than under low choice. This result is also compatible with self-perception theory. For participants who could attribute their arousal to an unrelated event (having taken the pill), no difference between high choice and low choice was found; however, for those participants who had expected the pill to be relaxing, the dissonance effect was even stronger than in the control condition. Note that self-perception theory cannot explain the different results in the three conditions as the self-perceived behaviour is identical in all three conditions. In contrast, the results support the assumption of an unpleasant state of arousal created by attitude-discrepant behaviour. Taken together, the results indicate that attitude-discrepant behaviour induced a negative state of dissonance on the one hand and attitude change on the other.

Another study (Elliot & Devine, 1994) sheds more light on the behaviour-dissonance-attitude sequence. In two high-choice induced compliance conditions, both affect and attitude were assessed either after participants had committed themselves to writing a counter-attitudinal essay (but before they started writing), or after they had completed the counter-attitudinal essay. In a baseline condition, affect and attitude ratings were taken before participants had agreed to write an essay. The crucial finding was that committing to write the essay already caused negative affect as evident from higher ratings as compared to the baseline condition (Figure 7.3).

The attitudes, however, were as negative as were attitudes in the control group. By contrast, participants who were asked for their ratings at the end of the experiment (i.e. after having written the essay) showed the reverse pattern. Their attitudes were more positive, but negative affect did not differ from baseline. In line with the theory, agreeing to perform a counter-attitudinal behaviour initially creates negative affect. Once the attitude has aligned with the behaviour, however, the negative affect reverts to baseline. Interestingly, attitude change is not the only way to compensate for the negative affect. If it is easy to deny one's responsibility after dissonance aroused, negative affect is also reduced (Gosling *et al.*, 2006). After all, if one did not commit the behaviour out of one's own free will but because of external reasons beyond one's control, one can still hold consistent cognitions. In turn, dissonance should be strongest if one actively, publicly and freely commits to the behaviour. It is but one step further to predict that dissonance increases with personal investment (time, effort, money, etc.) in a behaviour, a phenomenon widely known as **effort justification**.

In an early study by Aronson & Mills (1959), participants had to take an initiation test in order to join a discussion group. They were told that the group discussion was about sex and that it was necessary to find out if they could speak frankly about the topic. Therefore, part of the initiation would be that they had to read sexually explicit words aloud. In one group, the words were mildly embarrassing (e.g. petting), whereas in the other group, the words were more embarrassing (e.g. cock), which was thought

Effort-justification hypothesis: The assumption that people often come to like what they had to suffer for as a result of reducing the dissonance caused by high effort invested despite low attractiveness of the outcome.

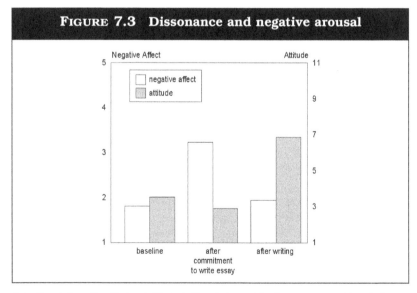

FIGURE 7.3 Dissonance and negative arousal

Note: Reported negative affect and attitude at different stages of the dissonance-arousal-to reduction sequence (data from Elliot & Devine, 1994)

to cost them more effort. Participants later listened to a discussion held by the group to which they allegedly had been admitted. They rated the discussion as more interesting when admittance costs were higher.

In this vein, dissonance theory has been successfully applied in different domains (cf. Figure 7.4). In one study (Axsom & Cooper, 1985) overweight women who were trying to lose weight were asked to perform cognitive and perceptual tasks that were either difficult (high effort) or easy to perform (low effort). Apart from these pseudo interventions, which had nothing to do with any established therapy or theory of weight loss, the women were simply asked to keep track of the food they ate and were weighed at regular intervals. The results showed that women in the high-effort group lost more weight than those in the low-effort group, and this difference was maintained over a one-year period. These and other findings (e.g. Axsom, 1989) indicate that therapies which include hard work, even if this is unrelated to the therapeutic goal, seem to be more effective than therapies that are less effortful for the client (for a review, see Draycott & Dabbs, 1998).

Taken together, the empirical evidence supports the notion that cognitive dissonance goes together with an unpleasant feeling and that it can lead to attitude change. To be clear, this does not mean that findings in support of dissonance theory exclude self-perception as a relevant mechanism in attitude formation. For instance, if a person only holds a very weak attitude towards an issue, or maybe does not hold an attitude towards an issue at all, behaviour is unlikely to evoke dissonance. Self-perception theory, however, is still applicable in this case, and would predict that a new attitude will be inferred that fits with the behaviour (for an integration of dissonance and self-perception theory, see Fazio *et al.*, 1977), but cannot accommodate the full range of empirical findings (see Harmon-Jones & Harmon-Jones, 2007).

Nor is dissonance theory the only way to explain the results obtained. For example, it has been argued that dissonance reflects the cognition that the behaviour is incompatible with one's sense of moral integrity (e.g. Steele, 1988). As a consequence, dissonance may actually be reduced by mechanisms other than attitude change, such as reaffirming oneself by focusing on values more important to the self (Steele & Liu, 1983). The **self-affirmation explanation** is empirically supported by findings showing that in many dissonance studies, the mediating negative affect is better described as guilt than some discomfort (Kenworthy *et al.*, 2011), but cannot accommodate the full range of empirical findings (see Harmon-Jones & Harmon-Jones, 2007).

Self-affirmation theory: A theory whose main assumption is that threats to the integrity of a person's self-concept (such as engaging in counterattitudinal behaviour) instigate a motivation to reaffirm the self.

Nevertheless, dissonance theory motivated much empirical research and together with other theories of cognitive consistency (e.g. Abelson, 1968; Aronson, 1968; Bem, 1972; Heider, 1946; Newcomb, 1953), it provided a key understanding of human psychological processes, paving the way for many current psychological theories (Gawronski & Strack, 2012). And despite the differences between the different consistency theories, the common denominator – the consistency motive – has not been disputed (Greenwald *et al.*, 2002).

That said, not all attitudinal structures are free from contradictions. Earlier in this book, we already pointed out that attitudinal conflicts often exist: ice cream may be linked with both, good and bad. On the one hand, it feels so good on the tongue, on the other hand, it hurts so much on the hips (cf. Kaplan, 1972). Early work by Rosenberg (1960), for instance, proposes that attitudes are often characterised by an *evaluative-cognitive inconsistency*. What is meant here is that one's affective attitude basis does not align with the cognitive basis – a phenomenon that is grounded in the proverb of being torn between one's head and one's heart. But doesn't the consistency motive imply that we hold consistent attitude structures? Shouldn't we minimise inner conflict by changing some of the cognitions until we can clearly state that this caramel brownie ice cream is from heaven or from hell? In the following section we will deal with the question of when incompatible cognitions yield attitude change and when they should not, with an emphasis on how much conflict awareness has to be involved.

DO PEOPLE UNCONSCIOUSLY STRIVE FOR CONSISTENT ATTITUDE STRUCTURES?

Since the birth of consistency theories, researchers tried to address whether the formation of consistent attitude structures requires awareness (Brock & Grant, 1963; Cohen & Zimbardo, 1962; Rosenberg & Hovland, 1960). In the beginning, this question was approached empirically by the use of hypnosis techniques. Hypnotised participants were given instructions that potentially created dissonant cognitions. Effects of these instructions were then interpreted as evidence for some unconscious dissonance. For example (Brock & Grant, 1963), participants had to eat sauces, whereby half of the participants had some thirst-arousing hot sauce, but the other half had some diluted ketchup arousing little thirst. All participants were then placed under hypnosis. Whereas control participants were told they would feel just tired after the hypnosis, the experimental group was told that upon waking up they would 'feel extremely bloated with water' but would not remember the experimenter telling them this (Brock & Grant, 1963, p. 55). The researchers assumed that dissonance can occur without awareness, and hypothesised that in the experimental condition, dissonance arises because feeling thirsty would conflict with the cognition of feeling satiated for water. In line with their expectations, participants in the 'tired' control group drank more water after having eaten the hot sauce than the mild sauce. In the experimental 'bloated' group, however, the effect reversed. Participants who had previously eaten the hot sauce drank even less water, both during the hypnotic episode and after having woken up. According to the authors, thirst – particularly strong thirst – should have conflicted with the feeling of bloatedness. The resulting dissonance would have been eliminated by reducing the thirst drive. Although not directly related to the domain of attitudes, Brock and Grant's results imply that cognitive dissonance might

Box 7.1   Green grass for consistent capuchins

Folk wisdom states that things we do not possess always appear more valuable. Dissonance theory, however, suggests that in the long run 'the grass is usually *not* greener on the other side' (Festinger, 1962, p. 3). If we choose one option over another – say, studying psychology instead of biology, or moving to the countryside rather than the city – we usually experience some degree of **post-decisional dissonance**. Negative features of the chosen alternative and positive features of the rejected alternative are inconsistent with our choice. Especially if two options are initially equally attractive – both options have a similar ratio of positive to negative aspects – it is likely that dissonance will be aroused. One way of reducing this dissonance is to enhance the chosen alternative, but to devaluate the rejected one. Early experimental demonstrations with adult participants support this idea (Brehm, 1956). Over the years, evidence for post-decisional dissonance accumulated, showing that effects on preferences are stable over periods as long as three years (Sharot *et al.*, 2012).

However, until recently, it was unclear at which developmental stage – phylogenetic and ontogenetic – the basis for post-decisional dissonance would evolve. To answer this research question, Egan *et al.* (2007) tested children, using a modified version of the original procedure by Brehm (1956). In a pre-test phase, 4-year-olds were asked to rate various stickers on a child-oriented scale (i.e. displaying different degrees of smile). Triads of equally liked stickers (e.g. a dolphin, a dragonfly and a ladybug) were then used in the main study. In a first phase, children were presented with two stickers – say, the dolphin and the dragonfly. In the choice condition, they were asked to choose the preferred stickers out of the two. In the no-choice condition, they were shown the stickers, but received one at random. In the next phase, children were asked to choose another sticker to take home. The choice set now consisted of the formerly rejected or not given sticker (e.g. the dragonfly) and the formerly not presented, novel sticker (e.g. the ladybug). The results are shown in Figure 7.5.

In the no-choice condition, children chose one out of the two stickers by chance, which is not surprising given the children had initially rated these stickers as equally attractive. In the choice condition, however, children showed a preference for the novel stickers. Apparently, children aligned their evaluation of the sticker with their behaviour, which means that the previously rejected sticker became devaluated. The authors concluded that cognitive dissonance would be experienced at an early stage of human development. But would we expect cognitive dissonance, even in non-human species? A conceptual replication with a capuchin monkey sample aimed at answering this question. In a pre-test phase, monkeys were presented with M&Ms of different colours, whereby initial colour preference was operationalised by how much time the monkeys took to pick the respective sweet. In the main study, the capuchins were seated in front of two boxes, each containing one M&M of similarly liked colours. In the no-choice condition, only one of the boxes was accessible, but in the choice condition, capuchins had access to both M&Ms, but once they had taken one, access to the non-chosen one became restricted. As can be retrieved from Figure 7.5, a similar pattern was obtained as in the study with the children. In the critical test phase, the capuchins took the novel M&M – that is, an M&M not presented in the preceding choice phase. Notably, there was a reverse effect in the no-choice condition. Here, capuchins actually preferred the colour they had not been allowed to choose.

Thus, the grass might become greener on the other side of the fence if the monkey is prevented from accessing it (cf. Chapter 10 on resistance). However, once the capuchin has rejected the green grass, it seems to lose its appeal. It is premature to conclude from this that youngsters and capuchins formed an attitude. The experiments, however, provide evidence for the self-consistency motives at early developmental stages.

FIGURE 7.4   Consistency motives may increase job satisfaction

Note: Reprinted with permission from Universal Uclick

FIGURE 7.5   Choice of the novel option for subjects who had previously made a choice themselves or had been assigned an option

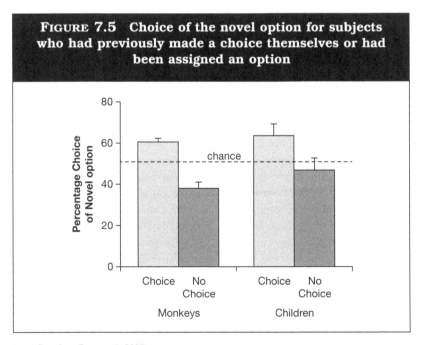

Post-decisional dissonance: Unpleasant state of inconsistency in beliefs arising after an individual has taken a decision, brought about by negative aspects of the chosen alternative and positive aspects of non-chosen alternatives.

Note: Data from Egan *et al.*, 2007

not be the outcome of some conscious reflection about the compatibility of different cognitions. More closely related to the domain of attitudes, more recent research invigorated the idea of dissonance-induced attitude change in the absence of conflict awareness. For instance, amnesic patients who were unable to form consciously retrievable memories were asked to evaluate a set of art prints. In a second phase, they indicated which paintings they chose to take home (Lieberman *et al.*, 2001). To assess attitude change, participants then evaluated the paintings again. As was expected from dissonance theory, chosen prints were evaluated more positively, but rejected prints were evaluated more negatively as compared to the initial evaluations (cf. Box 7.1). Notably, this was the case even though the participants could not remember their choices when evaluating the paintings, suggesting that dissonance may arise without being aware of the cognition that causes the conflict (here, 'I had rejected this picture').

The results obtained from studies using hypnosis as well as studies with amnesic participants imply that individuals need not become aware of the inconsistency between their cognitions, but nevertheless they will form consistent attitude structures. However, this interpretation is not iron-clad. Brock & Grant (1963) had to admit that the hypnosis technique perhaps had not prevented participants from processing the conflicting cognitions in a conscious manner. In a similar vein, amnesic patients might have consciously processed a conflict during or immediately after the choice. The resulting attitude may just have persisted longer than the conscious memory for the choice behaviour (for findings on attitude stability in memory-impaired samples, also see Haddock *et al.*, 2011). Thus, the debate whether dissonance-induced attitude change requires awareness of the dissonant cognitions remained open. With the rise of the implicit measures, this debate actually heated up further. In view of the various approaches on implicit attitude measures, researchers formulated models that tackle the spontaneity with which consistent attitudes are formed, thereby moving the debate from a merely empirical to a theoretical one. Theorising on implicit attitude (measures) actually produced opposing positions regarding the condition under which individuals will change their attitudes in order to form consistent attitude structures. Some researchers proposed that individuals may automatically form consistent structures (e.g. Cvencek *et al.*, 2012; Greenwald *et al.*, 2002). From this perspective, individuals do not have to be aware of conflicting cognitions, but mere associative learning operates according to some logical rules which guarantee balanced structures. In harsh contrast to a spontaneous dissolution of logical inconsistency, other researchers (e.g. Gawronski & Bodenhausen, 2006, 2007, 2011; Strack & Deutsch, 2004) proposed that higher order processes are necessary for detecting incompatible cognitions. Only if the conflicting cognitions are known could mechanisms proposed in dissonance theory (e.g. substitution or rejection) be applied to solve the perceived conflict and establish consistency.

The consistency principle in implicit measures

Pertinent to the debate on the processes underlying the formation of consistent attitude structures, the outcomes of implicit measures are assumed to be independent of respondents' conscious deliberation about the object (cf. Chapter 3). Thus, despite different perspectives on what exactly is revealed by implicit measures, it is common sense that due to time constraints, individuals may not consciously address a logical inconsistency. For instance, imagine a smoker taking an IAT is requested to react upon the stimulus 'cigarette'. While taking the IAT, he will lack the time to have two thoughts: 'Cigarettes are great' as well as 'Cigarettes cause heart disease'. Even if so, he would be unable to elaborate on that the latter cognition was logically inconsistent with the former, given that he also believes that 'health is important'. Even less would he come up with the conflict-solving cognition 'Health is not as important as pleasure!', all before pressing the key within less than a second. In this vein, researchers applied implicit measures to assess whether or not conflicts and their solution could be shown in the absence of conscious logical reasoning. We will exemplify the current debate by reviewing two theoretical accounts, starting with a theoretical account favouring the idea of some unconscious balancing – that is, the Balanced Identity Theory (Greenwald *et al.*, 2002).

Balanced Identity Theory

A strong theoretical claim in favour of *unconscious* balancing was made by Greenwald *et al.* (2002) who proposed that even unaware attitudinal structures adhered to the consistency principle. So how should consistent attitude structures form, if not by deliberate reflection about their components? First, objects are assumed to be – more or less – directly linked with evaluations, an assumption we already met in Chapter 5 (see Figure 5.1). Importantly, Greenwald and colleagues claim two principles underlying the formation of associative networks. First, if two unlinked nodes are related to the same node, a link between the two will be formed. For instance, a smoker associating himself with cigarettes and himself with 'good' should also start to associate cigarettes with 'good'. Second, it is predicted that the network avoids forming *direct links* between two semantically opposing nodes. Thus, in a network in which cigarettes are directly linked with the 'good' node, the link with the 'bad' node can only be indirect as, for instance, mediated by a node representing the warning mother. This is important, because it suggests that the associative network shapes itself according to logical rules. In this model, if cigarettes are good, they cannot be bad – at least not to the same degree.

In line with these two assumptions, several studies found that attitudes in implicit measures are highly compatible with the consistency principle as proposed in Heider's balance theory (for reviews, see Greenwald *et al.*,

2002; Cvencek *et al.*, 2012). Recall that balance theory predicts a multiplicative function of three related concepts. A balanced structure then requires that the third relation follows from the multiplication of the other two. If a (p)erson likes the (o)ther, and the (o)ther dislikes issue x, it follows that the (p)erson dislikes the issue x. Greenwald *et al.* (2002) proposed that this multiplicative function between three related concepts should also be evident in associations, as revealed by implicit measures. Using adapted IATs, they assessed the associations between the self and valence, the self and several groups (e.g. male vs. female) as well as the association between the group and valence. In line with a balanced representation, the products of the self-valence and self-group scores closely predicted the group-valence scores. The finding is not only in line with the social identity literature stating that self-esteem (i.e. a self-valence association) depends on the perceived status of the group to which one belongs (cf. Tajfel & Turner, 1979). It also suggests that attitudes expressed in implicit measures can be quite coherent. Similar findings were obtained when one of the relations was manipulated (Horcajo *et al.*, 2010), showing that the associations are malleable and create balanced states. Identifying yourself with psychology, therefore, should result in a positive implicit self-evaluation as long as psychology is associated with good things. As soon as psychology's reputation suffers, however, your self-evaluation will suffer automatically. Taken together, these results indicate that the balance principle is not only evident in explicit measures, but in implicit measures, too. Indeed, Greenwald and colleagues observed that the balance principle was more closely reflected in implicit than in explicit measures, a fact that might be caused by explicit measures being biased due to limited introspection or socially desirable responding. However, the notion of an automatic balancing process has been challenged by proponents of the Associative-Propositional Evaluation Model (Gawronski & Bodenhausen, 2006), which we will introduce below.

Associative-Propositional Evaluation Model (APE): Dual-process model to explain implicit–explicit consistency. Different from explicit meassures, implicit measures are (mostly) unaffected by propositional processes. Under specifiable conditions, associative processes and propositional processes result in different evaluations. If so, the correspondence between implicit and explicit measures is reduced.

The Associative-Propositional Evaluation Model

The **Associative-Propositional Evaluation (APE) Model** (Gawronski & Bodenhausen, 2006, 2011) was originally formulated to account for the different findings obtained from explicit and implicit measures. As you may remember from Chapter 3, correlations between implicit and explicit measures may vary to a large degree. The APE model explains these variations as reflecting that evaluative judgements in implicit versus explicit measures are guided by distinct processes of information integration (Gawronski & Bodenhausen, 2006, 2007, 2011). More concretely, the model distinguishes between *associative* and *propositional* processes (cf. Chapter 5). As put forward in the APE model (and its precursor, the Reflective–Impulsive Model, Strack & Deutsch, 2004; see Box 13.1), associative processes follow the principle of spreading *activation*. Upon encounter, a stimulus will activate related contents in memory, and the valence attached to them. The net valence of the activated memory content will then yield an *affective* response. As implied by the word 'net' valence, this response is univalent in nature. With respect to the introductory example, the burger will trigger a positive affective response ('Yummy!').

The authors further proposed that it is this associative process that 'drives responses on measures of implicit evaluations' (Gawronski & Bodenhausen, 2011, p. 62), a crucial assumption that stipulates how to empirically test some of the model's contentions. Notably, the model also accommodates situational influence. As retrieval is context-dependent (cf. Chapter 6) not all related memory content will be activated at the same time. For instance, right after having eaten a bad-tasting burger, negative memory contents of a burger may be activated and thus yield some negative affective response. On the measurement level, this means that implicit attitude scores are not considered to reveal an enduring attitude but may be influenced by the situation due to specific retrieval processes. But aside from situations that may trigger situation-specific content, usually the burger would activate the chronically accessible memory content, which in our example would cause a positive affective response.

A second process that may operate in addition to the associative process is of propositional nature. Different from an association, such propositions (e.g. 'Burgers are great!') can be judged as true or false. The model states that propositional processes *validate* cognitions by comparing them to other relevant cognitions ('Burgers are unhealthy'; 'Burgers cause animal suffering', etc.). This comparison of cognitions can yield contradictions; thus the APE predicts that cognitive dissonance cannot arise without propositional processes.

Central to the APE model, associative and propositional processes interact with each other in different ways. Per default, a stimulus should associatively activate an immediate evaluation. Coming back to the burger example, the predominant associative response was positive. In the second step, propositional processes would kick in and try to confirm the input obtained from the associative process by checking other relevant cognitions. Some of the relevant cognitions, however, might be incompatible with the immediate evaluation. You may think that 'Burgers make me fat'. Cognitive dissonance could then be reduced by consciously rejecting one of the propositions. The initial input whereupon the burger is good, might then be disconfirmed. The evaluation on explicit measures should then yield that you dislike burgers.

Indeed, there is a large body of evidence in line with the APE model's predictions whereupon people's immediate evaluations are associative, but do not consider logical relations such as a negation (for a review, see Gawronski & Bodenhausen, 2011). For instance, experimental participants were trained to overcome stereotypes towards blacks (Gawronski *et al.*, 2008). For this purpose, they were presented with black or white faces accompanied by a positive or negative trait. Half of the participants were instructed to affirm trials in which blacks were presented with positive words. The other half of participants, however, were instructed to negate trials in which blacks were depicted with negative words. Later, participants worked on an implicit measure, meant to reveal the associative evaluation. This IAT showed that those who had affirmed positive trials showed a more favourable evaluation of blacks as compared to baseline. However, those who had reacted to negative statements showed an even more negative response towards blacks, even though they had negated the respective combinations. It thus appears that, for the latter participants, blacks became associated with the negative statements and the negation itself, if anything, added negativity. Presumably, the logical relation between two concepts is not spontaneously taken into account.

Assuming that contradictions are detected by reflective processes, Gawronski and Strack (2004) hypothesised that dissonance-induced attitude change should be evident in verbal reports, but not in the IAT. In an induced-compliance paradigm, participants were informed about a new scholarship policy, a plan to allocate more funding to African American students. Experimental participants were then asked to argue in favour of the policy, yet situational pressure varied between groups. Concretely, half of the participants were told that they had been randomly assigned to the experimental group that had to list arguments supporting the policy. The other half of the participants was free to list arguments for either position, but were told that the experimenter would be pleased if they came up with pro-arguments because enough arguments against the policy had already been collected. The authors found that explicit attitudes towards African Americans were more favourable in the induced than in the forced compliance condition, a finding in line with dissonance-induced attitude change. IAT scores, however, remained unaffected by the manipulation. Interpreting the results from the perspective of the APE model, associative evaluations had been the same among all participants whereas propositional thoughts differed between the groups. Participants in the forced condition could justify the position they advocated in the experiment by the experimental instruction, so they should not have experienced dissonance. As a consequence, they validated the input obtained from the associative process. However, participants who voluntarily engaged in the behaviour had to disconfirm the initial input and to change their evaluation. In line with this interpretation, correlations between the implicit and the explicit measure were higher in the forced than in the induced compliance condition. One may therefore conclude that dissonance-induced attitude change is based on higher order, propositional processes because only these processes are able to signal the conflict between contradictory cognitions.

But didn't Greenwald and colleagues' findings show that there is automatic balancing, following logical rules? Or can the APE explain that implicit measures reflect Heider's balance principle, a finding repeatedly obtained by Greenwald and colleagues? Indeed, Gawronski & Bodenhausen

(2011) argued that it could be explained by associative processes, without assuming higher order processes that resolve logical contradictions. Consider the phenomenon of US revaluation we described in Chapter 5. This holds that an evaluative conditioning effect may reverse, if the US changes its valence after the CS and US had been paired. Importantly, as pointed out by Gawronski and Bodenhausen (2011), this phenomenon does not require propositional processes but can be explained by associative stimulus–stimulus learning – that is, participants in Greenwald and colleagues' studies did not necessarily form direct links between self, group and valence, but the self might have been linked with valence via 'group' or vice versa. Consistent attitude structures, thus would not reflect the outcome of an automatic goal-directed process – memory networks actively avoid forming contradictory associations – but a by-product of stimulus–stimulus learning. Finally, the results may also be explained by the mutual interplay of associative and propositional processes as proposed in the APE model. More precisely, the APE does not imply that the propositional process can correct the outcome of the associative one only in explicit measures. In some cases, propositional processes may come first and influence the associative process, thereby affecting implicit measures, too. For example, repeatedly thinking that 'Smoking causes cancer' might render it so accessible that the immediate affective response becomes negative, even for a smoker.[2] In a similar vein, elaborating about one's attitude can render the attitude more automatically accessible, and thereby increase the correspondence between implicit and explicit attitude (Karpinski *et al.*, 2005). Thus, propositional processes may cause the formation of new associations.

Notably, the multitude of interactions between associative and propositional processes as proposed in the model seems suitable to describe the complex nature of evaluation processes. However, it also means that it is hard to come up with a critical test, that may falsify the model. At least, it raises doubts whether implicit measures are suitable to test the processes at work during the formation as opposed to the retrieval of an attitude (cf. de Zilva *et al.*, 2013; Sweldens *et al.*, 2014). The same holds for studies using hypnosis or amnesic samples; thorough reflection might have taken place before assessing the attitudes via implicit measures. The debate, therefore, is unlikely to settle soon. However, it is only by scientific debate that our understanding of attitude change advances. As demonstrated in the example, negative arousal of cognitive dissonance theory, some of the most conclusive tests follow decades after the theory had been proposed.

CONCLUDING COMMENT: CONSISTENT CAPUCHINS AND ASSOCIATIVE APES

In this chapter, we have seen that individuals strive for cognitive consistency. As soon as they realise that cognitions contradict each other, an unpleasant state will be aroused, which then motivates individuals to solve this conflict.

To form a more consistent attitudinal structure, then, individuals often have to give up or even change their attitudes. What is changed finally depends on what can be changed most easily (Gosling *et al.*, 2006; Heider, 1958). Most people who think that SUVs cause unnecessary pollution would nevertheless not distance themselves from a friend, once he bought an SUV. For them, SUVs would become more positive. A hard-core environmentalist, however, would become more distant to his friend and cool down the relationship.

Consistent evaluative behaviour is not only evident in humans, but also in capuchins, not only in explicit, but also in implicit measures, not only in non-clinical but also in amnesic samples. To what extent conscious processes are a necessary condition for individuals to realise the contradictions in their attitudinal representations and then change them therefore seems difficult to answer. Whereas some theories suggest that consistency is mostly based on an automatic process, others suggest that it requires some logical reflection. Yet, the answer may lie in between (cf. Petty & Briñol, 2012; Petty *et al.*, 2007). In a closer look at attitudinal ambivalence effects on implicit measures, De Liver and colleagues (De Liver *et al.*, 2007) indeed made an interesting observation. In a single-category IAT (cf. Chapter 3), they measured response latencies for objects towards which participants indicated ambivalence. They showed that these objects could be quickly categorised as positive, but also as negative. Thus, the immediate response may not be univalent in nature, but already indicate the conflict. The key to understanding when inconsistent representations trigger the formation of consistent attitude structures, therefore, might lie in considering two steps. Incompatible attitude structures might signal some conflict, without people becoming aware of the opposing cognitions that cause it. Yet only if people become aware of what causes the conflict might they figure out the cognitions that solve this conflict, thereby creating consistent attitude structures.

Yet the question of why people hold incompatible beliefs, attitudes or cognitions finally does not only depend on the question of awareness. Some people can live pretty well with their contradictory attitudes (Newby-Clark *et al.*, 2002). Furthermore, as follows from a joint consideration of dissonance theory and a constructivist perspective on attitudes (cf. Chapter 6), depending on the situation, people may consider one or the other cognition as unimportant or irrelevant, thereby creating consonance. An important question, therefore, is what attitudes are good for. Hence, ambivalent attitudes become mainly stress-arousing, if people cannot stay uncommitted, but have to decide one way or the other (De Liver *et al.*, 2007; Harmon-Jones & Harmon-Jones, 2007, 2015; van Harreveld *et al.*, 2009). From time to time, individuals may just be okay being in a love–hate relationship with ice cream and accept that it is fattening but tasty. At the ice-cream parlour, however, you had better solve the conflict.

CHAPTER SUMMARY

1   Several consistency theories proposed that people inherently strive for logically consistent attitude structures. Some of these theories are rather specific and focus on inter-attitudinal structures relating the self and some other person to an impersonal attitude object; others are very broad and comprise of all kinds of cognitions (including beliefs and attitudes).

2   Cognitive dissonance theory, in particular, states that logically incompatible cognitions induce negative arousal. People tend to reduce this arousal by creating logical consistency.

3   According to dissonance theory, attitude change can be the consequence of a behaviour one has shown. This will be the case if the behaviour is a) at odds with one's initial attitude, b) hard to change and c) not justified by some external cause. This hypothesis has been tested in various experiments using the induced compliance technique.

4   A prominent critique of cognitive dissonance theory, the self-perception theory, suggests that individuals do not change their attitudes in order to reduce dissonance. Instead, it is assumed that people may feel uncertain about their attitudes, therefore behaviours are used as a basis to infer them.

5   Although many studies are compatible with both dissonance and self-perception theory, dissonance theory has received empirical support by studies supporting the unique assumption whereupon attitude–behaviour discrepancy should evoke negative arousal.

6   According to the APE model, an attitude object will yield an initial affective response, which is evident in implicit measures. Subsequent propositional processes can signal inconsistency and may reject the response's implication for an evaluation. The evaluation endorsed in explicit measures therefore often diverges from implicit measures.

7   The question of deliberation in both, the inconsistency detection and solution, remains at the centre of ongoing scientific debate. To date, there is evidence that the formation of coherent attitude structures, at least can occur without conscious memory of the incompatible cognition. In line with the APE model, however, there is no conclusive evidence showing that dissonance-induced attitude change could occur without propositional reasoning.

Exercises

1   Let us assume that you had always wanted to study psychology because of your strong interest in the subject. Your friend, however, was not sure whether to choose psychology or biology instead. According to dissonance theory, how much would you and your friend like psychology after you both had enrolled? Would it make a difference if

your friend had enrolled for psychology after having received a rejection by the biology department? Would it make a difference if you had to work hard in order to pass an entrance test?

2   Think of your attitudes towards luxury. Start by completing the evaluative proposition of 'luxury is ____!' Then, write down the propositions relevant to this attitude. Probe the propositions and check how it feels.

3   Please remember the findings on affect-as-information (Chapter 4), according to which mood serves as an indicator for one's life satisfaction, but only if the true source of the mood is not evident. How could these findings be explained as an interplay of associative and propositional processes as proposed in the APE model?

Further reading

The Associative-Propositional Evaluation Model:

Gawronski, B. & Bodenhausen, G. V. (2011). The associative-propositional evaluation model: theory, evidence, and open questions. In J. M. Olson & M. P. Zanna (eds), *Advances in Experimental Social Psychology, 44,* 59–127. San Diego, CA: Academic Press.

For an extension of the Theory of Cognitive Dissonance:

Harmon-Jones, E., Harmon-Jones, C. & Levy, N. (2015). An action-based model of cognitive-dissonance processes. *Current Directions in Psychological Science, 24*(3), 184–189.

Notes

1   Self-perception theory makes the assumption that people are often unaware of their attitudes. It therefore applies if attitudes are weak or do not exist at all. In contrast, dissonance theory presumes that people already hold an attitude with sufficient certainty. Else, behaviour could not be at odds with it and cause the unpleasant feeling. Thus, the two theories may have different areas of validity.

2   The debate once more illustrates that data interpretation is strongly tied to the theoretical context. Often, different models may accommodate the same results, yet with different implications. In this vein, one might also reinterpret the data by Gawronski & Strack (2004) against the MODE model (Fazio, 1995). Recall that the implicit scores did not differ between conditions. From a MODE model perspective, one might say that the manipulation did not cause any attitude change at all. One might speculate that instructions in the induced-compliance condition influenced the explicit ratings – for example, that participants inferred

that the experimenter held a positive attitude towards African American students and for reasons of social desirability adjusted their reported attitudes. When interpreting the results as motivated distortions, the explicit measure would reveal a hypocritical answer rather than an endorsed attitude.

Part III

The social nature of attitude change

Social psychology is to a large extent concerned with the way people influence each other's thoughts, feelings and behaviours (Allport, 1942). Obviously, attitudes are a prime subject for social influence. As we already alluded to in Chapter 5, attitudes may be transmitted via social learning. People may form and adjust their attitudes depending on the attitudes in their social circle. This does not even require the others' intention to exert an influence. But of course, there are many instances where others purposefully and actively try to influence our attitudes (cf. Figure III.1). This may be so in private encounters or in public debates. Advertising, political and social campaigns are prime examples of a huge and massive industry with the sole goal of changing our attitudes – and our behaviour. In principle, all the mechanisms discussed so far are applicable for this purpose and are actually applied. Advertising uses evaluative conditioning, mood and mere exposure, for example. But arguably the lion's share in influencing strategies pertains to more explicit appeals. Part III will begin with a chapter on persuasion, which has been defined as an influence on attitudes or behaviour resulting from a message (Bohner & Dickel, 2011; McGuire, 1973), which may be conveyed orally, textually or visually. Persuasion is indeed as old as the Bible:

> The woman said to the serpent, 'We may eat fruit from the trees in the garden, but God did say, "You must not eat fruit from the tree that is in the middle of the garden, and you must not touch it, or you will

die.' 'You will not certainly die,' the serpent said to the woman. 'For God knows that when you eat from it your eyes will be opened, and you will be like God, knowing good and evil.'

(Genesis, 3: 2–5)

Most people know what happened next. Eve picked the apple from the forbidden tree: the crafty serpent had succeeded in persuading her. The story of Adam and Eve is certainly not the only historical example dealing with persuasion, but throughout history humans seem to have been fascinated by the topic. Persuasion is central to many stories. The Greeks and the Romans even had goddesses for persuasion, Peitho and Suada respectively. But what is so fascinating about persuasion? For one thing, it is interesting because of the associated effects: as demonstrated by the biblical example, a competent persuader can get others to want what she wants them to desire. In other words, the ability of persuading others means having control, it means having power. Not surprisingly, therefore, professionals from political propagandists to marketers have long shown great interest in

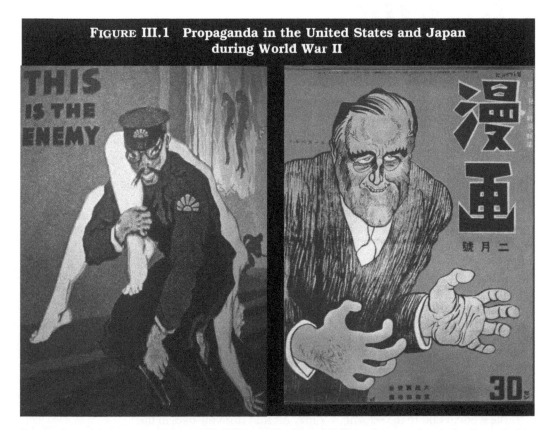

FIGURE III.1   Propaganda in the United States and Japan during World War II

Note: American anti-Japanese propaganda poster. World History Archive / Alamy (left); Roosevelt propaganda poster from Japan, Invalides Army Museum, Paris, France. Archivart / Alamy (right)

understanding the underlying mechanisms – that is, to understand the psychology of persuasion.

And of course, the power associated with persuading others is not restricted to professional fields, but persuasion competence is also quite beneficial in everyday life. For instance, think of all the situations in which you tried to persuade your parents. As an adolescent, did you manage to persuade them into giving you more pocket money? Were you able to convince them that your favourite music is no worse than theirs? Similarly, writing an essay in school: did your teacher like it, did she buy your story? And today, do you sometimes find yourself being especially polite when you want someone to do you a favour?

Social psychology has much to say about persuasion, and research addresses the question of how attitudes are formed and changed as a result of information processing, usually in response to messages about the attitude object. Attitude change in response to persuasive messages has been widely studied, with a particular focus on persuasion processes at the level of the individual message recipient (for overviews, see Chaiken *et al.*, 1996; Petty & Briñol, 2010). This may not be surprising, as unilateral persuasion attempts with a clearly identifiable message source are almost omnipresent in our 'age of advertising' (McGuire, 1985). It is this level of analysis we emphasise in the present section: in Chapter 8, we will review major theories of persuasion, informing the reader about how messages encourage receivers to like or dislike what the persuader wants them to like or dislike.

In Chapter 9, we will broaden this perspective and also look at multiple influences and how they play out over repeated processes. We will look at basic phenomena of social influence in groups and at the societal level. In Chapter 10 you will learn why messages sometimes fizzle out. For instance, in folk wisdom persuasion is typically associated with subtleness; in some translations of the Bible, the serpent is described as subtle rather than crafty. As we will see in this part, subtle persuasion might sometimes be the key to persuade a certain target person, simply because the person does not notice the persuasive attempts and therefore does not put up any protective shield. In other words, this part deals with when and why message recipients are resistant to attitude change, but also introduces some of the tactics proposed to break resistance.

Chapter 8

PERSUASION: MAKING OTHERS LIKE WHAT YOU WANT THEM TO LIKE

We have already learned in previous chapters about some of the basic mechanisms underlying attitude formation and change. For instance, mood, mere exposure and current goals all affect how objects are evaluated, and suggest a number of ways to compose a persuasive appeal. However, there is more to say about persuasion. Conceived as an act of communication, it requires that persuaders understand how a certain message will be understood by the receiver.

MESSAGE RECEPTION AND TRANSFORMATION

The importance of processing message content was first emphasised by Hovland and his colleagues at Yale University in their **message-learning approach** (Hovland *et al.*, 1953). This approach does not represent a unitary theory; rather, it can be understood as an eclectic set of working assumptions, influenced by learning theory and other contemporary theoretical perspectives. Its proponents assumed that learning and recall of message content mediates attitude change. Their research focused on various elements of the persuasion setting that would affect message learning. Following the guiding question 'Who says what to whom through what channel with what effect?' (Smith *et al.*, 1946), the classes of independent variables examined by the Yale group were the message source (e.g. its expertise or trustworthiness), the message (e.g. its length and structure), recipient characteristics (e.g. self-esteem or intelligence) and the channel (or medium) of communication (e.g. written versus spoken). Internal mediating processes that were studied include attention to the message, comprehension of its content, rehearsal of arguments and yielding to the message position. The dependent variables assessed were changes in beliefs, attitudes and behaviours. The major tenet of the message-learning approach – attention to and comprehension of a message would mediate persuasion

Message-learning approach: Conceptual framework for studying persuasion, focusing on source, message, channel and recipient as elements of the persuasion process and on the learning of message content as the primary mediator of attitude change.

– was developed into a more comprehensive information approach by McGuire (1969, 1985). As reception was assumed to be reflected in the recall of message content, high correlations between message recall and attitude change ought to be the rule. Empirically, however, memory for message content turned out to be a poor predictor of persuasion (see Chapter 6 of Eagly & Chaiken, 1993, for a review).

Given the equivocal evidence for message learning as a mediator of attitude change, researchers turned their attention to other cognitive mediators of attitude change, which emphasised not the passive reception but the active transformation, elaboration and generation of arguments. Because idiosyncratic cognitive activity is central to these approaches, Petty and Cacioppo (1981) labelled them *self-persuasion approaches*. Research in this direction includes work on role-playing as a persuasion technique (Janis & King, 1954; King & Janis, 1956), forewarning and inoculation (McGuire & Papageorgis, 1962; McGuire, 1964; see Chapter 10) as well as the work by Abraham Tesser (1978) on the **mere thought effect** (see Chapter 6).

Mere thought effect: Polarisation of an attitude caused by merely thinking about the issue without acquiring external information.

In the classic studies on *role-playing* (Janis & King, 1954) participants were asked to generate and present arguments on an issue, while other participants were instructed to listen to the same arguments. Those who had actively generated arguments showed greater attitude change in the direction of these arguments than participants who merely listened to the arguments. King and Janis (1956) further showed that the crucial process mediating attitude change in role-playing was the active improvisation of arguments: students who improvised a speech based on arguments they had previously read showed greater attitude change than others who had read externally generated arguments either into a tape recorder or silently to themselves. A process that seems to be at the core of this effect is what Janis (1959) called the biased scanning of evidence on one side of the issue in preparing one's speech. Later studies (Janis & Mann, 1965) using this paradigm showed that heavy smokers could be induced to reduce their cigarette consumption from 24 to 14 cigarettes daily, one month after the role playing session. They merely had to improvise for one hour the role of a lung cancer patient who is facing hospitalisation and death, whereas participants in the control group of equally heavy smokers merely listened to a tape-recording of the role-playing session (they also reduced consumption but to a lesser extent from 22 to 17 cigarettes daily). Importantly, this effect was maintained in follow-up interviews over an 18-month period (Mann & Janis, 1968). In the light of more recent research, a caveat is in place here: biased scanning should lead to attitude change in the direction of the position advocated mainly if generating the speech feels subjectively easy; if it is too difficult to come up with improvised arguments, the improvisation technique might backfire.

Ease-of-retrieval effect: The more easily information comes to mind subjectively, the higher is its impact on the judgement.

Numerous studies on the **ease-of-retrieval effect** (for a review, see Wänke, 2013) show that people rely on the implications of the retrieved arguments when the retrieval felt easy but less so when the retrieval felt difficult. One well-known paradigm to induce easy or difficult retrieval is to vary the amount of the to-be-retrieved arguments. For example, retrieving one reason why to prefer a BMW over a Mercedes is easy and consequently participants reported a higher preference for a BMW over a Mercedes (Wänke *et al.*, 1997). Retrieving ten arguments, however, is difficult and consequently participants reported lower preference for BMW. Paradoxically, then, retrieving more pro arguments often makes for less positive attitudes and retrieving more contra arguments makes for more positive arguments.

Research by Tesser and associates revealed that even in the absence of a persuasive message, simply thinking about an attitude object can lead to more extreme attitudes. Starting from an initially mild attitude (e.g. a somewhat negative attitude towards your neighbours), cognitive schemata will direct the thoughts and render the crucial attributes of the objects more salient (e.g. your neighbours called the police to stop the party).

The cognitive response approach

The accumulating evidence for the importance of active thought processes in both attitude change and resistance to change (cf. Chapter 10) as well as the Yale researcher's focus on message processing as a key to understanding persuasion, are combined in the **cognitive response approach** to persuasion (Greenwald, 1968; Petty *et al.*, 1981). Its assumptions may be summarised as follows:

Cognitive response approach: Theoretical orientation in persuasion research that conceives of attitude change as mediated by an individual's evaluative thoughts about a message or issue.

1 Individuals who are exposed to a persuasive message actively relate the content of this message to their issue-relevant knowledge and pre-existing attitude towards the message topic, thereby generating new thoughts and cognitive responses.
2 Attitude change is mediated by these cognitive responses.
3 The extent and direction of attitude change are a function of the cognitive responses' valence in relation to the message's content and position. In this sense, cognitive responses can be a) favourable, b) unfavourable or c) neutral.
4 The greater the proportion of favourable responses and the smaller the proportion of unfavourable responses evoked by a message, the greater the attitude change in direction advocated by the message should be.

The focus of the cognitive response approach, then, is not on the arguments per se, but the thoughts evoked during the active, deep processing of these arguments. To test the assumptions concerning the mediational role of cognitive responses in persuasion, a new methodology was introduced – the *thought-listing technique* (Brock, 1967; Cacioppo *et al.*, 1981; Greenwald, 1968). Research participants are asked to list within a given time – say, three minutes – any thoughts that come to mind while they read or hear the persuasive message. These thoughts are later content analysed and categorised according to their favourability (or other criteria; see Petty and Cacioppo, 1986a, pp. 38–40). For example, students who listened to a message that advocates the fluoridation of drinking water may list thoughts such as 'The arguments concerning the reduction of tooth decay were convincing' (a favourable thought); 'I don't want more chemicals in drinking water' (an unfavourable thought); 'I still need to do this reading assignment' (an irrelevant thought).

The role of thoughts about the message is nicely illustrated in a study by Petty *et al.* (1976). The authors presented students with good or poor arguments for an increase of tuition fees at their university. While listening to the arguments, students also had to record the position of an 'X' which appeared on a monitor. Depending on condition, the 'X' actually appeared 0, 4, 12 or 20 times per minute, thus varying the level of distraction. The finding was that participants in the good argument condition reported fewer positive thoughts and also less favourable attitudes at high levels than at low levels of distraction. Note that this finding is also compatible with a message-learning approach but does not require that people form cognitive responses towards the arguments. The findings in the weak argument condition, however, rule out that message-learning is sufficient to get the intended persuasion effects. Students who had listened to the weak arguments showed the reverse pattern: they generated fewer positive thoughts and less positive attitudes if distraction was low rather than high (Figure 8.1).

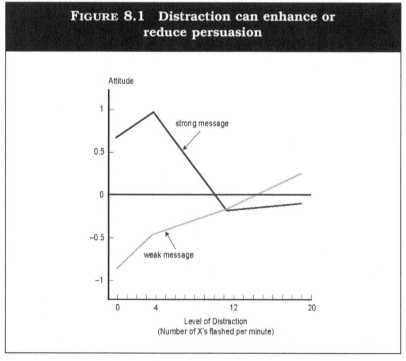

FIGURE 8.1   Distraction can enhance or reduce persuasion

Note: Distraction may decrease persuasion when arguments are weak (data from Petty *et al.*, 1976)

Apparently, low distraction enabled them to think about the arguments, but their cognitive responses had been unfavourable, therefore supporting the idea of active thought. At the same time, however, several research questions could not be solved by the cognitive response approach. For example, it had been shown that attitude change was not necessarily due to thoughts about the attitude object, but sometimes thoughts about the communicator characteristics (e.g. likeability) are better predictors of attitude change (Chaiken & Eagly, 1983). Also, it was unclear why the same variables sometimes helped, but sometimes hindered persuasion. Furthermore, persuasion-induced attitude change was sometimes consequential and sometimes not. Apparently, the impossibility of integrating the diverse findings had been so agonising that at the same time different researchers, Shelly Chaiken (together with Alice Eagly) and Richard Petty (together with John Cacioppo), were developing theoretical solutions (for a detailed report on the evolution of persuasion models, cf. Briñol & Petty, 2012). And although the researchers worked independently of each other, their conclusion was very much alike: a **dual-process model of persuasion**.

DUAL-PROCESS MODELS OF PERSUASION

Most persuasion research since the mid-1980s has been based on theories that incorporate the assumptions of the cognitive response approach about active, effortful processing, but also include hypotheses about persuasion based on effortless processing. These dual-process models are the elaboration likelihood model (ELM; Petty & Cacioppo, 1986a, b; Petty & Wegener, 1999; Petty & Briñol, 2012) and the Heuristic-Systematic Model (HSM; Bohner *et al.*, 1995; Chaiken, 1987; Chaiken *et al.*, 1989; Chaiken & Ledgerwood, 2012; Chen & Chaiken, 1999). In the following, we present these two dual-process models including a small selection of the enormous amount of empirical investigations they had inspired. Since the two models have much in common, we start by describing one of the models, the ELM, in detail and then shortly introduce the HSM by highlighting the major differences.

The Elaboration-Likelihood Model (ELM)

As one of the most comprehensive models of persuasion, the ELM is too complex to be fully described in this textbook. Yet, to give you some introduction, let us summarise the core ideas[1] (cf. Petty & Briñol, 2012; Wagner & Petty, 2011). First, it is assumed that people try to hold correct attitudes that can fulfil a utilitarian attitude function (see Chapter 1) – that is, people are motivated to hold correct attitudes which help to regulate approach and avoidance behaviour, although this correctness motive might sometimes be undermined by conflicting motives (e.g. trying to impress others or trying to be self-consistent; see Chapter 10). Second, the ELM states that persuasion occurs in different ways depending on the amount of

Dual process models of persuasion: Theories of persuasion that postulate two modes of information processing which differ in the extent to which individuals engage in effortful thought about message arguments and other specific information on an attitude object. The mode of information processing is assumed to depend on motivation and ability.

Elaboration likelihood model: Comprehensive theory positing that attitude change is mediated by two modes of information processing: central-route processing and peripheral-route processing. Elaboration denotes the extent to which an individual engages in central-route processing of issue-relevant arguments rather than being influenced by processes that characterise the peripheral route to persuasion (e.g. heuristic processing). Elaboration likelihood is determined by motivation and ability.

elaboration or thought involved. The amount of elaboration might take any value on a continuum ranging from low to high. Third, the ELM distinguishes between two prototypical classes of processes which depend on whether elaboration is relatively high or low. The two processing modes are called the *central route*, in which persuasion is mediated by effortful scrutiny of message arguments and other relevant information, and the *peripheral route*, which features the influence of peripheral cues (i.e. non-content aspects like the message source) and includes a variety of less effortful mechanisms such as, for instance, identification with the source, heuristics or mere exposure. Fourth, the ELM posits that any persuasion variable (e.g. the attractiveness of the source) can play multiple roles (e.g. act as a peripheral cue or as a central argument). Fifth, the amount of elaboration during attitude change affects how strong and consequential an attitude is (cf. Chapters 10 and 13). Simply speaking, it is predicted that attitudes that are generated via the central route to persuasion are more persistent over the course of time, are more resistant to change and are also better predictors of behaviour.

Which route does one take?

Generally, elaboration likelihood varies along a continuum and is a function of two factors: *motivation* and *ability* to process a given message. If motivation and ability are relatively high, elaboration likelihood increases, and the greater should be the impact of effortful processing of issue-relevant information, including message arguments. At the same time, the impact of peripheral cues on the formation of and change of attitudes should reduce. Thus, the ELM's two routes were conceived as antagonistic in their impact on persuasion outcomes. As the impact of central route processing increases, the impact of peripheral processes was bound to decrease (Petty & Cacioppo, 1986a, b).

These core hypotheses about the nature of central and peripheral route processing gave rise to many empirical studies. For an empirical test, many researchers manipulated a) processing motivation and/or capacity, b) argument quality and/or c) the valence of a peripheral cue. The principal idea, then, is that for low capacity (e.g. due to distraction) or motivation (e.g. due to little issue involvement) conditions the peripheral cue should affect the persuasion outcome; but as arguments are not carefully processed their quality should not be relevant to the persuasion outcome. By contrast, for conditions in which participants are able and motivated to process the persuasive appeal, the outcome should depend on argument quality, but peripheral cues should have little influence.

Issue involvement

Perhaps the most prominent motivational variable is issue involvement, the degree to which the recipients perceive an issue as personally relevant (e.g. Petty & Cacioppo, 1979; Petty *et al.*, 1981; for a review, see Johnson & Eagly,

1989). Recipients who are highly involved in an issue should be motivated to elaborate a message more than recipients who are not involved. In one experiment addressing this hypothesis, Petty *et al.* (1981) asked undergraduates to listen to a message stating that mandatory comprehensive examinations would be introduced in their area of study. Using a 2 × 2 × 2 factorial design, the authors varied issue involvement, source expertise and argument strength. Adopting a technique that was introduced by Apsler and Sears (1968) they told students in the high involvement condition that the new exam policy would take effect in the following year (and thus affect them personally), whereas students in the low involvement condition heard that it would be ten years before the policy would be implemented. To induce high versus low source expertise, the message was said to come either from 'the Carnegie Commission of Higher Education' or from a local high school class. Finally, the comprehensive exam proposal was supported with either strong or weak arguments.

After listening to the message, participants reported their attitudes towards comprehensive exams. Confirming the authors' predictions regarding central route processing under high issue involvement, attitudes were strongly affected by argument quality if the topic was personally relevant than if it was not. Participants in the low involvement condition, however, were affected by the source status lending further support to the notion that low involvement leads to peripheral route processing. In the high involvement condition, by contrast, the effect of the source was negligible. Building on the idea that involvement increases elaboration depth, Petty and Wegener (1998a) also reinvestigated the functional matching hypothesis (see Chapter 1). They argued that appeals matching the recipients' attitude function would be more persuasive because recipients became more engaged and therefore processed messages more deeply. In support of their claim, they showed that the advantage of function matching depends on argument quality: messages fitting the central attitude functions are more persuasive (e.g. image concerns with people high in self-monitoring) only if the arguments conveyed are strong. However, if the arguments are weak, functional matching leads to decreased effects (for related findings, Lavine & Snyder, 2000).

NEED FOR COGNITION

For another prominent variable affecting the degree of message elaboration, let us consider the **need for cognition** (NFC; Cacioppo & Petty, 1982; Cacioppo *et al.*, 1996; Petty *et al.*, 2009). The NFC can be understood as a person's intrinsic motivation to engage in and enjoy effortful thinking. This inter-individual difference variable is assessed via self-report, and respondents are asked to describe themselves on a number of face-valid statements such as 'Thinking is not my idea of fun', or 'I only think as hard as I have to' (Cacioppo *et al.*, 1996) on a Likert Scale. The construct developed closely in line with the ELM and, right from its start, it was meant

Need for cognition (NFC): An individual difference variable reflecting the extent to which a person enjoys and engages in thoughtful processing.

to predict differences in elaboration likelihood (Cacioppo & Petty, 1982). Speaking to the construct validity, individuals high in NFC have been shown to elaborate the arguments on a deeper level (e.g. Bless et al., 1994; Cacioppo et al., 1983; Putrevu, 2008). Also, these individuals seem less susceptible to peripheral cues (Bakker, 1999; Haugtvedt et al., 1992; Keller et al., 2000). For instance, Haugtvedt et al. (1992) varied the attractiveness of an endorser in an advertisement for a calculator – in the 1990s calculators were still machines one could buy rather than a function in a phone. This manipulation showed an effect on individuals low in NFC: an attractive endorser – a peripheral cue in this context – caused a more positive attitude towards the calculator than an unattractive one. High NFC recipients' attitudes towards the product remained unaffected by the manipulation of endorser attractiveness. Taken together, elaboration likelihood also depends on inter-individual differences. However, the construct of NFC should always be considered in combination with situational demands. At extreme levels of situational motivation (e.g. very high personal relevance), low and high NFC individuals should show the same extent of effortful thinking (Cacioppo et al., 1996).

MOOD

Finally, one variable that can increase or decrease persuasion by affecting message scrutiny is the recipient's mood. In Chapter 5 we learned that many mood effects on attitudes are best explained by assuming that mood serves an informative function. People may form attitudes based on a 'How do I feel about it?' heuristic, often mistaking a pre-existing mood state for a reaction to the attitude object. Current mood may not only signal how we feel about an object but also more broadly whether the current situation is threatening or benign. Positive mood signals a benign, unproblematic situation, whereas negative mood indicates a problematic state of affairs (Frijda, 1988). This in turn regulates how much cognitive effort will be invested in information processing in the situation (for reviews, see Bless & Fiedler, 2006; Schwarz, 2002).

Such mood effects on information processing have also been shown in the persuasion domain. Accordingly, a person who is feeling happy when encountering a persuasive message may not feel the need to invest much effort in processing its arguments and rely instead on a salient peripheral cue. A person who feels bad, on the other hand, may perceive the situation as problematic or threatening, which may motivate her or him to invest considerable effort in message processing. Various studies conducted within the dual-process framework produced results in line with these assumptions (e.g. Bless et al., 1990; Kuykendall & Keating, 1990; Worth & Mackie, 1987; see Handley & Lassiter, 2002; Hullett, 2005; Wegener et al., 1995 for a refined perspective integrating the affective tonality of the information). In a study by Bless et al. (1990), students were asked to recall and describe either a happy or a sad life event, ostensibly to help with the construction of a life-

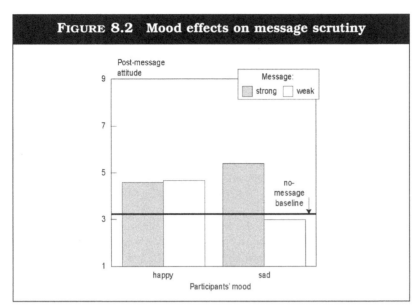

FIGURE 8.2   Mood effects on message scrutiny

Note: Positive mood reduces the impact of message quality on persuasion (data from Bless *et al.*, 1990). As positive mood signals that a situation is benign, people spend less effort to process carefully

event inventory. This task unobtrusively put them into a positive or negative mood. Later, as part of a purportedly independent second study, participants listened to a tape-recorded message that contained either strong or weak arguments in favour of an increase in student services fees. To study the impact of mood states on the spontaneous processing of a persuasive message, participants were told that this second study was concerned with language comprehension. After listening to one of the taped messages, they reported their attitudes towards an increase in student services fees and listed their cognitive responses to the message. To obtain an attitude baseline, students in the control group were exposed neither to a mood manipulation nor to a persuasive message, but simply reported their attitude towards student services fees.

As shown in Figure 8.2, participants in a negative mood reported more favourable attitudes towards the proposed fee increase when they were exposed to strong arguments than when they were exposed to weak arguments. Participants in a positive mood, on the other hand, were not differentially affected by strong versus weak arguments, but showed a moderate degree of attitude change in comparison to the baseline condition regardless of message content. Similarly, expert sources elicited more persuasion relative to non-expert sources when recipients were in a happy compared to a neutral mood (Worth & Mackie, 1987).

The findings summarised in the previous paragraph not only show that the general functions of mood can be integrated into the domain of message processing, but also support one of the ELM's core ideas: one variable can play different roles. In the next section, we will give a brief overview of these functions.

Multiple roles of persuasion variables

One role a variable can play according to the ELM is directing *the amount of thought*. As with the example of mood, a negative state may induce recipients to think thoroughly about the message, thereby increasing the impact of argument quality. Positive mood, by contrast, may favour peripheral route processing. In line with the notion of multiple roles, the positive mood then also *serves as a peripheral cue* – it enhances the liking of the attitude object by some effortless process (e.g. implicit misattribution; cf. Chapter 5).

Whether a variable affects the amount of thought or acts as a peripheral cue for one thing depends on the potential processing motivation (Petty & Wegener, 1998b). Let's assume that a recipient starts with a medium level of motivation to process. Prior to message reception, an attractive endorser may then engage the recipient to pay attention to what is said, thus increasing elaboration likelihood. For a recipient low in processing motivation, however, the attractive endorser will simply act as a peripheral cue, thus increasing the liking for the attitude object. Further, the role of the variable has to be considered within context. Sometimes, a salient cue may have an informative value and therefore *become an argument*. Endorsing a beauty product, the attractiveness of the person giving the testimonial is a relevant argument. Hence, an attractive endorser might be more persuasive than an unattractive one (see also Chapter 10), as mediated by thoughts about the cue rather than some affect misattribution or a simple beautiful-is-good heuristic. Finally, it is stated in the ELM that a variable may *bias elaboration*. An attractive endorser may make you focus more on the positive attributes of the attitude object (e.g. the shampoo makes your hair shine), but disregard the negative ones (e.g. the shampoo comes at an exorbitant price). Thus, the function of a variable is not bound to its physical or modal nature. Just as a salient cue can become an argument under high elaboration, arguments can serve as peripheral cues if elaboration likelihood is low. In this vein, it has been shown that the number of arguments (rather than their quality) affects persuasion outcomes if recipients are not involved (Petty & Cacioppo, 1984).

Finally, the flexibility of the ELM does not end with the multiple roles of persuasion variables; the ELM also states that central and peripheral processes may co-occur at mid-levels of elaboration (Petty & Wegener, 1998a). Yet the exact nature of their interplay remains unclear (e.g. Does a peripheral cue add to the argument? Is its effect reduced as compared to low elaboration?), which renders the assumption hard to test. This question of how low- and high-effort processes jointly determine persuasion outcomes has been addressed more directly in the other famous dual-process theory of persuasion: the Heuristic-Systematic Model of persuasion.

The Heuristic-Systematic Model

Like the ELM, **the Heuristic-Systematic Model (HSM)** of persuasion features two modes of persuasion: an effortless heuristic mode and a more effortful systematic mode (Bohner *et al.*, 1995; Chaiken *et al.*, 1989; Chen & Chaiken, 1999; Chaiken & Ledgerwood, 2012). Systematic processing is defined in a similar way as central route processing: Chaiken *et al.* (1989, p. 212) 'conceive of systematic processing as a comprehensive, analytic orientation in which receiver access and scrutinize all informational input for its relevance and importance to their judgement task, and integrate all useful information in forming their judgments'. The HSM differs from the ELM in the definition of the low-effort mode and its assumptions about the interplay of processing modes. We will address these issues in turn.

The low-effort mode: heuristic processing

The HSM's low-effort mode is a narrower and more specific mode than the ELM's peripheral route. As the name suggests, the low-effort mode is tied to the use of heuristics. Heuristics are simple rules of thumb about what can be inferred from an external cue. In this vein, persuasion outcomes might depend on the endorser's age in a population which had stored the heuristic that 'old people are wise', or the likeability of a source may contribute to persuasion because recipients think that 'you shouldn't agree with people you dislike'.

The presence of the external cue, however, is not sufficient on its own to exert influence, but the heuristic also has to be accessible, which might depend on the given situation. In a study reported in Chaiken (1987, pp. 27–28), different heuristics about what can be inferred from likeability were primed. In a first phase, students memorised statements that were designed to either strengthen or undermine the perceived reliability of the liking-agreement heuristic (e.g. 'when people want good advice, they go to their friends' versus 'best friends do not necessarily make the best advisers'). Participants in a control condition memorised unrelated statements. Later, all participants took part in an apparently unrelated experiment in which either a likeable or dislikeable communicator argued that people should reduce their sleeping time. Further, the need for cognition was assessed as an index of processing motivation. Participants high in the need for cognition (i.e. people motivated to process) were unaffected by this manipulation. For participants low in the need for cognition, attitudes towards reduced sleep time depended on the likeability of the communicator and the reliability manipulation – that is, the likeable communicator tended to be more persuasive than the dislikeable communicator in the high reliability and control group. In the group in which statements suggested a different rule of thumb, this trend was slightly reversed (Figure 8.3).

Heuristic-Systematic Model: A dual-process model of persuasion, positing that attitude change can be mediated by two modes of information processing – namely, heuristic and systematic processing. When individuals are unmotivated or unable to invest much cognitive effort, they are likely to rely on heuristics in forming an attitude judgement; when motivation and ability are high, they also scrutinise message arguments and all other potentially relevant information to form a judgement.

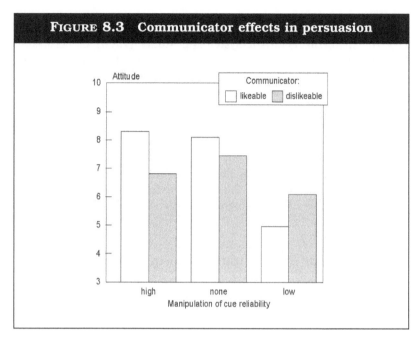

FIGURE 8.3   Communicator effects in persuasion

Note: The effects of communicator likeability and reliability of the likeability on the attitudes of a recipient being low in need for cognition (data from Chaiken, 1987)

Interplay of processing modes: the co-occurrence hypotheses

In contrast to the ELM, the two processing modes in the HSM are not antagonistic. Instead, the low-effort heuristic mode is assumed to operate at every level of motivation and capacity. However, if motivation and capacity are high, the high-effort systematic mode will kick in as well. The exact interplay of the two modes depends on the nature of arguments in the message and is summarised in the so-called **co-occurrence hypotheses** (Bohner *et al.*, 1995).

Co-occurrence hypotheses: A set of assumptions in the Heuristic-Systematic Model about the interplay of its processing modes.

If the external cue and the arguments do not contradict each other (e.g. an expert provides good arguments), then heuristic and systematic processing will exert two independent main effects (*additivity hypothesis*). This hypothesis was supported in various studies (Bohner *et al.*, 1998; Chaiken & Maheswaran, 1994; Maheswaran & Chaiken, 1991). However, because systematic processing often yields more, and subjectively more relevant, information, the additional effects of heuristic processing may be obscured. In other words, this would equal the outcome of some high-effort processing as proposed in the ELM, in which the argument quality, but not a peripheral cue would determine persuasion. This *attenuation hypothesis* also received extensive support (e.g. Chaiken & Maheswaran, 1994; Maheswaran & Chaiken, 1991). If a message is ambiguous in its implications or mixed (i.e. contains good and bad arguments), initial heuristic inferences may guide the interpretation of the message, leading to cognitive responses and attitudes that are in line with the valence of the heuristic cue (*bias hypothesis*). Finally, the arguments provided in the message may contradict the implications of the external cue. If so, the HSM predicts contrast effects (*contrast hypothesis*). In line with this assumption, Bohner *et al.* (2002) found that information about high or low communicator expertise may evoke clear expectations that the message will be strong or weak. If message content contradicted these expectations, a bias opposite in valence to the expectation was induced. For example, a message ascribed to a renowned expert that contained weak arguments led to less positive cognitive responses and attitudes than the same message ascribed to a non-expert – a contrast effect. In the case of ambiguous arguments, however, participants' expertise-based expectations led to biased assimilation of cognitive responses and attitude judgements.

DUAL-PROCESS MODELS: SOME OPEN QUESTIONS

Both dual-process accounts, the ELM and the HSM, constitute comprehensive frameworks for understanding persuasion. With their help, many of the findings obtained from tests of the earlier accounts such as the message-learning approach could be integrated. And without any doubt, few theoretical accounts in the domain of attitude formation have inspired so much empirical and theoretical advance as these models have.

A great deal of this advance is due to the introduction of some key variables, in particular the variation of motivation and ability as well as the variation of argument quality. Yet criticisms have been raised concerning both – the theoretical assumptions as well as the paradigmatic approaches.

What is a strong argument?

Although variation of argument quality is a clever methodological tool, it goes with some problems. A standard method for determining argument quality is pre-testing the arguments. For instance, participants are exposed to various arguments in favour of an issue and their thoughts towards the arguments are registered. Those arguments evoking mainly positive thoughts are then included in the strong message. Arguments eliciting negative thoughts are then selected to be included in the weak message (Petty & Cacioppo, 1986a), or participants are provided with diverse arguments and asked to rate their quality (Axsom *et al.*, 1987). The empirical approach is straightforward and builds the basis for a large body of empirical investigations. Yet it also points to some ambiguities about the construct of attitude quality, with important implications for both researchers and practitioners. The way in which argument quality is defined at the operational level raises the question of whether at the theoretical level argument quality might actually capture two independent constructs – namely, argument strength and argument valence (Areni & Lutz, 1988). Argument strength suggests a differentiation between arguments of the same valence, such as more or less important arguments in favour of an issue. For example, with regard to a mobile phone, long battery life might be a strong argument, but receiving an additional pair of earphones might be a weak, less important one. However, argument valence refers to a differentiation between pro- and counterarguments. One may argue whether a monochrome display is indeed a weak argument in favour of the phone or actually an argument against the phone. Defining weak arguments by the elicitation of negative responses, therefore, involves the danger of selecting counter-arguments, rather than weak arguments in favour of the issue.

Other researchers criticised that argument quality is defined by an effect (e.g. on a participant's thoughts; O'Keefe & Jackson, 1995). It was therefore impossible to a priori define general aspects of an argument that renders it as a strong argument. This becomes even more problematic in light of contextual variables that may affect the quality of an argument (see Box 8.1). In defence of the dual-process models, we acknowledge that the issue of argument construction lies beyond the scope of a model of persuasion processes. Nonetheless, the critique highlights that the models are not sufficient alone to create persuasive appeals, but users have to consider further psychological models as well as topic knowledge in order to craft persuasive arguments.

How many routes does persuasion take?

The assumption of two qualitatively distinct processes has been the topic of a long-lasting and controversial debate, in the domain of persuasion (e.g. Kruglanski & Thompson, 1999) and beyond (e.g. Evans & Stanovich, 2013; Keren & Schul, 2009; Kruglanski & Orehek, 2007; Osman, 2004). A thought-provoking alternative to the dual-process models of persuasion has been introduced by Kruglanski and Thompson (1999): *the uni-model of persuasion*. Kruglanski and Thompson argued that the assumption of two qualitatively different processes is not necessary to account for the results of the studies in the dual-process paradigm. As denoted by the prefix 'uni', the authors suggest that persuasion can be reduced to a single process. Both heuristic cues (e.g. an expert argues against genetically modified food) and message arguments (e.g. 'genetically modified food weakens the immune system') can serve as evidence and are functionally equivalent.

Processing motivation and ability, then, does not affect which of two qualitatively distinct processes (i.e. different ways of information trans-formation) will occur, but merely how much of the persuasive information will be processed. If motivation or ability is low, recipients will draw on the information that can be processed most easily, be that a cue or an argument. If effort is high, recipients will think longer and integrate more information, and therefore perhaps arrive at different conclusions.

Box 8.1 What makes an argument persuasive: fit and fluency

In many cases the persuasiveness of an argument may seem very evident. Providing an individual 24-hour tutor for every student seems a strong argument for a tuition increase whereas extending library opening hours for 15 minutes does not. Often, however, argument quality is not so clear-cut. What may be convincing for you, may be irrelevant for someone else. As we alluded to in Chapters 4 and 6, whether or not an argument is persuasive also depends on the recipient's attitudes and goals. In this sense, low fuel consumption may be either a more or a less convincing argument for buying a car, depending on external conditions (e.g. fuel price) and internal conditions (e.g. the current goal of saving money or one's attitude towards energy conservation). A skilled persuader will be able to anticipate what is relevant for the respective target group and craft her arguments accordingly. It helps that in addition to any idiosyncratic differences, other influences systematically affect what is convincing. For example, Construal Level Theory (see Chapter 6) holds that inessential features are weighted less in the distant future compared to the near future. Accordingly, such a feature (e.g. the clock on the radio) may be a weaker argument when forming a judgement about an object in the distant compared to the near future.

In particular, the *regulatory fit* hypothesis (Higgins, 2000, 2005) provides a useful framework for understanding the effects of message content on persuasion outcomes. This hypothesis is based on a broader theory of self-regulation (Higgins, 1997) that differentiates between two different orientations during goal-pursuit: a *promotion* and a *prevention focus*. The promotion focus suggests that organisms strive towards aspiration and accomplishment. It is associated with sensitivity to possible gains (vs. non-gains), but also risk-seeking. The prevention focus refers to striving for safety and security. Individuals in a prevention focus are sensitive to possible losses (vs. non-losses). People experience regulatory fit when their current (chronic or situational) regulatory focus fits with the current goal-pursuit strategies often induced by situational affordances (cf. Figure 8.4).

Specifically applied to advertising, people experience regulatory fit when the manner in which they process information is in line with their current regulatory focus (see Cesario *et al.*, 2008 for a review of regulatory fit effects in persuasion). One crucial consequence of fit is that the processing feels more fluent and the resulting response 'feels right'. The fit that results from the message processing and the person's regulatory orientation focus may be based on the content of the message or argument (Keller, 2006; Werth & Förster, 2007). For example, promotion-focused individuals were shown to be more persuaded by advertising that emphasised the comfort compared to the safety of a product and vice versa for prevention-oriented individuals (Werth & Förster, 2007). More interestingly, fit can result from framing. Consider the following argument from a message advocating an after-school programme: 'The primary reason for supporting this programme is because it will *advance* [secure] children's education and *support* [prevent] more children to *succeed* [from failing]'. Among promotion-focused individuals phrasing in promotion terms (italics) found more support than in prevention terms (brackets) and the reverse was true among prevention-focused individuals (Cesario *et al.*, 2004). Furthermore, because promotion focus corresponds with more high-level construal and prevention focus with low-level construal, a fit can also be caused by a match between the regulatory focus of a message recipient and the abstractness versus concreteness of the message's language. After an appeal to exercise, promotion-focused individuals reported a higher intention to exercise when the appeal was phrased in more abstract language (e.g. 'Sports also increase your endurance') compared to concrete language ('You can endure more if you exercise') whereas prevention-focused recipients showed the opposite pattern (Semin *et al.*, 2005). In sum, these studies showed that recipients are more responsive to persuasion appeals when the message content, its language or framing match the recipient's regulatory focus. Moreover, independent of the recipients' goals, messages that address promotion topics (e.g. 'get energised') are more persuasive when they are also framed accordingly – that is, when they emphasise the benefits of taking action (e.g. 'get energised) rather than the costs of not taking action (e.g. 'don't miss out on getting energised') whereas prevention topics (e.g. 'prevent clogged arteries') are more persuasively communicated when the emphasis is on the costs of not taking action (e.g. 'don't miss out on preventing clogged arteries') rather than the benefits of taking action (e.g. 'prevent clogged arteries') (Lee & Aaker, 2004).

The idea of fit was extended to a more general match between the current processing mode and the properties of the processed information. For example, six months from a campaign launch a political candidate was evaluated more favourably when the campaign message emphasised high-level, abstract, concepts (values, reasons, ideals, ultimate goals) relative to when the message featured low-level elements that emphasised how the candidate would govern. Conversely, when the election campaign was expected to begin in a week, a message featuring low-level elements yielded more favorable attitudes relative to a message featuring high-level elements (Kim *et al.*, 2009). Again, it is assumed that the match between the mind-set due to the temporal distance and the content of the message induces a feeling of fluency and a sense of 'feeling right'. Similarly, such a match also increased the credibility of statements (Hansen & Wänke, 2010; Wright *et al.*, 2012).

After the examples given in Chapter 4 suggesting that the perceptual fluency of an object increases its likeability, it should not come as a surprise that the fluency of a message may also increase its persuasiveness. Beyond the examples of fluency resulting from (regulatory) fit, any other variable that increases the fluency of a persuasive message may also increase its persuasiveness. For example, advertising slogans were shown to be more persuasive when they used familiar – and thus easy to process – proverbs (e.g. 'Don't put all your eggs in one basket') rather than more literal forms (e.g. 'Don't risk everything on a single venture') (Howard, 1997).

Interestingly, in classic studies the cue (attractiveness, status, expertise, etc.) is often the information that is easier to process but also the information that is presented first. Recipients are therefore unlikely to process additional information. In contrast, when arguments were presented first they moderated the processing of the cues (Erb *et al.*, 2007).

To be clear, by assuming that a persuasion variable can play multiple roles the ELM may well accommodate all these findings. However, as one requirement of a scientific model is parsimony, the question remains whether the assumption of a second process allows for predictions beyond what can be explained by logical reasoning about cues. Arguably, some

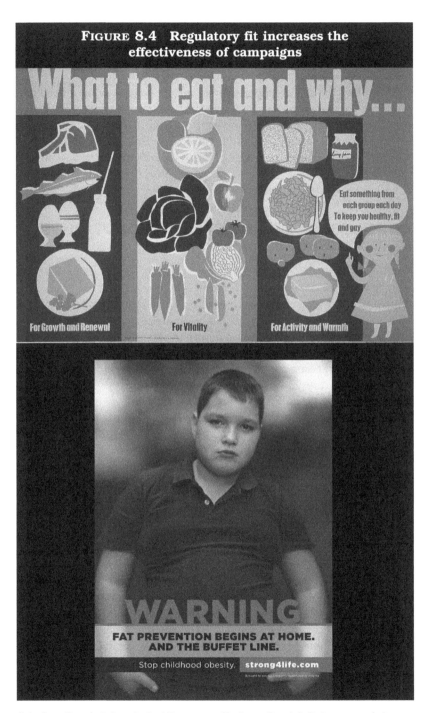

FIGURE 8.4   Regulatory fit increases the effectiveness of campaigns

Note: Promotion-oriented people should be more sensitive to growth and vitality (upper campaign). Prevention-oriented people are sensitive to negative outcomes, therefore warnings (lower campaign) may appeal especially to them

mechanisms – mere exposure, priming and even evaluative conditioning – are better described by simpler processes (but see De Houwer, 2014). In this respect the ELM provides a much broader framework by subsuming these mechanisms within the peripheral route to persuasion.

Given that the processes summarised under the term of peripheral and central route processing can be further differentiated (e.g. the distinction between various mechanisms underlying evaluative conditioning, Chapter 5), one might alternatively unfold the two routes into many, many mechanisms. It therefore remains a trade-off between fulfilling different standards of theory development – parsimony on one hand and compatibility with a maximum of empirical findings on the other.

CONCLUDING COMMENT: A REVOLUTION NEVERTHELESS

Every day you are the target of persuasion. Some people tell you why to spend more time studying, and others why you should spend less. Persuaders explain why to buy their products, why to donate blood or why to vote for their party. In explaining why, they provide arguments – strong or weak. In this chapter we have introduced you to the psychological processes underlying the processing of persuasive messages. Often you will be persuaded by the content of the arguments. However, according to the dual-process models, this will require that you are motivated to scrutinise them closely. In many situations, however, you will lack time or involvement, and it is in these situations that being persuaded has little to do with how good the arguments were. Easily processed information will then take over and open the door for logically unwarranted attitudes.

This insight is supported by a large body of empirical research that was based on the influential dual-process models of persuasion. Whether or not the mechanisms are best understood as two classes of processes is a question for future investigations. Considering the developments of the ELM, however, it appears that the two-route metaphor fades more and more into the background. Instead, its proponents today have turned the spotlight to a set of processes that predict the effectiveness of arguments' quality at different levels of involvement and at different stages in the persuasion process (Petty & Briñol, 2008, 2012). Independent of how many processes actually are involved, the dual process models were a serious progress: the key variable of processing depth has advanced the understanding of persuasion outcomes, resistance (Chapter 10) and behaviour predictions (Chapters 12 and 13). Moreover, it also influenced most of the later accounts, dealing with topics from evaluative conditioning to implicitly assessed attitudes.

CHAPTER SUMMARY

1   Persuasion theories deal with attitude change in reaction to messages about an attitude object.

2   The cognitive response approach stated that message arguments may elicit internal responses which in turn determine the persuasion outcome.

3   Dual-process models – the ELM and the HSM – locate persuasion processes along a continuum ranging from low-effort mechanisms to the kind of high-effort, issue-related thinking featured in the cognitive response approach. Both models portray high-effort processing as a function of motivation and capacity.

4   The models account for different functions of any variable in the persuasion process. Specifically, any persuasion variable may motivate persons to engage in deeper processing, work as a peripheral (or heuristic) cue, work as an argument or bias the interpretation of message arguments.

Exercises

1   Advertisement signs are often seen on the fly (e.g. when driving on the highway). Which effects can be expected according to the cognitive response approach? Which effects can be expected according to dual-process models?

2   Imagine you were to cast an anti-smoking advertisement. What would your campaign look like, given that you have strong arguments? Would you use positive cues such as celebrity endorsers? If so, at which stage of the ad?

Further reading

The development of persuasion theories:

Briñol, P. & Petty, R. E. (2012). A history of attitudes and persuasion research. In A. W. Kruglanski & W. Stroebe (eds), *Handbook of the History of Social Psychology* (pp. 283–320). New York: Psychology Press.

Fit effects and persuasion:

Cesario, J., Higgins, E. T. & Scholer, A. A. (2008). Regulatory fit and persuasion: Basic principles and remaining questions. *Social and Personality Psychology Compass, 2,* 444–463.

Note

1   In the previous edition of this book, the authors (Bohner & Wänke, 2002) presented a more detailed description of the ELM. For the sake of presenting novel developments, in the present book the authors chose to present a more condensed description, derived from the core ideas presented by Petty & Briñol (2012) as well as a description of the correctness postulate (Petty & Cacioppo, 1986), which we will pick up in Chapter 10, again.

Chapter 9

SOCIAL INFLUENCE ON OUR ATTITUDES

Up until this chapter, this book has focused on the *intra-personal* processes involved in attitude formation. Even persuasion research, that by definition studies how social communication affects attitudes, is to a large extent more concerned with how individuals process these persuasive messages (and how these processes in turn determine the content and strength of the persuasion target's attitude) than inter-personal processes and group dynamics. But, of course, attitudes do not emerge in a vacuum but in a social context. Persuasive arguments do not appear out of thin air but usually have a source that is somehow related to the persuasion target. In this respect, it may matter whether a friend or someone you dislike is trying to persuade you, whether this person is high or low in status, or whether the persuader is someone with whom you must continue working or will never see again, to list just a few examples. Nor is persuasion and influence a one-trial experience with one persuader and one persuasion target in only one situation. For example, you may hear your mother's arguments about why marijuana should be legalised every time the issue comes up or you may discuss an issue with different people either over various occasions or in one setting. The latter is often the case when groups try to form an opinion or reach a decision (see also Nijstad, 2009). In such instances it may also matter whether most of the fellow group members share your view or you find yourself in a minority. In short, attitudes are clearly a social product. In this chapter we will illustrate a few of the phenomena in this regard.

ATTITUDES ACQUIRED THROUGH SOCIAL INFLUENCE

Parents may deliberately reinforce their children for expressing attitudes that the parents themselves approve of. However, parents may also unintentionally influence the attitudes of their children by providing a role model. Overhearing parents' pejorative remarks about a social group, political party or any attitude object are likely to provide a foundation for negative attitudes towards these attitude objects in children. Likewise, observing parents or others behaving in a friendly or respectful manner towards a group or person may instigate more positive attitudes. Assimilating others' attitudes is an on-going process that continues throughout a person's life-span and is certainly not restricted to childhood, nor is it simply a process of imitation. One may easily imagine that modelled behaviour will in turn be reinforced if it meets the expectation of the social environment, or punished if it violates the respective social norms. One of the most influential studies in this area was conducted at a US liberal women's college, Bennington, in the 1930s. In this study, young women were observed over the four years they attended Bennington. During this time, they became continuously more liberal in their views, and this adoption of the college's values was greater the more they identified with the college (Newcomb, 1943). Other researchers have observed that newcomers to an organisation gradually accept its predominant values and attitudes over time. For example, American police recruits became more authoritarian (Carlson & Sutton, 1974), and white police officers became more anti-black as they progressed through the police academy (Teahan, 1975).

The observation that people apparently adopt the attitudes of their peers and social environment does not tell us exactly how those attitudes are transmitted. Actually, we do not even have to assume *one* single process. Considering the Bennington students (or the police officers), one may assume that they had new experiences and gathered new information during their education that shaped their attitudes. Moreover, and more relevant to the topic of social influence, it seems likely that over the years these students discussed various political and social issues with fellow students and were convinced by some of the arguments. Perhaps some simply adopted their peers' attitudes to feel closer to them or to win their approval. Expressing similar attitudes as their peers – whether based on true conviction or simply peer pressure – was likely to be reinforced and in the long run shaped these cohorts' attitudes.

To understand why social influence works – independent of its transmitting processes – it is worthwhile to look once more at attitude functions (see Chapter 1). On one hand, people strive to have valid attitudes. If attitudes serve a knowledge function it is crucial that the attitude is 'correct'. Others, or more precisely other people's attitudes, provide one cue to the attitude's validity. If you dislike a band that everybody else is raving about you may begin to wonder whether you are missing something. If others also detest their music you would feel that you were right all along. Others provide social validation of our views or what Robert Cialdini refers to as social proof (see Box 9.1). In this regard it may also be important whether any other person will do and provide social proof, or whether some people have more validity than others (see Box 9.1).

A second function of attitudes, as you may recall from Chapter 1, is that they can help to maintain or establish one's social identity. By and large people experience a need to belong. By sharing other people's attitudes one

Box 9.1   Six principles of social Influence

In 1993 eminent social psychologist Robert Cialdini was among the first academic scholars to write a popular psychology book, in his case on – you may have guessed – social influence. He describes six different principles that are based on different psychological processes and the supporting evidence comes from different theoretical paradigms. Although the psychological processes guiding these principles do not necessarily involve attitude change, we think that these classics should not be missing in a section dealing with social influence. Hence, we want to offer at least a brief summary. For many more applied examples we recommend the original book.

Reciprocity

Tit for tat is a very strong social norm in many – if not all – cultures. We tend to return favours and feel obliged when others do something for us or give us a present. How many wines would you taste at a free tasting before feeling the social obligation to buy a bottle? The bike shop may not bill you for helping you to mend a tyre in hope that such customer care will make you return with bigger business. Reciprocity is also the driving force of a sales-person trick, the *door in the face technique*. If a remote relative asks to crash on your couch for the next three months and bring his two dogs as well, you may not react enthusiastically (and in fact say no). 'Okay', he understands, 'but what about one month' (and the dogs stay home)? Many examples show that refusing a 'big' initial request (a large favour) makes people more susceptible to a reduced request than if the smaller request had been presented in the first place. To some extent this may be because by comparison it seems smaller (contrast effect) but moreover the reduction of the request can be conceived as a concession, which then calls for also making a concession.

Commitment and consistency

As you may recall from Chapter 7, people try to honour their commitments and behave consistently. Having persuaded them to yield a little may be the first step in a larger shift (foot-in-the-door effect). Cialdini also describes an effect he refers to as *low balling*, where people stick to a deal even when, after the deal was made, the conditions were changed ('Sorry, I just heard that I cannot give you the rebate I promised').

Social proof

As described in this chapter, consensus provides social validity or proof. Facebook's 'I like button' is a powerful tool in this respect as more 'likes' may work like an objective quality proof.

Liking

People are more persuaded by people they like. Besides physical attractiveness another source of liking is attention, such as compliments. Moreover, similarity breeds liking. Mentioning some biographical or attitudinal similarity may help to influence others. Cialdini reports that identifying similarities before or during negotiations reduced the chances of a deadlock from 30 per cent to 6 per cent.

Authority

People yield to authority. Power and status obviously represent influential strength. So does expertise (see also Chapter 8). Experts are authorities who know what is best. Experts are particularly influential if they are considered trustworthy.

Scarcity

People like what they cannot have or what is hard to get (see Chapter 10). Raising the age limit for a book or a film (adults only) will raise interest. What is scarce is also special and more valuable. Limiting supply may therefore induce demand.

will feel more like one of them. Moreover, expressing similar attitudes provides a social lubricant that makes other people more attentive and makes interactions more pleasant. In contrast, disagreeing may risk social exclusion or punishment. A classic study that is also a model example of realism and ecological validity in lab experiments provided evidence for this phenomenon. Stanley Schachter (1951) set up 32 clubs at the University of Michigan. There were four types of clubs and students indicated how interested they were in joining these clubs. According to these preferences they were either assigned to a club they valued highly or were not very interested in joining. The actual experiment was conducted at the first meeting of these clubs where the club members were to discuss the case of a juvenile delinquent, Johnny Rocco, and to give a recommendation on how to deal with him. After reading the case, each of the five to seven group members first gave his (there were only male students involved) recommendation based on seven alternative options that were provided, ranging from treating him with love and affection to harsh punishment. Three confederates of the experimenter who played different roles then gave their recommendation. One confederate (the 'mode') favoured the alternative that the modal number of real participants had recommended. During the following discussion he also adjusted his position to be always in agreement with the modal position. Another confederate, the 'deviant', chose an extreme position and held it during the remaining 25 minutes of discussion. In contrast, the 'slider' also began with an extreme position but gradually shifted to the modal position during the discussion. After the discussion, club members were told that for the following meetings it might become necessary to reduce the group size. In order to do so it would be helpful to know which group members would like to remain together and therefore everybody should rank the other members in order of preference to stay in the group. Whereas ratings for the 'slider' did not differ from those of the 'mode' and both did not differ from the average rank, the deviant was ranked significantly lower. Moreover, when it came to distributing committee jobs he was also less likely to be assigned to desirable functions but more likely to be assigned to jobs nobody else wanted to do. Some of these effects were stronger for clubs that were highly valued than those that the members cared less about. Based on such observations it is reasonable to assume that adopting the group attitude will make life more pleasant than deviance. And indeed people yield to group influence. You may be familiar with the classic studies by Asch (1951) where a participant in a small group heard every other group member (in reality, the other group members were confederates of the researcher) give a blatantly wrong answer (e.g. choosing the second longest line in an array of five lines when asked which line was longest). As a result, the real participants to some extent also chose this option. Although these studies did not pertain to attitude reports, the group dynamic is similar for attitudinal judgements.

The distinction between adopting other people's attitudes in order to hold 'correct' attitudes or to feel accepted reflects a classic and quite influential distinction between informational and normative influence (Deutsch & Gerard, 1955). By accepting information obtained from other people or groups as evidence about reality, others exert **informational social influence**, and by conforming to other people's expectations, others exert **normative social influence.** Put together, assimilation to other people's opinions has a lot going for it, but obviously social influence may pull a person in many directions. For example, your parents may say smoking is bad, but some of your peers may smoke whereas others may not. Additionally, health campaigns stress the link between smoking and cancer whereas the tobacco industry tries to make you believe that smoking is the ideal way to express your true self. To whom do we yield or, more precisely, which are the factors that determine the resultant attitude?

Informational social influence: Following others because one believes their responses are valid and correct.

Normative social influence: Following others because one seeks their approval.

MODERATORS OF SOCIAL INFLUENCE

As we have mentioned, social influence may be exerted via different means and processes. On a very general level and independent of the particular processes involved, social impact theory (Latané, 1981) holds that the degree to which people are influenced depends on a) the number of sources, b) their strength and c) their immediacy. We will define each aspect more closely in the following.

Number

The more people or, more generally speaking, the more influences that tug a person in one direction, the stronger the resultant influence and the more likely this attitude will be adapted (controlling for everything else). From a social validation perspective, it may be rational to rely on the majority or the *social consensus* as it provides more social proof. If everyone agrees, chances are that they are correct. Taking the minority position is certainly more risk-prone.

It is not necessary to actually experience the influence of the majority. Students at a university in the USA who had reported their attitude towards African Americans were given bogus feedback that either 81 per cent or 19 per cent of this university's students agreed with their attitude (Sechrist & Stangor, 2001). The crucial finding was that participants' attitudes became stronger as indicated by higher accessibility when they thought other students would share them. Furthermore, this also translated to behaviour (see Chapter 13). Those who had reported a negative attitude and also believed that a majority shared their prejudice chose a seat further away from the African American student than those prejudiced participants who were led to believe they were in the minority. In contrast, students who were low in prejudice sat closer to the target when they believed they shared the majority view compared to the minority view. Majority claims are often used in persuasion, when persuaders claim – for example, 'surely most people will agree with me, when I say that . . .', or advertisers stress that their brand is the most preferred brand in the nation, or that '8 out of 10 users would buy brand X again'. The underlying argument here is that if so many people agree they are likely to be right. However, consensus information can also exert normative influence, particularly when the referent group is the in-group as in the study by Sechrist and Stangor reported above.

The majority sets a norm in so far as this is what people usually do or think. In their Focus Theory of Normative Conduct, Cialdini and colleagues (Cialdini *et al.*, 1990; Cialdini *et al.*, 1991) refer to these norms as **descriptive norms**. Interestingly, persuasive appeals, warnings or media reports often stress the shockingly high incidence of an undesirable behaviour or attitude in order to mobilise counter-action – for example, how many children are sent to school without having eaten breakfast or how many college students think drinking and driving is okay. However, as Cialdini and colleagues pointed out, such numbers may inadvertently draw attention to the prevalence of the undesired behaviour and recipients may draw the undesired conclusion that if so many people are doing it, they themselves might just as well do so too. From this perspective, such well-meant campaigns may backfire. Alarms about rising anti-Semitism in Europe may actually contribute to it by highlighting the appalling trend. What is important is to communicate the desired behaviour or attitude, or what Cialdini and colleagues refer to as the **injunctive norm** (e.g. drinking and driving is irresponsible and unacceptable).

Descriptive norm:
Norm oriented on frequency of occurrence (e.g. is the attitude endorsed by the majority?).

Injunctive norm:
Norm oriented on a theoretical ideal (e.g. is it morally desirable to hold a certain attitude?).

People will be more likely to change if they feel that they are not alone but are supported by a large number of others. A fascinating application of the law of numbers was provided by a field study on reducing energy consumption (Schultz *et al.*, 2007). First the researchers obtained the consumption levels of 290 households. These households were then randomly assigned to two conditions. Half households received feedback on how they compared to the average in their neighbourhood. Thus the descriptive norm was activated. As would be desired, those households that had been told that they were using more energy than the average decreased their consumption considerably over the following three weeks (no later measures were taken). However, attesting to the fact that descriptive norms may backfire and supporting the model, those that now found out that they had used less energy than their neighbours increased their consumption. This is where the other condition comes into play. The other half of the households not only received descriptive feedback but the feedback also included a smiley face for those that were below average and a frowney face for those that were above average. It was assumed that thereby the injunctive norm (wasting energy is bad, conserving energy is good) was communicated. Indeed, the combination of descriptive and injunctive norms was equally successful in decreasing consumption of previously above-average households, and, most importantly prevented the below-average households from increasing their consumption.

Undoubtedly, the number of influencers plays a large role in social influence. But if more sources have more impact, does this mean that the majority always wins? We will turn to this interesting issue in a later section.

Strength of the influence

The strength of the source may come in many different forms. For example, as you have seen in the previous chapter, strong arguments exert more influence (under certain conditions) than weaker arguments. Also, reinforcement or punishment for expressing certain attitudes may be stronger or weaker. The more power a person has in rewarding (or punishing) others, the more likely it will be that others will yield to this person's influence. In this respect, it is not surprising that out-group members have less influence than in-group members (e.g. Stangor *et al.*, 2001). When we referred to the message-learning approach in Chapter 8, we already mentioned expertise (see also studies regarding the ELM) and trustworthiness (see also Chapter 10) as two source characteristics that may determine whether recipients yield to a persuasive message or not. Many studies in the paradigm of the message-learning approach as well as the ELM provided evidence for the impact of other source characteristics. For example, when students at a campus were approached by another student who argued that the university should stop serving meat in the dining halls, they were more likely to agree when the persuader was attractive compared to less attractive

(Chaiken, 1979). When the endorsers in a restaurant ad were attractive compared to unattractive, more ad recipients were interested in the restaurant (e.g. Shavitt *et al.*, 1994). The fact that celebrities are popular as endorsers in advertising speaks to the effectiveness of celebrity status in persuasion and controlled experiments attested the persuasive power of celebrities compared to non-celebrities (e.g. Petty *et al.*, 1983). Celebrities may work so well because they are usually liked. In sum, due to different underlying processes, source characteristics may moderate the impact of the influence (see also Box 9.1).

Immediacy

People with whom one has more contact have more opportunities to exert their influence. The police cadets in the above example were particularly prone to the influence of their peers with whom they interacted for several hours everyday. Immediacy does not necessarily equal proximity as in the modern world technology allows for frequent and intensive contact over long distances. What this property also symbolises is that social influence is not a one-shot process but every occasion of social contact may tug at our attitudes. People with whom we are in close contact will exert their influence – intentional and unintentional – quite frequently.

FROM INDIVIDUAL ATTITUDES TO PUBLIC OPINION

As already mentioned before, attitude research as well as social psychology at large have focused on the individual and have rather neglected processes and phenomena at the macro level. Having said this, we have to acknowledge – and you will see in this section – that attitude researchers have produced a host of findings and theories on attitude formation in small groups, such as was described above with Schachter's classic study. Yet, we know relatively little about how attitudes emerge or change in whole societies – for example, what caused attitudes towards homosexuals to change so dramatically over the last 30 years. One exception is a model developed as a dynamic extension of Social Impact Theory, the Dynamic Theory of Social Impact (Nowak *et al.*, 1990; see also Vallacher & Nowak, 2007). It provides a framework to describe and predict attitude change in groups, small or large. We will first describe the model and its predictions. We will then discuss some of the phenomena in more detail.

Dynamic Theory of Social Impact

In a social network, be that a society at large, an organisation or a small group, in principle each member exerts influence on other members and is also the target of others' influence. This is the base of the Dynamic Theory of Social Impact (Nowak *et al.*, 1990). This model is an attempt to capture the result of these mutual influences and make predictions for the system as a whole. In order to do so, it relies on the same parameters as Social Impact Theory: number, strength and immediacy. Most importantly, it pays tribute to the fact that social influence is a repeated process. People do not stop to influence each other after the first occasion. Whereas most other research only looks at such one-trial situations – for example, attitude change after one persuasive message – the dynamic model takes such reiterations into account. Computer simulations show how attitudes in a social network change after some iterations given certain initial parameters, such as number, strength and immediacy, and some simple rules regarding their impact.

The following example described by Vallacher & Nowak (2007) illustrates the power of the dynamic process. Each individual was described by an initial attitude (pro vs. con depicted by light and dark shades respectively in Figure 9.1a; for the sake of simplicity this example comprises only pro vs. con attitudes but more fine-grained positions can also be simulated), influential strength of the person (depicted by the height of the blocks) and his or her position in the social space. Individuals depicted by higher blocks will exert more influence and will be better able to resist external influence. To start the simulation, one individual is chosen at random from which his or her influence spreads. Using an algorithm in which more immediate contacts and those of higher influential strength are weighted more heavily than less immediate and weaker sources (for details, see Vallacher & Nowak, 2007) the simulation determines the overall strength and direction of the influence for each individual in the system. If the resulting influence that is exerted upon one individual is stronger than the individual's current attitude, the individual changes his or her position accordingly. This procedure is reiterated until after several rounds the system reaches a stable state and further repetitions do not change individual positions any more. Figure 9.1a depicts a random distribution of a majority (60 per cent) and minority position (40 per cent). In each group the relative proportion of strong and weak members is the same. Figure 9.1b shows the distribution after six simulations, after which the system reached an equilibrium and further rounds did not result in further switches.

Two things can be easily detected from Figure 9.1b. First, the former majority grew even more. Now 90 per cent endorse the 'light grey' position and the minority position is only held by 10 per cent. As a whole, the system shifted towards the majority position, and whereas the average opinion was initially moderately positive (remember light grey stands for pro) the average later became more extreme. This phenomenon, referred to as polarisation, is well known in small group research and we will discuss it below.[1]

Second, and perhaps somewhat astonishing after what we discussed above about the influence of numbers, the system did not completely shift.

FIGURE 9.1   Spread of majority attitudes

FIGURE 9.1A

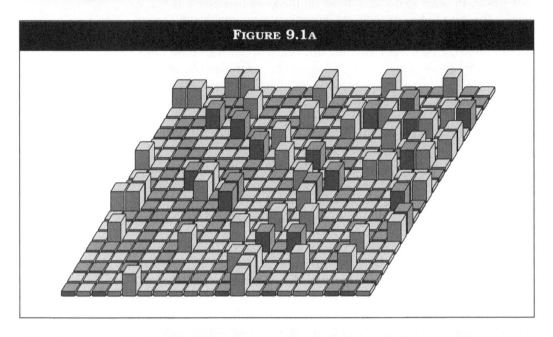

FIGURE 9.1B

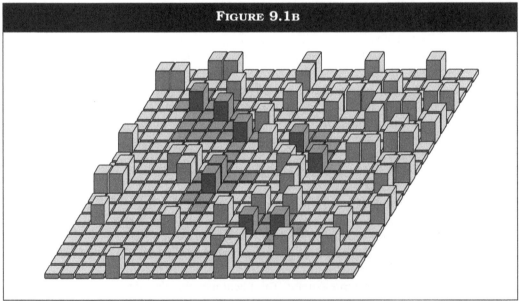

Note: Initial (A) and final (B) distribution of attitudes in a society. The minority attitude (dark grey bars) is marginalised by the majority (light grey bars). Minority attitudes survive centered around strong minority members. (Graph from Vallacher & Nowak, 2007)

The minority's number reduced but some minority clusters remained, centred by strong sources. Such a pattern reflects that also in the real world people who are close to each other often share opinions. It also suggests that minority positions can survive because in a local niche (in a particular social circle) this position is actually the majority position. As long as this niche manages to insulate itself from other influences it will survive. To the extent that people who hold different opinions do not interact, discuss the issues that divide them, or are at least exposed to each other's views, they will hardly influence each other. On the positive side, this may secure the survival of minority opinions. On the downside, this also means that seclusion may foster division and cause people to grow apart. In this respect, it may be either a comforting or an unsettling thought that today's technology makes it easy to find one's very own social niche (see Chapter 11 on selective exposure). Virtual social networks and media provide social reinforcement for even the most outlandish positions. Whereas social networks should drive the spread of opinions, they will only do this to the extent that the members are interconnected (Christakis & Fowler, 2010). With members clustered together but few connections between the clusters, influence will not spread beyond the respective clusters and within the clusters polarisation will occur. As a result the opinion gap between clusters will grow (see also Vallacher, 2015).

Group polarisation (and group consensus)

Important decisions are rarely made by a single individual. In most organisations, whether they are in business, politics, education or other domains, people meet in teams, committees, boards, commissions and the like to discuss the issue at hand and to come to a conclusion. Supposing that people bring different opinions to the table, one might assume that in such a mix the different viewpoints may balance each other out and therefore groups would tend to arrive at more moderate, middle-of-the-road positions. This, however, is not usually the case. In groups where the individual members have an initial tendency towards one or the other side, the group tends to shift towards this pole and the position of the group's position tends to be more extreme than the average initial position of its members. A classic study that demonstrated this effect was conducted in France and involved two attitude objects: the French president at the time, Charles de Gaulle, and North Americans (Moscovici & Zavalloni, 1969). On average, participants initially had positive attitudes about the former and slightly negative attitudes about the latter. They then discussed their attitudes in groups. After the group discussion, individual attitudes were again assessed but this time the average attitude towards de Gaulle was even more favourable whereas the average attitude towards North Americans had become considerably less favourable. Numerous other studies in small groups (e.g. juries) attest to this effect, called *group polarisation* (for a classic review, see Lamm & Myers, 1978). The label 'group polarisation' is often misunderstood as when members disagree and opinions diverge after group discussions, but it is meant to express that group opinions become more extreme.

With the many findings, quite a number of explanations of the effect have been brought forward but the accumulated evidence favours only two (for a review, see Isenberg, 1986). One is founded in the social identity function (others exert normative social influence) whereas the other pertains to the motivation to hold valid attitudes (others exert informational social influence).

Imagine you attend a group discussion on an issue about which you feel mildly positive. Not knowing how the others feel you carefully test the waters with a slightly positive but non-committal statement. To your relief, your opinion is met with agreement and the others also seem to be favourably inclined. Driven by the desire to meet the others' approval and acceptance, you become more daring and venture another and perhaps more supportive claim. By doing so, you communicate to the group that you are a good group member that adheres to shared opinion (Brown, 1974). If everyone follows suit and tries to top the others, a shift to the more extreme can easily be accounted for.

Of course, it is also possible that you are convinced by the arguments you hear. Whereas before the discussion you had only thought of one reason to support the issue, you have now learned new arguments. Moreover, the doubts you may also have harboured have been washed away by some of the others' arguments.

Support for this latter account comes from findings that polarisation increases to the extent that the arguments presented in the group discussion are convincing and novel (e.g. Vinokur & Burnstein, 1978). In support of the group norm account, findings suggest that merely hearing the other members' position, even when this position is not backed up by an argument, suffices to produce group polarisation – albeit to a smaller extent (Isenberg, 1986). Presumably, both accounts – normative and informational social influence – contribute to the polarisation effect.

The processes contributing to group polarisation also cause groups to become uniform in their opinions. Although in the computer simulation depicted in Figure 9.1b a small minority remained, one can easily imagine that in small groups minority positions may not survive. It is difficult if not impossible to form an isolated niche in a small group. Both consensus and polarisation may contribute to a phenomenon in small groups called group-think. In a nutshell, group-think refers to the fact that groups (intentionally or unintentionally) may strive for consensus and agreement, thereby ignoring important information and making suboptimal – if not disastrous – decisions (see Esser, 1998).

The dynamics that govern opinion formation in groups must not be neglected when evaluating the outcome. For example, a popular method in opinion research is to bring people together in a so-called *focus group* where they are supposed to focus on one issue and discuss it. It is important to bear in mind that the results do not represent the average opinion of the members, nor would such groups reveal an adequate picture of the diversity of opinions, as groups tend to converge to a consensus.

At this point one may wonder, is this really the whole story? What about *12 Angry Men*? In this classic movie (by Sydney Lumet, 1957; a remake was released in 1997), one jury member, played by Henry Fonda, is initially the sole dissenter favouring acquittal in an otherwise unanimous jury. Slowly he succeeds in turning the jury around until they reach the unanimous verdict of 'not guilty'. Is this merely a Hollywood fairy tale?

THE MAJORITY ALWAYS WINS?

So far it does not look good for minority positions. The computer simulation suggests that minorities become marginalised, and small group research suggests that members advocating positions counter to the group may be punished or the mere threat may silence them. Obviously, this cannot be the whole story. A look at history easily provides examples of how initial minority positions became mainstream thinking. Christianity began with just 12 followers and a few hundred years later it had spread all over Europe. Many other social movements have over the last decades changed how the majority looks at things. How did the minority become a sizeable force or even a majority? Well, number is not everything.

Again, a computer simulation may be a first step in understanding the respective dynamics. Note that in the example above (Figure 9.1a) the majority and the minority had exactly the same proportion of strong sources. But what if the minority's influencers were slightly stronger than those of the majority? Perhaps adherents to a minority position are better trained to communicate their point or they try harder. Perhaps they are higher in charisma, expertise or power, and can thereby exert a stronger influence. So minorities may make up in strength what they lack in numbers. Moreover, the algorithm used in the simulation above assumed the same immediacy for majority and minority members. But perhaps minorities aim to reach more people; after all, these rebels have a cause and they may be motivated to push it. Perhaps they receive more media attention. When Leonardo di Caprio bought a Prius (an eco-friendly car), it made headlines. Sometimes Zeitgeist or external events play into a minority's hands. In the years before 2011 the number of people vehemently opposed to nuclear power in Germany was never above 26 and usually below (Köcher, 2011). Then Fukushima happened. After the Japanese reactor blew up, the number shot to a whopping 42 per cent (note, vehemently opposed) (Köcher, 2011). Within days, the German government completely reversed its energy policy as a result.

In sum, there are many reasons why the power of social influence may be tilted slightly towards the minority (sometimes). Does this help? When

FIGURE 9.2   Shifting distributions of attitudes in a society

FIGURE 9.2A

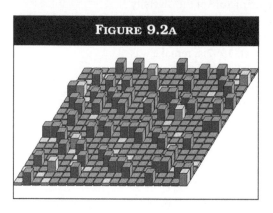

FIGURE 9.2B

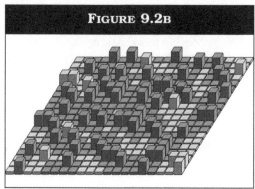

FIGURE 9.2C

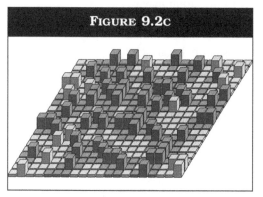

FIGURE 9.2D

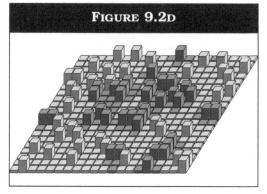

Note: Minorities may become majorities and vice versa (see explanation in text)

the algorithm in the computer simulation was changed to give the minority position a slight advantage, a very different picture emerged. Figure 9.2 (Vallacher, 2015) shows the results of such a simulation (the bias was induced independent of strength or immediacy but by adding a constant favouring the minority position). Panel A depicts a 10 per cent minority, randomly distributed among the population. Assuming the same rules for minority and majority influence, the minority position would further reduce and perhaps be wiped out because minority members are rather isolated and will find it difficult to cluster. Introducing a bias favouring the minority position, however, helped to form some clusters (Panel B) that continued to grow around majority clusters (Panel C) until after 40 iterations the former minority became the new majority of 80 per cent (Panel D). It is interesting to note that the new minority is strategically in a better position than the minority in panel A. When times are changing and provide favourable conditions (external events, charismatic leaders, good campaigning, etc.) it will be easier for them to strike back and win back some lost ground. And perhaps the pattern will shift again.

By capturing the dynamic component of social influence, such computer simulations make fascinating predictions regarding attitudinal shifts in larger social entities. Vallacher (2015) points out that there are many real world examples of rather dramatic swings of public opinion. In the immediate aftermath of the break up of the communist regimes in Eastern Europe, the communist parties suffered severe losses in most countries but were often able to swing back in the following election.

But what exactly are the secret weapons minorities can use in their favour? We have already mentioned some in passing. External events can play into the minority's hands and catalyse change but obviously such events cannot be planned and do not lend themselves as a reliable strategy. Acquiring influential endorsers – meaning those that have high influential strength and/or are well linked – will also help. Paul Lazarsfeld (1944) even assumed that influence was mediated to the masses by such opinion leaders.[2] Psychological research identified what William Crano (2012) refers to as the holy trinity: persistence, consistency and unanimity. As these aspects on practical grounds are sometimes hard to distinguish from one another, they are commonly lumped together as consistency.

Consistency (persistence and unanimity)

The first systematic studies on minority influence in small groups were conducted by Serge Moscovici and his colleagues (Moscovici *et al.*, 1969). The experimental set-up reversed the classic Asch experiments on majority influence. Whereas in the Asch experiments one real participant was confronted with the diverging view of a majority consisting of research confederates, in Moscovici's minority studies a group of four real participants were confronted with the diverging view of two research confederates. All group members were asked to name the colour shown on 36 slides. The colour was unambiguously blue, not teal, not turquoise, not green-blue, but blue, and in a pretest everybody had said so. However, in one condition the two confederates, who were the first to give their judgement, consistently – that is, 36 out of 36 trials – named the colour as green. As a result, about 8 per cent of the other group members' judgements also shifted to green. That this was due to the consistent divergence could be inferred from the comparison with a condition where the minority only judged green in 24 out of the 36 trials. Then, only about 1 per cent of the majority judgements followed. Influencing colour perception – just as rating the length of lines – may be considered a long way from influencing attitudes, but similar results have been shown in the attitude domain from early work by Mugny (1975) to fairly recent examples (e.g. Martin & Hewstone, 2008; for a review, see Martin & Hewstone, 2010). Moreover, a meta-analysis across 97 studies also corroborated the importance of consistency, showing more minority influence with higher consistency (Wood *et al.*, 1994).

Persistence. Note that in the colour perception studies consistency referred to always giving the same response to an identical stimulus (the same colour). In one, the consistent, condition the confederates never changed their view. In this example, the behaviour may have also been described as persistent. The minority members insisted on their view over and over again. Consistency (never diverging from the message) and persistence (continuously pushing the message) usually go hand in hand and both are helpful when it comes to social influence. Minority members are well advised to keep nagging and pushing their point. It may not necessarily make them popular, but it may cause others to think more about the minority's point (see below). After all, constant dripping wears the stone.

Unanimity. Unanimity means consistency among the minority members. If one of the members had called the colour yellow and the other one green we would have had two minorities and their impact would be even smaller. Technically, we might consider them together as the non-blue minority, but if you try to imagine this situation, it will probably become intuitively clear that chances to convert any other member to non-blue would be dismal. 'All they say is that it is not blue, despite a majority seeing blue, but they can't even agree on what they see instead of blue.' When many diverse groups challenge the majority, it becomes much easier for the majority to dismiss these alternative views, in particular if they contradict each other. Moreover, splitting the dissent will also weaken its impact according to the rules of social impact. The maxim 'divide et impera' (divide and rule) owes its presumed effectiveness to this dynamic.

Other moderators of minority influence

The experimental examples pertained to minorities in a strictly numerical sense. Fewer group members endorsed position A and more group members endorsed position B. It may not seem significant that the only division between the two camps is their views on A and B, but this may easily become a major divide when it comes to important issues. However, dissenting views also often relate to group status insofar as from the majority's perspective the majority is the in-group and the minority is the out-group. It is beyond the scope of this book to go into the huge area of intergroup processes (e.g. Brewer, 2003), but it probably is still easy to see why it is even harder for a double minority to make their mark.

Why do majorities change?

Although describing some of the tools that may make minorities successful may have already provided a flavour of the processes by which minorities affect attitudinal change, we have not yet provided a process account. In short, many different theories have been put forward over the years. They are often hard to compare because different models take different assumptions into account – for example, whether they pertain to a numerical or a social minority. To some extent most models were influenced by Moscovici's **conversion theory** (1980, 1985). Moscovici assumed that minority messages would be scrutinised in more detail and processed more systematically, whereas majority messages would be processed in a more superficial manner. After all, siding with the majority is usually beneficial and therefore does not require much thought. Minority positions, however, are not simply put aside or ignored. As they stand out they may elicit a desire 'to see what the minority saw, what it understood' (1980, p. 215). In this respect, the effects of consistency come into play as a consistent (and persistent) message will attain more attention and will also be more likely to convey the commitment and coherence of the group (Moscovici, 1968), which will lend their position more credibility and help to establish that it should be taken seriously. Later research showed that minorities do indeed elicit more systematic processing than majorities, but this may be confined to messages regarding attitudes of medium importance (see Chapter 10; for reviews, see Crano & Seyranian, 2009; Martin & Hewstone, 2008). For highly important attitudes, the majority was more influential, although presumably in both cases systematic processing occurred. For attitudes very low in importance, apparently the heuristic to go with the majority was applied.

A somewhat provocative account was put forward by Nemeth (1995), whose *convergent–divergent theory* suggested that minority and majority influence elicits different thinking styles. When the majority holds an attitude counter to one's own this may be considered as threatening and may narrow one's focus. Attention and thoughts converge on the majority's view but leads to only a superficial exploration of the issue. Counter-attitudinal positions of a minority, however, may instigate divergent thinking – that is, thoughts will go beyond what was presented by the minority. Minority positions may thereby trigger the emergence of creative and novel perspectives. Although there is supporting evidence for Nemeth's perspective, most of her, as well as other people's, work is not concerned with attitudes but problem solving, and we therefore will not explore this account in detail.

Conversion theory:
Conversion theory holds that positions that diverge from the majority cause attention and may cause individuals to analyze the minority's arguments. As a consequence attitude conversion may occur.

CONCLUDING COMMENT: PERSUASION AS A SOCIAL PROCESS

We began this chapter by mentioning that classic persuasion research often neglected the social nature of persuasion. Although persuasion is often defined as a form of communication – in the eyes of McGuire, it is one of the more interesting forms (McGuire, 1973, p. 216) – and this definition is also reflected in the classical approaches in persuasion research that conceptualise the effects of source, message and recipient (e.g. Hovland *et al.*, 1953; see Chapter 8) the dynamics that come from the social interaction between persuader and participant did not play a major role. As McCann and Higgins (1992) noted, persuasion researchers conceived of communication mainly as an information transmission device and restricted the role of persuasion targets as passive recipients of communication. But clearly, persuasion recipients actually do more than message processing. In this concluding section we would like to look at persuasion from a social viewpoint.

By signalling their reactions they may make the persuader change his or her approach. In a debate people exchange arguments. As you may well know, this does not simply mean that Bill presents a pro argument and Liz a contra argument and then they go home and elaborate on each other's arguments but the elaboration will be part of the exchange. They will refute and challenge the other's arguments while pressing the opponent to accept one of theirs. In some respect, argumentation is like a negotiation (Rips, 1998). However, once you are successful and have persuaded your opponent to concede a point, the consistency principle (see Box 9.1) implies that the opponent cannot go back on this. This may mean that you have a foot in the door (see Box 9.1) and may press for more. Yet, accepting a fact does not automatically mean conversion and you may still wrestle about the conclusions from the claim.

Communication is also interactive insofar as both sides take the other's characteristics into account and tailor the message or the strategy accordingly (see Chapter 10). Communication entails that there is a shared goal towards which progress can be made and recorded. Communication also rests on the mutual understanding that every contribution is relevant to the purpose of the communication (Grice, 1978; for a review, see Wänke, 2007). Based on this assumption, Wänke and Reutner (2010) proposed that a message or claim may be persuasive merely because it is perceived as intended to persuade. The first task of a listener in communication is to understand what the speaker means (Clark & Schober, 1992), and the same is true for persuasion (Albaracín, 2002). In order to understand the message of the persuader and interpret its meaning, recipients may rely on the speaker's purpose – namely, persuasion. This would render every piece of information that is presented as potentially supporting the persuader's goal. Indeed, they found that consumers considered the same amount of an unhealthy ingredient – for example, 3 grams of fat – as a subjectively lower amount when it was communicated by an advertisement for the product than by a neutral source that had no persuasive intention. The reverse was found for healthy ingredients. As a result, the products were considered as healthier when the nutritional information was claimed in an advertisement compared to a neutral source. Apparently, recipients had no clear conception of whether the amount was high or low and therefore relied on the fact that it was presented in order to induce people to buy the product, and therefore must represent a benefit. In other words, they followed the heuristic: if they advertise it, it must be good. However, this is not to say that persuaders have recipients eating out of the palm of their hand. Instead, people may try to avoid being persuaded, which is an issue we will deal with in the next chapter.

CHAPTER SUMMARY

1   People may adopt others' attitudes due to many different processes. In general, adjusting one's attitudes to those of others may be due to informational social influence as well as normative social influence. The former refers to the fact that other people serve as social proof. The latter refers to the fact that others provide social acceptance and can punish deviants. Both influences can be realised by what other people actually do (descriptive norms) and what they preach (injunctive norms).

2   The three key variables in social influence are number, strength and immediacy.

3   Social influence is rarely a one-trial process but occurs repeatedly, with different or the same contact persons. Models need to take this dynamic into account to make predictions about attitudinal shift at the societal level.

4   In groups, attitudes tend to become more uniform among members and to shift to a more extreme position (group polarisation).

5   Minorities can influence majorities. One strategy that helps them do this is to push persistently, to argue consistently and to convey that there is consensus within the minority. Different models have been put forward to explain minority influence. The models all agree that minority and majority positions elicit different processes. The exact nature of this relationship depends on many other factors, such as the status of the minority and relevance of the attitude.

6   Although persuasion is defined as communication, the principles of communication have been rather neglected in persuasion research but may well give rise to novel hypotheses and insights.

Exercises

1   Think of discussions with your peers. Can you remember episodes when you changed your opinion?

2   Design a campaign for recycling using injunctive norms and descriptive norms.

3   Novel music, dance or fashion trends often cause suspicion or even ridicule. Try to explain why underground trends become mainstream, even though the majority is usually opposed to them at first.

Further reading

For a popular psychology book on minority influence:

Crano, W. (2012). *The Rules of Influence: Winning When You Are in the Minority.* New York: St Martin's Press.

For a more academic text:

Martin, R., Hewstone, M., Martin, P. & Gardikiotis, A. (2008). Persuasion from majority and minority groups. In W. D. Crano & Prislin, R. (eds) *Attitudes and Attitude Change* (pp. 261–384). New York: Psychology Press.

Notes

1   We cannot help commenting at this point that polarisation is rather a misnomer as the system does not become *less* but *more uniform*. However, this is the term used in the literature.
2   Although his model did not especially pertain to minority influence.

Chapter 10

RESISTANCE: STUBBORN RECEIVERS AND HOW TO PERSUADE THEM

Imagine Carlos, who is in favour of nuclear power. Lily, an environmentalist classmate, confronts him with information about the nuclear disaster in Fukushima, Japan: 'It's time to wake up! These incidents clearly demonstrate the potential danger of nuclear power plants. It is a force beyond human control. Now is definitely the time to change your opinion!' Carlos takes some time to think about it, and finally agrees on the potential danger involved in nuclear power. 'Well, I see that things could go wrong. But that does not mean that nuclear power is not a good thing. We just need higher safety standards.' You also have probably tried to convince someone that her or his opinion was wrong, but then had to accept that it was impossible to change that person's mind. You might have wondered how people can be so ignorant and just stick with their attitude despite all the arguments against it. In order to understand how one can be so 'ignorant' and stick to one's attitude irrespective of facts and arguments, it can help to put yourself in their position. How would you feel knowing that someone was trying to manipulate your opinions? Would you easily give up your attitudes?

WHAT MOTIVATES US TO RESIST PERSUASION?

Early scholars already pointed out the necessity of studying resistance in order to come up with a comprehensive understanding of how persuasion works (Brehm, 1966; McGuire, 1964). Strikingly – part of what makes the psychology of persuasion so exciting – it can be presumed that senders and receivers of persuasive messages have conflicting motives. Whereas the sender aims at changing the receiver's attitude, the receiver aims at maintaining the status quo.

   One motive to resist persuasive attempts is that we do not want to be someone else's puppet, but would prefer to enjoy psychological freedom. According to Brehm's **Theory of Psychological Reactance** (1966), people resent restrictions and strive to maintain their freedom to behave as they

Theory of Psychological Reactance: Approach whose core assumption is that individuals are motivated to restore restricted freedom by enhancing the value of 'forbidden' or otherwise blocked objects or behavioural alternatives.

want to. When this psychological freedom is threatened, they react with psychological reactance. Thus, if someone takes away our behavioural options (e.g. smoking) or tries to prescribe how we should think, we show counter-reactions. For instance, we will start devaluing the source of the message. Or we will oppose the position they are seeking to promote and thereby regain our sense of self-determination (e.g. Worchel & Brehm, 1971; Wright, 1986).

In principle, any persuasive attempt can be regarded as manipulative and a means of commanding someone else's thoughts or behaviours. Thus, any persuasive attempt has the potential to evoke reactance. However, we would expect reactance to be highest when the messages include strong, imperative requests. In this vein, reactance theory has been applied to explain the paradoxical effects of restrictions and censorship on people's attitudes. In one study (Worchel & Arnold, 1973), students were led to believe that they would hear a tape-recorded speech advocating a ban of police from university campuses – a topic hotly debated at the time of the US Vietnam War, when confrontations between protesting students and the police were not uncommon. They then learned, however, that unfortunately they would not hear the tape either due to a technical malfunction or because some other student group had objected to the tape being used in the experiment. Students who were denied access to the tape reported attitudes more in line with a police ban than students in a control group, who had never expected to hear any speech. The effect was even more pronounced for the group led to believe that the denial of access to information was intended and thus, this finding is in line with reactance theory.

Another early approach tackling the motivation underlying resistance was McGuire's Inoculation Theory (McGuire, 1961). Similar to reactance theory, Inoculation Theory assumes that being the target of a persuasive attempt causes threat. In contrast to reactance theory, however, McGuire suggested that this threat results from becoming aware that one might have to give up existing attitudes. As such, the resistance motive applies only to the case when there is already an attitude towards an object. Nevertheless, the crucial question in this case is why do people not want their attitudes to be changed. Shouldn't we sometimes give up our long-standing attitudes and replace them with new and more accurate ones? Wouldn't this render our attitudes more useful? There are at least two ways of understanding why people do not want to give up their attitudes.

The first becomes evident when we consider attitude functions besides the utilitarian function (cf. Chapter 1). Recall that attitudes not only show us whether to approach or avoid the attitude object, but attitudes also help us express ourselves and position ourselves in the social world. For an environmentalist, for instance, giving up his pro-environmentalist attitude would mean losing part of his identity, and might even perhaps lead to conflict or break-up with his friends and acquaintances. Trying to maintain their identity, people therefore may resist attitude change, though valid arguments against their position do exist (Sherman & Cohen, 2002, 2006;

Steele & Liu, 1983). The counter-intuitive implication would be that a strong personality is not the one who resists, but who dares changing her attitude. Complimenting this idea, people affirmed of their selves become more open to change their mind (Cohen *et al.*, 2000; Correll *et al.*, 2004).

The second argument concerns our need for self-consistency, which is represented in a coherent attitudinal structure (cf. Chapter 7). Whenever new counter-attitudinal information comes our way, it is likely to conflict with existing attitudes, thereby creating cognitive dissonance, a negative state which people try to reduce. In line with these ideas, the dual-process models have explicitly incorporated receiver motives. Other than the motive to hold correct attitudes (see Chapter 8), the most pertinent to resistance is the **defence motive** (e.g. Chaiken *et al.*, 1989; note that although the defence motive is part of both, the ELM and the HSM, its role has been emphasised more in the HSM). In contrast to accuracy motivation, defence motivation will lead to biased message processing, an attempt to invalidate and discount counter-attitudinal information and to enhance pro-attitudinal information (see Chapter 11).

Defence motive: People are intrinsically motivated to keep their attitudes, an assumption made in prominent dual-process models of persuasion (e.g. the Heuristic-Systematic Model).

Thus, receivers' defence motives and their struggle for self-determination can explain why it is sometimes so difficult to persuade them. Importantly, knowing why people may want to resist persuasive attempts allows us to understand the characteristics that render attitudes either more or rather less resistant to persuasion. As you will see, to some extent this question can be answered by considering the various indicators of attitude strength, which we discussed in the first chapter. Indeed, strong attitudes have been hypothesised or even defined as being resistant to change (e.g. Petty & Krosnick, 1995). In this context research has focused on how attitudes develop that are most likely to be unaffected by persuasion, an issue we will deal with in the following section, before turning to some essential social processes at work during the persuasion episode.

WHAT MAKES AN ATTITUDE RESISTANT TO CHANGE?

For a real soccer fan, few things can be worse than if one's favourite club is involved in one of the biggest corruption scandals in the history of the game. The famous club and former Italian champions, Juventus, or more precisely their General Manager Luciano Moggi, was accused in 2006 of bribing referees and fixing matches, to name just some of the charges. Given the very solid state of evidence, in July that year Juventus were dismissed from the most prestigious team competition in Europe, the UEFA Champions League. Even at the national level, Juventus were relegated to the second division, Serie B. It was no surprise that all this corruption and the subsequent relegation caused many fans to stay away and the number of spectators at Juventus games dropped significantly. However, and perhaps more noteworthy, despite being in the second division, Juventus could still count on 20,000 spectators per match, much more than other second league clubs. Apparently, some of the supporters maintained their love for 'the old lady' – as the Juventus fans call their club – despite the breakdown of moral and sporting values they had witnessed.

Sometimes, attitudes can be very strong. Although it appears that every rational argument speaks against it, and it feels very hard to maintain the attitude in question, still, these attitudes resist change. Some things we just love, in good times as in bad. You also probably have some attitudes you would never contemplate changing. We already discussed in Chapter 1 some indicators of strong attitudes. In the following chapter we will consider how these strong attitudes emerge and why they are so hard to change.

Inoculation Theory

Early in the development of psychology of attitudes, McGuire (1964) raised the question of how attitudes could be strengthened. He adopted a biological metaphor to illustrate how attitudes could become more resistant. The basic notion was that just as mild doses of a virus train the body to defend against an infectious disease, small doses of counter-attitudinal information might inoculate attitudes against a severe *counter-attitudinal attack.*

Inoculation Theory:
Theory stating that exposures to smaller doses of counter-attitudinal information strengthen the attitude, thereby inoculate against subsequent counter-attitudinal persuasion attempts.

In the original formulation of **Inoculation Theory**, McGuire assumed that the effect of inoculation was restricted to defending beliefs that are not controversial. Thus, his inoculation studies dealt exclusively with cultural truisms (e.g. 'Mental illness is not contagious'; McGuire, 1964, p. 201), beliefs so widely shared that people neither doubted them nor wondered how these could be attacked. In a study by McGuire and Papageorgis (1961), participants reported their agreement with four truisms after three of these truisms had been attacked. Some days earlier, they had received treatments to help them resist two of the three messages: an 'inoculation' or 'refutational defense' treatment in which counterarguments had been presented and subsequently refuted, and a 'supportive defense' treatment in which arguments in favour of the truism had been presented. No defence for the third truism had been provided, and the fourth truism was neither defended nor subsequently attacked. The results (Figure 10.1) showed that post-message agreement was strongly affected by the counter-attitudinal attack when no defence treatment had been given. Compared to the attack-only condition, a good deal of resistance was conveyed by the inoculation treatment, whereas beliefs in the supportive condition did not differ significantly from those in the attack-only condition. Thus, having already been confronted with counterarguments, the mind becomes immune against them. To date, there is ample evidence that inoculation treatments render attitudes less vulnerable to counter-attacks as compared to no-treatment control groups and even groups receiving arguments supportive of their position. These studies, moreover, demonstrate that inoculation is also effective with controversial topics such as the legalisation of marijuana, hand-guns and gambling (Pfau *et al.*, 1997), animal testing (Nabi, 2003) or genetically modified food (Wood, 2007).

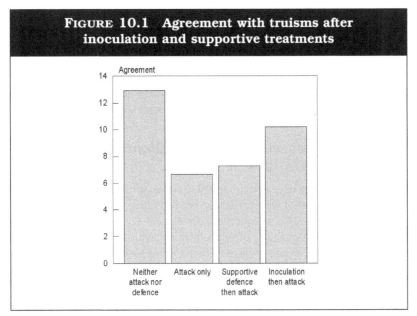

FIGURE 10.1   **Agreement with truisms after inoculation and supportive treatments**

Note: Beliefs/attitudes can be inoculated against attacks (data from McGuire & Papageorgis, 1961; adapted from a table by McGuire, 1964)

But how could one increase resistance against some unknown virus? In contrast to biological inoculation, it is not necessary that the mild dose involved contains the same virus as the attack. Early work by McGuire & Papageorgis (1961) already suggested that refutational-different inoculation might be equally as effective as refutational-same treatments. Indeed, results from a more recent meta-analysis (Banas & Rains, 2010) confirmed that the arguments of the counter-attack need not be included in the inoculation treatment, but confrontation with different counterarguments also helps defend against the subsequent attack to one's beliefs.

Complementing this notion, other means that stimulate the generation of counterarguments show the same bolstering effect as inoculation. More precisely, attitudes can be invigorated by *forewarning* recipients that a message may transport some persuasive intent (McGuire & Papageorgis, 1962; Petty & Cacioppo, 1977; Wood & Quinn, 2003).

Although McGuire and his associates emphasised the role of counter-arguing in explaining resistance, they did not directly propose the cognitive mediators of the resistance outcome. However, their work inspired much research on the cognitive underpinnings of resistance, over and above the particular phenomenon of inoculation. Building upon McGuire's work, various studies explored how inoculation treatments affect the different constructs summarised under the umbrella of attitude strength. In particular, Pfau and his colleagues were able to show that inoculation treatments increase the accessibility of an attitude (Pfau *et al.*, 2003). Moreover, they demonstrated that inoculation led to changes in the associative network representing the attitude in question. For participants who had received an inoculation treatment, the number of nodes in the attitude-relevant network had increased as compared to a no-treatment control group (Pfau *et al.*, 2005). As we will see in the next section, a clearer understanding of inoculation effects in particular and resistance in general, emerges when the concept of attitude strength is taken into account (cf. Chapter 1).

Inoculation effect:
Metaphorical term describing that resistance to persuasion is increased when, prior to a persuasion attempt, other counterattitudinal arguments have been successfully refuted.

Explaining resistance with indicators of attitude strength

A plethora of studies have demonstrated that the various indicators of strong attitudes are correlated with the resistance to counterattacks. Due to space considerations, we cannot reiterate them all here. Instead, we will concentrate on how strong resistant attitudes develop, with an emphasis on meta-cognitive processes. In particular, we will focus on how thinking about one's attitudes determines **attitude certainty** which refers to the confidence with which one holds an attitude (Festinger, 1954; Gross *et al.*, 1995).

Attitude certainty:
Meta-attitudinal experience, referring to the confidence with which an attitude is held.

Argument elaboration

As stated in the dual-process models (Chaiken 1987; Petty & Cacioppo, 1986a, b; see Chapter 8) persuasion may occur via different processes. One postulate in the original version of the ELM already stated that attitudes formed through elaborate processing of the persuasive message (i.e. via the central route) are more endurable and more resistant to change. In support of this hypothesis, Haugtvedt and Petty (1992) found that a message created more resistant attitudes in people who presumably engaged in systematic processing (i.e. individuals with a high NFC) than in people who process information more superficially (i.e. individuals low in NFC). With the ELM in mind, Haugtvedt and colleagues also proposed that arguments rather than content-unrelated affective cues might yield a more resistant attitude. This idea is also in line with Inoculation Theory because the resulting knowledge structure enables defence against counterarguments. In a study by Haugtvedt *et al.* (1994), a cover story asked participants to evaluate a new cartoon series. For this purpose, participants saw comic drawings. With the comic drawings, they were also exposed to some advertisements one of which advertised the focal product – the Omega 3 pen. Pertinent to the formation of resistant attitudes, the researchers varied the way the focal product was advertised. In the baseline condition, the pen was only advertised once. In a mere repetition condition, the pen was advertised three times by the same advertisement. In another two conditions, the pen was also advertised three times. However, either the three ads for the pen varied with respect to some affective background cues or, as was the case in a last condition, the variation was substantial – that is, the pen was advertised in three ads, but the argument was changed in each of the ads. To investigate whether the manipulation had an effect on the initial attitudes, participants rated the focal as well as some distractor products right after the experiment. After one week, participants were exposed to some product evaluations including a mildly negative consumer report about the Omega 3 pen. Subsequent attitude ratings served for measuring resistance to the counter-attitudinal message. Results revealed that repeated ad exposure led to initially more favourable attitudes towards the pen than single exposure – a result that is in line with mere exposure effects (see Chapter 4). However, all the repetition strategies were similarly effective. Interestingly, however, subsequent to the counter-attack, participants equipped with the different arguments showed a more positive attitude towards the object than participants in the other conditions. Thus, the findings show that there are different ways to form a positive attitude. However, depending on the way the attitude formed, resistance may vary. Specifically, the same summary evaluation will be more resistant if it is based on a more elaborate structure.

The question of why increased elaboration should yield more resistant attitudes, however, cannot be answered in a single sentence. For one thing, cognitive elaboration may enrich one's knowledge about the attitude object (Holtz & Miller, 2001; also cf. mere thought effect in Chapter 8). If attitudes are based on a lot of knowledge rather than a little, one may possess the argumentative repertoire to counter-argue and thereby defend one's attitude. For instance, you may have some knowledge suggesting that a counter-argument is wrong. In this vein, the defence mechanisms themselves are also based on deliberation about hard facts of the attitude object. Yet there is a more abstract way to think about a rich knowledge base. If your representation of an attitude is linked with many positive instances, a single negative argument may not have the weight to turn the overall evaluation into negative. Moreover, the vested effort and the profound representation may make you feel more certain about your attitude. Indeed, attitude certainty has been shown as a predictor of resistance to change (Bassili, 1996; Tormala & Petty, 2002). Relevant to the formation of resistant attitudes, attitude certainty has been found to increase with the amount of cognitive elaboration (Smith *et al.*, 2008). Crucially, the effect of cognitive elaboration on certainty was mediated by perceived knowledge rather than an actual knowledge increase. Thus, upon encounter of counter-attitudinal information (see also Chapter 11) because you believe that there is good reason for you to hold this attitude. From this perspective it becomes obvious that there are more ways to strengthen an attitude than by careful thinking. Other factors affecting attitude certainty should show similar effects.

Certainty does not need arguments

Several factors have been proposed to increase attitude certainty. For example, attitude certainty increases with direct experience with the attitude object (Fazio & Zanna, 1978; Krosnick *et al.*, 1993). You will feel more

---

Box 10.1   Can freedom be too much?

Is a wide variety of products always more enticing than a limited one? Results of the following field experiment by Iyengar and Lepper (2000) cast some doubt. In a supermarket a brand of jams was promoted at a stall. Customers were invited to taste the jams. The crucial manipulation was the variety of choice. In one condition, customers faced a rather small variety, six different flavours. In the other condition a wide variety of as many as 24 flavours were offered. Indeed, choice per se was attractive. Whereas about 60 per cent of the passers-by stopped for the large set, only 40 per cent stopped to taste some jam when the set was small. However, people in the large-set condition did not try more jams than their counter-parts in the small set condition. Moreover, these customers were not more likely to buy one of the brand's jams. Instead, only 3 per cent purchased a jam of the display compared to about 30 per cent in the small-set condition. Finally, and alarmingly from the provider as well as the customer perspective, further analysis showed that satisfaction was lower after having made a choice from a large assortment, compared to a small. Thus, providing large freedom of choice may be suitable to circumvent reaction, but it comes at the risk of customers feeling overcharged, and can decrease post-choice satisfaction.

---

confident that someone is an idiot if you personally heard him say stupid things than if you learned about his stupidity second-hand. Certainty, however, does not only increase after exposure to the attitude object, but also to the attitude itself. Repeatedly expressing an attitude renders it more accessible and it also increases attitude certainty (e.g. Holland *et al.*, 2003). Hence, accessibility can be experienced and serve as an indicator for how certain we are about our evaluations.

The multiple paths to attitude certainty become more evident if we consider a more fine-grained consideration of this construct. Petrocelli *et al.* (2007) proposed that attitude certainty actually consists of two distinct components: attitude clarity and correctness. The former refers to the fact that we are sure how we evaluate an object. In this vein, repetition results in our attitudes becoming clearer; saying how much you like your favourite song does not take you much time – you probably have a clear and reliable position. Thus, becoming clear about our attitudes is partly due to the meta-cognitive experience resulting from perceived stability: 'Since I expressed the same attitude over time, it appears that this attitude is really reliable' (cf. Box 10.1).

Just as people can perceive the clarity or say reliability of their attitudes, they may experience varying degrees of validity, which is captured by the term 'attitude correctness'. For some of your attitudes, you might think that they are correct and well justified (see correctness motive, Chapter 8), and others should have the same attitude, too. But how can we know if our attitude is correct? One piece of information people use to judge whether something is true or not is consensus (Asch, 1951), as we explained in Chapter 9. If everyone likes baggy pants, there must be something to them. Petrocelli *et al.* (2007) tested the impact of consensus on perceived attitude correctness in the following experiment. Students were asked to indicate their attitude towards a new identification card policy at their university. Half of the participants were led to believe that their opinion about the topic was shared by most of their peers, while the other half was led to believe that they belonged to the minority holding this attitude. In line with their predictions, attitude correctness increased when the consensus was high. This effect was not caused by increased clarity, corroborating the necessity to distinguish between the two components. In a further experiment, again consensus and attitude repetition were varied, and clarity and correctness were assessed. Subsequently participants were confronted with some relevant arguments opposing their attitude. For instance, a person who was against the new student card would have been told that the card helped preventing non-members misusing university resources. In line with the authors' reasoning, both repeated expression and high consensus increased resistance to change. Specifically, they showed that repeated attitude expression caused higher resistance due to increased attitude clarity. In contrast, participants who learned that other students shared the same opinion had more resistant attitudes because they were confident that their attitude was correct. The findings therefore demonstrate that different ways in which attitudes are strengthened may increase resistance, but through different mechanisms. It is an open question, then, whether previous findings on vested thought on attitude certainty may be reinterpreted as the effects of attitude correctness or of attitude clarity, or both.

Inferring attitude certainty from resistance

The relation between attitude certainty and resistance, however, is by no means unidirectional. How certain would you feel about your attitude when you realise that you can defend it against a strong attack? Tormala & Petty (2002) argued that certainty might also be the outcome of resistance. The idea is that resisting a counter-attitudinal attack will be accompanied by meta-cognitions, such as 'The fact that I did not change my attitude despite the counterarguments shows that my attitude must be reliable and valid'. In an experimental investigation, the authors showed that after resisting a counter-attack, participants did not change their attitude towards a personally relevant issue. In line with the authors' hypotheses, however, participants resisting attitude change felt more certain of their initial attitudes. Notably, this was only the case when participants were told that the counterarguments were strong. Participants who had been led to expect that the arguments were weak did not feel more certain than a control group. From an inoculation perspective, one might argue that ostensibly strong attacks should cause more counter-arguing. However, there was no evidence that the variation of ostensible argument quality affected the amount or content of arguing against the attack. Therefore, the authors concluded that certainty arises from the meta-cognitive insight that one was able to defend a potentially powerful attack. It should be added that resisting persuasion does not always increase certainty. Sometimes people may resist persuasion, though being able to defend against an attack, they may realise that it required severe effort to do so. Thus, when people experience the fact that resisting was difficult, attitudes may stay the same but become less certain (Tormala *et al.*, 2006). As explained by Barden and Tormala (2014), attitude certainty, a meta-cognitive construct, can be inferred from another meta-cognitive construct, here *perceived* ease of resistance. In a similar vein, attitude certainty must not increase due to actual elaboration, but it could result if one actually thinks that one had elaborated deeply (cf. Smith *et al.*, 2008).

To sum up, attitudes vary in their strength depending on how they are formed initially as well as how they are *maintained*. Attitude strength therefore is a useful construct for understanding resistance to persuasion. It should be noted, however, that the predictions do not only hold for deliberate persuasion but also for the way that people deal with attitude-relevant information, an issue we will deal with in the chapter on selective information processing (Chapter 11). Before we turn there, however, the remainder of this chapter will address which social inference processes are involved during the reception of persuasive communication.

EXPLAINING RESISTANCE WITH SOCIAL INFERENCES

So far, we have focused on properties of the attitude to predict resistance to persuasion. For a more comprehensive understanding of resistance, however, it is important to consider resistance in the course of social interactions. Several authors have highlighted the fact that persuasion is a dynamic interaction between an agent and an active target person (see also Chapter 9). Receivers do not only reason about the message content, but also about the sender, which in turn causes the interpretation of the information given (e.g. Hovland *et al.*, 1949; Friestad & Wright, 1994).

Attribution theory:
A conceptual framework that deals with people's explanations of behaviour and events.

Inspired by **attribution theory**, persuasion research has explored a receiver's inferences about the source's motives. Core assumptions of the attributional approach to persuasion are that a message recipient may infer different reasons why a communicator presents a certain position, and inferred positions moderate the impact of the statements on recipient's attitudes. As Kelley (1967) noted, the recipient may conclude that a communicator's message actually reflects external reality, in which case it is regarded as valid and likely to be accepted. However, often there are other plausible causes for a communicator's statement. It may be attributed to characteristics of the communicator (her goals, desires, etc.), to the particular situation, or to the audience at which the statement is targeted – including the recipient himself. For the attitude change to occur, it is crucial that the statement is attributed to the external reality rather than the sender's intention. For example, we would be more likely to accept the statement that a certain product offers high quality if this statement comes from an independent testing agency rather than the company marketing the product (but see Chapter 9 on receiver inferences about unclear conceptions).

Various studies have supported this principle. Eagly *et al.* (1978) found that a communicator who advocated a pro-environmental policy was more likely to change recipients' attitude when his background suggested a pro-business affiliation (or when his audience was described as business people) than when he was portrayed as someone with pro-environment affiliations (or when his audience was described as environmentalists). Thus, when either the communicator's vested interest or his concern to please the audience constituted plausible alternative reasons for the communicator's statements, external reality was discounted as a potential cause for his behaviour. Conversely, when the communicator's position opposed what would be expected based on his own interest or his audience, external reality was inferred with even greater confidence as the cause for the communicator's behaviour – an augmentation effect (see Finchham & Hewstone, 2001; Kelley, 1972). Similar attribution principles seem to operate in minority influence (see also Chapter 9). Research suggests that influence may be reduced via discounting if a communicator argues for a position that serves the interest of a social minority he or she belongs to, for example, a gay person promoting gay rights (Maas *et al.*, 1982). Thus, in many instances, resistance will be the outcome of a social inference process. Realising that the source of a message has a manipulative intent, recipients become suspicious of the source credibility and will doubt the validity of message content.

The social inference perspective on resistance also becomes evident in more recent research on reactance. Silvia (2006) presented participants with a persuasive message. As is typical of experiments on reactance, it was manipulated whether participants' freedom was threatened in the message or not. Thus, in one experimental condition, participants' freedom was threatened right at the beginning of the message. Participants in this condition not only increased counter-arguing, but also became suspicious of the source's credibility – that is, participants did not only reason about the quality of arguments, but they engaged in thoughts about the source validity. In turn, participants showed more disagreement with the attacking message's position. Moreover, the effects from another experimental condition suggest that reactance effects do not necessitate counter-arguing, but can reflect a mere social phenomenon. Participants in the second experimental condition were threatened at the end of the message. These participants also showed less agreement than the control group. However, the effect could not have been explained by processing of the arguments or the source characteristics, but appeared instead to reflect a direct effect of psychological reactance on resistance: participants merely contrasted their position with that of the endorser who was threatening their freedom. Thus, one strategy is direct opposition: recognising that a person is trying to manipulate our attitudes, one suitable strategy to restore our autonomy is simply to do the opposite – that is, endorsing a position that contradicts the endorser's. When parents forbid their adolescent children to get a tattoo, children may like tattoos even more simply to oppose their parents.

Receivers have persuasion knowledge, at least a bit

Persuasion knowledge: Beliefs about others' motives and tactics within a persuasion episode.

Whether or not recipients perceive a manipulative intent, ultimately depends on the person's **persuasion knowledge**. Friestad & Wright (1994) proposed that recipients hold belief systems about how persuasion works. These beliefs comprise knowledge about the agents' motives and persuasion tactics. Imagine a sales person tells you that a pair of jeans suits you extremely well. If identifying flattery as a persuasion strategy, you would be likely to correct for the pleasant feelings caused by the compliment. In this vein, tactics knowledge may moderate whether shopping malls profit from the use of pleasant music and smells or whether people show counter-reactions against this type of manipulation. In this sense, it can be assumed that accurate persuasion knowledge constitutes an advantage in a persuasion interaction. Friestad and Wright (1994) demonstrated that despite some divergence, lay persuasion knowledge often converges with the expert's knowledge, such as the knowledge of professional marketers. Persuasion knowledge seems to exist for a variety of cues and domains (see also Kirmani & Campbell, 2009). For instance, Vogel *et al.* (2010) showed that physical attractiveness is a variable considered as fostering persuasion success. Crucially, their studies suggest that lay people consider that the positive effect of physical attractiveness in persuasion is moderated by the recipient's processing motivation. More precisely, participants did not rely on sender attractiveness when predicting persuasion effects, if the target of persuasion was presumably high in processing motivation. Recall that research on the Elaboration Likelihood Model (see Haugtvedt *et al.*, 1992 in Chapter 8), had indeed revealed that attractiveness effects in persuasion are reduced if the receiver NFC is high rather than low. The results therefore indicate that lay beliefs about persuasion not only converge with the knowledge of professional applicants, but also with scientific theorising.

Third-person-effect: People consider themselves less susceptible to persuasion than others.

However, it cannot be expected that lay individuals have a comprehensive understanding of how persuasion works (e.g. Vogel *et al.*, 2010). A well-documented phenomenon termed the **third-person-effect** refers to the observation that people consider themselves less vulnerable than others (Davison, 1983; Perloff, 1999). You may agree that if everyone considers him- or herself more resistant to persuasion than others, at least some of them must be wrong. To explore the nature of this bias, Douglas and Sutton (2004) compared post-persuasion attitudes with remembered pre-persuasion attitudes. Whereas pre-persuasion attitudes were remembered correctly for others, pre-persuasion attitudes for oneself were biased towards the post-persuasion attitude (see also Chapter 11). Apparently, people recognised that others' attitudes changed over the course of the persuasion episode. However, they did not recognise a change in their own attitudes but thought they had always held these attitudes beforehand, which was obviously wrong. Thus, when occupying the role of the target themselves, lay people will often have a self-enhancing perception of invulnerability and underestimate the impact of professional agents.

Ultimately, persuasion knowledge is supposed to differ between individuals. Since persuasion knowledge is assumed to develop in the course of life, one inter-individual difference factor that should determine persuasion knowledge is age (Boush *et al.*, 1994; Wright *et al.*, 2005). Hence, children constitute a group particularly vulnerable to advertisements because of their lack of persuasion knowledge. In line with this reasoning, it has been found that older children are more likely to distinguish commercials from other forms of television programme (John, 1999). However, although even 4-year-old children realise that commercials do not belong to the main programme (Butter *et al.*, 1981), this differentiation is primarily based on perceptual cues. The sensitivity for the manipulative intent behind commercials, by contrast, appears not to develop before the age of 7 or 8 years. For marketing forms subtler than TV adverts, persuasion knowledge may be acquired even later in life. In one study, children's awareness of sponsorship was assessed in a theme park (Grohs *et al.*, 2012). Among children younger than 9 years, only one-third agreed that companies placed their logos in order to increase purchase intentions. During adolescence, marketplace persuasion knowledge about the psychological and behavioural goals held by advertisers becomes more sophisticated. Among 12-year-olds, more than 90 per cent were aware that sponsors were pursuing their own interests.

Importantly, recognising persuasive intents does not guarantee for effective coping with persuasive attempts, neither for children nor for adults. Accessibility of persuasion knowledge also varies across situations. The different beliefs comprised in persuasion knowledge are often tacit, but certain situational demands can activate the knowledge and increase its impact in coping with persuasive attempts. In addition, persuasion knowledge can be more or less accessible (Campbell & Kirmani, 2000; for a review, see Kirmani & Campbell, 2009). A sales person flattering a customer prior to a purchase decision almost inevitably activates persuasion knowledge: the sales person is pursuing her or his own interest. However, when a sales person flatters a customer after the purchase has been made, their intent might be less accessible. Motivation and capacity might be needed to come up with the less accessible knowledge about tactics and goals such as building customer relationships.

THE ARMS RACE: ACTIVE PERSUADERS VERSUS ACTIVE RECEIVERS

With the stubborn receiver, persuasion becomes a new challenge. Rather than use appeals to evoke positive reactions in the target person, persuasion also means avoiding or minimising negative reactions (e.g. Knowles & Linn, 2004; Knowles & Riner, 2007). In other words, when engaging in a persuasive attempt, senders should take into account the fact that the active receiver might be motivated to resist and, if so, possesses a repertoire of defensive strategies.

In this vein, it has been proposed that persuaders might circumvent reactance by providing participants with the freedom of choice. When promoting a certain product on the Internet, for instance, you might not simply state certain facts, but enable homepage users to request it on their own by clicking on various topics (cf. Schlosser & Shavitt, 2009). As long as customers experience freedom and not the agony of choice, you can expect positive effects (see Box 10.1).

Also, communicators aiming at persuasion might want to suggest that institutions tried to forbid or censor their products (including films, video games, etc.) or opinion. The target might then see the possibility of restoring his or her freedom by choosing the forbidden fruit (see Figure 10.2). This strategy is also nicely illustrated by a pro-continuance appeal from the late 1920s directed towards the citizens of New Zealand. In this campaign, liquor traders portrayed prohibition as a threat to New Zealanders' freedom of choice. In a similar vein, yet more subtle, the modern entertainment industry suggests that institutions prohibit adolescents from choosing their music. On-package signs on films, music albums or computer games offer prominent warnings of violent and sexually explicit content, and ask not to distribute the media to minors.

Even cannier, persuaders might use the paradoxical effects of reactance and pressure receivers to disagree with them. In one study reported by Knowles and Linn (2004, Experiment 2), students read expert statements about some issues relevant to their group. For instance, an expert source was cited stating the following: 'Parking at the University of Kansas is cheaper than at most universities.' For half the participants, the sentence was preceded by an ostensible disclaimer: 'I know you will not want to agree with this, but parking at the University of Kansas is cheaper than at most universities.' These students, in fact, were more likely to agree with the statement than were their counterparts. Thus, when the default is set to disagreement, agreement will feel as the behaviour reflecting the free will.

Other strategies primarily concentrated on preventing targets' distrust in the source. As suggested by research on persuasion knowledge and the discounting principle in particular, persuaders may profit from hiding their true motive. For positive information about an object to be trusted, the sender of the information must be considered sincere. A prominent strategy to evoke source credibility is so-called **two-sided persuasion** (Hovland *et al.*, 1949). Rather than solely presenting desirable attributes of a product,

Two-sided persuasion: Persuasive attempt that contains both pro- and counterarguments.

FIGURE 10.2   Consuming forbidden fruits makes birds feel free

Note: According to reactance theory, prohibition will result in boomerang effects. The forbidden fruit becomes more attractive because consuming it restores freedom

communicators can also mention some shortcomings of the object. Presenting the flipside of the coin then leads to a receiver inferring honesty in the sender, thereby increasing the impact of the message. There is a trade-off, however, between this enhancing effect of two-sided messages and the potential decrease in persuasion that may be caused by revealing the shortcoming at all. Supposedly, a car seller who admits that the engine was broken will appear trustworthy, but she will not make you buy the car. Therefore, if negative aspects are mentioned in adverts, they usually pertain to relatively unimportant aspects of the product. In some case, the negative aspects may even underline the validity of the positive aspects (Bohner *et al.,* 2003; Pechmann, 1992). As illustrated by Bohner *et al.* (2003), consider a restaurant, aiming at promoting the freshness of their meals. In addition to stating that meals are always freshly cooked, the restaurant might apologise for some inconveniences. For example, the restaurant might apologise for noise from the highway nearby. Or it might warn guests of long waits until their orders are served. What do you expect to be more efficient? On their own, both facts are negative and therefore can be expected to increase the credibility of the source. However, long waiting times are logically related to freshly prepared food, and therefore serve to augment the impact of the freshness argument, in turn leading to increased persuasiveness. Interestingly, such a logical conclusion requires some elaboration and target persons motivated to think about message content are even more likely to be persuaded by the logically related negative information.

An alternative strategy for avoiding resistance is to embed persuasive messages in non-persuasion settings. This will not only prevent defiance. As suggested by the *Transportation Imagery Model* (Green & Brock, 2000, 2002), when a message is conveyed in a narrative, even counter-arguing can be reduced (cf. Box 10.2). Different elements might explain why it is so difficult to refute a statement conveyed in a story. For one thing, following a story is taxing, therefore little capacity will be left for counter-arguing. Whereas we can focus on the argument quality when arguments are presented in a list, we have problems thinking about argument quality while following a story (Escalas, 2007). More importantly, being transported into a story means that receivers leave their external reality. The story takes us into a different world which then for a while constitutes our reality. In real life, we may doubt that BMWs or Aston Martins resist fire, but while embedded in a James Bond film we will take such a fact as given. Furthermore, accepting the story's reality then builds the basis for becoming immersed. We start feeling with the protagonists, and experience attitude objects much like they do – and after having read a novel on the exciting sex life of a sadomasochist couple, or having watched a film involving white sharks attacking divers, abstract representations of sadomasochism or scuba-diving will not only become positive or negative, but also self-referential experiences.

Crucially, however, part of the reality will persist over and above the end of the story. A statement once accepted as true in the story's reality is more likely to be considered true in real life. Consistent with the model's

Box 10.2   Reducing the impact of counterarguments

Sometimes persuaders may lack good arguments, and therefore cannot avoid unfavourable thoughts and counter-arguing by the receiver. Imagine you and your friend were debating about where to go for dinner. Contrary to your friend, you prefer the Italian over the Thai restaurant, even though it is more expensive and its reputation is not great. The few arguments you can come up with – 'You can never go wrong with pasta' and 'Italy is the home of pasta!' – do not even convince yourself. Lacking convincing arguments, could you perhaps profit from enhancing your friend's mood? From all you have learned about the dual-process models of persuasion in Chapter 8, you might want to try inducing a positive mood by, say, reminding her that she just received an A in an exam. If she were in a positive mood, she would be less likely to elaborate carefully and would not recognise the flaws in your argument. Once she has already taken the peripheral route, you may further benefit from the fact that her happy mood serves as information while evaluating your suggestion.

However, given her interest in the decision she is going to scrutinise every word you say about the restaurant. Would cheering her up still have an effect? According to the **self-validation hypothesis** (Petty *et al.*, 2002), a later extension of the ELM, incidental states (and simple cues) may indeed affect persuasion outcomes under high-elaboration conditions. The hypothesis is based on the assumption that cognitive responses can mediate the effects of arguments on persuasion outcomes, only if recipients have confidence in their own thoughts. If recipients, however, doubt their own thoughts, their cognitive responses will have only small effects. In this way, incidental experiences can affect the recipient's confidence, thereby qualifying the effect of the cognitive responses elicited by the persuasive message. This, however, is not to say that you would actually benefit from reminding your friend of her recent success. Research on the self-validation hypothesis actually suggests the opposite.

In one study by Briñol and Petty (2003), participants listened to information about a new student card to be introduced on campus. Depending on the experimental condition, the message contained either strong (e.g. the card allows you to securely access your grades via the Internet) or weak arguments (e.g. the card saves time so security guards have more time for lunch). In addition to the variation of argument strength, the authors also manipulated participants' head movements. Half of the participants were instructed to move their head horizontally, the other half were told to move their head vertically. The vertical movement which is associated with agreement (i.e. nodding) and was therefore predicted to validate the recipients' cognitive responses. By contrast, the horizontal movement which is associated with disagreement (i.e. head shaking), and was therefore hypothesised to invalidate the recipient's thoughts.

The self-validation hypothesis therefore predicts an interaction between argument strength and head movement. A person listening to the strong arguments should generate positive thoughts. As the impact of these thoughts should be higher if people feel validated, the attitudes towards the new ID card should be more favourable for nodding participants than for head-shaking participants. Crucially, the opposite prediction holds for the weak argument condition. If a person has negative thoughts, but feels confident about them, the resulting attitude should be rather negative. If the negative thoughts, however, become doubted, they

Self-validation hypothesis: Positive (negative) persuasion variables validate or invalidate one's thoughts about a persuasive message.

are less likely to determine the attitude. Briñol and Petty (2003) therefore predicted that for weak arguments, head shaking leads to more favourable attitudes than nodding. The results confirmed their predictions (see Figure 10.3). Thus, according to the self-validation hypothesis, two minuses may yield a plus: negative thoughts and negation behaviour will lead to relatively favourable results.

The self-validation hypothesis is not restricted to the domain of embodiment effects, but other variables associated with confidence showed similar findings. For instance, it seems that when recipients feel self-sufficient and have trust in their own competences, thought quality has a higher effect. In this vein, it could be shown that strong arguments work better with recipients who experience high rather than low power status (Briñol et al., 2007). With weak arguments eliciting negative responses, however, the effect reversed: attitudes were more in line with the advocated position for recipients who experienced low as compared to high power. Apparently, the latter participants had more confidence in their negative thoughts than participants who felt low in power.

An important finding in this line of research is that the role of the persuasion variable – here, power status – depends on when it enters the persuasion process. Strong messages showed stronger effects for powerful as opposed to powerless people, only if power was manipulated *after* the message presentation – that is, participants reflected on the arguments, and their cognitive responses were then validated or invalidated, depending on the power they felt. By contrast, participants who felt powerful *before* message receipt were less persuaded than their powerless counterparts. This can be explained by a consideration of the processing routes put forward in the ELM (Chapter 8): those who felt powerful in the very beginning were self-confident and trusted in their opinion. They therefore did not even process the message arguments in depth.

The self-validation hypothesis has repeatedly retrieved empirical support (Briñol et al., 2004; Briñol et al., 2007; Horcajo et al., 2010; Petty et al., 2002; Tormala et al., 2006, 2007; see Briñol & Petty, 2009 for an overview). Related to the introductory question, the findings have also been obtained in experiments in which mood was manipulated after message exposition (Briñol et al., 2007). Positive mood may also boost confidence in one's responses. So again, would you try to lift your friend's mood to make her accompany you to the Italian restaurant? Realising that your friend is not convinced by the fact that 'Italy is the home of pasta', you might not necessarily win her over by lifting her mood. Once she has confidence in her counterarguments, she will be come even more resistant.

assumptions, the degree of agreeing with a position endorsed in the story can be predicted from the extent to which story readers felt transported into the story (Green & Brock, 2000), a state that seems to depend on the general propensity to immerse into a story (Dal Cin et al., 2004; Mazzocco et al., 2010).

Maybe you are inclined to deny that your reality is shaped by dubious statements conveyed by fictitious stories. You may feel that as soon as you leave the cinema, you will also leave this untrue reality. And indeed, empirical evidence supports the idea that right after the confrontation

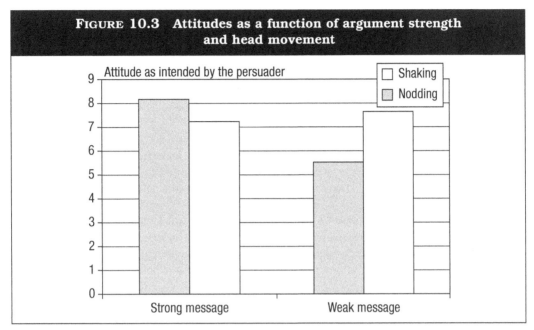

FIGURE **10.3**   **Attitudes as a function of argument strength and head movement**

Note: Body movements associated with disagreement (i.e. nodding) reduce the impact of counter-arguments caused by a weak message (data from Briñol & Petty, 2003)

the effect of story statements on truth assumptions is comparably small. However, as has been reported by Appel and Richter (2007), narrative persuasion produces so-called **sleeper effects** (Hovland *et al.*, 1949) – that is, persuasion effects become stronger after a certain time has passed. The explanation for sleeper effects is that people are often good at remembering what was said, but forget where they know it from (Hovland & Weiss, 1951; see Kumkale & Albarracín, 2004 for a review). As a consequence, the source is no longer discounted and counter-arguing against the ostensible facts becomes unlikely. Hence, associations of overweight persons as lovely and clumsy will impact our attitudes, once they pop up as detached from the comedies in which they were originally encountered. This may become even more problematic when media products portray harmful and criminal behaviour in a positive way. For example, one may wonder whether the frequent portrayal of torture in the much acclaimed US TV series *24* led viewers to become more accepting of torture and other violations of sacred laws (Green, 2005).

In this vein, strategic devices such as product placement – presenting a certain product in the course of a film, video game or book – go beyond evaluative conditioning (Chapter 5). Rather than a mere transfer of valence, product placement is likely to break down resistance towards the advertiser's claims.

Sleeper effect:
Phenomenon which describes that a persuasive effect unfolds over time.

CONCLUDING COMMENT: KNOWING THE RECEIVER

Individuals try to and actually do defend their existing attitudes. Resistance to some extent reflects individuals' avoidance of being manipulated. Persuading others therefore not only involves creating positive associations towards an attitude object; it also necessitates breaking down existing barriers in the receiver (Knowles & Riner, 2007). Various strategies have been proposed to overcome resistance mechanisms, ranging from two-sided persuasion to product placement. These strategies may be combined to persuade the receiver. For instance, the brand Patagonia ran an advertising campaign 'Do not buy this jacket'. The advertisement informed viewers that the production of the jacket and all of Patagonia's goods were bad for the environment. Consumers apparently rewarded this honesty as Patagonia's sales increased by 40 per cent in the following year. However, as canny as these tactics might appear, none of the tactics named above are free from the risk that reactance will be aroused. One cannot exclude the possibility that lay people recognise the manipulative attempt behind two-sided persuasion, product placements, etc. With increasing persuasion knowledge, the likelihood increases that tactics become identified, opening the door for boomerang effects.

Resistance, however, can also be understood as the logical consequence of some attitude properties, summarised in the concept of attitude strength: when attitudes are strong, persuasive attempts may fail. In this chapter we have concentrated on attitude certainty, but similar patterns have been obtained for other indicators of attitude strength. For instance, people tend to resist change for attitudes that are personally important (e.g. Pomerantz *et al.*, 1995). But what strategies do people employ to avoid being influenced? For one thing, they avoid attitude change by focusing on information that supports their views, for another they might come up with some idiosyncratic interpretations of the information given. We will deal with this issue in more detail in the following chapter.

CHAPTER SUMMARY

1   Persuasion often fails because individuals are motivated to defend existing attitudes, or because the manipulation of attitudes is perceived as a restriction of freedom.

2   Persuasion becomes difficult if receivers of the message already hold strong attitudes opposing the message. Attitudes become stronger after inoculation treatments (i.e. exposure to mild counterarguments), high cognitive elaboration during attitude formation, direct experience with the attitude and repeated attitude expression. One way of explaining these factors' effects on resistance is that they increase attitude certainty.

3   Individuals draw inferences about a communicator's motives. Recognising that the communicator holds self-interests, receivers tend to discount his or her credibility. The inferences drawn may vary across individuals and domains, depending on the recipient's persuasion knowledge and whether it is activated during the persuasion episode.

4   A prominent strategy to avoid resistance is by embedding persuasive messages in non-persuasion settings. This may help preventing reactance and counter-arguing.

Exercises

1   Look up adverts from the 1950s. How has advertising changed? Do you find more restrictive messages in old ads than in more recent ones?

2   Recall experiments exploiting the induced-compliance paradigm (Chapter 7). Try to reframe the results in terms of reactance theory.

3   Think of an actor you like and one you dislike. Does your impression of the actors depend on real-world knowledge about them or is it influenced by the character they played?

Further reading

Knowles, E. S. & Riner, D. D. (2007). Omega approaches to persuasion: overcoming resistance. In A. R. Pratkanis (ed.), *The Science of Social Influence: Advances and Future Progress* (pp. 83–114). New York: Psychology Press.

Tormala, Z. L. & Petty, R. E. (2004). Resistance to persuasion and attitude certainty: a metacognitive analysis. In E. S. Knowles & J. A. Linn (eds), *Resistance and Persuasion* (pp. 65–82). Mahwah, NJ: Lawrence Erlbaum.

Part IV

Consequences of our attitudes

In the preceding chapters we examined the origins of attitudes, from simple by-products in everyday life to an outcome of systematic manipulation. In this final part of the book we turn to the consequences of individuals' attitudes on thoughts and overt behaviour. As described in Chapter 10, people try to resist attitude change. But how do they do this? Although Chapter 10 introduced some strategies, there is more to discover in Chapter 11, in which we will address the influence of attitudes on information search and information processing. As you will see, your attitudes change the way you see the world. In the subsequent chapter, we will turn to attitudinal consequences regarding how people actually deal with an attitude object. Does a positive attitude towards Christianity indicate whether one will attend church? Would one use condoms because one agrees that safer sex is a good thing? A preliminary answer to these questions is: 'Yes!' A more refined answer, however, would be 'Yes, to some extent' or 'Yes, but it depends'. Hence, beginning with Chapter 12, we will explore the attitude–behaviour relation and elaborate on which moderating variables predict whether attitudes result in behaviour. However, as social psychologists have produced so much valuable knowledge on this issue, we think it is worth dedicating more than just one chapter to this issue, which is also of high practical relevance. Thus, in Chapter 12 we will review classic theoretical approaches on the attitude–behaviour relationship, but continue with a thirteenth chapter to report more novel insights, with an emphasis on the cognitive underpinnings of the attitude–behaviour relationship.

Chapter 11

THE WORLD IS NOT WHAT IT USED TO BE: ATTITUDE INFLUENCES ON INFORMATION PROCESSING

Freedom of opinion is the hallmark of democratic societies. Not only do people in free societies hold opinions that may differ from their neighbours, but they can also express them. Free societies enjoy a plurality of media products that range from different books, newspapers, magazines, films, plays, TV and radio shows, to new formats such as Internet blogs and postings. Never in the history of mankind has it been so easy to inform oneself about different perspectives and be exposed to a variety of views – at least in democratic societies. Virtually with the click of a finger we have access to a vast amount of facts, opinions and arguments, although it is certainly true that some pieces of information are easier to come by than others, and not all information may indeed be available or digestible. This large-scope availability of information might suggest that people are better equipped to come to well-founded opinions, that claims need to be based on solid evidence, and that persuasive arguments contain substantial and undisputable facts. Moreover, one might expect that given exposure to a plurality of opinions, differences abate and the different opinions become less extreme. This would only follow, however, if people sample information (opinions as well as supporting evidence) in an unbiased way and then process it in an unbiased manner. The respective evidence sheds some doubt on this premise, as we will highlight in this chapter. People tend to shun information that is contradictory to their views. If they come into contact with such information they distort it, interpret it in a way that is more compatible with their views or discredit it. Depending on other conditions, such information may also be remembered less well. In sum, attitudes may both bias our interpretation of social reality and affect the intensity of our information processing. Furthermore, these effects of attitudes may also contribute to stabilising and reinforcing our existing attitudes.

THEORETICAL ASSUMPTIONS GUIDING RESEARCH ON ATTITUDE-PROCESSING LINKS: CONSISTENCY, FUNCTION AND STRUCTURE

The effects of attitudes on thinking have been hypothesised to occur at all stages of information processing, including a) *attention, encoding and exposure*, b) *judgement and elaboration* and c) *memory* (see Eagly & Chaiken, 1998). The influence can occur unintentionally (e.g. having one's attention involuntarily drawn towards an attitude object) or may represent a more deliberative strategy primarily in order to bolster or defend one's attitudes (e.g. actively seeking and elaborating on attitude-consistent information).

The latter example attests to the phenomenon that people strive for consistency, and indeed much research on attitudinal effects on the processing of new information has been guided by the principle of cognitive consistency (see also Chapters 7 and 10). A basic tenet characterising this approach is that people attempt to maintain consistency of their cognitive structure by seeking out new information in line with their existing attitudes, and screening out new information that might challenge their attitudes (Festinger, 1957, 1964). This should result in what has been termed *attitudinal selectivity effects* at several stages of processing, including attention, elaboration and memory. However, other accounts besides the need for consistency have also been suggested.

One alternative (or additional) approach to predict and explain attitude effects on different stages of information processing is based on the functional analysis of attitudes. As explained in Chapter 1, attitudes provide structure and inform the individual about the hedonic relevance of attitude objects. Both aspects were taken up by Pratkanis (1989) as part of his socio-cognitive model of attitude structure. From this perspective, an attitude representation consists of an attitude-object category, an evaluative summary and a supporting knowledge structure. These structural elements cause two types of information processing effects: *heuristic* and *schematic* effects. Using an attitude like a *heuristic* means that the link between attitude object and evaluative summary (cf. Fazio, 1995) is applied like a simple general rule for problem solving that could be paraphrased as 'things I like are good'. Applying this rule means that liked objects will be approached, favoured, defended, etc., whereas disliked objects will be avoided, opposed, attacked, etc. (Pratkanis, 1989, p. 76). This notion is similar to the utilitarian function, or the cognitive functions ascribed to attitudes by early theorists (see Chapter 1), such as the object-appraisal function (M. B. Smith *et al.*, 1956) or the knowledge function (Katz, 1960). We review some of the effects of using an attitude as a heuristic in the section on attitudinal influences on judgement.

The schematic function in Pratkanis's (1989) model refers to information-processing effects that are caused by the attitude-supporting knowledge structure. Although different conceptualisations were proposed, we can highlight two central properties of a schema (see Fiske & Morling, 1995):

1   A schema is *abstract*, representing general knowledge about a domain
    or category and emphasising the similarities between special cases, thus
    simplifying reality.
2   A schema *affects the processing of new information* by establishing
    expectations, facilitating encoding and guiding inferences; a person using
    a schema may 'go beyond the information given' in any particular
    situation (Bruner, 1957).

Applying these criteria to attitudes, we should expect that having an
attitude both simplifies and guides information processing in predictable
ways. For example, a person who strongly dislikes meat should (1) easily
encode and remember information fitting his attitudinal schema (e.g. a report
on cases of food poisoning caused by spoiled meat), (2) be prepared to
respond negatively to any novel object he encodes as an exemplar of the meat
category (e.g. an ostrich steak), and (3) make negative inferences and judgements about this object (e.g. regarding its smell, taste or nutritional value).

The effects ascribed to the schematic properties of knowledge structures
about an attitude object are useful to understand attitudinal effects on
memory. We will address this in the last section.

In the sections to follow, we will discuss the effects of attitudes on each
of the stages in information processing.

ATTITUDE EFFECTS ON ATTENTION, ENCODING AND EXPOSURE

Some effects of attitudes on attention and encoding happen quickly and
efficiently, sometimes outside a perceiver's conscious awareness, and may
be difficult to control. Such automatic effects can be beneficial as they
help individuals to notice and process objects that are of hedonic relevance,
enabling them to respond appropriately without requiring much cognitive
capacity (Fazio, 2000). As there are a vast number of stimuli that impinge
on an individual every day, natural selection should favour a highly adaptive
orienting function of attitudes that helps to rapidly encode stimuli into
hedonically meaningful categories as well as to attend to certain important
stimuli. In ancestral times, individuals who quickly identified a perceptual
object as an enemy (or a source of food or a potential mate) and reacted
to it in a proper way (e.g. by fleeing or approaching) were more likely to
survive and reproduce than those who didn't. We will first discuss automatic
effects of attitudes on attention and categorisation; then we will turn to more
strategic aspects of selective attention and exposure to information that
supports existing attitudes.

Automatic attention

Which of the pictures in Figure 11.1 did you notice first? If you are a horse
lover it was probably the photo of the horses. Likewise, a soccer fan will have

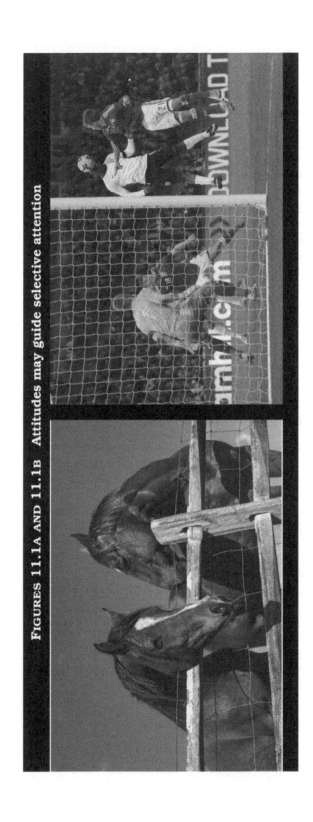

FIGURES 11.1A AND 11.1B Attitudes may guide selective attention

first noticed the soccer photo. And if you are neither you may ask, 'What photos?' What this example is meant to illustrate is that things we like attract attention. However, should you detest horses (but who would?) your attention was probably also drawn to this picture, as not only likes but also dislikes attract attention. Actually, negatively evaluated stimuli elicit even more attention that positive stimuli (e.g. Smith *et al.*, 2003). If we contend that attitudes help to regulate approach and avoidance it makes sense that attitudes also help us to notice the to-be-approached and to-be-avoided objects in the first place. Beyond this example there is also experimental evidence for the orienting value of attitudes (Roskos-Ewoldsen & Fazio, 1992).

When members of a Jewish organisation were instructed to focus their gaze on a briefly shown central item that was surrounded by eight other items, they later recalled fewer of the surrounding items if the central item was either a swastika or a Star of David compared to when it was a neutral object (Erdelyi & Appelbaum, 1973). At the very least, this demonstrates that affective stimuli are better at holding perceivers' attention and make it more difficult for distractors. Evidence that attitudes actually direct attention to attitude relevant objects comes from studies involving a visual search task (Roskos-Ewoldsen & Fazio, 1992). The dependent variable was the time it took a participant to detect a target object (or to indicate that the target object was not displayed) in an array of six objects. Importantly, participants were told in advance that the target object would appear in only three out of six positions on the screen, whereas items in the remaining three positions could safely be ignored. As you may have guessed, the distractor items that appeared in the to-be-ignored positions were attitude objects. Participants had previously rehearsed their attitudes towards these objects in order to make these attitudes highly accessible or had made non-evaluative judgements about them (control items). This manipulation ensured that the objects were identical but what differed was the accessibility of the attitudes towards these objects. The main finding was that it took participants significantly longer to perform the visual search task when the distractors were high accessibility objects than when they were control objects. This finding suggests that at least strongly attitude-evoking objects involuntarily attract attention even if a person is trying to ignore the stimulus (for a review of related evidence, see Fazio, 2000).

Automatic effects of attitude encoding

Another way in which attitudes may automatically affect processing is by accentuating hedonically meaningful categories for encoding a stimulus (see Fazio, 2000). Most objects can be categorised in numerous ways. For example, a car can be seen as a means of transportation or as a status symbol (Ennis & Zanna, 2000), while pizza may be viewed as a tasty snack or as an unhealthy food item. Theories of categorisation assume that which of the possible attributes of an object is used for categorisation may depend on the allocation of attention to these attributes (e.g. E. R. Smith

& Zárate, 1992). Just as a highly accessible attitude towards an object in the visual field may direct further attention to that object (Roskos-Ewoldson & Fazio, 1992), a highly accessible attitude towards one of many potential categories in which a stimulus may be categorised can facilitate that the category is used.

How would you categorise yoghurt? Is it a healthy food? Is it a dairy product? When attitudes to either of the two categories had been rehearsed to make them more accessible, the category to which an attitude had been rehearsed was more likely to be chosen (Smith *et al.*, 1996).

The issue of which categories people use and how attitudes towards the categories affect categorisation becomes more socially relevant when we think of social categories. Whether Angela Merkel is categorised as a head of state or as a woman determines how others respond to her. Fazio and Dunton (1997) studied the influence of attitudes to socially relevant categories. They first measured participants' implicit attitudes towards black versus white people. A week later, the same participants rated the similarity of pairs of target persons who were depicted in photos that included cues to their occupation (e.g. a tool or a uniform). Thus, information was present on each target's sex, race and occupation. Participants with strong positive or strong negative racial attitudes towards black people were more likely to base their similarity judgements on race (as opposed to sex or occupation) compared to people with more neutral racial attitudes.

In sum, object categories for which a perceiver holds strong and accessible attitudes are more likely to be used in categorising an object or person. Moreover, these spontaneously activated, attitude-related categories may be used implicitly as input to other types of judgements, even if neither the attitude nor the category in question form part of the explicit judgement task. In the next section, we will address more deliberate decisions about the allocation of attention to attitude-related information.

Strategic effects of attitudes on attention and exposure

A recent meta-analysis on selective exposure (Hart *et al.*, 2009) begins with the example that former US Vice President Dick Cheney (Republican) demanded all the television sets in his hotel rooms to be preset to the Fox News Channel (a political conservative channel; *The Smoking Gun*, 2006). This anecdote is both illuminating and disconcerting in at least two ways. First, it illustrates nicely that people are motivated to avoid other views (*hostile* or *uncongenial* information) and seek information consistent with their beliefs and attitudes (*congenial* information). This has been termed **selective exposure, congeniality bias** or **confirmation bias**, and we will report some of the relevant research findings in this section. Second, it also documents that there is a media catering to those demands. Newspapers, TV channels and the like spin the information and slant it according to their audiences' preferences.

Congeniality bias (also confirmation bias): Tendency to seek information that provides support to one's attitude.

Besides the anecdote about the US Vice President, there is a great deal of evidence from everyday life. How often do you talk to people whose opinions radically differ from yours about these issues? Presumably it is less often than discussions with similar others. Which news outlets do you prefer and why? If people only had the motive to hold attitudes that are accurate (in an objective way – e.g. is psychology really the best subject for me?) they should be interested in sampling many different views to arrive at an unbiased conclusion. But as was already pointed out in the previous chapters, people also have the motive to uphold and bolster their attitudes and to defend them against counter-attitudinal influences. According to the principle of cognitive consistency (Chapter 7), consciously considering information that challenges one's attitudes should cause an aversive state of arousal (e.g. Festinger, 1964). It follows that people should actively search for and pay close attention to information that matches their existing attitudes, and should try to avoid or ignore information that is incompatible with their attitudes.

A meta-analysis (Hart *et al.*, 2009) of about 300 studies found a moderately sized congeniality bias. Virtually all the studies reviewed in this meta-analysis measured whether participants selected information that was favourable or unfavourable to their views or a previously made decision. Some of the studies involved self-reports on real issues. For example, in the early 1970s the US President Richard Nixon was involved in the Watergate scandal. Nixon supporters reported paying less attention to the media coverage and discussing it less than other persons (Sweeney & Gruber, 1984). Most experimental studies, however, involve a paradigm in which participants are allowed to choose information – for example, newspaper articles, product tests, etc. They have to make their choice only on the basis of titles, summaries or headlines that do not give any details but clearly express whether the information is favourable or unfavourable to a particular perspective. Sometimes there are also additional cues such as the source of information.

In their meta-analysis, Hart and colleagues (2009) also identified several moderators. As would be expected, people who were high on the inter-individual difference measure closed-mindedness showed a larger congeniality bias. For these people, counter-attitudinal information holds a threat whereas more open-minded people may enjoy a challenging debate (e.g. Altemeyer, 1998). The congeniality bias was also larger when the information available for selection was of high (e.g. coming from an expert) or moderate quality (e.g. coming from a journalist) compared to low (e.g. a non-expert such as a passer-by). Obviously, an expert source will be a better source of confidence in the case of confirmation, but likewise a higher threat in the case of disconfirmation. The bias was reduced when the respective attitude had been supported prior to the information selection, compared to no or challenging information. For example, participants may have learned that the majority (support) or the minority (challenge) shared their attitude (e.g. Nemeth & Rogers, 1996). With regard to attitude strength, the bias was larger the higher the commitment to attitude was, the more relevant the issue was to one's values, but the lower one's confidence in the attitude was. Unfortunately, the meta-analysis did not code for attitude accessibility, which is a further indicator of attitude strength. One study (Knobloch-Westerwick & Meng, 2009) reports that attitude accessibility, measured by the time it took participants to indicate their attitudes to several political topics, such as gun control, abortion, healthcare and minimum wages, increased choices of counter-attitudinal messages. Apparently, these different indicators of attitude strength (see Chapters 1 and 10) have different effects.

All these moderators are well in line with a defence motivation (Chaiken *et al.*, 1989; Petty & Cacioppo, 1986a, b; cf. Chapter 10). The motivation for defence is stronger when the information is more difficult to discard or devalue. It is stronger for issues in which one has invested and cares about but does not feel confident enough to withstand a counter-attitudinal attack.

Defence motivation would also predict that that selectivity should be most pronounced *after* a behavioural decision based on the attitude (e.g. to buy a certain product) but not before a decision (cf. Chapter 7). Once one has made a decision one should be more committed to the underlying attitude (Festinger, 1957). Although an often-cited study confirmed this expectation (Frey & Rosch, 1984), the meta-analysis did not. Depending on the specific details of the analysis, the congeniality bias was actually larger when reversal was possible (Hart *et al.*, 2009). Perhaps the ability to reverse one's position may particularly induce a motivation to defend why one does not engage in a reversal. But different explanations are possible (see Hart *et al.*, 2009) and have yet to be tested.

So, is there no evidence that people search for information in an unbiased way to arrive at valid conclusions and decisions? Recall that the dual-process theories of attitude change not only claim a defence motive, but also an accuracy motive which might work against the congeniality bias. One might expect that for important decisions – that is, decisions that carry some consequences – this would be the case. Again, although there are some studies in line with this hypothesis (e.g. Lowe & Steiner, 1968) the meta-analysis (Hart *et al.*, 2009) found no difference in the congeniality bias, regardless of whether outcome relevance was high or low. Apparently, additional factors moderate the effect. More insights have been gained from a closer inspection that not only considers whether information is outcome relevant or not, but which information (congenial or uncongenial) is more relevant to the outcome. Indeed, people do select uncongenial information – namely, when it was particularly useful for a present goal (Hart *et al.*, 2009). For example, uncongenial information is more useful than congenial information when one has to prepare for a debate (e.g. Canon, 1964).

Most studies on selective exposure only looked at which information is selected. A few studies also looked at how intensively the information is processed, but different hypotheses are possible. On one hand, one might expect uncongenial information to be neglected not only in selection but also in processing depth. On the other hand, one could also expect that if counter-attitudinal information is processed at all (either because it is chosen or cannot be avoided), counter-attitudinal messages instigate more rather than less processing because partisans try to refute the message. And, indeed, in studies that made participants read congenial and uncongenial information, participants spent more time on a piece of uncongenial compared to congenial information (e.g. Edwards & Smith, 1996). For example, when exposed to medical recommendations including pro- and anti-alcohol information, message recipients took longer to read the information that was inconsistent with their attitude towards alcohol (Kiviniemi & Rothman, 2006). More direct evidence for the more elaborate processing of uncongenial information comes from an analysis of participants' thoughts. Message recipients reported more, and more opposing thoughts for an uncongenial than congenial message (Eagly *et al.*, 2000; Edwards & Smith, 1996). Apparently, once recipients could not avoid the counter-attitudinal information, they engaged in defensive processing. Motivation alone is, however, not sufficient. Defensive processing would also require the ability and capacity to do so. In line with this, Taber and Lodge (2006) found that more politically sophisticated participants took longer to read counter-attitudinal than pro-attitudinal messages regarding gun control and affirmative action, whereas participants low in political sophistication took less time for counter-attitudinal messages. Presumably, those with sufficient political knowledge were able to elaborate on the uncongenial information. (Yet, as political sophistication is not an experimental factor, it could have been the other way round: open-minded people become politically sophisticated.)

As shown above, the congeniality bias is moderated by attitude strength in a complex manner. One indicator of weak attitudes that has received considerable attention in recent years is attitudinal ambivalence (cf. Chapters 1 and 7). In line with consistency theories reported in Chapter 7, people try to reduce attitudinal ambivalence. Yet, there are different ways of solving the conflict, which presumably depend on the initial starting point. For a person who feels highly torn between different positions (i.e. the summary evaluation is close to zero), defence motivation might not be strong enough. Instead, triggered by the uncertainty of how to evaluate the object, a highly ambivalent attitude-holder should engage in deep processing of the given information, including uncongenial information (Conner & Sparks, 2002). However, for a person who holds an ambivalent attitude, which already points in one direction – either positive or negative – the simplest way was to focus on congenial information, thereby reducing discomfort but strengthening the position. In line with this, ambivalent attitude-holders show pronounced congeniality biases (e.g. Clark *et al.*, 2008), especially if ambivalence turns into feelings of discomfort (Nordgren *et al.*, 2006).

Although we mentioned above that the effect size of the congeniality bias is moderate according to the meta-analysis, the review of several moderators implies that the effect may be considerably larger in some cases. Attitudes to which people feel committed or that touch on central values show stronger effects. In this regard it is not surprising that issues involving politics or religion showed the largest effects (Hart *et al.*, 2009). Also, when real issues were used compared to artificial scenarios the effect was higher. This suggests that the effect may actually be larger in real life than in many research studies. One finding is particularly noteworthy in this regard: the effect was much higher when the research participants were not university or high school students. In sum, we can state that people tend to select information in a manner that allows them to keep their beliefs and opinions and avoid challenging views. Although perhaps healthy for their personal well-being – after all, a consistent belief system has a hedonic advantage (see Chapters 1 and 7) – it is disconcerting for the hope that free access to information may be able to eradicate misconceptions and prejudice.

ATTITUDE EFFECTS ON JUDGEMENT AND ELABORATION

Once a person has attended to external information – be that congenial, uncongenial or neutral – questions arise regarding how that information is perceived and interpreted, and how it is used in forming a judgement. A given piece of information can usually be interpreted in more than one way, and 'seeing both sides of things' can be unpleasant, as it requires high cognitive effort and may slow down decision making (see Figure 11.2 for an extreme case). By contrast, holding a positive or negative attitude may focus our view on one side of an issue and make us lean towards attitude-consistent interpretations. In other words, attitudinal selectivity comes into play at these stages of information processing as well. As reported in Chapter 1, attitudes, especially highly accessible ones, can simplify decision-making processes, enhance the quality of decision making and free cognitive resources. In this regard, an attitude may serve a heuristic function (Pratkanis, 1989). We will first briefly outline this concept before we turn in more detail to attitude-congruent information interpretation and elaboration.

Effects of using an attitude as a heuristic

As mentioned above, Pratkanis (1989) proposed that attitudes may work as a heuristic. In this manner, attitudes would affect interpretations and explanations, expectations and inferences, the formation of attitudes towards other objects and persons, as well as predictions of the future. An overview of these effects, some of which we already talked about in earlier chapters, is given in Box 11.1.

Some of these effects may, however, also be explained by selective exposure (see section above) and selective memory (see section below). For example, Pratkanis (1988) presented research participants with pairs of factual statements about public figures (e.g. US President Ronald Reagan). One statement was correct, whereas the other was not. He also varied

FIGURE 11.2 Seeing both sides of things can be vexing

Box 11.1 The attitude heuristic

In a review chapter on the cognitive representation of attitudes, Pratkanis (1989) presented 11 examples of heuristic effects of attitudes. Taken together, these phenomena provide strong evidence for the power of the attitude concept in explaining social judgement.

- *Interpretation and explanation.* Among the things that people judge in accordance with their attitudes are the credibility of news items (G. H. Smith, 1947), events on the football field (Hastorf & Cantril, 1954, see Chapter 1) and the causes and motives for other people's actions (Regan *et al.*, 1974).
- *Halo effects.* We expect that people we like possess positive characteristics, whereas people we dislike are expected to have negative traits (e.g. Lott & Lott, 1972). Survey research shows that positive events are often associated with positive expectations about the future, even in unrelated domains (Katona, 1975).
- *Syllogistic reasoning.* A person's attitude towards the conclusion of a syllogism may influence his judgement about the logical validity of the syllogism (Thistlethwaite, 1950). This effect may be explained as a heuristic inference based on the rule 'what I believe is true'.
- *Responses to persuasive communications.* Prior attitudes can bias message recipients' cognitive responses to persuasive messages, with positive attitudes increasing favourable responses and negative attitudes increasing counter-arguing (for a review, see Petty *et al.*, 1981).
- *Interpersonal attraction.* We tend to like people who hold attitudes similar to our own and to dislike people with dissimilar attitudes (e.g. Byrne, 1971; Newcomb, 1961; Pilkington & Lydon, 1997).
- *Judgement of social stimuli.* Attitudes may be used as a reference point for judging social stimuli. For example, survey respondents judged the position of their preferred presidential candidate on several issues to be very similar to their own (Granberg & Jenks, 1977). However, opposite effects have also been obtained (cf. the 'hostile media effect', discussed below).
- *False consensus of opinion.* People often tend to overestimate the percentage of others who share their opinions (e.g. Gilovich, 1990; Ross *et al.*, 1977).
- *Fact identification.* An attitude may be used to infer the accuracy of factual statements (Pratkanis, 1988; see discussion in this chapter) or to reconstruct past events (see section on memory in this chapter).
- *Estimates of own behaviour.* People often reconstruct or revise their past behaviour to fit in with their current attitudes. For example, Ross *et al.* (1981) exposed participants to persuasive messages that either promoted or criticised daily tooth brushing. Later, participants who had heard the anti-tooth brushing message reported that they brushed their teeth less often than participants who had heard the pro-tooth brushing message.
- *Information error technique.* This can be seen as a variant of the fact identification effect. When asked to indicate which of two factually incorrect alternative statements is correct, people tend to select the statement whose implications correspond to their attitude (Hammond, 1948).
- *Prediction of future events.* Simply holding a particular attitude may lead to attitude-congruent predictions; this is well documented for predictions about the results of US presidential elections, where partisans usually overestimate the share of votes for their preferred party's candidate (Granberg & Brent, 1983).

whether the true statements were favourable or unfavourable (e.g. 'got an A in college' vs. 'got a C in college'). Participants were less likely to identify a true positive statement as correct when they disliked the person than when they liked the person. It is possible that participants had previously attended more to positive information about people they liked. This illustrates that the effects of memory and those of active construal are not always separable. We may regard cognitive tasks as falling somewhere on a continuum that ranges from inferring or generating novel information on one end to explicit remembering of previously learned material on the other.

Pratkanis's (1988) results and his collection of examples regarding the attitude heuristic (Pratkanis, 1989) convincingly show that there is a close link between holding certain attitudes and making judgements and decisions. Thereby attitudes may simplify information processing. The benefits have been illustrated in Chapter 1: people who can rely on highly accessible attitudes as a basis for their decisions showed lower autonomic arousal during decision making compared to people with less accessible attitudes, who presumably have to construct their decisions on-line (Blascovich *et al.*, 1993).

However, these benefits of efficient decision making and reduced stress may come at a cost. Specifically, people with accessible attitudes may be rather close-minded regarding the processing of information that is incongruent with their attitude. Furthermore, an attitude object may change over time, and relying on the automatic activation of a well-rehearsed evaluation may prevent a person from detecting such change. Fazio *et al.* (2000) demonstrated this in a series of studies. For example, in the first phase of one study, participants were repeatedly exposed to photographs of people and were asked either to rehearse their attitudes towards each photo or to perform a control task. In the second phase they were presented with both the original photos and computer-generated 'morphs' of these photos. Participants with more (vs. less) accessible attitudes were less likely to view a morph as a photo of a novel person and more likely to view it as a different photo of a person seen before. Thus, individuals with more accessible attitudes had greater difficulty detecting change and perceived relatively less change in the attitude object than individuals with less accessible attitudes. This might also imply that well-established and often rehearsed attitudes towards objects may not change even if the object changes.

Attitude-congruent interpretation and elaboration

Several lines of theorising allow for the possibility that a person's attitude introduces a motivational or cognitive bias into their processing of information that is related to the attitude. These approaches include cognitive consistency theories (e.g. Festinger, 1957; see Chapter 7), social judgement theory (e.g. Sherif & Hovland, 1961), dual-process models of persuasion (Chaiken & Trope, 1999; see Chapter 8) and theories of motivated social cognition (e.g. Kunda, 1990).

In the section on selective exposure, we saw that people often avoid contact with information that might clash with their attitudes (Hart *et al.*, 2009). However, in everyday life, exposure to hostile information cannot always be avoided. Festinger (1957) proposed that under these conditions of 'forced exposure', people would tend to distort opposing information, whereas their perception of congenial information would be more accurate. These processes would jointly minimise cognitive dissonance. *Social judgement theory* (e.g. Sherif & Hovland, 1961) assumes that people represent their own attitudes as well as other attitudinal positions along an evaluative dimension. The positions along the evaluative continuum that a person rates as acceptable define the *latitude of acceptance*, whereas those that the person judges as objectionable define the *latitude of rejection*, and all remaining positions constitute the *latitude of non-commitment*. People were thought to minimise the discrepancy between their own attitude and attitudinal positions falling within their latitude of acceptance, but to accentuate the perceived distance of positions that fall within their latitude of rejection.

Following early observations that attitudes can severely affect people's interpretation of ambiguous events (Hastorf & Cantril, 1954), several studies have provided evidence consistent with social judgement theory's predictions of assimilation and contrast effects. People on opposing sides of a debate overestimate the extent to which they disagree (e.g. Dawes *et al.*, 1972; Robinson & Friedman, 1995; Robinson *et al.*, 1995; Thompson, 1995), in particular when the issues are central to partisans' belief-systems (Chambers *et al.*, 2006). They also see disagreeing opinions as more extreme than their own. An interesting example of an attitude-based contrast effect in perception has been labelled the **hostile media phenomenon**. It refers to a tendency of partisans in a political issue to judge media reports as biased against their own side. This was first demonstrated by Vallone *et al.* (1985), who examined how 'pro-Israel' and 'pro-Arab' students perceived TV coverage of the killing of civilians in Palestinian refugee camps in Lebanon by the Lebanese Christian militia. Each group perceived the same news items as hostile to their own position and supporting the other side (for similar results, see Giner-Sorolla & Chaiken, 1994; Perloff, 1989). This effect was replicated for media coverage regarding sports events where the reports were perceived as biased against the own team (Arpan & Raney, 2003). The most comprehensive study was based on the coverage regarding various social groups in the US, such as Catholics, born-again Christians, blacks, Hispanics, members of labour unions, and the two political parties in the US, Democrats and Republicans. For each group, those who belonged to the group judged the media reports to be less favourable to their group than those who were not involved (Gunther, 1992). Moreover, juxtaposing the two opposing parties, Democrats and Republicans, each group also felt that the coverage of the other group was too favourable.

The contrasting interpretation of positions that diverge from one's own may actually help perceivers to disparage these positions. Once perceived as extreme it is easy to dismiss the arguments of the other side as ridiculous

Hostile media phenomenon:
Tendency to view media as biasing information, away from one's position.

and not worth dealing with. Would more elaborate processing of opposing arguments lead to more balanced opinions and more agreement?
One might optimistically expect so, but remember that people are not very
willing to give up their opinions. In the ELM (Petty & Cacioppo, 1986b) and
in the HSM (Chaiken *et al.*, 1989; Chaiken *et al.*, 1996; see Chapter 8), the
two most prominent persuasion models, defending one's position is a
strong motivator for critically examining and dissecting counterarguments
(see also Eagly *et al.*, 2000; Edwards & Smith, 1996). Thus, if such information is indeed elaborated and processed systematically, information that
is less than perfectly convincing is likely to be dismissed allowing the bias
to remain. Given that successfully refuting attempts of attitude change may
fortify these attitudes (see Chapter 10) the bias may even grow stronger.

Evidence that conflicts with one's own views may be processed very
thoroughly and even meticulously, as illustrated by a study on scientific peer
reviewing (Mahoney, 1977). Not only were expert reviewers more critical
of the methodology of a scientific study when the study's conclusion conflicted with their own paradigms, but they were also more likely to find a
severe typo in the manuscript. This experimental paradigm of evaluating
research articles was borrowed for the best-known study on this topic (see
Box 11.2).

The comments in Table 11.1 illustrate that the same piece of information
may be interpreted and evaluated rather differently depending on whether
it supports or challenges one's attitudes. Similarly, identical evidence

---

Box 11.2   Again: what is a strong argument?

Lord *et al.* (1979) asked students who initially either opposed or
favoured capital punishment to read and evaluate two (fictitious)
research articles. One article supported the conclusion that the death
penalty was an effective deterrent to murder, whereas the other article
provided evidence favouring the opposite conclusion. Students first
read the conclusions of the studies and then indicated the extent to
which this information influenced their attitudes towards capital
punishment. Following their initial judgement they then received more
details about the studies, including the research procedure, the
rebuttal of possible criticism, data in the form of tables and graphic
displays, etc. They rated how convincing they thought the evidence
was and were also asked to discuss the evidence in a free format.
Finally, they again judged the extent to which the evidence impacted
their beliefs. Overall, the students rated the evidence that was
consistent with their own attitude as more convincing than the
information that questioned their attitude. Table 11.1 shows two
examples of respective comments.

TABLE 11.1   Comments on a pro- and an anti-deterrence study as a function of attitudes towards death penalty

	Comments on pro-deterrence study	Comments on anti-deterrence study
Proponent of death penalty	'The experiment was well thought out, the data collected was valid, and they were able to come up with responses to all criticisms.'	'There were too many flaws in the picking of the states and too many variables involved in the experiment as a whole to change my opinion.'
Opponent of death penalty	'The study was taken only 1 year before and 1 year after capital punishment was reinstated. To be a more effective study they should have taken data from at least 10 years before and as many years as possible after.'	'The states were chosen at random, so the results show the average effect capital punishment has across the nation. The fact that 8 out of 10 states show a rise in murders stands as good evidence.'

Source: Adapted from Lord *et al.* (1979)

regarding the assassination of John F. Kennedy was judged as evidence for a conspiracy by conspiracy theorists but as evidence against it by detractors (McHoskey, 1995); and after watching the 1996 pre-election debate between US presidential candidates Bill Clinton and Bob Dole, viewers' pre-debate attitudes determined whom they considered to be the winner of the debate and who had the better arguments (Munro *et al.*, 2002).

Biased assimilation:
Tendency to interpret arguments as supportive of the own position.

The degrading of arguments that support opposing views is referred to as **biased assimilation**. Such biased assimilation has been found to be stronger for more extreme (Edwards & Smith, 1996; McHoskey, 1995; Miller *et al.*, 1993), stronger (Taber & Lodge, 2006) and more accessible attitudes (Houston & Fazio, 1989). In sum, attitude strength (see Chapters 1 and 10) is an important moderator of biased assimilation. Strong attitudes are likely to be more central to one's belief system and thereby the motivation to uphold and defend them is higher than for less cared about attitudes.

Another – and perhaps counterintuitive – finding by Lord and colleagues (see Box 11.2) showed that the more of the 'two-sided' information the students had read, the more pronounced the differences between proponents' and opponents' attitudes became. Thus, somewhat paradoxically, exposure to mixed evidence did not mitigate initial attitudes but rather led to their polarisation. In the light of the biased assimilation – that is, the degrading of counter-attitudinal arguments – this may be easily explained. If the arguments are not deemed convincing they may not only have no influence but, at a meta-cognitive level, they may elicit contrast effects: 'If that is the best they can come up with, I'm even more convinced that I'm right.' It should be noted, though, that evidence is mixed regarding attitude polarisation after exposure to both sides of the camp. The effect is stronger for self-reported attitude shifts than for actual attitude change as assessed by a pre-post measure (Miller *et al.*, 1993; Munro & Ditto, 1997; Munro *et al.*, 2002; for a pre-post measure effect, see Taber & Lodge, 2006).

As was also the case for biased assimilation, attitude polarisation is moderated by attitude strength with stronger (Taber & Lodge, 2006) and more committed attitudes (Pomerantz *et al.*, 1995) showing larger polarisation. Again, this makes sense from a defensive motivational perspective, as the defensive motivation should be stronger for central and important attitudes.

Outside of the persuasion domain, researchers have also proposed that specific motives and goals may affect reasoning (for a review, see Kunda, 1990). In line with this approach, Schaller (1992) demonstrated that group-related attitudes can motivate the allocation of processing effort to statistical reasoning tasks. Take a look at Table 11.2. It suggests a correlation between gender and leadership ability. Table 11.2B clarifies that the relationship at the aggregate level is due to the fact that executives have better leadership abilities than workers, and that more men than women are executives. Within each job category there is no correlation between gender and leadership ability. When confronted with these data, female participants invested greater processing effort than male participants and were more likely to detect the correlation within the job categories.

When Schaller (1992, Experiment 2) repeated this study with stimulus material in which the spurious correlation between gender and leadership ability was to the advantage of women, the men used more complex reasoning and were more likely to conclude that there is no real relation between gender and leadership. In contrast, the women were more likely to accept the positive correlation at face value.

TABLE 11.2   Stimulus information reflecting a spurious correlation between gender and leadership ability

A. Aggregate data

	Good leaders	Bad leaders
Male	13	7
Female	7	13

B. Broken down by job category

	Executives		Office workers	
	Good leaders	Bad leaders	Good leaders	Bad leaders
Male	12	3	1	4
Female	4	1	3	12

Source: Adapted from Schaller (1992, Table 1, p. 64)

The studies we reviewed in this section indicate that attitudes can lead to selective interpretation of attitude-relevant information. The processes underlying these effects may vary. They may be triggered unintentionally by strong and accessible attitudes and reflect relatively simple perceptual distortions, but may also involve considerable cognitive effort and elaboration. Furthermore, individuals may be content with an initial judgement based on low-effort processing if it matches their attitude-based expectations or preferences, but they may step up their processing effort if superficial processing does not yield the desired results.

ATTITUDE EFFECTS ON MEMORY

> When a subject is being asked to remember, very often the first thing that emerges is something of the nature of attitude. The recall is then a construction, made largely on the basis of this attitude, and its general effect is that of a justification of the attitude.
>
> (Bartlett, 1932/1995, pp. 206–207)

When it comes to personal recollections one's current attitudes provide a strong retrieval cue or perhaps, in line with Bartlett, we should better say construction guide. As Michael Ross (1989) has illustrated in a fascinating review, people tend to report previous attitudes and behaviours as congruent with their present attitudes. Experimental studies in this domain first change attitudes and then ask people to recall earlier attitudes and behaviours (for a review, see Ross, 1989) but support also comes from historical – albeit rather indirect – data. Reiter (1980) analysed survey data collected in the US between 1952 and 1972, where Democrats and Republicans were asked whether they had ever identified with the other party. According to these data, a majority of African Americans and Jews recalled being Democrats prior to the 1930s. Although the individual data cannot be verified, the data contradict historical records, which indicate that during the 1920s the vast majority of African Americans and Jews were Republicans. It was only during the New Deal era in the 1930s that these groups flocked to the Democratic Party. Reiter interprets the later reported party affiliation as a projection of their current partisanship.

Beyond autobiographical memory, Bartlett's notion also bears some relevance for the recall of externally presented information. Depending on their attitudes, people are likely to hold either more or less favourable representations of the attitude object. As suggested by recent research, this even pertains to the visual representation of an attitude object (Dotsch *et al.*, 2008). In this vein, the look of a political candidate is remembered as more favourable among partisans than among his opponents (Young *et al.*, 2014). The major part of research concerned with attitude effects on memory, however, studied the representation of abstract knowledge, an issue we will deal with in the remainder of this section.

Congeniality bias in recall?

As explained above, the conception of attitudes as schemas implies that the knowledge structure representing the attitude guides information processing. From this perspective one may expect that congenial information is more easily encoded because it fits readily into the available knowledge structure. As a result, pro-attitudinal information may also enjoy a recall advantage. Early research produced evidence largely consistent with this proposal. For example, Levine and Murphy (1943) presented information that was favourable or unfavourable towards the Soviet Union to communist and anti-communist participants. In several recall tests conducted over a five-week period, the anti-communists recalled the content of an anti-Soviet text passage much better than the communists did.

However, two factors would provide an argument against a pro-attitudinal memory bias. First, as stated earlier in this chapter, attitude-relevant objects receive more attention than irrelevant, and this also holds true for counter-attitudinal objects (Roskos-Ewoldsen & Fazio, 1992, 2008). Extending this thought to attitude-relevant *information*, one might predict that more attention would be paid to congenial, but also uncongenial information than attitude-irrelevant information. As a consequence, some attitudes may be represented by a bipolar structure (Pratkanis, 1989) that not only encompasses information about the favoured side but that of both sides. This is likely to be the case for issues that are controversially discussed in one's social environment. For such attitudes with bipolar structures, one would thus expect that pro- as well as counter-attitudinal information would fit easily into relevant memory structures and should therefore be easily processed and recalled. To test this notion, Judd and Kulik (1980) had students read belief statements concerning several political issues (e.g. 'Majority rule would only complicate the lives of most South Africans'). Participants were asked to indicate how much they agreed with each statement and how favourable or unfavourable it was. The response times for each of these judgements were measured, and at a later stage the students were asked to recall as many statements as they could. The results showed that more extreme statements, in terms of both subjective agreement and objective favourability, were processed faster and were more likely to be recalled than less extreme statements. This was equally true for statements opposed to and in line with participants' own position. Thus, information may fit an attitude schema to the extent that it is located near either pole of a bipolar evaluative continuum.

A second factor that works against a congenial memory advantage is, as you may recall, that there is also evidence that if counter-attitudinal information is attended it is also processed more thoroughly (e.g. Eagly *et al.*, 2000; Edwards & Smith, 1996), presumably due to a defensive strategy. From all we know, deeper processing should result in better recall (Craik & Lockhart, 1972). So perhaps it is not too surprising that in their study, Eagly and colleagues (2000) found better recall for uncongenial information.

Note that defensive processing does not necessarily involve better recall for uncongenial than congenial information. While it may boost recall of the uncongenial information through elaborate processing, congenial information may not necessarily require thorough processing to be remembered. Because congenial information fits the person's beliefs, it can be more easily integrated with existing memory structures. In combination, congenial and uncongenial information may be recalled equally well, albeit for different reasons.

In sum, whether there is a memory bias for congenial information should depend on the attitude representation and on how deeply message recipients processed the uncongenial information. Accordingly, a meta-analysis on selective memory (Eagly *et al.*, 1999) found a considerable heterogeneity of effects. Overall, averaging across 65 studies, there was a small recall advantage for congenial over uncongenial information, but 26 out of 65 studies point in the direction of a recall advantage for uncongenial information.

Whether or not these recall biases for uncongenial information are due to defensive counter-arguing could not be answered by the meta-analysis. But in line with the predictions that controversial attitudes tend to be represented bipolarly, the meta-analysis found that for highly controversial attitude topics, recall was more even-handed as would be expected for bipolar representations. Moreover, other research found that independent of the message's congeniality, activists as well as participants with stronger attitudes (Eagly *et al.*, 2000) and those for whom the attitudes were important (Holbrook *et al.*, 2005) had better memory. One may easily imagine that these people have more bipolar attitude structures as they are often involved in debates with the other camp. Also in line with the assumption that a coherent representation in memory is crucial in whether only pro-attitudinal or also counter-attitudinal information is integrated and recalled, message recipients with high compared to low knowledge showed overall better recall (Wiley, 2005). More importantly, they showed no congeniality bias, whereas participants low in knowledge did.

As a last note on the issue of attitudinal influences on memory, we would like to emphasise two aspects. First, in all the reviewed studies participants did not actively seek the counter-attitudinal information. In real life, selective exposure may prevent encountering counter-attitudinal information in the first place. Second, although in some cases counter-attitudinal information enjoyed a recall advantage, this does not imply persuasion. On the contrary, if the recall advantage was due to counter-arguing one would expect no persuasion or even contrast (see Chapter 10).

CONCLUDING COMMENT: SHORT-SIGHTED IN ONE EYE, BLIND IN THE OTHER

During the 2008 presidential race in the USA rumours came up alleging that the candidate Barack Obama was a Muslim. According to some sources, about 12 per cent of Americans believed this rumour and the numbers did not change very much over a three-month period despite extensive attempts to correct the misperception (Hollander, 2010). The research findings we reviewed in this chapter may illuminate why it is often rather difficult to correct false information, make people consider opposing evidence and change their beliefs. Put together, people may not even encounter challenging information. Even if they cannot avoid it, they may deal with it in a defensive manner. They may doubt its validity, devalue it, distort it or dismiss it. Even if it is processed, it is likely to be refuted. As a consequence, change in beliefs is not highly likely (see also Chapter 10).

We began by pointing out the plethora of information in this day and age. In the light of the demand for congenial information, the dark side of this seemingly positive development becomes evident. Such a smorgasbord affords that everyone can find the information that caters to her or his opinions. To be sure, this alone is not problematic even if it facilitates avoidance of counter-attitudinal information. However, the demand for confirming information may lead to a more polarised media at the expense of a more balanced range of media (see also Mullainathan & Shleifer, 2005; Prior, 2005). It may not be a coincidence that in the US the news channel CNN is increasingly marginalised by channels positioned on more extreme sides of the ideological continuum. This example may illustrate that the phenomena described in this chapter may have societal consequences beyond individual processing.

CHAPTER SUMMARY

1   The idea that attitudes affect information processing has its roots in cognitive consistency theory, in the functional analysis of attitudes and in theorising on attitude structure.

2   Attitudes may influence the attention to attitude objects, the use of categories for encoding information and the interpretation, judgement and recall of attitude-relevant information. These influences tend to be more powerful for strong attitudes, which are easily accessible and based on an elaborate knowledge structure.

3   Attitudes may guide attention and encoding automatically, even if the individual is pursuing unrelated goals. However, people may also seek out attitude-congruent information in a more strategic fashion, especially after a behavioural decision.

4   Attitudes may affect perception and judgement in various ways. Pratkanis distinguishes between heuristic effects of attitudes, where inferences are drawn from a summary evaluation ('What I like is good'), and the schematic effects of attitudes, where inferences are based on a more complex attitudinal knowledge structure.

5   Accessible attitudes provide the benefits of efficiency and stress reduction, but come at the cost of close-mindedness. They may inhibit the detection of change in an attitude object.

6   Forced exposure to attitude-incongruent information may lead to biased interpretation and elaboration. Processing information on both sides of an issue under the guidance of a prior attitude can result in a more extreme attitude, and people may strategically use more or less effortful reasoning strategies depending on what outcome they desire based on their attitudes.

7   There are at least two types of attitude effects on memory: bipolar attitudes may facilitate recall of information that fits either pole of a bipolar evaluative continuum; congeniality effects are characterised by better recall of attitude-consistent than attitude-inconsistent information. On balance, there is only weak evidence for congeniality effects for memory.

8   The processes mediating attitudinal selectivity in processing and recall may vary both qualitatively, including selective inattention and selective counter-arguing, and quantitatively along a continuum of processing effort.

Exercises

1   Can you think of examples for the attention-grabbing nature of strong attitudes in everyday life?

2   What are the similarities and differences between heuristic and schematic effects of attitudes?

3   What is the hostile media effect and under what conditions is it most likely to be observed?

4   Would informing people about the potentially biasing effects of their attitudes help them in forming unbiased judgements and decisions? Why or why not?

Further reading

A narrative review of work on selective exposure:

Smith, S., Fabrigar, L. & Norris, M. (2008). Reflecting on six decades of selective exposure research: progress, challenges, and opportunities. *Social and Personality Psychology Compass, 2*(1), 464–493.

A quantitative review on selective exposure:

Hart, W., Eagly, A., Lindberg, M., Albarracin, D., Brechan, I. & Merrill, L. (2009). Feeling validated versus being correct: a meta-analysis of selective exposure to information. *Psychological Bulletin, 135*, 555–588.

An excellent, although somewhat dated, cognitive-structural account for attitudinal effects on information processing:

Pratkanis, A. R. (1989). The cognitive representation of attitudes. In A. R. Pratkanis, S. J. Breckler & A. G. Greenwald (eds), *Attitude Structure and Function* (pp. 71–98). Hillsdale, NJ: Erlbaum.

A quantitative review on attitude effects on elaboration and memory:

Eagly, A. H., Chen, S., Chaiken, S. & Shaw-Barnes, K. (1999). The impact of attitudes on memory: an affair to remember. *Psychological Bulletin, 125,* 64–89.

Chapter 12

DO ATTITUDES PREDICT BEHAVIOUR?

Perhaps the major reason why attitudes are studied is the assumption that attitudes guide behaviour. On one hand, this assumption seems obviously correct: we eat food that we like and avoid people we dislike; we vote for the political party whose aims we find most appealing, and so forth. On the other hand, behaviour often seems to be at odds with attitudes: we may drive to work even if we resent air pollution, practice unsafe sex even if we abhor sexually transmitted diseases, or cheat on our partners even if we love them. Quite unsurprisingly, early research trying to establish if a close relationship between attitudes and behaviour exists produced mixed results. It turned out that attitudes sometimes predicted behaviour quite well, whereas at other times it was hard to detect any relationship between the two. Therefore, a second generation of research was devoted to delineating the conditions under which attitudes predict behaviour more or less closely. A further generation of research, which extends to the present, addresses the cognitive processes involved in the attitude–behaviour link (see Zanna & Fazio, 1982, in Chapter 13).

EARLY DISENCHANTING RESULTS ON THE ATTITUDE–BEHAVIOUR RELATION

Early pessimism about the idea that attitudes guide behaviour was nourished in an article by LaPiere (1934). The author went on an extensive tour across the USA in the company of a Chinese couple. Given the prejudice against Asians that prevailed in the United States in the 1930s, LaPiere expected that his Chinese travel companions would often be refused service by hotels or restaurants. To his surprise, however, this happened in only one of the 251 establishments they visited. What is even more astonishing is the result of a mail survey that LaPiere conducted six months later. He wrote to all the hotels and restaurants visited, asking if they would accept 'members of the Chinese race' as guests. In total contrast to their prior behaviour, 118 (92 per cent) of the 128 places that returned the questionnaire responded that they would not serve Chinese customers. LaPiere concluded from this enormous discrepancy between stated attitude and overt behaviour that questionnaire responses are not valid indicators of a person's true attitude. He suggested that the use of questionnaire measures of attitude, as they measure merely 'symbolic' responses, should be limited to issues that remain symbolic – for example, predicting voting behaviour from political attitude surveys.

Viewed in the light of contemporary methodological standards, there are, of course, a number of flaws in LaPiere's (1934) study: respondents' attitudes were assessed long after the behaviour in question; it was unclear if the people who responded to the mailing were the same as those who had admitted the Chinese guests; and the attitude object, an English-speaking couple accompanied by a white American, may not have been identified as 'members of the Chinese race' to begin with. However, other studies, which suffered less from methodological problems, also failed to find a high correlation between attitudes and behaviour (see Ajzen & Fishbein, 1970; Corey, 1937). These accumulated findings contributed to a generally pessimistic view on the possibility of predicting behaviour from attitudes in the 1960s and early 1970s (e.g. Wicker, 1969).

But rather than giving up the study of attitude–behaviour relations, researchers began examining the reasons for why, in some studies, the prediction of behaviour from attitudes was quite successful (e.g. Fishbein & Coombs, 1974; Newton & Newton, 1950; for a review, see Ajzen & Fishbein, 1977), whereas in others it was not (see Box 12.1 for the results of attitude–behaviour studies conducted over more than 60 years). The variability of empirical findings suggested that the question *if* attitudes predict behaviour was too broad and undifferentiated. Therefore, researchers began asking more specific questions: what are the conditions that need to be present in order to find a strong association between attitudes and behaviour?

Box 12.1 Predicting behaviour from attitudes in various domains

The correlation between attitudes and behaviours largely varies across content domains. This variation is nicely illustrated in a meta-analytic review by Eckes and Six (1994). In some domains, such as altruistic behaviour or family planning, correlations were low to moderate, whereas in other areas, such as using (both legal and illegal) drugs, the predictive power of attitudes was substantial.

Another notable finding of this quantitative review was that the findings varied considerably within domains as well. Statistical tests of heterogeneity showed that in all but one of the areas depicted in Figure 12.1, the variability in correlation coefficients across studies was greater than would be expected by chance. Thus, it is likely that moderator variables affected the strength of the attitude–behaviour relation in varying degrees.

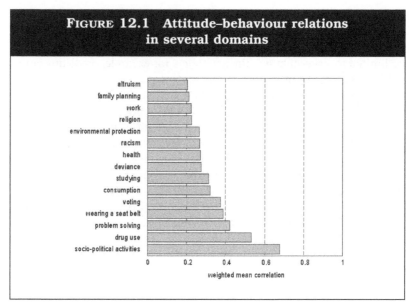

FIGURE 12.1   Attitude–behaviour relations in several domains

Note: The bars represent the weighted mean of correlation coefficients reported in studies conducted between 1927 and 1990. Only domains represented by more than five studies are shown (data from a meta-analysis reported by Eckes & Six, 1994)

APPROPRIATE MEASURES INCREASE ATTITUDE–BEHAVIOUR RELATION

As mentioned above, early studies did not necessarily meet the required scientific standards. Thus, one way to improve attitude–behaviour consistency was by advancing methodological rigour.

The correspondence principle

One reason for a weak association between attitude and behaviour may lie in the lack of correspondence (or compatibility) of the two measures. Ajzen and Fishbein (1977) noted that both attitudes and behaviours can be described with respect to four characteristics:

1   The *action element*: what behaviour is being studied – e.g. voting, donating or attending?
2   The *target element*: what is the target of the behaviour – e.g. a political party, a charity or a lecture?
3   The *context element*: in what context is the behaviour being performed – e.g. a totalitarian or democratic society, in public or in private, at university or evening school?
4   The *time component*: at what point in time is the behaviour occurring – e.g. immediately or over the following year?

It is impossible to predict with accuracy any specific behaviour (e.g. 'attending the soccer match of one's local team next weekend') from a global measure of attitude (e.g. a questionnaire on general attitudes towards soccer). Although this point may almost seem self-evident, it is precisely the questionable link between global attitude and specific behaviour that was examined in most early studies, with LaPiere's (1934) investigation being one famous example.

According to Ajzen and Fishbein (1977), close relations between attitude and behaviour can be expected only if both measures agree in their degree of specification. Their review of attitude–behaviour studies supported this reasoning: the reported correlations between attitude and behaviour are indeed larger to the extent that the specification of both measures was similar. Some years later, reviews yielded identical conclusions (Eckes & Six, 1994; Kim & Hunter, 1993; Kraus, 1995). To illustrate the **correspondence principle**, let us consider a study by Davidson and Jaccard (1979). These researchers predicted women's contraceptive behaviours from attitudinal measures that varied in specificity. As Table 12.1 shows, the predictive power of the attitude measure increased dramatically with increasing correspondence of attitude and behaviour.

It should be noted, however, that this method of increasing the prediction of specific behaviours entails a shift on the predictor side from *attitudes towards objects* to the narrower concept of *attitudes towards behaviour*. This shift is inherent in current expectancy x value models of the attitude–behaviour relation, although other researchers have continued to use attitudes towards objects as predictors of behaviour (see Chapter 13).

Correspondence principle: Attitudes best predict behaviour when both are measured at the same level of specificity.

TABLE 12.1   Correlations of attitude measures that vary in specificity with a specific behaviour (use of birth control pills during a two-year period)

Attitude measure	Correlation with specific behaviour
Attitude towards birth control	.083
Attitude towards birth control pills	.323
Attitude towards using birth control pills	.525
Attitude towards using birth control pills during the next two years	.572

Note: Based on a sample of 244 women (data from Davidson and Jaccard, 1979)

The aggregation principle

Aggregation principle: Global attitudes are better predictors of aggregated behavioural measures than of any specific behaviours.

Although measures of general attitudes towards objects are poor predictors of single, specific behaviours, they fare better at predicting behaviour over a wider range of situations and contexts. As a complement to the strategy of maximising specificity, Fishbein and Ajzen (1974) thus proposed to assess and aggregate multiple behaviours to increase the predictive power of global attitude measures. In Chapter 2 we mentioned that reliability increases with a larger number of items in a scale (Cronbach, 1951). Similarly, if we sample and aggregate a large number of behaviours – and assume that the attitude remains fairly stable over the assessment period – then any determinants of behaviour other than attitude should cancel each other out in the aggregate score. Going back to our earlier example, people who differ in their global attitude towards soccer should also differ in predictable ways regarding a range of related behaviours taken as a whole, like playing soccer, attending matches, watching soccer programmes on television, wearing team colours, and so on.

This reasoning is supported by research findings. Fishbein and Ajzen (1974) successfully predicted an aggregate measure of self-reported religious behaviours from general attitudes towards religion. In an extensive field study, Weigel and Newman (1976) provided another powerful illustration of the aggregation principle. These researchers used a 16-item scale to assess town residents' general attitudes towards the environment. Then, over an extended period of time, they arranged opportunities for the residents to engage in various pro-environmental behaviours. For example, the respondents were visited in their homes and asked to sign and circulate petitions for various environmental causes, and a kerbside waste-recycling programme was set up specifically for the purpose of the study. Participation in each of these activities was unobtrusively recorded and behavioural measures at different levels of aggregation were derived from these observations. As Table 12.2 shows, the general attitude did not reliably predict most of the specific behaviours; however, its correlation with a fully *aggregated* measure of environmental behaviour was a remarkable .62.

Of course, as anticipated in Chapter 6, the variability of the attitude itself constrains the magnitude of the attitude–behaviour correspondence. The more the attitude itself is subject to change over the assessment period, the lower its association with behaviour should be.

In sum, the principles of correspondence and aggregation show that levels of measurement are important in determining attitude–behaviour relations. Specific attitudes predict equally specific behaviours, whereas global attitude measures predict behaviours aggregated across contexts and points in time. Thus, when trying to predict whether people will attend church next weekend or recycle waste, you should ask for their attitude towards these specific behaviours. In order to predict a whole set of behaviours related to religion or environment, a more economic global measure will work well.

TABLE 12.2   General attitude as a predictor of behavioural criteria varying in generality

Correlations of environmental attitude (16-item measure) with . . .

Single Behaviours	r	Categories of Behaviour	r	Fully Aggregated Behaviour Index	r
Offshore oil	.41**	Petitioning	.50**		
Nuclear power	.36*	behaviour			
Auto exhaust	.39**	scale (0–4)			
Circulate petitions	.27				
Individual participation	.34*	Litter pick-up	.36*		
Recruit friend	.22	scale (0–2)			
				Comprehensive	.62***
Recycling				behavioural index	
week 1	.34*				
week 2	.57***				
week 3	.34*	Recycling			
week 4	.33*	behaviour scale	.39**		
week 5	.12	(0–8)			
week 6	.20				
week 7	.20				
week 8	.34*				
Unweighted average	.31		.42		.62

Note: N = 44 (data from Weigel and Newman, 1976). * p < .05; ** p < .01; *** p < .001.

EXPECTANCY-VALUE MODELS: ATTITUDES TOWARDS BEHAVIOUR AND OTHER DETERMINANTS OF BEHAVIOUR

The previous sections have shown that, if measured appropriately, attitudes are a major determinant of behaviour. But researchers also recognised the importance of other influential factors, most notably social norms, but also habits, skills and abilities. They developed a family of theories in which *attitudes towards behaviour* (rather than attitudes towards targets of behaviour) are located within a network of other predictor variables

Expectancy-value principle: A feature of various theories in motivation and attitude–behaviour research. It says that an individual assesses the desirability of an object (or course of action) by considering the sum of its features (or expected outcomes) weighted by their subjective probability.

Theory of reasoned action (TRA): A model whose core assumption is that attitudes towards a given behaviour in combination with subjective norms influence the intention to perform that behaviour, which in turn influences behaviour.

(e.g. Ajzen, 1991; Bagozzi, 1992; Bentler & Speckart, 1979; Fishbein & Ajzen, 1975). These are called **expectancy-value models** (see Feather, 1982) because attitudes are defined in these models as expectancy by value products.

The theory of reasoned action

The initial model, Fishbein and Ajzen's (1975) **theory of reasoned action** (TRA), is displayed in Figure 12.2 (top panel). According to this model, the immediate cause of behaviour is *behavioural intention*, which is a conscious decision to engage in a certain action. Any influences on behaviour that the theory accounts for are assumed to be mediated by this construct. The two determinants of intention are *attitude towards the behaviour* and *subjective norm*. Attitude towards the behaviour is defined as the sum of expectancy x value products. Each of these products consists of the subjective probability (= expectancy) that the behaviour has a certain consequence, multiplied by the subjective value attached to this consequence. For example, a person may expect that by studying economics she will perhaps find a prestigious, well-paid job (a very positive consequence with moderate subjective likelihood) but will have to put up with boring maths in her courses (a somewhat negative consequence with very high likelihood). These two aspects combined would yield a moderately positive attitude towards studying economics.[1]

The second determinant of behavioural intention is the construct of subjective norm. It is also defined as a sum of products, with each product consisting of the belief that a significant 'referent' (i.e. another person or group) thinks one should perform the behaviour and the motivation to comply with this referent. For instance, a student may believe that her father thinks that she should not get a tatoo, but she may not be willing to comply with her father; she may also believe that her partner would strongly approve of her being tattooed and she may be inclined to comply with her partner. If only these two referents were considered, the resulting subjective norm would be positive and would increase the intention of going to the tattooist. This aspect holds an interesting implication for instigating behavioural change. Changing personal attitudes towards the behaviour is one way to achieve behavioural change. Alternatively (or additionally), one may also try to change people's behaviour by influencing social norms.

In the TRA, only the constructs described above were included, whereas any other, more distal variables, such as demographic variables, personality traits and even attitudes towards targets, were considered 'external' to the theory. This means that they were thought to influence behaviour only indirectly, by affecting the attitude towards the behaviour and the subjective norm, or by moderating these factors' impact on the intentions built.

For an illustration of such an influence, let us consider how cultural variation can be embedded in the TRA. As proposed by cultural psychologists (Markus & Kitayama, 1991), people in Eastern cultures are likely to

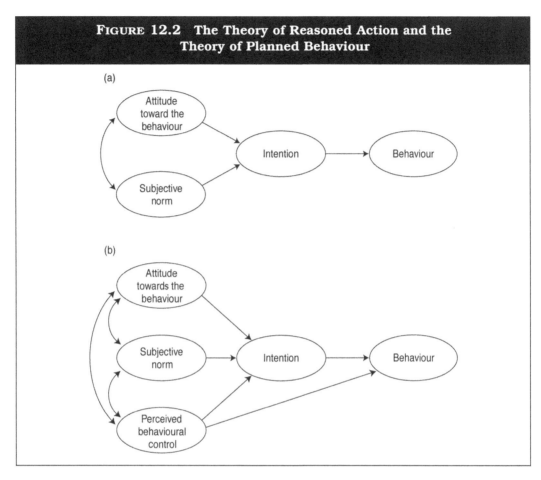

FIGURE 12.2   The Theory of Reasoned Action and the Theory of Planned Behaviour

Note: Schematic depiction of the theory of reasoned action (top panel) and the theory of planned behaviour (bottom panel); (adapted from Ajzen and Madden, 1986)

define themselves by their relations with other persons such as friends or family members. By contrast, people in Western cultures (e.g. Americans) construe themselves as rather independent of others. Thus, their identity is primarily based on internal characteristics, such as their own feelings, thoughts, goals and achievements. These differences might be evident beyond self-construal, and people in an Eastern, collectivist culture should be more likely to behave in line with their in-group norms than people in a Western, individualist culture (Mills & Clark, 1982; Triandis, 1994; Triandis & Suh, 2002). Building on the cultural differences proposed above, Bagozzi and colleagues (Bagozzi *et al.*, 2000) modelled the relations between attitudes, norms and behavioural intentions in the domain of fast food consumption. Their study included Eastern and Western samples that were assumed to vary gradually on the independent–interdependent self dimension, as well as on the individualism–collectivism dimension (i.e. Americans, Italians, Japanese and Chinese). Confirming their predictions, attitudes were the strongest predictor of behavioural intentions in the American sample, but path coefficients were still significant for the Italian and the Japanese sample. However, among the Chinese, which was the most collectivist culture among the samples under study (Hofstede *et al.*, 2010), this path was not significant. For the latter sample, as was expected, intentions were most strongly affected by subjective norms.

Similar to cultural variables, personality variables can be considered to cause a shift of the relative importance of attitudes as compared to subjective norms, when predicting behavioural intentions, which in turn predicts behaviour. One such trait that affects the relative importance of attitudes (versus other factors) in guiding behaviour is *self-monitoring* (cf. Chapter 1). People low in self-monitoring, whose social behaviour is generally more reflective of their internal states (Snyder, 1974), show higher attitude–behaviour correlations than people high in self-monitoring. High self-monitors' behaviour, on the other hand, is guided more by situational demands and the expectations of others. Part of this difference might be due to the fact that low self-monitors prefer and seek out situations in which attitudes can be openly expressed and enacted (Snyder & Kendzierski, 1982). However, the moderating role of self-monitoring on the attitude–behaviour relation can be reconstructed in terms of the TRA as an effect on the relative weighting of the attitude and subjective norm components. For low self-monitors, the attitude is more important, whereas for high self-monitors, the subjective norm is the major determinant of a behavioural intention.

The relative importance of attitudes versus norms may, of course, also vary across situations depending on whether they direct one's attention towards oneself or others. This was tested in studies by Froming *et al.* (1982). Participants who favoured punishment as a method of teaching but thought that others would oppose it (or vice versa) were given the task of applying electric shocks to a 'learner'. Depending on the experimental condition, participants' attention was focused either on their private self by facing a mirror, or on their public self by facing an audience. The results showed that participants' punishing behaviour was more in line with their attitudes in the former condition, but more in line with the perceived social norm in the latter. Taken together, 'external factors' may moderate the relative impact of the attitudes and the subjective norms on behavioural intentions. Sometimes, their impact might be hydraulic and high normative influence may reduce the predictive value of the attitudes on behaviour. Indeed, there is empirical evidence to suggest that this will be the case. A meta-analytic review (Wallace *et al.*, 2005) showed that the attitude–behaviour correlation was substantially reduced in studies in which participants perceived social pressure to show the behaviour, and in which the behaviour was difficult to perform. It is worth noting that, at the mean level of social pressure and difficulty, the meta-analysis still found an attitude–behaviour correlation of .41, attesting the importance of considering the attitude construct when predicting behaviours. However, without equating social pressure with subjective norms as conceived in the TRA, the findings at least imply that further, external factors should be taken into account. Indeed, the TRA has been extended in various ways, with the most prominent extension paying respect to the difficulty to perform a behaviour.

Extending the TRA: the theory of planned behaviour

The most prominent extension to the TRA was proposed by Ajzen (1991, 2012; Ajzen & Madden, 1986). His **theory of planned behaviour** (TPB) features one additional predictor variable: *perceived behavioural control* (see Figure 12.2, bottom panel). This extension was assumed to enhance prediction especially for those behaviours over which a person does not have complete voluntary control, including complex behaviours that require extensive planning or preparation (e.g. running a marathon). Perceived behavioural control was conceptualised as the expected ease with which the intended behaviour can actually be performed (cf. the concept of self-efficacy; Bandura, 1977). It was hypothesised to affect behaviour either indirectly, via the behavioural intention, or directly, to the extent that it is an accurate reflection of the actual control a person has over the behaviour in question. For example, a person who thinks it will be difficult to run a marathon should be less likely to form a behavioural intention of doing so; in addition, once she has formed an intention to act, she may be less likely to succeed.

Theory of planned behaviour (TPB): An extension of the theory of reasoned action. In addition to attitudes and subjective norms, perceived behavioural control is included as a predictor of behavioural intention and behaviour.

Ajzen and Madden (1986, Experiment 2) conducted a study whose aim was to demonstrate the predictive superiority of the theory of planned behaviour over the theory of reasoned action. Their participants were business students, and the target behaviour was getting an 'A' (the best grade) in a course. At two points in time – both early in the semester and one week prior to final examinations – the researchers measured students' attitudes towards 'receiving an "A" in this course', students' subjective norms regarding this behaviour and their perceived control over this behaviour. Attitude was assessed by asking students to evaluate, on a good–bad scale, ten salient consequences of getting an 'A' (e.g. obtaining a sense of personal accomplishment; increasing one's grade point average), and to rate the probability of each of these consequences on a scale from unlikely to likely. A belief-based measure of attitude was then formed by summing the products of these two ratings over all ten consequences. To measure subjective norm, the students indicated how much each of five referents (e.g. the instructor; their classmates) would *approve* versus *disapprove* of their getting an 'A', and how much they were willing to comply with each referent (scale from very much to not at all). A belief-based measure was formed by

---

Box 12.2   Strengthening the link between intention and behaviour

Many people think that the outcome of exercising such as looking good and feeling better, overall, is quite desirable. Or, to sum up in terms of the TRA, they hold a positive attitude towards exercising. In turn, they form the clear-cut intention to go to the gym regularly. Nevertheless, they often do not follow through with their intentions, but stay on the couch or go to the cinema instead. On many occasions it does not even occur to them that they could go exercising because the resolution to exercise more often is not at the top of their mind. One option to overcome this problem is by implementation intentions (Gollwitzer, 1999). Implementation intentions are if–then rules that not only comprise the intended behaviour (e.g. going to the gym), but also define the situation in which the behaviour could be executed. 'After having watched the 7pm news, I pick up my dumbbells for half an hour.'

Research revealed that people who have formed implementation intentions have a better prospective memory – that is, they are able to retrieve the intentions when needed in the future (e.g. Cohen & Gollwitzer, 2008; McCrea *et al.*, 2015; for a review, see Chen *et al.*, 2015).

But there is another reason why implementation intentions overcome the intention–behaviour gap. Every once in a while, intentions fail to translate into behaviour because we can fool ourselves and postpone the planned behaviour: 'For sure, I will exercise. But not today.' Implementation intentions, however, are too concrete, and having specified the concrete situation, procrastination would cause dissonant feelings and thoughts. Then, the best way of avoiding dissonance is by going to the gym. Thus, implementation intentions can counter procrastination (e.g. Owens *et al.*, 2008). Or, put differently, procrastination actually is 'the avoidance of the implementation of an intention' (Van Eerde, 2000, p. 374).

To date, there are multiple studies attesting the effectiveness of implementation intentions, including its positive effects on physical activity (Bélanger-Gravel *et al.*, 2013). Thus, if your plan is to get in shape before the next summer, you had better plan *when* to go running, otherwise you will stay on the couch until fall.

---

summing the products of these two ratings over all five referents. Finally, perceived behavioural control was assessed by summing over eight beliefs about the presence versus absence of facilitating and inhibiting factors (e.g., possessing the relevant skills; being involved in extracurricular activities).

The dependent variables were behavioural intentions, assessed with three items (e.g. 'I intend to get an "A" in this course'), and behaviour, i.e. the actual grade obtained. For each dependent variable, the researchers performed two-step hierarchical regression analyses at each time of measurement. The first step of the regression represented a test of the theory of reasoned action and its second step provided a test of the theory of planned behaviour. Thus:

1   Behavioural intentions were predicted from attitude and subjective norm (step 1), and then jointly from these two predictors and perceived behavioural control (step 2).
2   Behaviour (i.e. the grade obtained) was predicted from intention (step 1) and then jointly from intention and perceived control (step 2).

Ajzen and Madden (1986) assumed that early in the semester perceptions of behavioural control would not reflect actual control very well. The inclusion of perceived behavioural control would therefore improve the prediction of actual behaviour only indirectly, via behavioural intentions, but not directly. However, the researchers hypothesised that, late in the semester, students' perceptions of control should become more accurate as they learn more about factors facilitating or inhibiting success; this would lead to improved predictions of actual behaviour from perceived control both indirectly via intentions and directly.

Both hypotheses were supported. When measured early in the semester, attitudes and subjective norm were substantially related to behavioural intention (multiple R = .48), confirming the validity of the theory of reasoned action. But this multiple correlation was significantly increased (to R = .65) when perceived behavioural control was added as a predictor. Furthermore, intention was significantly correlated with the grade actually obtained (R = .26), and including perceived behavioural control as an additional predictor did not increase the magnitude of this coefficient.

When measured late in the semester, attitude and subjective norm together predicted intentions (R = .49); and again, this coefficient was significantly increased (to R = .64) when perceived behavioural control was included in the model. Finally, when measured late in the semester, perceived control also significantly improved the prediction of the actual grade obtained, from R = .39 when intention was the sole predictor, to R = .45 when intention and perceived control were used as concurrent predictors.

One could argue, however, that the difficult behaviour investigated in Ajzen and Madden's (1986) study, 'getting an A in a course', includes a *consequence* of behaviour rather than just describing the behaviour proper (i.e. studying for the course). Therefore, perceived behavioural control could be more parsimoniously subsumed in the TRA's concept of attitude, as it refers to the subjective likelihood of a behavioural consequence. Nevertheless, a meta-analytic review of 185 studies confirmed the conclusion suggested by Ajzen and Madden's study that the construct of perceived behavioural control accounts for a significant amount of variance in intention and behaviour over and above subjective norm and attitudes towards the behaviour. The inclusion of the variable thus improves the predictions (Armitage & Conner, 2001).

Further extensions of the TRA and the TPB

Other extensions of the TRA's list of predictor variables have been proposed (see Eagly & Chaiken, 1993). Some theorists noted that behaviour is affected by *previous behaviour* or *habit*, and that these influences are not necessarily mediated by attitudes, subjective norms or intentions (e.g. Bentler & Speckart, 1979; Triandis, 1980; cf. Ajzen, 1991). A meta-analysis (Ouellette & Wood, 1998) indicates that past behaviour does significantly contribute to the prediction of future behaviour. Interestingly, it does so along either of two mediational pathways. Well-practised behaviours that are performed in stable contexts (e.g. using a seatbelt) recur because the processing that controls them becomes automatic; the frequency of prior behaviour is then reflected in habit strength, which directly affects future behaviour. However, behaviours that are less well learned or occur in unstable contexts tend to remain under conscious control; under these circumstances, past behaviour influences future behaviour indirectly via behavioural intentions. (For how to bridge the intention–behaviour gap, see Box 12.2.) While most studies that predict behaviour from past behaviour are correlational, Albarracín and Wyer (2000) provided the first experimental evidence for a causal impact of past behaviour. Using an elaborate cover story, they made participants believe that they had voted in favour of or against the introduction of comprehensive exams on what was said to be a subliminal measure of unconscious behavioural tendencies (in fact, no subliminal measures of voting were taken). This subjective perception of past behaviour influenced later voting behaviour via its influence on attitudes. When participants were capable of thinking about the implications of introducing comprehensive exams (i.e. engaging in the kind of outcome-related cognitions that are emphasised in the TRA/TPB), perceived past behaviour influenced attitudes both directly and also indirectly, through its impact on outcome-related cognitions. Importantly, however, past behaviour still had a direct effect on attitudes when participants were distracted from thinking about the implications of introducing comprehensive exams.

Also, researchers have proposed subdividing the construct of perceived behavioural control into the components of self-efficacy (the perception of own skills and ability) and perceived control (the perception of controllability of environmental constraints on behaviour – e.g. Armitage & Conner, 1999). Yet other proposed variables to extend the list of predictors of behaviour are belief salience, moral norms and self-identity (for a review, see Conner & Armitage, 1998). Extending the concept of the subjective norm i.e. what is perceived others want one to do, Rivis and Sheeran (2003) also looked at the concept of descriptive norm (i.e. what is perceived that others are actually doing; see Chapter 9). In their meta-analysis, descriptive norms significantly improved predictions from intentions after attitudes, subjective norm and perceived behavioural control had been taken into account, and explained an additional 5 per cent of the variance.

Last but not least, several extensions of the expectancy-value approach aimed at distancing themselves from the concept of humans as rational agents, a concept which is implied in the TRA and the TPB (e.g. Richard *et al.*, 1998). These extensions include the suggestion of assessing affective aspects in addition to the more rational, evaluation-based beliefs (e.g. Conner & Armitage, 1998; Conner *et al.*, 2003; Manstead & Parker, 1995; Wolff *et al.*, 2011). In particular, it was proposed that *anticipated regret* might cause people to form behavioural intentions. For instance, a person could decide to buy an expensive concert ticket because she imagines the regret she would feel if the tickets were sold out later. In support of this notion, several studies showed that a model, including anticipated regret, explained more variance as compared to the original model (for a review, see Sandberg & Conner, 2008). However, whether the inclusion of anticipated regret, or affect more generally speaking, requires an extension of the model remains debatable. As discussed by Ajzen (2011), neither the TRA nor the TPB denies the influence of affect, but attitudes might actually contain the anticipation of affective outcomes. In this sense, attitudes towards smoking might depend on the expectation that smoking will feel great. In a similar vein, a person may anticipate the regret thinking of the poor health caused by smoking cigarettes. Thus, a modification of the TPB in order to accommodate effects of anticipated affect may not be necessary, but the TPB might suffice to explain it if a more refined attitude measure was used – a measure which explicitly asks for the affective outcomes associated with the behaviour. A further suggestion regarding the measure of attitudes follows from the particular conception of anticipated regret as a negative affect resulting from inaction (Abraham & Sheeran, 2003; but see Pieters & Zeelenberg, 2007 for an alternative conception). Ajzen (2011) argued that previous research may have shown an incremental use of including anticipated regret because attitude measures asked for an action, but the assessment of behavioural intentions asked for an inaction (e.g. attitude towards smoking, but intention not to smoke). Experimental evidence is in support of this interpretation. Anticipated regret only explained variance over and above the traditional TPB variables if there was a mismatch between the assessments of the attitude and the intention, such as when attitudes towards eating fast food were used to predict the behavioural intentions towards not eating fast food (Ajzen & Sheikh, 2013).

To sum up, the TPB may embed affective factors without giving up its parsimonious structure. However, assuming that attitudinal influence on behaviours is mediated by behavioural intentions, the model has problems explaining some unintended effects of our attitudes on behavioural out-comes (e.g. Fazio, 1986). Thus, alternative models were developed in order to account for more impulsive behaviours, an issue we will deal with in the next chapter.

CONCLUDING COMMENT: OPTIMISM IS WARRANTED

While very early research on the attitude–behaviour relationship yielded disenchanting results, methodological and theoretical advances helped to overcome this scientific depression. Expectancy value theories have relegated the attitude concept to the background as one among many predictors of behaviour, focusing on a narrow definition of attitude towards behaviour. Today, the TRA and its later extension, the TPB, received overwhelming empirical support in literally thousands of studies (Ajzen, 2011). Several meta-analyses that reviewed correlational as well as experimental studies bear witness to their validity. In a meta-analytic review of 87 studies, Sheppard *et al.* (1988) found an overall multiple correlation of R = .66 for predicting behavioural intentions from attitudes and subjective norms, and a mean correlation between intention and behaviour of r = .53 (also see, Sutton, 1998). The idea that behaviour follows from formed intentions is further corroborated by an analysis of 47 experimental studies (Webb & Sheeran, 2006).

The theories have been successfully applied to predicting diverse behav-iours, ranging from strategy choices in laboratory games (Ajzen, 1971) over consumer behaviours like purchasing toothpaste (D. T. Wilson *et al.*, 1975) to personally significant decisions such as having an abortion (Smetana & Adler, 1980). Most of all, they became an integral part of health psychology. Several meta-analyses show that they are applicable to the prediction of health-related behaviours such as condom use (e.g. Albarracín *et al.*, 2001), donating blood (Pomazal & Jaccard, 1977), exercising (Hausenblas *et al.*, 1997) or attending screening programmes (Cooke & French, 2008). The TPB, for instance, proved to be successful for predicting health-related behaviours as is evident from a review of as many as 206 articles (McEachan *et al.*, 2011). Pessimism therefore seems unwarranted. Instead, the TPB – with attitudes being one of just three determinants – is one of the most powerful social psychological theories, building the scaffold for many eclectic models customised to specific content domains. With the latter being said, we want to add that the theory fares better in some domains than in others. For example, more variance can be explained in studies on physical activity than in studies on safer sex or drug use (McEachan *et al.*, 2011), One might speculate therefore, that it is better applicable to behaviours that are performed as a consequence of conscious deliberation. Attitude–behaviour theories that are more comprehensive by including explanations for spontaneous behaviour will be discussed in the next chapter.

CHAPTER SUMMARY

1   A major reason why attitudes are studied is the belief that they guide behaviour. But many early studies failed to provide evidence for a close link between attitudes and behaviour, leading some scholars to suggest abandoning the attitude construct altogether.

2   The attitude–behaviour relation is high if both concepts are measured at the same level of specificity (the correspondence principle). General attitude measures poorly predict single behaviours, but are good predictors of aggregate measures of behaviour (the aggregation principle).

3   Expectancy-value models – most notably, the theory of reasoned action and the theory of planned behaviour – conceptualised behavioural intentions as the major determinant of behaviour. Intentions are in turn thought to be influenced by attitudes towards the behaviour and subjective norms regarding the behaviour. Additional predictors have been suggested as well (e.g. perceived behavioural control, prior behaviour, affective beliefs). These models explain a substantial amount of variance in a range of deliberate and intentional behaviours.

Exercises

1   For which of the following attitudes and behaviours would you expect higher correlations and for which lower ones?

   Attitudes: (A1) Towards studying at university.
   (A2) Towards the specific course 'X'.

   Behaviours: (B1) Attending course X regularly.
   (B2) Attending course X on a given day.
   (B3) Attending all classes regularly.

2   What other variables have been found to influence behaviour besides attitudes?

Further reading

Behaviour prediction:

Ajzen, I. & Fishbein, M. (2005). The influence of attitudes on behavior. In D. Albarracín, B. T. Johnson & M. P. Zanna (eds), *The Handbook of Attitudes* (pp. 173–221). Mahwah, NJ: Erlbaum.

A review of the theory of planned behaviour:

Ajzen, I. (2012). The theory of planned behavior. In P. M. Van Lange, A. W. Kruglanski & E. Higgins (eds), *Handbook of Theories of Social Psychology* (Vol. 1, pp. 438–459). Thousand Oaks, CA: Sage Publications.

An application in health psychology:

Conner, M. & Norman, P. (2005). *Predicting Health Behaviour*. Maidenhead, UK: McGraw-Hill Education.

Note

1   Students attending our courses on attitudes sometimes complain about the mathematical nature of the model. To be clear, attitudes in the TRA do not require people to enter decimals in a calculator. Instead, the model has to be understood as an 'as-if-model' – that is, attitudes and subjective norms are composed as if people holding the attitudes multiplied subjective expectancies with subjective values.

Chapter 13

WHICH ATTITUDES PREDICT BEHAVIOUR AND WHY

In the previous chapter, you learned that attitudes do indeed serve as predictors of behaviours. However, you will remember that attitudes are not always reliable predictors, but that measurement aspects may moderate the attitude–behaviour correlation. If there was a mismatch between attitude and behaviour measure – for example, with respect to specificity – correlations may only be weak. As we showed in the previous chapter, much of the failure to predict behaviour from attitudes (alone) can be explained by weak measure correspondence. It is noteworthy that the correspondence principle, more broadly conceived, allows for many predictions beyond the measure itself. More generally speaking, attitudes and behaviour are more closely related if the aspects of the attitude that are highly accessible at the time of attitude measurement are also accessible at the time the behaviour is performed (Shavitt & Fazio, 1991; Tesser & Shaffer, 1990; Wilson & Dunn, 1986; Wilson et al., 1989). To test this hypothesis with respect to attitude functions, Shavitt and Fazio (1991) examined students' attitudes towards two brands of soft drink: 7-Up lemonade and Perrier mineral water. Pilot testing had shown that attitudes towards each drink typically served distinct functions. Perrier was liked mainly because of the trendy image it imparts (social image function), whereas 7-Up was liked foremost for its taste (utilitarian function; see Chapter 1). In their experiment, Shavitt and Fazio primed either image or taste before participants were asked to evaluate each drink: specifically, some participants judged the social impression that each of 20 behaviours would create, whereas others rated 20 food items for their taste. Later, all participants reported their attitudes towards both 7-Up and Perrier along with their intentions to buy each of these drinks. Shavitt and Fazio hypothesised that attitudes would more strongly predict behavioural intention if the primed attitude function matched rather than mismatched the function that is normally associated with the attitude object. As shown in Figure 13.1, the data supported this prediction. Students' intentions to purchase Perrier were more highly correlated with attitudes towards Perrier when they had thought about social impression rather than taste just prior to attitude measurement. By contrast, students'

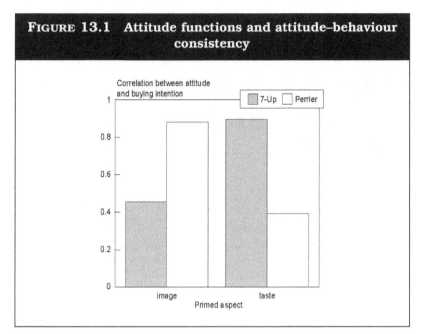

FIGURE 13.1   Attitude functions and attitude–behaviour consistency

Note: The matching of primed attitude aspects and object-bound attitude functions determines the magnitude of attitude–intention relations (data from Shavitt & Fazio, 1991)

intentions to buy 7-Up were more highly correlated with their attitudes towards 7-Up when they had previously thought about taste rather than social impression. Therefore, marketers should not only consider how to influence an attitude, but should also take the conditions at the point of sale into account. Creating a positive attitude which serves a symbolic function may not affect purchase if in the purchase situation more utilitarian attitudes prevail. To profit from the positive attitude, it might then be worthwhile to further activate thoughts about social situations.

Other findings suggest that thinking about the reasons *why one holds a certain attitude* can either increase or decrease the attitude–behaviour correlation (Wilson & Dunn, 1986; Wilson *et al.*, 1984; Wilson *et al.*, 1989). For example, in one study (Wilson *et al.*, 1984), dating partners were asked to evaluate their romantic relationship on a series of items assessing how happy their relationship was and how they felt about their future. Before doing so, however, participants in the experimental condition were asked to analyse the reasons and to explain why they felt positively or negatively about the relationship. About six months later, the authors asked participants whether they still dated their partners. In the control group, this behavioural measure was indeed correlated with the previously assessed attitudes. However, for participants who had provided reasoned attitude judgements, the attitudes did not predict the later relationship status. These results can also be understood as an instance of matching of attitude aspects. Given that thinking about *reasons* accentuates an attitude's cognitive aspects, it should elevate the attitude–behaviour correlation if mainly cognitive aspects are relevant at the time of performing the behaviour. Conversely, the attitude–behaviour association should be weakened by introspection about reasons if the behaviour is performed in a situation where the affective attitude component is most salient (see also Millar & Tesser, 1986). It is the love you feel and not a list of pros and cons that tells you that you want to spend your life with your partner.

Yet, as we will see throughout this chapter, there is more to say about the boundary conditions that allow attitudes to forecast behaviour. We will start this chapter by summarising some general aspects of the attitude – in particular, indicators of attitude strength – suggesting whether or not an attitude will guide behaviour. Focusing on the particular indicator of attitude accessibility, we will then revisit a model that you met in Chapter 6 (i.e. the MODE model; Fazio, 1995), in order to account for the influence of situational demands on attitude–behaviour relations.

STRONG ATTITUDES GUIDE BEHAVIOUR

As we saw in Chapter 1, research on attitude strength entailed the hypothesis that strong attitudes are better predictors of behaviour than weak attitudes (see Petty & Krosnick, 1995). From Chapters 1 and 10, you may remember that attitude strength is not only characterised by the attitude's consequences that researchers and practitioners want to predict. The various indicators of attitude strength also comprise antecedents of an attitude (i.e. how our attitudes have been formed), its representation (i.e. what and how quickly we may retrieve the attitudes) and some meta-attitudinal aspects (i.e. how we think and feel about our attitudes). Almost all of them have been shown to affect attitude–behaviour consistency (for meta-analytic reviews, see Cooke & Sheeran, 2004; Glasman & Albarracín, 2006; Kraus, 1995). Yet, as space does not permit discussion of all the indicators of attitude strength, we will focus on a subset of variables which are most directly related to the theoretical constructs we discussed in the chapters on persuasion (Chapter 8), balance (Chapter 7) and malleability (Chapter 6).

Cognitive effort in attitude formation

As we discussed in Chapter 8, the way in which attitudes are formed is at the core of dual-process models of persuasion (see Bohner *et al.*, 1995; Chaiken *et al.*, 1989; Petty & Cacioppo, 1986 a, b). According to these models, high motivation and ability foster the formation of attitudes through effortful processing of all potentially relevant detail information, whereas low motivation or low ability leads to lower processing effort and judgements based on simple rules. These different routes to attitude formation have been linked to different degrees of attitude–behaviour consistency. Within the ELM framework, Petty and Cacioppo (1986 a, b) proposed that attitudes that were formed via the central route should be more predictive of behaviour than attitudes formed via the peripheral route. In line with this hypothesis, various research findings have shown that the attitudes of people who processed under conditions of high personal relevance when forming their attitudes were more predictive of behaviour than those of people who processed under conditions of low relevance (Haugtvedt & Priester, 1997; Leippe & Elkin, 1987; Petty *et al.*, 1983; Shavitt & Brock, 1986; Sivacek & Crano, 1982).

This idea is complemented by research investigating attitude–behaviour consistency as a function of the *need for cognition* (Cacioppo & Petty, 1982; Cacioppo *et al.*, 1996). Because people high in need for cognition tend to engage in greater processing effort when forming an attitude, they should form stronger attitudes, which are relatively persistent, resistant to change and predictive of behaviour. In support of this view, Cacioppo *et al.* (1986) found that the degree to which students' attitudes towards US presidential candidates predicted their voting behaviour was a direct function of these students' need for cognition.

Attitude stability

As reported earlier, it is advisable to assess attitudes and behaviour in close temporal proximity, in order to obtain predictive attitude information (Ajzen & Fishbein, 1977). This makes perfect sense because the longer the interval between the attitude assessment and the observation of the behaviour, the more likely the attitude changes in between (Thurstone, 1931). Thus, stable attitudes, those that are reluctant to change, might be good predictors of behaviours, even if substantial time has elapsed between the attitude assessment and the behaviour observation. To test this assumption, Schwartz (1978) measured attitudinal stability as well as some attitude-relevant behaviours. More precisely, students responded to a plethora of items dealing with attitudes towards altruistic behaviours, one of which was assessing their attitudes towards helping blind people. The same questionnaire was administered three months later, to see whether their attitude had changed or was stable across the period. Accordingly, depending on the difference between altruistic attitudes in t1 and t2, attitudinal stability was classified as high, moderate or low. Then, another three months later, participants were asked whether they would be willing to tutor a programme for blind children. Attitudes towards caring for the blind as assessed three months before the behaviour significantly predicted the willingness to participate in the programme. Further, in support of the central hypothesis, attitude stability moderated the attitude–behaviour consistency – that is, the correlation was highest among students high in attitudinal stability. Among students holding moderately stable attitudes, the attitude–behaviour correlation was reduced, but still significant. In the group of students with the lowest attitude stability, however, attitudes did not predict the behaviour of interest.

To date, there is a large body of literature demonstrating the effect of attitudinal stability on attitude–behaviour correlations. While the construct of attitudinal stability is interesting on its own, it can be further applied to explain various other well-known moderators of the attitude–behaviour relation. For example, attitudinal ambivalence – another indicator of attitude strength – has yielded similar results (e.g. Jonas *et al.*, 2000) – that is, despite the same overall evaluation, ambivalently held attitudes are less predictive of behaviour than univalent attitudes. This can be explained by the retrieval phenomena we reported in Chapter 6 because ambivalent representations should yield intertemporally instable evaluations. Whenever a radio station airs a country song, a person who holds a univalent negative attitude towards country music will be likely to switch the station. However, for a person who holds an ambivalent attitude representation of country music, situational factors may activate either the more negative or the more positive associations. During a road trip, when the sun is setting, a person with mixed feelings towards country music may keep on listening and enjoy the song to the very end.

The notion of stability as the mediating construct between ambivalence and attitude–behaviour consistency is also suggested by a comparison of the behavioural consequences of one- and two-sided persuasion (Glasman & Albarracín, 2006). As reported in Chapter 10, two-sided persuasion may be efficient because sources that provide counterarguments appear more credible and trustworthy than sources that only present arguments in favour of the attitude object. However, two-sided messages may also create a more ambivalent representation of the attitude object. In line with this idea, Glasman and Albarracín (2006) found that two-sided (vs. one-sided) messages create less stable attitudes, which in turn decrease the attitudes' effect on corresponding behaviours.

In a similar vein, attitudes are less implicative of behaviour if there is incongruence between its affective and cognitive components, a phenomenon that has been termed evaluative–cognitive consistency (Chapter 7). Early work by Rosenberg (1968) showed that an attitude's high evaluative-cognitive consistency (ECC) is positively related to its temporal stability and resistance against persuasion attempts. Norman (1975) found support for the related hypothesis that ECC moderates the magnitude of the attitude–behaviour relation. In a series of studies, he assessed the ECC of students' attitudes towards volunteering for experiments. Several weeks later, the same students were asked to sign up for an experiment that did not provide any monetary reward or course credit. Norman found that across studies, attitudes of high ECC participants strongly predicted behaviour (with correlation coefficients between .47 and .62), whereas attitudes of low ECC participants did not reliably predict behaviour (*r*s between –.28 and .24).

To sum up, the stability of an attitude is a good predictor of the attitude–behaviour relation. The arguments listed above should have also clarified that the different aspects of attitude strength are likely to overlap with each other, and it is by the joint consideration of each of the pieces that a coherent picture of the attitude formation to attitude–behaviour process emerges. Thus, the moderating role of effortful elaboration about the object, internal consistency or stability across situations on attitude–behaviour correspondence may not necessarily reflect independent mechanisms. Instead, one might understand the process by considering that higher elaboration leads to more consistent attitude structures, which renders the attitude more stable. In a similar vein, reflection about an object and its evaluation may increase the attitude accessibility, which in turn predicts whether an attitude has the power to guide behaviour. Such processes are often accompanied by higher attitude certainty (see Chapters 1 and 10), which on its own can increase the attitude–behaviour relation (Tormala & Rucker, 2007): being certain that your favourite music band is the best in the world will ensure that you will buy their new album.

Attitude accessibility

The role of attitude accessibility as a moderator of the attitude–behaviour relation has been highlighted by Fazio (1986, 1990, 1995). Initial research on this approach addressed the role of direct experience with the attitude object. According to Regan and Fazio (1977), direct behavioural experience creates attitudes that are held with greater clarity, confidence and stability compared to attitudes formed via indirect information about the attitude object. Because of these attributes, experience-based attitudes are thought to be more accessible and, ultimately, to be more powerful determinants of future behaviour. These hypotheses were supported in numerous studies (for an overview, see Fazio & Zanna, 1981). In a field study conducted by Regan and Fazio (1977), first year students at Cornell University were asked for their attitudes towards alleviating a housing crisis and were then provided with the opportunity to engage in some related activities. Importantly, the study was conducted in a period when there was not enough student housing, so some students had to stay in temporary dormitories. In line with the authors' expectations, these students (who had direct experience) showed greater attitude–behaviour consistency in their attempts to alleviate the crisis than students who held similar attitudes but had no direct experience. In a related laboratory experiment, the same authors systematically varied the type of experience through which students formed attitudes to a number of intellectual puzzles: some students gained direct behavioural experience by working through examples of the puzzles, whereas others gained only indirect experience by looking at examples of puzzles that had already been solved. Later, when the students were free to play with any of the puzzles, attitudes towards each puzzle predicted playing behaviour more closely for students in the direct-experience condition than for those in the indirect-experience condition.

The central process that is assumed to mediate this effect is the attitude's accessibility, which is operationally defined as the speed with which an attitude can be expressed (Fazio, 1986). At the conceptual level, accessibility indicates the strength of association between the representation of the attitude object and its evaluation stored in memory. This evaluation can guide behaviour only if it is activated and a stronger associative link from the attitude object to its evaluation increases its likelihood of being activated. Fazio and others have shown that attitudes that are based on behavioural experience are indeed more accessible (e.g. Fazio *et al.*, 1982); furthermore, greater attitude accessibility goes along with greater attitude–behaviour consistency (e.g. Fazio & Williams, 1986). In addition to direct experience, repeated expression of an attitude has also been shown to increase its accessibility (Fazio *et al.*, 1982; Powell & Fazio, 1984). As an illustration of the spontaneous attitude–behaviour link proposed by Fazio, consider the results of a study by Fazio *et al.* (1989). These researchers asked participants to express their attitudes towards 100 familiar consumer products, using a computerised assessment that included reaction time measures. Later, participants could choose several of the products (e.g. a Snickers, a package of Sun-Maid Raisins) to take home. This behavioural measure was more highly correlated with the expressed attitude, the faster the attitude judgement had been given – i.e. the more accessible the attitude was. This shows that simply having an attitude may be insufficient for guiding behaviour; in order to determine behaviour, it is necessary that the attitude is accessible.

Another intriguing applied study looked at voting in political elections. Bassili (1993) asked several hundred respondents which party they would vote for in an up-coming election (voting intention) and also assessed the time it took them to answer this question and name their party (attitude accessibility). Moreover, respondents were asked whether their decision was final or open to change (attitude certainty). The respondents were called back after the election and asked which party they had actually voted for, which permitted an analysis of the effects of attitude certainty and accessibility on whether prior voting intention and actual voting corresponded. The speed with which respondents could name their intended party as well as whether they thought their decision was final co-occurred with a higher likelihood of voting in line with the voting intention. Regression analysis actually revealed that attitude accessibility was a better predictor of participants' actual votes than attitude certainty.

The moderating role of attitude accessibility on attitude–behaviour consistency has received substantial support (for reviews, see Cooke & Sheeran, 2004; Kraus, 1995). Yet, high accessibility of an attitude alone does not seem to guarantee high attitude–behaviour consistency. Instead, attitude accessibility may interact with conditions present in the situation in which the behaviour could potentially be shown. In some situations, individuals may actively control for attitudinal influence on behaviours, an issue with which we deal next.

ATTITUDES AND THE PREDICTION OF UNINTENDED BEHAVIOURS

To account both for situations that are characterised by conscious deliberation and for those in which people act relatively spontaneously, researchers came up with dual-process and dual-system models. In these models, attitudes towards objects (rather than attitudes towards behaviour as in TRA or TPB) are back at centre stage as antecedents of behaviour.

One exemplar of such a dual-process model is the MODE model (Motivation and Opportunity as DEterminants model; Fazio, 1990, 2007; Fazio & Towles-Schwen, 1999; Olson & Fazio, 2008; Figure 13.2; also see Chapter 6), which we introduced in detail in Chapter 6. As for dual-system models, the most prominent exemplar focusing on the attitude–behaviour relation is the Reflective–Impulsive Model (RIM, Strack & Deutsch, 2004, 2014; Box 13.1).

Both models converge regarding the moderators of attitude–behaviour consistency. And both predict that controlled behaviour requires higher order processing. Whereas the RIM is more explicit regarding the cognitive processes, the MODE model is more parsimonious and therefore easier to

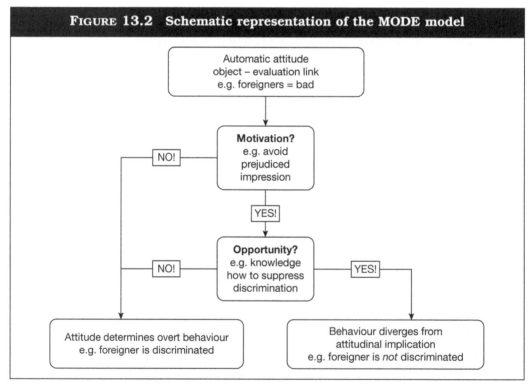

FIGURE 13.2   Schematic representation of the MODE model

Note: In the MODE model (Fazio, 1990), it is proposed that automatically accessible attitudes cause spontaneous behaviour. However, a person may adjust to situational demands if she/he is motivated (e.g., make a positive impression on others) and has the opportunity to do so (e.g., knows how to modify the behaviour). Graph is adapted from Olson & Fazio, 2009

Box 13.1 From moderators to cognitive processes

Whereas the MODE model can accommodate a wide range of findings on the attitude–behaviour relationship, it is rather mute about the cognitive processes involved, in either spontaneous or deliberative behaviour. A prominent model that has even found its way into the applied fields is the Reflective-Impulsive Model by Strack and Deutsch (2004, 2014). It distinguishes between two separable systems, which follow different rules. The lower order impulsive system relies on associative activation, an assumption that built the basis for the later Associative-Propositional Evaluation Model (APE; Gawronski & Bodenhausen, 2006, see Chapter 7). For example, a hamburger activates a 'delicious' response if that is what is most closely related in an associative network for a particular person. The impulsive system then may even trigger experiential aspects such as the smell or the taste of the burger. Crucially, the impulsive system automatically motivates an approach (or, in the case of negative associations, avoidance) reaction. Complementing the activation of the associated responses, you would go for the burger, take it and eat it (see Strack *et al.*, 2006).

In addition to the impulsive system, a higher order reflective system is able to categorise the attitude object and to consider knowledge about it. Just as in the APE Model, this system processes the relations between different concepts (i.e. propositions, Chapters 5 and 7). It is by this process that attitude objects can be clustered into categories, which in turn will provide further knowledge about the object. In our example, the reflective system may yield that this delicious object is, after all, a burger and burgers are known to be unhealthy and fattening.

An interesting notion is that only the reflective system can represent the future. It is by this system that we imagine and order events in time. The reflective system is thus responsible for higher goals and for overcoming habits. And it is only this system that is able to *form an intention* of how to behave towards the object. Mechanisms such as the ones described in the TRA or the TPB, therefore, would require that the reflective system is active.

Whether this will be the case is a question of available cognitive resources. Whereas the impulsive system is fast and requires little cognitive resources, the slower reflective system depends on resources. Just as the lower order heuristic process in the Heuristic-Systematic Model (Chapter 8), the impulsive system will always operate. Only if cognitive resources are rather unconstrained by external factors (e.g. time pressure, distraction), the reflective system will kick in. If so, it can potentially reverse the behavioural implications. Hence, this system has the potential to control the input by the impulsive system at different stages of the attitude–behaviour process. For example, you may feel the impulse to have a burger, but by categorising it as an unhealthy high-calorie food, it conflicts with your goal of losing weight. It is this goal that motivates the behaviour of not eating the burger, and you may decide to resist the temptation but form the intention to eat something healthier and ultimately choose a salad instead. Crucially, this involves several steps, and the behavioural implication from the impulsive system may compete at different stages (Hofmann *et al.*, 2009). Even if you had already thought of the burger as unhealthy junk food, when at the diner, talking to your friends could distract you again. Then, impulses win over again and make you go for the bacon cheese burger.

As you may have noted, in the description of the RIM, we did not use the word 'attitude'. This reflects the road attitude research has taken: From models that tried to predict attitudes over models that used attitudes as antecedences, to ultimately a newer class of models that is no longer explicit about what an attitude is, but concentrates on the qualitatively distinct cognitive processes that contribute to our summary evaluations (see Table 13.1 on p. 252). However, it also shows that the ideas accumulated in the history of attitude research still have their place in this research – that is, motivation and capacity as focal variables prevailed since the 1980s. Nevertheless, different models conceive differently of motivation and capacity, and their respective roles. Whereas dual-process models of persuasion refer to the motivation and capacity to process information, the MODE model concentrates on the motivation and capacity to show a certain behaviour. Finally, in the RIM, processing capacity is the determinant of the motivation to show a certain behaviour – an impulsive behaviour or an intended one which is based on goals and decisions.[1]

comprehend. Given that you are already familiar with the MODE model, we will use this model to review some of the literature demonstrating the impact of motivation and opportunity on the attitude–behaviour relation.

To start with, remember that the MODE model predicts that if there is neither motivation nor opportunity, attitudes are thought to directly activate behaviour. According to the model, this should be true mainly for highly accessible attitudes. Thus, merely encountering or considering an attitude object may trigger a behavioural response of approach or avoidance, depending on the valence of the attitude. The phenomenon of selective attention and some of the effects of attitudes on information search that we discussed in Chapter 11 may be subsumed under this class of attitude–behaviour processes. No deliberate reflection or reasoning about the appropriate course of action seems to be involved here; the individual may not even be aware that he is attending more closely to attitude-congruent information or criticising attitude-discrepant material. Fazio's concept of the automatic effects of attitudes on behaviour is consistent with accumulating evidence showing that social behaviour may be profoundly affected by unconscious influences (for an overview, see Bargh, 2007).

The spontaneous process of accessible attitudes to behavioural response can be contrasted with a more deliberate process in which more detailed evidence about possible behavioural alternatives is carefully evaluated, leading to a conscious intention to act. The theory of reasoned action (Fishbein & Ajzen, 1975) and the theory of planned behaviour (Ajzen, 1991) exemplify this type of processing. As this more deliberate process requires motivation and opportunity, it is assumed to depend on various external variables such as time, resources and cognitive capacity.

Sanbonmatsu and Fazio (1990) empirically examined the moderating role of motivation and opportunity. Their research participants received information about two department stores. One, 'Brown's', was described as rather good overall but as having a poor camera department; the other, 'Smith's', was portrayed quite negatively overall, but the description of its camera department was positive. Later, participants were asked to decide in which of the two stores they would buy a camera. If these decisions were based on the overall attitudes towards the stores, Brown's should have been chosen more frequently; however, if participants recalled and processed the specific attributes of each store instead, Smith's should have been chosen more often. The conditions under which participants made their decisions were varied in a 2 × 2 design, involving both motivation and opportunity to deliberate. High accuracy motivation was induced by telling participants that they would have to explain their decisions, whereas in the low motivation condition, no such instructions were given. Opportunity was varied by introducing high versus low degrees of time pressure.

Sanbonmatsu and Fazio (1990) found that participants who were both highly motivated and did not experience time pressure were more likely to make an attribute-based decision (choosing Smith's) than participants in any other condition. These findings support the MODE model: if either opportunity or motivation to deliberate was lacking, overall attitudes seemed to guide behaviour; but if both motivation and opportunity were present, behavioural decisions were guided by more effortful processing of relevant detail information. Similar conclusions can be drawn from studies in which accessibility had been induced experimentally (e.g. Schuette & Fazio, 1995). In recent decades, the majority of studies to test the model's predictions was based on measures to assess the automatic attitudes (i.e. the implicit measures).

Predicting behaviour from implicit and explicit attitude measures

Please recall that Fazio postulates that some objects are so strongly tied to an evaluative response that upon an encounter, they yield an automatic, inevitable evaluative response (Fazio, 2007; Olson & Fazio, 2009). The IAT and the evaluative priming paradigm are thought to best reveal this response, because these measures leave little opportunity to alter the behavioural response according to situational demands (cf. Chapter 6). In this sense, the model predicts that implicit measures allow for better predictions of spontaneous, unintended behaviours than explicit measures because the latter may reflect motivational aspects. For instance, high accuracy motivation may cause the person to consider additional inform-ation, or high affiliation motivation may cause the person to express a desirable response. With the latter being said, the predictions have been studied extensively in domains in which social norms suggest that certain behaviours are inappropriate (e.g. racial discrimination).

Subtle prejudice and discrimination

A prime example for such a domain of behaviours is the discrimination of minority- or out-group members (cf. Dovidio *et al.*, 2009): social norms

TABLE 13.1 Dual-Process and Dual-System Models in Attitude Research

Model	Lower order process/system	Higher order process/system	Interplay between modes	Role of implicit measures	Central role of attitude	Predicted outcomes
Elaboration-Likelihood Model (Petty & Cacioppo, 1986b)	*Peripheral route* Cues determine relatively weak attitudes by various simple processes	*Central route* Quality of information determines relatively strong attitudes	Antagonistic	–	Outcome	Attitudes; attitude strength
Heuristic-systematic model (Chaiken et al., 1989)	*Heuristic processes* Cues determine attitudes according to simple rules-of-thumb	*Systematic processes* Switch off or modify the implication of the heuristic process, depending on information quality	Hierarchical	–	Outcome	Attitudes
Unimodel (Kruglanski & Thompson, 1999)	*Single process* High effort increases the extensity of information processing, but is not qualitatively distinct from low-effort processing	–	–	–	Outcome	Attitudes

Motivation-and-Opportunity-as-Determinants Model (Fazio, 1990)	*Automatic attitudes* Stored, highly accessible object-evaluation links instigate (evaluation) behaviour	*Ad hoc evaluation* Information in the given context alters the behaviour if opposing the attitudinal implication	Hierarchical	Reveal automatically accessible attitude	Antecedent	Behaviour
Reflective–Impulsive Model (Strack & Deutsch, 2004)	*Impulsive system* Associations and automatic approach-avoidance tendencies instigate behaviour	*Reflective system* Facts, knowledge and goals alter the behaviour if their implications oppose the impulsive implication	Hierarchical	Reveal outcome of impulsive system	Not explicitly defined	Behaviour
Associative-Propositional Evaluation Model (Gawronski & Bodenhausen, 2006)	*Associative processes* Spontaneous affective reactions guided by the principle of spreading activation determines the evaluation	*Propositional Processes* Facts, knowledge and goals alter the evaluation if they invalidate the outcome of the associative process	Hierarchical	Reveal outcome of associative process	Not explicitly defined	Evaluation

Note. Table 13.1 summarises models in attitude research building on the central assumption that the effects of an input on an outcome are moderated by motivation and capacity. In the ELM, the resulting processing modes are antagonistic. In hierarchical models, lower order processes always take place. Capacity-consuming higher order processes (or systems) can kick in and can correct for the input obtained from the lower order mode. In most models, the higher order process has the final say on the outcome. In some models (e.g. the RIM), the outcome is determined by the system with the stronger behavioural implication. In more recent models, the conception of an attitude has become less explicit, but the focus is on cognitive processes (for a biological perspective, see Cunningham & Zelazo, 2007; for a possible synthesis of the MODE and the APE model, see Petty *et al.*, 2007) typically hold that one should not disadvantage persons due to their ethnicity or race, a norm that is even established in many countries' laws. The necessity of establishing anti-discrimination laws, however, already indicates that discrimination does exist. Whether or not such laws may actually fulfil their goals, however, partly depends on how much individuals are actually able to control these behaviours. As proposed by social psychologists (e.g. Dovidio & Gaertner, 2004; Gaertner & Dovidio, 1986), prejudice may often be rather subtle, and people may sometimes even be unaware of their racial bias and discrimination it causes. Thus, people may not necessarily engage in overt offence towards minority group members, but discrimination might be evident in some spontaneous non-verbal behaviour, such as avoiding eye contact. Accordingly, researchers have investigated the predictive validity of implicit attitude measures on non-verbal discrimination. In line with the MODE model perspective, white participants' eye contact with a black relative to a white experimenter was correlated with implicit attitudes towards black people as assessed via a priming measure, but it was not correlated with an explicit rating on a prejudice scale (Dovidio *et al.*, 1997; for related results using an IAT, see McConnell & Leibold, 2001). Whereas the meaning of subtle discrimination may appear harmless at first glance, it is not. Targets of subtle, non-verbal discrimination show typical reactions of threat and its associated consequences including cognitive impairment (e.g. Murphy *et al.*, 2013; Richeson & Shelton, 2003; Shelton *et al.*, 2006), which demonstrates the importance of attitude models that incorporate the prediction of unintended behaviours.

The incremental validity of the implicit measures in predicting racial discrimination, however, has been debated. Whereas an initial meta-analysis led to the conclusion that IAT scores outperform explicit measures in predicting interracial interactions (Greenwald *et al.*, 2009), a later meta-analysis led to a different conclusion (Oswald *et al.*, 2013): the IAT was not a better predictor than explicit measures. Moreover, across studies dealing with non-verbal behaviours in inter-racial interactions, the IAT was not a reliable predictor. Yet, the variance of the effects across samples was substantial, therefore suggesting that procedural conditions had moderated the effects. From the perspective of the MODE model, it appears particularly plausible to consider variation in the motivation and the opportunity to control non-verbal discrimination. And indeed, experimental studies suggest that these factors are promising candidates for explaining variability across studies (e.g. Dasgupta & Rivera, 2006; Hofmann *et al.*, 2008).

Hofmann *et al.* (2008), for example, studied inter-racial interactions in an interview situation. Italian students were initially administered a race IAT. Then, in an ostensibly unrelated experiment, the same students were asked to take the position of the candidate in an interview that served as a training exercise for interviewers from the sociology department. In total, they met two interviewers, one was Italian and one was African. Crucially, the authors also sought to vary participants' opportunity to voluntarily modify the behaviour. Building on an assumption shared by the MODE model and the RIM, they argued that resources to exert control over one's behaviour would be reduced if individuals were busy with a cognitively demanding task. Thus, half of their participants received a list of words and were asked to memorise as many as possible, but the other half of participants did not. In full support of the authors' predictions, the manipulation, which aimed to vary available cognitive resources, moderated the effects of the IAT on non-verbal behaviours. The IAT scores only predicted visual contact towards the African experimenter among participants who had to allocate resources to the memory task. The findings therefore attest to the role of opportunity to take control over one's behaviour as a moderator of the effects of implicit attitudes on non-verbal behaviours,[2] shedding further light on the controversial findings in this domain. In this sense, the variability of effects across previous studies on non-verbal discrimination may be partially explained by unintended variations of participants' available cognitive resources.

Do we need implicit measures?

Similar conclusions about the moderating role of cognitive resources on the predictive value of the implicit measures can be drawn from other studies, using different resource manipulations and considering behaviours other than discrimination. For example, in one experiment (Hofmann & Friese, 2008), participants' attitudes towards certain candies were measured using an adapted version of the IAT. All participants then had an orange juice, but depending on the condition the juice was pure or contained a considerable amount of vodka. After working on some filler tasks, participants were asked to taste sweets, whereby grammes of consumed sweets served as the dependent measure. The result was that the sweet consumption was not only higher among participants who had had the vodka than it was among their sober counterparts. Crucially, and in line with the idea that alcohol reduces control resources, implicit measures predicted sweet consumption only in the vodka condition. In the control condition, however, consumption correlated with an explicit measure of restrained eating (see also Hofmann *et al.*, 2007). Similar effects were obtained in a study in which resources were varied using a cogni-tively demanding task (for related findings using a different manipulation of cognitive resources, see Hofmann *et al.*, 2007). In a similar vein, Friese *et al.* (2008) found that scores from a chocolate (vs. fruit) IAT were a better predictor for choosing chocolate over fruit when participants were put under high rather than low cognitive load. Explicit attitudes, however, were a better predictor in the low rather than the high load condition. Complementing the crucial role of capacity in moderating the predictive value of implicit and explicit measures, similar findings have been obtained for variations of time pressure (Friese *et al.*, 2006)[3] or depletion of cognitive resources (Friese *et al.*, 2008).

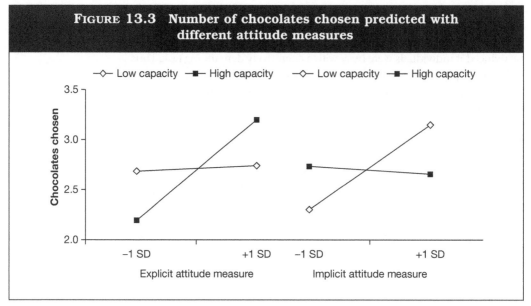

FIGURE 13.3   **Number of chocolates chosen predicted with different attitude measures**

Note: Different attitude measures (implicit vs. explicit) show different correlations with the behaviour, depending on the capacity manipulation (low vs. high). The x-axis denotes attitude scores one standard deviation (SD) above and below the mean. (Data from Friese *et al.*, 2008)

Thus, implicit measures were better predictors of behaviour when participants had to act quickly or when participants were exhausted due to preceding cognitive activities compared to when cognitive capacity was high whereas explicit measures were better predictors when capacity was high compared to low (for a review of the predictive validity of implicit measures in the consumer domain, see Friese *et al.*, 2009; for a review of the predictive validity in political elections, see Gawronski *et al.*, 2015).

Thus, highly accessible attitudes towards an object often directly and automatically influence our behaviour. Importantly, in situations where the accuracy of behavioural decisions is important and our capacity to deliberate is relatively unconstrained, more controlled processing may override the effect of automatic attitude activation. Subsequently, more detailed considerations of the attitude object, and also other relevant information (e.g. normative pressures) comes into play, reducing the magnitude of the relation between automatically accessible attitudes and behaviour. In that case, explicit ratings often do better in predicting the behaviour. The crucial implication is that the explicit measures – despite higher reactivity – should not simply be replaced by less economic implicit measures (cf. Chapter 3). Instead, they seem to do better if the conditions during behaviour assessment match the conditions when the evaluation has been assessed: concretely, explicit ratings will be good predictors if external factors affecting the individual's motivation and ability to show a certain behaviour are stable across situations. As such, much of the double dissociation of implicit vs. explicit measures in predicting spontaneous versus controlled behaviourscan be reframed in terms of the correspondence principle we dealt with in the previous chapter. If the conditions for assessing an attitude and for showing the respective behaviour are alike, the attitude–behaviour correlation should increase. Nevertheless, models including the distinction between spontaneous and deliberative processes (e.g. Fazio, 2007; Fazio & Towles-Schwenn, 1999; Strack & Deutsch, 2004, 2014) fleshed out the abstract idea of the correspondence principle and pointed to the important conditions that have to be met for both the assessment of attitude and behaviour. In this way, they have strongly enriched the understanding of how to predict behaviours from attitudes.

CONCLUDING COMMENT: TRUE LOVE AND BEHAVIOUR

In this last chapter, we stressed, once more, that not all attitudes are equal. Therefore, they are not all alike when guiding behaviour. In particular, strong attitudes can be considered good predictors of behaviour. One reason for this is that strong attitudes are characterised by high accessibility. The most accessible attitudes are even able to guide unintended behaviours. It can be regarded as part of the attitudes' adaptive nature, that in situations in which people are unable to reflect on how to behave, they instigate approach or avoidance. That being said, this chapter also highlighted reasons to study and use the implicit measures. Independent of whether these measures reveal stored object-evaluation links (cf. Olson & Fazio, 2003) or associative processes (cf. Gawronski & Bodenhausen, 2006; Strack & Deutsch, 2004), their predictive validity has been shown in several empirical demonstrations. Whereas they may not have an incremental value per se, they might be better when predicting behaviours occurring in the absence of executive control (for reviews, see Friese *et al.*, 2008; Perugini *et al.*, 2010). Another reason is that strong attitudes are predictive of behaviour due to their high stability and internal consistency. In this vein, they are less likely to vary across situations, therefore triggering the same behavioural response across different situations.

Finally, implicit measures have been shown to be more predictive if they yield the same or a similar outcome than the explicit measures (Perugini, 2005; Greenwald *et al.*, 2009). If your immediate response towards your partner is positive and upon reflection you still say that you love your partner, whom else would you marry?

CHAPTER SUMMARY

1   The correspondence principle is not limited to methodological issues. Understanding attitude–behaviour consistency involves integrating attitude functions and the situational factors present when the behaviour is performed.

2   Stronger attitudes are better predictors of behaviours than weak ones. This can partially be explained by their heightened stability and accessibility.

3   The MODE model expands the scope of attitude–behaviour relations by integrating two processes by which attitudes can guide behaviour: the deliberate formation of intentions, which requires both motivation and opportunity, and the immediate activation of behaviour through highly accessible attitudes, which may operate without intention or awareness. Motivation may include the subjective norms as conceived of in the TRA and opportunity may include behavioural control. Yet motivation and opportunity are moderators of the attitude–behaviour link but do not contribute independently.

4   From the perspective of the reflective-impulsive model (RIM), the impulsive system is fast and requires little resources. This system is the major driving force behind evaluations in the implicit measures as well as spontaneous behaviours shown when resources are scarce (e.g. after depletion). The reflective system requires more resources. It is at work when evaluating explicitly, it is able to represent goals and to form behavioural intentions.

5   At the methodological level, implicit measures tend to be better predictors of spontaneous rather than deliberative behaviour. Instead, intended behaviours are better predicted from explicit measures.

Exercises

1   Name a few variables that moderate the attitude–behaviour link and explain why they do so.

2   Advertisers and campaigners who aim at changing recipients' behaviour attempt to influence the favourability of attitudes. Explain why they should also try to influence the attitude's accessibility. How could they achieve this?

3. According to the MODE model, when would attitudes affect spontaneous behaviour and when would they affect well-considered behaviour?

Further reading

A review of the MODE model:

Olson, M. A. & Fazio, R. H. (2009). Implicit and explicit measures of attitudes: The perspective of the MODE model. In R. E. Petty, R. H. Fazio & P. Briñol (eds), *Attitudes: Insights from the New Implicit Measures* (pp. 19–63). New York: Psychology Press.

A review of the reflective-impulsive model:

Strack, F. & Deutsch, R. (2014). The reflective impulsive model. In J. W. Sherman, B. Gawronski & Y. Trope (eds), *Dual-Process Theories of the Social Mind* (pp. 92–104). New York: Guilford Press.

For a controversial empirical debate on predicting behaviours from the IAT:

Greenwald, A. G., Poehlman, T., Uhlmann, E. & Banaji, M. R. (2009). Understanding and using the implicit association test: III. Meta-analysis of predictive validity. *Journal of Personality and Social Psychology*, *97*(1), 17–41.

Oswald, F. L., Mitchell, G., Blanton, H., Jaccard, J. & Tetlock, P. E. (2013). Predicting ethnic and racial discrimination: a meta-analysis of IAT criterion studies. *Journal of Personality and Social Psychology*, *105*(2), 171–192.

Notes

1   Implicitly, motivation is also a determinant of whether the reflected system becomes active. According to the RIM, the activation of the reflective system requires an appropriate level of arousal. If arousal was too high, capacity might become constrained and the reflective system would break down. This implies a curve-linear relation between motivation and system activity. If motivation becomes too high, only the impulsive system will take command.

2   Here, the focus is on hard to control involuntary non-verbal behaviours. For various intended and reflected non-verbal behaviours, explicit attitudes should constitute valid predictors according to the models treated above.

3   This effect of time pressure was not obtained for participants high in implicit–explicit consistency.

EPILOGUE

You have reached the end of the book, and hopefully you had some inspiring, sometimes even joyful moments while reading it. We hope that a picture emerged and there are some ideas you will take home.

As you have learned, people do not hold attitudes for their own sake, but attitudes are helping tools that organise your everyday life, including your social relations. Though not easy to measure, attitudes can be measured. It's by the careful construction and application of both classic survey standards as well as sophisticated indirect measures that you can get insights in how people evaluate what they encounter in their lives. These attitudes do not come out of thin air. Besides a biological basis, attitudes are shaped in the course of life, elicited by co-occurring events and objects, transmitted via affective and bodily sensations, transformed by the thoughts you have about the object and the attitudes themselves. They are also affected by others, sometimes on purpose. Whether or not you are trying to resist this change, the final attitudes are influential and affect your thoughts as well as your behaviour. We think that the research reviewed in this book makes strong evidence for all of the points listed above.

However, from time to time it might have been difficult to form a clear picture and to reach definite conclusions. Perhaps, you then experienced some kind of an 'Ouch, that's tough!' We truly sympathise with you, and agree that sometimes the matter is complex and often there was not just one answer. Does evaluative conditioning require awareness? When do implicit and explicit attitudes converge? Are low- and high-effort modes of persuasion antagonistic or do they interact? Moreover, although providing you with the basic definition of attitudes as summary evaluations, we left it up to you to form your personal opinion of what an attitude is. Is an attitude the stable part of your evaluations or do you conceive attitudes as the evaluation at a given point in time? However, ambiguity and open questions drive our discipline by demanding better models and more conclusive research. And debate and controversy is what science is all about.

With that being said, although you have reached the end of the book you did not reach the end of what there is to say about the formation, manipulation and consequences of our attitudes. We therefore encourage you to follow up on whatever puzzled you, to cultivate your critical thoughts and to creatively develop new ideas so that eventually you may perhaps even contribute to what it is going to be the future of attitude research.

Glossary

Accessibility: The ease with which information (e.g. an attitude) comes to mind.

Aggregation principle: Global attitudes are better predictors of aggregated behavioural measures than of any specific behaviours.

Ambivalence: Holding conflicting feelings or beliefs towards one object.

Assimilation: Evaluation of a stimulus is shifted towards the valence of a context stimulus.

Associative link: Type of link between concepts in a semantic network. The activation of one concept (e.g. news anchor) leads to an activation of another (e.g. war), depending on how strong the associative link is.

Associative-Propositional Evaluation Model (APE): Dual-process model to explain implicit–explicit consistency. Different from explicit measures, implicit measures are (mostly) unaffected by propositional processes. Under specifiable conditions, associative processes and propositional processes result in different evaluations. If so, the correspondence between implicit and explicit measures is reduced.

Attitude: Summary evaluation of an object of thought.

Attitude certainty: Meta-attitudinal experience, referring to the confidence with which an attitude is held.

Attitude function: The purpose that holding an attitude serves for an individual.

Attitude object: This can be anything a person discriminates or holds in mind – e.g. things, persons, groups or abstract ideas.

Attitude strength: Reflects the intensity of an individual's feelings or beliefs as manifested in attitude extremity, accessibility, certainty and other indicators.

Attitude structure: Representation and organisation of different attitudes (inter-attitudinal structure) or of components belonging to one attitude (intra-attitudinal structure) in memory.

Attitudes-as-constructions perspective: A theoretical orientation positing that individuals construct evaluative judgements on the basis of chronically and temporally accessible information.

Attribution theory: A conceptual framework that deals with people's explanations of behaviour and events.

Balance theory: A cognitive consistency theory proposed by Heider, according to which individuals strive for consistency among the relations between cognitive elements (representations of self, others and objects).

Basking in reflected glory (BIRG): Identification with successful others, serving a positive self-evaluation.

Biased assimilation Tendency to interpret arguments as supportive of the own position.

Bogus pipeline technique: A procedure designed to reduce motivated response distortions in direct attitude measurement. The respondent is hooked up to fake psychophysiological machinery, which purportedly gives the experimenter access to the respondent's true attitudes.

Chronic versus temporary accessibility: The ease with which information comes to mind due to situational factors (temporary) or factors independent of the specific situation (chronic).

Classical conditioning: If the presence of a conditioned stimulus (e.g. a bell) covaries with the presence of an unconditioned stimulus (e.g. food), the presence of the conditioned stimulus alone will be sufficient to elicit the unconditioned response (e.g. salivation).

Cognitive response approach: Theoretical orientation in persuasion research that conceives of attitude change as mediated by an individual's evaluative thoughts about a message or issue.

Cognitive schema: A cognitive structure representing an individual's knowledge (including evaluative beliefs) about an object, person, group, situation or event. Schemata are abstractions containing attributes and relationships among attributes of the object.

Congeniality bias (*also* confirmation bias): Tendency to seek information that provides support to one's attitude.

Construal Level Theory: A theory stating that mental representations become more abstract with increasing psychological distance.

Contrast: Evaluation of a stimulus is shifted in a direction opposite to the valence of a context stimulus.

Conversion Theory: Conversion theory holds that positions that diverge from the majority cause attention and may cause individuals to analyze the minority's arguments. As a consequence attitude conversion may occur.

Co-occurrence hypotheses: A set of assumptions in the Heuristic-Systematic Model about the interplay of its processing modes.

Correspondence principle: Attitudes best predict behaviour when both are measured at the same level of specificity.

Cronbach's alpha: A popular coefficient of reliability based on the intercorrelations of items.

Defence motive: People are intrinsically motivated to keep their attitudes, an assumption made in prominent dual-process models of persuasion (e.g. the Heuristic-Systematic Model).

Demand characteristics: Cues in a research setting that participants may use to infer how they are expected to respond or behave.

Descriptive norm: Norm oriented on frequency of occurrence (e.g. is the attitude endorsed by the majority?).

Direct measuring techniques: Respondents are asked to evaluate the attitude object. It is assumed that attitudes can be retrieved via introspection.

Dual process models of persuasion: Theories of persuasion that postulate two modes of information processing which differ in the extent to which individuals engage in effortful thought about message arguments and other specific information on an attitude object. The mode of information processing is assumed to depend on motivation and ability.

Ease-of-retrieval effect: The more easily information comes to mind subjectively, the higher is its impact on the judgement.

Effort-justification hypothesis: The assumption that people often come to like what they had to suffer for as a result of reducing the dissonance caused by high effort invested and low attractiveness of the outcome.

Elaboration likelihood model: Comprehensive theory positing that attitude change is mediated by two modes of information processing: central-route processing and peripheral-route processing. Elaboration denotes the extent to which an individual engages in central-route processing of issue-relevant arguments rather than being influenced by processes that characterise the peripheral route to persuasion (e.g. heuristic processing). Elaboration likelihood is determined by motivation and ability.

Electroencephalography (EEG): A technique recording fluctuations in electric activity on the scalp. Fluctuations occur if respondents observe an object that differs in valence from previously shown objects.

Electromyography: A technique recording the contraction of facial muscles. Activity of the zygomatic muscles is considered an indicator of a positive evaluation; activity of the corrugator muscles is considered an indicator of a negative evaluation.

Error-choice method: A disguised attitude measure based on forced-choice questions that ostensibly measure knowledge but are in fact designed to infer respondents' attitudes.

Evaluative conditioning: Attitude change towards an object due to paired exposure with a valenced stimulus.

Evaluative priming: An attitude measure exploiting priming logic. An attitude object will facilitate the evaluation of stimuli that share the same valence, but slow down the evaluation of stimuli with a different valence.

Evolutionary psychology: Approach that conceives of human behaviour as adapted mechanisms which improve – or at one point in evolution improved – selective fitness.

Expectancy-value principle: A feature of various theories in motivation and attitude–behaviour research. It says that an individual assesses the desirability of an object (or course of action) by considering the sum of its features (or expected outcomes) weighted by their subjective probability.

File-drawer model: A theoretical perspective that characterises attitudes as enduring concepts which are stored in the memory and retrieved when needed for object evaluation.

Functional magnetic resonance imaging (fMRI): Technique to visualise activity in different brain areas. Certain areas (e.g. the amygdala) are involved when processing valenced information.

Functional matching hypothesis: Persuasive attempts are considered more effective if they adjust to the prime attitude function of the object and/or the target person.

Heritability factor: Expresses which proportion of the variance of a phenotype in a population is due to genetic variance in the population.

Heuristic: Simple rule that is used to form an (attitude) judgement with little cognitive effort (e.g. 'the majority is right' or 'experts' statements are valid').

Heuristic-Systematic Model: A dual-process model of persuasion, positing that attitude change can be mediated by two modes of information processing – namely, heuristic and systematic processing. When individuals are unmotivated or unable to invest much cognitive effort, they are likely to rely on heuristics in forming an attitude judgement; when motivation and ability are high, they also scrutinise message arguments and all other potentially relevant information to form a judgement.

Hostile media phenomenon: Tendency to view media as biasing information, away from one's position.

Implicit association test (IAT): A response-time based method designed to assess attitudes. It measures the differential association of two target concepts (e.g. 'blacks' versus 'whites') with positive versus negative evaluations (e.g. 'pleasant words' versus 'unpleasant words').

Implicit attitude measures: Summary evaluations expressed without deliberation.

Impression management: Actions aiming at being positively viewed by others (e.g. by acting consistent with one's attitudes; by uttering desirable attitudes).

Indirect measuring techniques: Measurements exploiting that attitudes can be inferred from behaviours other than the evaluation of the attitude object.

Induced compliance: A research paradigm used in testing cognitive dissonance theory. Research participants are subtly induced to perform a counterattitudinal behaviour in order to create dissonant cognitions.

Informational social influence: Following others because one believes their responses are valid and correct.

Injunctive norm: Norm oriented on a theoretical ideal (e.g. is it morally desirable to hold a certain attitude?).

Inoculation effect: Metaphorical term describing that resistance to persuasion is increased when, prior to a persuasion attempt, other counterattitudinal arguments have been successfully refuted.

Inoculation Theory: Theory stating that exposures to smaller doses of counter-attitudinal information strengthen the attitude, thereby inoculate against subsequent counter-attitudinal persuasion attempts.

Knowledge function: An attitude's function of providing structure for organising and handling an otherwise complex and ambiguous environment.

Likert Scale: A multi-item attitude scale that consists of several evaluative statements about an object or issue. Respondents are asked to express their degree of agreement with each statement along a numerical response scale.

Linguistic intergroup bias: Speakers tend to use more abstract terms to describe a prejudiced out-group. In this sense, language abstractness can be used as an indicator of negative attitudes towards groups.

Lost-letter technique: A behavioural measure of attitude that involves leaving addressed letters in public places as if they had been lost, and then recording the return rate and condition of the returned letters. The attitude object studied is reflected in the address printed on the letter.

Mere exposure effect: Increase in liking for an object caused by merely being exposed (repeatedly) to that object.

Mere thought effect: Polarisation of an attitude caused by merely thinking about the issue without acquiring external information.

Message-learning approach: Conceptual framework for studying persuasion, focusing on source, message, channel and recipient as elements of the persuasion process and on the learning of message content as the primary mediator of attitude change.

MODE model: Model on attitude-behaviour relations. It states that automatic attitudes guide behaviour as long as people want and can behave different from the attitudinal implication.

Mood-as-information hypothesis: When evaluating an attitude object, people's current mood informs them on how they feel about it. This information is used for the attitude, unless people are aware of the real mood source.

Need for cognition (NFC): An individual difference variable reflecting the extent to which a person enjoys and engages in thoughtful processing.

Normative social influence: Following others because one seeks their approval.

Overjustification effect: A decrease in intrinsic motivation caused by external rewards.

Persuasion knowledge: Beliefs about others' motives and tactics within a persuasion episode.

Post-decisional dissonance: Unpleasant state of inconsistency in beliefs arising after an individual has taken a decision, brought about by negative aspects of the chosen alternative and positive aspects of non-chosen alternatives.

Priming: Increasing the accessibility of a particular concept by activating it prior to a processing task or judgement.

Projective techniques: Family of indirect measures of attitude (and other constructs) that involve the presentation of unstructured or ambiguous material and an assessment of how individuals interpret this material.

Propositional link: Type of link between concepts in a semantic network. Propositional links consist of how a concept is semantically related to another and can be probed for their truth.

Proprioceptive feedback: Information that stems from an individual's perception of her own movements, muscle contractions or body posture.

Question order effect: The response to a question is influenced by the questions asked previously if they bring to mind relevant information that would not have been accessible otherwise.

Random error: Chance variations in measurement; a threat to reliability.

Reactivity: A change in response (e.g. a reported attitude) brought about by the mere fact that a measurement is taken.

Reliability: The extent to which a measure assesses a construct consistently.

Schema. See 'cognitive schema'.

Self-affirmation theory: A theory whose main assumption is that threats to the integrity of a person's self-concept (such as engaging in counterattitudinal behaviour) instigate a motivation to reaffirm the self.

Self-monitoring: An individual difference variable. High self-monitors adjust their behaviour to fit situational cues and the expectations of others, whereas low self-monitors act more in accordance with their internal states and dispositions.

Self-perception theory: Theory whose core assumption is that individuals infer their own attitudes by observing their own behaviour in context, just as they would do with other people.

Self-validation hypothesis: Positive (negative) persuasion variables validate or invalidate one's thoughts about a persuasive message.

Semantic differential: A multi-item attitude measure consisting of several bipolar adjective scales.

Single-item measure: An attitude measure consisting of a single question or statement.

Sleeper effect: Phenomenon which describes that a persuasive effect unfolds over time.

Subliminal exposure: Very brief exposure below the threshold necessary for consciously encoding a stimulus, which may nonetheless affect subsequent responses.

Symbolic function: Class of attitude functions that are related to the hedonic consequences of expressing a particular attitude (e.g. self-esteem maintenance).

Systematic error: The extent to which a measurement is consistently influenced by constructs other than the one that is intended to be measured; a threat to construct validity.

Terror management theory: An approach whose central claim is that humans' knowing about their mortality has the potential of creating fear or terror, which people cope with by emphasising their being part of a greater 'immortal' cultural group. Among other things, this may result in prejudice against members of other groups.

Theory of cognitive dissonance: A cognitive consistency theory proposed by Festinger (1957). It posts that people who hold incongruent cognitions experience dissonance (= unpleasant arousal) and subsequently strive to reduce dissonance. This is done by changing one or more cognitions – for example, attitudes.

Theory of planned behaviour (TPB): An extension of the theory of reasoned action. In addition to attitudes and subjective norms, perceived behavioural control is included as a predictor of behavioural intention and behaviour.

Theory of Psychological Reactance: Approach whose core assumption is that individuals are motivated to restore restricted freedom by enhancing the value of 'forbidden' or otherwise blocked objects or behavioural alternatives.

Theory of reasoned action (TRA): A model whose core assumption is that attitudes towards a given behaviour in combination with subjective norms influence the intention to perform that behaviour, which in turn influences behaviour.

Third-person-effect: People consider themselves less susceptible to persuasion than others.

Tripartite model: The assumption that affective, cognitive and behavioural responses are independent elements of an attitude.

Two-sided persuasion: Persuasive attempt that contains both pro- and counterarguments.

Unobtrusive technique: Measure of an attitudinal response whereby the 'respondent' is unaware that t he attitudinal response is being recorded.

Utilitarian function: An attitude's function of maximising rewards and minimising punishment.

Validity: The extent to which a measure assesses the construct it is supposed to assess.

REFERENCES

Abelson, R. P. (1968). *Theories of Cognitive Consistency: A Sourcebook*. Chicago, IL: Rand-McNally.

Abelson, R. P. (1988). Conviction. *American Psychologist, 43,* 267–275.

Abraham, C. & Sheeran, P. (2003). Acting on intentions: The role of anticipated regret. *British Journal of Social Psychology, 42,* 495–511.

Ajzen, I. (1971). Attitudinal vs. normative messages: An investigation of the differential effects of persuasive communications on behavior. *Sociometry, 34,* 263–280.

Ajzen, I. (1991). The theory of planned behavior. *Organizational Behavior and Human Decision Processes, 50,* 179–211.

Ajzen, I. (2011). The theory of planned behaviour: Reactions and reflections. *Psychology & Health, 26,* 1113–1127.

Ajzen, I. (2012). The theory of planned behavior. In P. M. Van Lange, A. W. Kruglanski & E. T. Higgins (eds), *Handbook of Theories of Social Psychology* (Vol. 1, pp. 438–459). Thousand Oaks, CA: Sage Publications.

Ajzen, I. & Fishbein, M. (1970). The prediction of behavior from attitudinal and normative variables. *Journal of Experimental Social Psychology, 6,* 466–487.

Ajzen, I. & Fishbein, M. (1977). Attitude–behaviour relations: A theoretical analysis and review of empirical research. *Psychological Bulletin, 84,* 888–918.

Ajzen, I. & Madden, T. J. (1986). Prediction of goal-directed behavior: Attitudes, intentions, and perceived behavioral control. *Journal of Experimental Social Psychology, 22,* 453–474.

Ajzen, I. & Sheikh, S. (2013). Action versus inaction: Anticipated affect in the theory of planned behavior. *Journal of Applied Social Psychology, 43,* 155–162.

Albarracín, D. (2002). Cognition in persuasion: An analysis of information processing in response to persuasive communications. In M. P. Zanna (ed.), *Advances in Experimental Social Psychology* (Vol. 34, pp. 61–130). San Diego, CA: Academic Press.

Albarracín, D., Johnson, B. T., Fishbein, M. & Muellerleile, P. A. (2001). Theories of reasoned action and planned behavior as models of condom use: A meta-analysis. *Psychological Bulletin, 127,* 142–161.

Albarracín, D. & Wyer, R. S. Jr. (2000). The cognitive impact of past behavior: Influences on beliefs, attitudes, and future behavioral decisions. *Journal of Personality and Social Psychology, 79*, 5–22.

Albarracín, D., Zanna, M. P., Johnson, B. T. & Kumkale, G. (2005). Attitudes: Introduction and scope. In D. Albarracín, B. T. Johnson, M. P. Zanna (eds), *The Handbook of Attitudes* (pp. 3–19). Mahwah, NJ: Lawrence Erlbaum Associates.

Allport, G. W. (1935). Attitudes. In C. Murchison (ed.), *Handbook of Social Psychology* (Vol. 2, pp. 798–844). Worcester, MA: Clark University Press.

Allport, G. W. (1942). The use of personal documents in psychological science. *Social Science Research Council Bulletin, 49*.

Altemeyer, B. (1998). The other 'authoritarian personality'. *Advances in Experimental Social Psychology, 30*, 47–91.

Alter, A. L. & Oppenheimer, D. M. (2006). Predicting short-term stock fluctuations by using processing fluency. *Proceedings of the National Academy of Sciences, 103*, 9369–9372.

Alwin, D. F., Cohen, R. L. & Newcomb, T. M. (1991). *Political Attitudes over the Life Span: The Bennington Women after Fifty Years*. Madison, WI: University of Wisconsin Press.

Anderson, J. R. (1983). A spreading activation theory of memory. *Journal of Verbal Learning and Verbal Behavior, 22*, 261–295.

Anderson, J. R. & Bower, G. H. (1972). Recognition and retrieval processes in free recall. *Psychological Review, 79*(2), 97–123.

Anderson, J. R. & Bower, G. H. (1973). *Human Associative Memory*. Washington, DC: Winston.

Anderson, J. R. & Bower, G. H. (1974). A propositional theory of recognition memory. *Memory & Cognition, 2*, 406–412.

Anderson, N. H. (1971). Integration theory and attitude change. *Psychological Review, 78*(3), 171–206.

Appel, M. & Richter, T. (2007). Persuasive effects of fictional narratives increase over time. *Media Psychology, 10*, 113–134.

Apsler, R. & Sears, D. O. (1968). Warning, personal involvement, and attitude change. *Journal of Personality and Social Psychology, 9*, 162–166.

Areni, C. S. & Lutz, R. J. (1988). The role of argument quality in the elaboration likelihood model. *Advances in Consumer Research, 15*, 197–203.

Armitage, C. J. & Conner, M. (1999). The theory of planned behaviour: Assessment of predictive validity and 'perceived control'. *British Journal of Social Psychology, 38*, 35–54.

Armitage, C. J. & Conner, M. (2001). Efficacy of the theory of planned behaviour: A meta-analytic review. *British Journal of Social Psychology, 40*(4), 471–499.

Aronson, E. (1968). Dissonance theory: Progress and problems. In R. P. Abelson, E. Aronson, W. J. McGuire, T. M. Newcomb, M. J. Rosenberg & P. H. Tannenbaum (eds), *Theories of Cognitive Consistency: A Sourcebook* (pp. 5–27). Chicago, IL: Rand-McNally.

Aronson, E. & Mills, J. (1959). The effect of severity of initiation on liking for a group. *Journal of Abnormal and Social Psychology, 59*, 177–181.

Aronson, E., Ellsworth, P. C., Carlsmith, J. M. & Gonzales, M. H. (1990). *Methods of Research in Social Psychology*. New York: McGraw-Hill.

Arpan, L. M. & Raney, A. A. (2003). An experimental investigation of news source and the hostile media effect. *Journalism & Mass Communication Quarterly*, *80*, 265–281.

Asch, S. E. (1951). Effects of group pressure upon the modification and distortion of judgments. In H. Guetzkow (ed.), *Groups, Leadership and Me: Research in Human Relations* (pp. 177–190). Oxford: Carnegie Press.

Asendorpf, J. B., Banse, R. & Mücke, D. (2002). Double dissociation between implicit and explicit personality self-concept: The case of shy behavior. *Journal of Personality and Social Psychology*, *83*, 380–393.

Associated Press (2012). *Racial Attitudes Survey*. Retrieved from: http://surveys.ap.org/data%5CGfK%5CAP_Racial_Attitudes_Topline_091820 12.pdf. Accessed: 7 January 2016.

Axsom, D. (1989). Cognitive dissonance and behavior change in psychotherapy. *Journal of Experimental Social Psychology*, *25*, 234–252.

Axsom, D. & Cooper, J. (1985). Cognitive dissonance and psychotherapy: The role of effort justification in inducing weight loss. *Journal of Experimental Social Psychology*, *21*, 149–160.

Axsom, D., Yates, S. & Chaiken, S. (1987). Audience response as a heuristic cue in persuasion. *Journal of Personality and Social Psychology*, *53*, 30–40.

Baeyens, F., Eelen, P. & van den Bergh, O. (1990). Contingency awareness in evaluative conditioning: A case for unaware affective evaluative learning. *Cognition and Emotion*, *4*, 3–18.

Baeyens, F., Hermans, D. & Eelen, P. (1993). The role of CS–US contingency in human evaluative conditioning. *Behaviour Research and Therapy*, *31*, 731–737.

Baeyens, F., Crombez, G., Van den Bergh, O. & Eelen, P. (1988). Once in contact always in contact: Evaluative conditioning is resistant to extinction. *Advances in Behaviour Research and Therapy*, *10* (4), 179–199.

Baeyens, F., Eelen, P., Crombez, G. & Van den Bergh, O. (1992). Human evaluative conditioning: Acquisition trials, presentation schedule, evaluative style and contingency awareness. *Behaviour Research and Therapy*, *30*, 133–142.

Baeyens, F., Eelen, P., van den Bergh, O. & Crombez, G. (1989). Acquired affective-evaluative value: Conservative but not unchangeable. *Behaviour Research and Therapy*, *27*, 279–287.

Baeyens, F., Eelen, P., Van den Bergh, O. & Crombez, G. (1992). The content of learning in human evaluative conditioning: Acquired valence is sensitive to US-revaluation. *Learning and Motivation*, *23*, 200–224.

Bagozzi, R. P. (1992). The self-regulation of attitudes, intentions, and behavior. *Social Psychology Quarterly*, *55*, 178–204.

Bagozzi, R. P., Wong, N., Abe, S. & Bergami, M. (2000). Cultural and situational contingencies and the theory of reasoned action: Application to fast food restaurant consumption. *Journal of Consumer Psychology*, *9*, 97–106.

Bakker, A. B. (1999). Persuasive communication about AIDS prevention: Need for cognition determines the impact of message format. *AIDS Education and Prevention, 11*, 150–162.

Banas, J. A. & Rains, S. A. (2010). A meta-analysis of research on inoculation theory. *Communication Monographs, 77*, 281–311.

Bandura, A. (1962). Social learning through imitation. In M. R. Jones (ed.), *Nebraska Symposium on Motivation* (pp. 211–269). Lincoln, NE: University of Nebraska Press.

Bandura, A. (1977). Self-efficacy: Toward a unifying theory of behavioral change. *Psychological Review, 84*, 191–215.

Banse, R. (1999). Automatic evaluation of self and significant others: Affective priming in close relationships. *Journal of Social and Personal Relationships, 16*, 803–821.

Banse, R., Schmidt, A. F. & Clarbour, J. (2010). Indirect measures of sexual interest in child sex offenders: A multimethod approach. *Criminal Justice and Behavior, 37*(3), 319–335.

Bar-Anan, Y. & Nosek, B. A. (2012). Reporting intentional rating of the primes predicts priming effects in the affective misattribution procedure. *Personality and Social Psychology Bulletin, 38*, 1194–1208.

Bar-Anan, Y. & Nosek, B. A. (2013). Misattribution of claims: Comment on Payne *et al.*, 2013. Retrieved from Open Science Framework, osf.io/sk5hr. Accessed 7 January 2016.

Barden, J. & Tormala, Z. L. (2014). Elaboration and attitude strength: The new meta-cognitive perspective. *Social and Personality Psychology Compass, 8*, 17–29.

Bargh, J. A. (1994). The four horsemen of automaticity: Awareness, intention, efficiency, and control in social cognition. In R. J. Wyer & T. K. Srull (eds), *Handbook of Social Cognition, Vol. 1: Basic Processes; Vol. 2: Applications* (2nd edn) (pp. 1–40). Hillsdale, NJ: Lawrence Erlbaum Associates.

Bargh, J. A. (2007). *Social Psychology and the Unconscious: The Automaticity of Higher Mental Processes*. New York: Psychology Press.

Bargh, J. A., Chaiken, S., Govender, R. & Pratto, F. (1992). The generality of the automatic attitude activation effect. *Journal of Personality and Social Psychology, 62*, 893–912.

Bargh, J. A., Chaiken, S., Raymond, P. & Hymes, C. (1996). The automatic evaluation effect: Unconditional automatic attitude activation with a pronunciation task. *Journal of Experimental Social Psychology, 32*, 104–128.

Baron, R. A. (1993). Interviewers' mood and evaluations of job applicants: The role of applicant qualifications. *Journal of Applied Social Psychology, 23*, 253–271.

Bartlett, F. C. (1932). *Remembering: An Experimental and Social Study*. Cambridge: Cambridge University Press.

Bartlett, F. C. (1995). *Remembering: A Study in Experimental and Social Psychology*. Cambridge: Cambridge University Press.

Bassili, J. N. (1993). Response latency versus certainty as indexes of the strength of voting intentions in a CATI survey. *Public Opinion Quarterly, 57*(1), 54–61.

Bassili, J. N. (1996). Meta-judgmental versus operative indexes of psychological attributes: The case of measures of attitude strength. *Journal of Personality and Social Psychology, 71*, 637–653.

Bassili, J. N. (2008). Attitude strength. In W. D. Crano & R. Prislin (eds), *Attitudes and Attitude Change* (pp. 237–260). New York: Psychology Press.

Bélanger-Gravel, A., Godin, G. & Amireault, S. (2013). A meta-analytic review of the effect of implementation intentions on physical activity. *Health Psychology Review, 7*(1), 23–54.

Bem, D. J. (1972). Self-perception theory. *Advances in Experimental Social Psychology, 6*, 1–62.

Bentler, P. M. & Speckart, G. (1979). Models of attitude–behaviour relations. *Psychological Review, 86*, 452–464.

Berntson, G. G., Bechara, A., Damasio, H., Tranel, D. & Cacioppo, J. T. (2007). Amygdala contribution to selective dimensions of emotion. *Social Cognitive and Affective Neuroscience, 2*(2), 123–129.

Berntson, G. G., Norman, G. J., Bechara, A., Bruss, J., Tranel, D. & Cacioppo, J. T. (2011). The insula and evaluative processes. *Psychological Science, 22*(1), 80–86.

Blaney, P. H. (1986). Affect and memory: A review. *Psychological Bulletin, 99*, 229–246.

Blascovich, J., Ernst, J. M., Tomaka, J., Kelsey, R. M., Salomon, K. L. & Fazio, R. H. (1993). Attitude accessibility as a moderator of autonomic reactivity during decision making. *Journal of Personality and Social Psychology, 64*, 165–176.

Bless, H., Bohner, G., Schwarz, N. & Strack, F. (1990). Mood and persuasion: A cognitive response analysis. *Personality and Social Psychology Bulletin, 16*, 331–345.

Bless, H. & Fiedler, K. (2006). Mood and the regulation of information processing and behavior. In J. P. Forgas (ed.), *Affect in Social Thinking and Behavior* (pp. 65–84). New York: Psychology Press.

Bless, H., Fiedler, K. & Strack, F. (2004). *Social Cognition: How Individuals Construct Social Reality*. Philadelphia, PA: Psychology Press.

Bless, H. & Schwarz, N. (2010). Mental construal and the emergence of assimilation and contrast effects: The inclusion/exclusion model. In M. P. Zanna (ed.), *Advances in Experimental Social Psychology* (Vol. 42, pp. 319–373). San Diego, CA: Academic Press.

Bless, H. & Wänke, M. (2000). Can the same information be typical and atypical? How perceived typicality moderates assimilation and contrast in evaluative judgments. *Personality and Social Psychology Bulletin, 26*, 306–315.

Bless, H., Wänke, M., Bohner, G., Fellhauer, R. & Schwarz, N. (1994). Need for cognition: Eine Skala zur Erfassung von Engagement und Freude bei Denkaufgaben. *Zeitschrift für Sozialpsychologie, 25*, 147–154.

Bluemke, M. & Friese, M. (2006). Do features of stimuli IAT effects? *Journal of Experimental Social Psychology, 42*(2), 163–176.

Bluemke, M. & Friese, M. (2008). Reliability and validity of the Single-Target IAT (ST-IAT): Assessing automatic affect towards multiple attitude objects. *European Journal of Social Psychology, 38*, 977–997.

Bodenhausen, G. V., Schwarz, N., Bless, H. & Wänke, M. (1995). Effects of atypical exemplars on racial beliefs: Enlightened racism or generalized appraisals? *Journal of Experimental Social Psychology, 31*, 48–63.

Bodenhausen, G. V. & Wyer, R. S. (1987). Social cognition and social reality: Information acquisition and use in the laboratory and the real world. In H. J. Hippler, N. Schwarz & S. Sudman (eds), *Social Information Processing and Survey Methodology* (pp. 6–41). New York: Springer.

Bohner, G. & Dickel, N. (2011). Attitudes and attitude change. *Annual Review of Psychology, 62*, 391–417.

Bohner, G., Einwiller, S., Erb, H. & Siebler, F. (2003). When small means comfortable: Relations between product attributes in two-sided advertising. *Journal of Consumer Psychology, 13*, 454–463.

Bohner, G., Frank, E. & Erb, H.-P. (1998). Heuristic processing of distinctiveness information in minority and majority influence. *European Journal of Social Psychology, 28*, 855–860.

Bohner, G., Moskowitz, G. & Chaiken, S. (1995). The interplay of heuristic and systematic processing of social information. *European Review of Social Psychology, 6*, 33–68.

Bohner, G., Ruder, M. & Erb, H. (2002). When expertise backfires: Contrast and assimilation effects in persuasion. *British Journal of Social Psychology, 41*, 495–519.

Bohner, G. & Schwartz, N. (2001). Attitudes, persuasion, and behaviour. In A. Tesser & N. Schwartz (eds), *Blackwell Handbook of Social Psychology: Individual Differences* (pp. 413–435). Oxford: Blackwell.

Bohner, G. & Wänke, M. (2002). Psychological gender mediates sex differences in jealousy. *Journal of Cultural and Evolutionary Psychology, 2*, 213–229.

Bornstein, R. F. (1989). Exposure and affect: Overview and meta-analysis of research, 1968–1987. *Psychological Bulletin, 106*, 265–289.

Bornstein, R. F. & D'Agostino, P. R. (1992). Stimulus recognition and the mere exposure effect. *Journal of Personality and Social Psychology, 63*, 545–552.

Bornstein, R. F. & D'Agostino, P. R. (1994). The attribution and discounting of perceptual fluency: Preliminary tests of a perceptual fluency/attribution model of the mere exposure effect. *Social Cognition, 12*, 113–128.

Bouchard, T. J., Jr. & McGue, M. (2003). Genetic and environmental influences on human psychological differences. *Journal of Neurobiology, 54*, 4–45.

Boush, D. M., Friestad, M. & Rose, G. M. (1994). Adolescent skepticism toward TV advertising and knowledge of advertiser tactics. *Journal of Consumer Research, 21*(1), 165–175.

Bower, G. (1981). Mood and memory. *American Psychologist, 36,* 129–148.

Brehm, J. W. (1956). Post-decision changes in desirability of alternatives. *Journal of Abnormal and Social Psychology, 52,* 384–389.

Brehm, J. W. (1966). *A Theory of Psychological Reactance.* New York: Academic Press.

Brendl, C. M., Markman, A. B. & Messner, C. (2003). The devaluation effect: Activating a need devalues unrelated objects. *Journal of Consumer Research, 29,* 463–473.

Brewer, M. (2003). *Intergroup Relations.* Buckingham, UK: Open University Press.

Briñol, P. & Petty, R. E. (2003). Overt head movements and persuasion: A self-validation analysis. *Journal of Personality and Social Psychology, 84,* 1123–1139.

Briñol, P. & Petty, R. E. (2009). Persuasion: Insights from the self-validation hypothesis. In M. P. Zanna (ed.), *Advances in Experimental Social Psychology* (Vol. 41, pp. 69–118). San Diego, CA: Elsevier Academic Press.

Briñol, P. & Petty, R. E. (2012). A history of attitudes and persuasion research. In A. W. Kruglanski & W. Stroebe (eds), *Handbook of the History of Social Psychology* (pp. 283–320). New York: Psychology Press.

Briñol, P., Petty, R. E. & Barden, J. (2007). Happiness versus sadness as a determinant of thought confidence in persuasion: A self-validation analysis. *Journal of Personality and Social Psychology, 93,* 711–727.

Briñol, P., Petty, R. E. & Tormala, Z. L. (2004). Self-validation of cognitive responses to advertisements. *Journal of Consumer Research, 30,* 559–573.

Briñol, P., Petty, R. E., Valle, C., Rucker, D. D. & Becerra, A. (2007). The effects of message recipients' power before and after persuasion: A self-validation analysis. *Journal of Personality and Social Psychology, 93,* 1040–1053.

Brock, T. C. (1967). Communication discrepancy and intent to persuade as determinants of counterargument production. *Journal of Experimental Social Psychology, 3,* 269–309.

Brown, R. (1974). Further comment on the risky shift. *American Psychologist, 29*(6), 468¬–470.

Brock, T. C. & Grant, L. D. (1963). Dissonance, awareness, and motivation. *The Journal of Abnormal and Social Psychology, 67,* 53–60.

Brown, J. D., Novick, N. J., Lord, K. A. & Richards, J. M. (1992). When Gulliver travels: Social context, psychological closeness, and self-appraisals. *Journal of Personality and Social Psychology, 62,* 717–727.

Bruner, J. S. (1957). On perceptual readiness. *Psychological Review, 64,* 123–152.

Brunner, T. A. & Wänke, M. (2006). The reduced and enhanced impact of shared features on individual brand evaluations. *Journal of Consumer Psychology, 16,* 101–111.

Buss, D. M. (2007). The evolution of human mating. *Acta Psychologica Sinica, 39*(3), 502–512.

Buss, D. M. & Schmitt, D. P. (1993). Sexual Strategies Theory: An evolutionary perspective on human mating. *Psychological Review, 100*(2), 204–232.

Butter, E. J., Popovich, P. M., Stackhouse, R. H. & Garner, R. K. (1981). Discrimination of television programs and commercials by preschool children. *Journal of Advertising Research, 21*, 53–56.

Byrne, D. (1971). *The Attraction Paradigm.* New York: Academic Press.

Cabanac, M. (1971). Physiological role of pleasure. *Science, 173* (4002), 1103–1107.

Cacioppo, J. T., Harkins, S. G. & Petty, R. E. (1981). The nature of attitudes and cognitive responses and their relationships to behavior. In R. Petty, T. Ostrom & T. Brock (eds), *Cognitive Responses in Persuasion* (pp. 31–54). Hillsdale, NJ: Erlbaum.

Cacioppo, J. T. & Petty, R. E. (1982). The need for cognition. *Journal of Personality and Social Psychology, 42*, 116–131.

Cacioppo, J. T., Petty, R. E., Feinstein, J. A. & Jarvis, W. B. G. (1996). Dispositional differences in cognitive motivation: The life and times of individuals varying in need for cognition. *Psychological Bulletin, 119*, 197–253.

Cacioppo, J. T., Petty, R. E., Kao, C. F. & Rodriguez, R. (1986). Central and peripheral routes to persuasion: An individual difference perspective. *Journal of Personality and Social Psychology, 51*, 1032–1043.

Cacioppo, J. T., Petty, R. E., Losch, M. E. & Kim, H. S. (1986). Electromyographic activity over facial muscle regions can differentiate the valence and intensity of affective reactions. *Journal of Personality and Social Psychology, 50*(2), 260–268.

Cacioppo, J. T., Petty, R. E. & Morris, K. J. (1983). Effects of need for cognition on message evaluation, recall, and persuasion. *Journal of Personality and Social Psychology, 45*, 805–818.

Cacioppo, J. T., Priester, J. R. & Berntson, G. G. (1993). Rudimentary determinants of attitudes: II. Arm flexion and extension have differential effects on attitudes. *Journal of Personality and Social Psychology, 65*, 5–17.

Campbell, M. C. & Kirmani, A. (2000). Consumers' use of persuasion knowledge: The effects of accessibility and cognitive capacity on perceptions of an influence agent. *Journal of Consumer Research, 27*, 69–83.

Canon, L. K. (1964). Self-confidence and selective exposure to information. In L. Festinger (ed.), *Conflict, Decision, and Dissonance* (pp. 83–96). Stanford, CA: Stanford Univerity Press.

Carlson, H. M. & Sutton, M. S. (1974). The development of attitudes as a function of police roles. *Personality and Social Psychology Bulletin, 1*, 113–115.

Carney, D. R., Jost, J. T., Gosling, S. D. & Potter, J. (2008). The secret lives of liberals and conservatives: Personality profiles, interaction styles, and the things they leave behind. *Political Psychology, 29*, 807–840.

Carver, C. S., Lawrence, J. W. & Scheier, M. F. (1996). A control-process perspective on the origins of affect. In L. L. Martin & A. Tesser (eds),

Striving and Feeling: Interactions Between Goals and Affect (pp. 11–52). Hillsdale, NJ: Erlbaum.

Cesarini, D., Dawes, C. T., Johannesson, M., Lichtenstein, P. & Wallace, B. (2009). Genetic variation in preferences for giving and risk taking. *Quarterly Journal of Economics, 124,* 809–842.

Cesario, J., Grant, H. & Higgins, E. T. (2004). Regulatory fit and persuasion: Transfer from 'feeling right'. *Journal of Personality and Social Psychology, 86,* 388–404.

Cesario, J., Higgins, E. T. & Scholer, A. A. (2008). Regulatory fit and persuasion: Basic principles and remaining questions. *Social and Personality Psychology Compass, 2,* 444–463.

Chaiken, S. (1979). Communicator physical attractiveness and persuasion. *Journal of Personality and Social Psychology, 37,* 1387–1397.

Chaiken, S. (1987). The heuristic model of persuasion. In M. P. Zanna, J. M. Olson & C. P. Herman (eds), *Social Influence: The Ontario Symposium* (Vol. 5, pp. 3–39). Hillsdale, NJ: Erlbaum.

Chaiken, S. & Eagly, A. H. (1983). Communication modality as a determinant of persuasion: The role of communicator salience. *Journal of Personality and Social Psychology, 45,* 241–256.

Chaiken, S., Giner-Sorolla, R. & Chen, S. (1996). Beyond accuracy: Defense and impression motives in heuristic and systematic processing. In P. M. Gollwitzer & J. A. Bargh (eds), *The Psychology of Action: Linking Cognition and Motivation to Behavior* (pp. 553–578). New York: Guilford.

Chaiken, S. & Ledgerwood, A. (2012). A theory of heuristic and systematic information processing. In P. A. M. Van Lange, A. W. Kruglanski & E. T. Higgins (eds), *Handbook of Theories of Social Psychology* (Vol. 1, pp. 246–266). Thousand Oaks, CA: Sage.

Chaiken, S., Liberman, A. & Eagly, A. H. (1989). Heuristic and systematic information processing within and beyond the persuasion context. In J. S. Uleman & J. A. Bargh (eds), *Unintended Thought* (pp. 212–252). New York: Guilford.

Chaiken, S. & Maheswaran, D. (1994). Heuristic processing can bias systematic processing: Effects of source credibility, argument ambiguity, and task importance on attitude judgment. *Journal of Personality and Social Psychology, 66,* 460–473.

Chaiken, S. & Trope, Y. (eds). (1999). *Dual-Process Theories in Social Psychology.* New York: Guilford.

Chaiken, S., Wood, W. & Eagly, A. H. (1996). Principles of persuasion. In E. T. Higgins & A. W. Kruglanski (eds), *Social Psychology: Handbook of Basic Principles* (pp. 702–742). New York: Guilford.

Chaiken, S. & Yates, S. (1985). Affective-cognitive consistency and thought-induced attitude polarization. *Journal of Personality and Social Psychology, 49,* 1470–1481.

Chaiken, S., Liberman, A. & Eagly, A. H. (1989). Heuristic and systematic information processing within and beyond the persuasion context. In J. S. Uleman & J. A. Bargh (eds), *Unintended Thought* (pp. 212–252). New York: Guilford.

Chambers, J. R., Baron, R. S. & Inman, M. L. (2006). Misperceptions in intergroup conflict: Disagreeing about what we disagree about. *Psychological Science, 17,* 38–45.

Chen, S. & Chaiken, S. (1999). The Heuristic-Systematic Model in its broader context. In S. Chaiken & Y. Trope (eds), *Dual-Process Theories in Social Psychology* (pp. 73–96). New York: Guilford.

Chen, X., Wang, Y., Liu, L., Cui, J., Gan, M., Shum, D. K., & Chan, R. K. (2015). The effect of implementation intention on prospective memory: A systematic and meta-analytic review. *Psychiatry Research, 226*(1), 14–22.

Christakis, N. A. & Fowler, J. H. (2010). *Connected: The Amazing Power of Social Networks and How They Shape Our Lives.* London: HarperPress.

Cialdini, R. B. (1993). *Influence: The Psychology of Persuasion* (rev. edn). New York: Quill/William Morrow.

Cialdini, R. B., Borden, R. J., Thorne, A., Walker, M. R., Freeman, S. & Sloan, L. R. (1976). Basking in reflected glory: Three (football) field studies. *Journal of Personality and Social Psychology, 34*(3), 366–375.

Cialdini, R. B., Kallgren, C. A. & Reno, R. R. (1991). A focus theory of normative conduct: A theoretical refinement and reevaluation of the role of norms in human behavior. In M. P. Zanna (ed.), *Advances in Experimental Social Psychology* (Vol. 24, pp. 201–234). New York: Academic Press.

Cialdini, R. B., Reno, R. R. & Kallgren, C. A. (1990). A focus theory of normative conduct: Recycling the concept of norms to reduce littering in public places. *Journal of Personality and Social Psychology, 58,* 1015–1026.

Clark, H. H. & Schober, M. F. (1992). Asking questions and influencing answers. In J. M. Tanur (ed.), *Questions about Questions: Inquiries into the Cognitive Bases of Surveys* (pp. 15–48). New York: Russell Sage Foundation.

Clark, J. K., Wegener, D. T. & Fabrigar, L. R. (2008). Attitudinal ambivalence and message-based persuasion: Motivated processing of proattitudinal information and avoidance of counterattitudinal information. *Personality and Social Psychology Bulletin, 34,* 565–577.

Clore, G. L., Schwarz, N. & Conway, M. (1994). Affective causes and consequences of social information processing. In R. S. Wyer & T. K. Srull (eds), *Handbook of Social Cognition* (2nd edn, Vol. 1, pp. 323–417). Hillsdale, NJ: Erlbaum.

Cohen, A.-L. & Gollwitzer, P. M. (2008). The cost of remembering to remember: Cognitive load and implementation intentions influence ongoing task performance. In M. Kliegl, M. A. McDaniel & G. O. Einstein (eds), *Prospective Memory: Cognitive, Neuroscience, Developmental, and Applied Perspectives* (pp. 367–390). Mahwah, NJ: Erlbaum.

Cohen, A. R. & Zimbardo, P. G. (1962). An experiment on avoidance motivation. In J. W. Brehm & A. R. Cohen (eds), *Explorations in Cognitive Dissonance* (pp. 143–151). New York: Wiley.

Cohen, G. L., Aronson, J. & Steele, C. M. (2000). When beliefs yield to evidence: Reducing biased evaluation by affirming the self. *Personality and Social Psychology Bulletin, 26,* 1151–1164.

Collins, A. M. & Loftus, E. F. (1975). A spreading-activation theory of semantic processing. *Psychological Review, 82,* 407–428.

Collins, A. M. & Quillian, M. R. (1969). Retrieval time from semantic memory. *Journal of Verbal Learning and Verbal Behavior, 8,* 240–247.

Conner, M. & Armitage, C. J. (1998). Extending the theory of planned behavior: A review and avenues for further research. *Journal of Applied Social Psychology, 28,* 1429–1464.

Conner, M., Smith, N. & McMillan, B. (2003). Examining normative pressure in the theory of planned behaviour: Impact of gender and passengers on intentions to break the speed limit. *Current Psychology: A Journal for Diverse Perspectives on Diverse Psychological Issues, 22,* 252–263.

Conner, M. & Sparks, P. (2002). Ambivalence and attitudes. *European Review of Social Psychology, 12,* 37–70

Converse, Philip E. (1975). Public Opinion and Voting Behavior. In F. I. Greenstein & N. W. Polsby (eds), *Handbook of Political Science* (Vol. 4, pp. 75–169). Reading, MA: Addison-Wesley.

Cook, S. W. & Selltiz, C. (1964). A multiple-indicator approach to attitude measurement. *Psychological Bulletin, 62*(1), 36–55.

Cooke, R. & French, D. P. (2008). How well do the theory of reasoned action and theory of planned behaviour predict intentions and attendance at screening programmes? A meta-analysis. *Psychology & Health, 23,* 745–765.

Cooke, R. & Sheeran, P. (2004). Moderation of cognition-intention and cognition-behaviour relations: A meta-analysis of properties of variables from the theory of planned behaviour. *British Journal of Social Psychology, 43,* 159–186.

Corey, S. M. (1937). Professed attitudes and actual behavior. *Journal of Educational Psychology, 28,* 171–280.

Correll, J., Spencer, S. J. & Zanna, M. P. (2004). An affirmed self and an open mind: Self-affirmation and sensitivity to argument strength. *Journal of Experimental Social Psychology, 40,* 350–356.

Craik, F. I. M. & Lockhart, R. S. (1972). Levels of processing: A framework for memory research. *Journal of Verbal Learning and Verbal Behavior, 11,* 671–684.

Crano, W. D. (2012). *The Rules of Influence: Winning When You're in the Minority.* New York: St Martin's Press.

Crano, W. D. & Seyranian, V. (2009). How minorities prevail: The context/comparison-leniency contract model. *Journal of Social Issues, 65,* 335–363.

Crocker, J. (1981). Judgment of covariation by social perceivers. *Psychological Bulletin, 90,* 272–292.

Cronbach, L. J. (1951). Coefficient alpha and the internal structure of tests. *Psychometrika, 16,* 297–334.

Crowne, D. P. & Marlowe, D. (1964). *The Approval Motive: Studies in Evaluative Dependence.* New York: Wiley.

Croyle, R. T. & Cooper, J. (1983). Dissonance arousal: Physiological evidence. *Journal of Personality and Social Psychology, 45,* 782–791.

Cunningham, M. R., Barbee, A. P. & Philhower, C. L. (2002). Dimensions of facial physical attractiveness: The intersection of biology and culture. In G. Rhodes, L. A. Zebrowitz (eds), *Facial Attrativeness: Evolutionary, Cognitive, and Social Perspectives* (pp. 193–238). Westport, CT: Ablex Publishing.

Cunningham, W. A., Johnson, M. K., Raye, C. L., Gatenby, J. C., Gore, J. C. & Banaji, M. R. (2004). Separable neural components in the processing of black and white faces. *Psychological Science, 15,* 806–813.

Cunningham, W. A., Preacher, K. J. & Banaji, M. R. (2001). Implicit attitude measures: Consistency, stability and convergent validity. *Psychological Science, 12,* 163–170.

Cunningham, W. A., Raye, C. L., & Johnson, M. K. (2004). Implicit and explicit evaluation: fMRI correlates of valence, emotional intensity, and control in the processing of attitudes. *Journal of Cognitive Neuroscience, 16,* 1717–1729.

Cunningham, W. A. & Zelazo, P. D. (2007). Attitudes and evaluations: A social cognitive neuroscience perspective. *Trends in Cognitive Sciences, 11*(3), 97–104.

Cvencek, D., Greenwald, A. G. & Meltzoff, A. N. (2012). Balanced identity theory: Review of evidence for implicit consistency in social cognition. In B. Gawronski & F. Strack (eds), *Cognitive Consistency: A Fundamental Principle in Social Cognition* (pp. 157–177). New York: Guilford Press.

Dal Cin, S., Zanna, M. P. & Fong, G. T. (2004). Narrative persuasion and overcoming resistance. In E. S. Knowles & J. A. Linn (eds), *Resistance and Persuasion* (pp. 175–191). Mahwah, NJ: Lawrence Erlbaum Associates.

Dannlowski, U. & Suslow, T. (2006). Test–Retest Reliability of Subliminal Facial Affective Priming. *Psychological Reports, 98*(1), 153–158.

Dasgupta, N. & Rivera, L. M. (2006). From automatic antigay prejudice to behavior: The moderating role of conscious beliefs about gender and behavioral control. *Journal of Personality and Social Psychology, 91,* 268–280.

Davidson, A. R. & Jaccard, J. J. (1979). Variables that moderate the attitude–behaviour relation: Results of a longitudinal survey. *Journal of Personality and Social Psychology, 37,* 1364–1376.

Davison, W. P. (1983). The third-person effect in communication. *Public Opinion Quarterly, 47,* 1–15.

Dawes, R. M., Singer, D. & Lemons, F. (1972). An experimental analysis of the contrast effect and its implications for intergroup communication and the indirect assessment of attitude. *Journal of Personality and Social Psychology, 21,* 281–295.

Dawkins, R. (1989). *The Selfish Gene* (2nd edn). Oxford: Oxford University Press.

DeBono, K. G. (2000). Attitude functions and consumer psychology: Understanding perceptions of product quality. In G. R. Maio & J. M. Olson (eds), *Why we Evaluate: Functions of Attitudes* (pp. 195–221). Mahwah, NJ: Erlbaum.

Dechêne, A., Stahl, C., Hansen, J. & Wänke, M. (2009). Mix me a list: Context moderates the truth effect and the mere-exposure effect. *Journal of Experimental Social Psychology, 45*, 1117–1122.

De Houwer, J. (2007). A conceptual and theoretical analysis of evaluative conditioning. *The Spanish Journal of Psychology, 10*, 230–241.

De Houwer, J. (2009a). The propositional approach to associative learning as an alternative for association formation models. *Learning & Behavior, 37*(1), 1–20.

De Houwer, J. (2009b). Conditioning as a source of liking: There is nothing simple about it. In M. Wänke (ed.), *Social Psychology of Consumer Behavior* (pp. 151–166). New York: Psychology Press.

De Houwer, J. (2014). Why a propositional single-process model of associative learning deserves to be defended. In J. W. Sherman, B. Gawronski & Y. Trope (eds), *Dual-Process Theories of the Social Mind* (pp. 530–541). New York: Guilford Press.

De Houwer, J., Gawronski, B. & Barnes-Holmes, D. (2013). A functional-cognitive framework for attitude research. *European Review of Social Psychology, 24*, 252–287.

De Houwer, J., Teige-Mocigemba, S., Spruyt, A. & Moors, A. (2009). Implicit measures: A normative analysis and review. *Psychological Bulletin, 135*, 347–368.

De Liver, Y., van der Pligt, J. & Wigboldus, D. (2007). Positive and negative associations underlying ambivalent attitudes. *Journal of Experimental Social Psychology, 43*, 319–326.

DeMaio, T. J. (1984). Social desirability and survey measurement: A review. In C. F. Turner & E. Martin (eds), *Surveying Subjective Phenomena* (Vol. 2, pp. 257–281). New York: Russell Sage Foundation.

Deutsch, M. & Gerard, H. B. (1955). A study of normative and informational social influences upon individual judgment. *Journal of Abnormal and Social Psychology, 51*, 629–636.

Deutsch, R. (2004). What Does It Take to Negate? How Processing Negated Information Affects Cognition and Behavior. *Psychology Science, 46*(4).

Deutsch, R., Gawronski, B. & Strack, F. (2006). At the boundaries of automaticity: Negation as reflective operation. *Journal of Personality and Social Psychology, 91*(3), 385–405.

De Zilva, D., Vu, L., Newell, B. R. & Pearson, J. (2013). Exposure is not enough: Suppressing stimuli from awareness can abolish the mere exposure effect. *PloS one, 8*(10), e77726.

Dickinson, A. & Brown, K. J. (2007). Flavor-evaluative conditioning is unaffected by contingency knowledge during training with color-flavor compounds. *Learning & Behavior, 35*, 36–42.

Dotsch, R., Wigboldus, D. J., Langner, O. & van Knippenberg, A. (2008). Ethnic out-group faces are biased in the prejudiced mind. *Psychological Science, 19*(10), 978–980.

Douglas, K. M. & Sutton, R. M. (2004). Right about others, wrong about ourselves? Actual and perceived self-other differences in resistance to persuasion. *British Journal of Social Psychology, 43*, 585–603.

Douglas, K. M. & Sutton, R. M. (2006). When what you say about others says something about you: Language abstraction and inferences about describers' attitudes and goals. *Journal of Experimental Social Psychology, 42*, 500–508.

Dovidio, J. F. & Gaertner, S. L. (2004). Aversive racism. In M. P. Zanna (ed.), *Advances in Experimental Social Psychology* (Vol. 36, pp. 1–52). San Diego, CA: Academic Press.

Dovidio, J. F., Kawakami, K., Johnson, C., Johnson, B. & Howard, A. (1997). On the nature of prejudice: Automatic and controlled processes. *Journal of Experimental Social Psychology, 33*, 510–540.

Dovidio, J. F., Kawakami, K., Smoak, N. & Gaertner, S. L. (2009). The nature of contemporary racial prejudice: Insight from implicit and explicit measures of attitudes. In R. E. Petty, R. H. Fazio & P. Briñol (eds), *Attitudes: Insights from the New Implicit Measures* (pp. 165–192). New York: Psychology Press.

Draycott, S. & Dabbs, A. (1998). Cognitive dissonance 1: An overview of the literature and its integration into theory and practice in clinical psychology. *British Journal of Clinical Psychology, 37*, 341–353.

Dunton, B. C. & Fazio, R. H. (1997). An individual difference measure of motivation to control prejudiced reactions. *Personality and Social Psychology Bulletin, 23*, 316–326.

Eagly, A. H. & Chaiken, S. (1993). *The Psychology of Attitudes.* Fort Worth, TX: Harcourt Brace Jovanovich.

Eagly, A. H. & Chaiken, S. (1998). Attitude structure and function. In D. Gilbert, S. T. Fiske & G. Lindzey (eds), *Handbook of Social Psychology* (4th edn, pp. 269–322). New York: McGraw-Hill.

Eagly, A. H. & Chaiken, S. (2007). The advantages of an inclusive definition of attitude. *Social Cognition, 25*(5), 582–602.

Eagly, A. H., Chen, S., Chaiken, S. & Shaw-Barnes, K. (1999). The impact of attitudes on memory: An affair to remember. *Psychological Bulletin, 125*, 64–89.

Eagly, A. H., Kulesa, P., Brannon, L. A., Shaw, K. & Hutson-Comeaux, S. (2000). Why counterattitudinal messages are as memorable as pro-attitudinal messages: The importance of active defense against attack. *Personality and Social Psychology Bulletin, 26*, 1392–1408.

Eagly, A. H., Wood, W. & Chaiken, S. (1978). Causal inferences about communicators and their effect on opinion change. *Journal of Personality and Social Psychology, 36*, 424–435.

Eckes, T. & Six, B. (1994). Fakten und Fiktionen in der Einstellungs-Verhaltens-Forschung: Eine Meta-Analyse [Fact and fiction in research on the relationship between attitude and behaviour: A meta-analysis]. *Zeitschrift für Sozialpsychologie, 25,* 253–271.

Edwards, K. & Smith, E. E. (1996). A disconfirmation bias in the evaluation of arguments. *Journal of Personality and Social Psychology, 71,* 5–24.

Egan, L. C., Santos, L. R. & Bloom, P. (2007). The origins of cognitive dissonance: Evidence from children and monkeys. *Psychological Science, 18,* 978–983.

Egloff, B. & Schmukle, S. C. (2002). Predictive validity of an Implicit Association Test for assessing anxiety. *Journal of Personality and Social Psychology, 83*(6), 1441–1455.

Elkin, R. A. & Leippe, M. R. (1986). Physiological arousal, dissonance, and attitude change: Evidence for a dissonance arousal link and a 'don't remind me' effect. *Journal of Personality and Social Psychology, 51,* 55–65.

Elliot, A. J. & Devine, P. G. (1994). On the motivational nature of cognitive dissonance: Dissonance as psychological discomfort. *Journal of Personality and Social Psychology, 67,* 382–394.

Ennis, R. & Zanna, M. P. (2000). Attitude function and the automobile. In G. R. Maio & J. M. Olson (eds), *Why We Evaluate: Functions of Attitudes* (pp. 395–415). Mahwah, NJ: Erlbaum.

Erb, H., Pierro, A., Mannetti, L., Spiegel, S. & Kruglanski, A. W. (2007). Biassed processing of persuasive information: On the functional equivalence of cues and message arguments. *European Journal of Social Psychology, 37,* 1057–1075.

Erdelyi, M. H. & Appelbaum, A. G. (1973). Cognitive masking: The disruptive effect of an emotional stimulus upon the perception of contiguous neutral items. *Bulletin of the Psychonomic Society, 1,* 59–61.

Eriksson, N., Wu, S., Do, C. B., Kiefer, A. K., Tung, J. Y., Mountain, J. L., Hinds, D.A. & Francke, U. (2012). A genetic variant near olfactory receptor genes influences cilantro preference. *Flavour, 1,* 1–22.

Escalas, J. E. (2007). Self-referencing and persuasion: Narrative transportation versus analytical elaboration. *Journal of Consumer Research, 33,* 421–429.

Esser, J. K. (1998). Alive and well after 25 years: A review of groupthink research. *Organizational Behavior and Human Decision Processes, 73,* 116–141.

Evans, J. T. & Stanovich, K. E. (2013). Dual-process theories of higher cognition: Advancing the debate. *Perspectives on Psychological Science, 8,* 223–241.

Fazio, R. H. (1986). How do attitudes guide behavior? In R. M. Sorrentino & E. T. Higgins (eds), *Handbook of Motivation and Cognition* (pp. 204–243). New York: Guilford.

Fazio, R. H. (1990). Multiple processes by which attitudes guide behavior: The MODE model as an integrative framework. *Advances in Experimental Social Psychology, 23,* 75–109.

Fazio, R. H. (1995). Attitudes as object-evaluation associations: Determinants, consequences, and correlates of attitude accessibility. In R. E.

Petty & J. A. Krosnick (eds), *Attitude Strength: Antecedents and Consequences* (pp. 247–282). Mahwah, NJ: Erlbaum.

Fazio, R. H. (2000). Accessible attitudes as tools for object appraisal: Their costs and benefits. In G. R. Maio & J. M. Olson (eds), *Why We Evaluate: Functions of Attitudes* (pp. 1–36). Mahwah, NJ: Erlbaum.

Fazio, R. H. (2007). Attitudes as object-evaluation associations of varying strength. *Social Cognition, 25,* 603–637.

Fazio, R. H., Chen, J., McDonel, E. C. & Sherman, S. J. (1982). Attitude accessibility, attitude–behaviour consistency, and the strength of the object-evaluation association. *Journal of Experimental Social Psychology, 18,* 339–357.

Fazio, R. H. & Cooper, J. (1983). Arousal in the dissonance process. In J. T. Cacioppo & R. E. Petty (eds), *Social Psychophysiology: A Sourcebook* (pp. 122–152). New York: Guilford Press.

Fazio, R. H. & Dunton, B. C. (1997). Categorization by race: The impact of automatic and controlled components of racial prejudice. *Journal of Experimental Social Psychology, 33,* 451–470.

Fazio, R. H., Jackson, J. R., Dunton, B. C. & Williams, C. J. (1995). Variability in automatic activation as an unobtrusive measure of racial attitudes: A bona fide pipeline? *Journal of Personality and Social Psychology, 69,* 1013–1027.

Fazio, R. H., Ledbetter, J. E. & Towles-Schwen, T. (2000). On the costs of accessible attitudes: Detecting that the attitude object has changed. *Journal of Personality and Social Psychology, 78,* 197–210.

Fazio, R. H. & Olson, M. A. (2003). Implicit measures in social cognition research: Their meaning and use. *Annual Review of Psychology, 54*(1), 297–327.

Fazio, R. H. & Powell, M. C. (1997). On the value of knowing one's likes and dislikes: Attitude accessibility, stress, and health in college. *Psychological Science, 8,* 430–436.

Fazio, R. H., Powell, M. C. & Williams, C. J. (1989). The role of attitude accessibility in the attitude-to-behavior process. *Journal of Consumer Research, 16,* 280–288.

Fazio, R. H., Sanbonmatsu, D. M., Powell, M. C. & Kardes, F. R. (1986). On the automatic activation of attitudes. *Journal of Personality and Social Psychology, 50*(2), 229–238.

Fazio, R. H. & Towles-Schwen, T. (1999). The MODE model of attitude–behaviour relations. In S. Chaiken & Y. Trope (eds), *Dual-Process Theories in Social Psychology* (pp. 97–116). New York: Guilford.

Fazio, R. H. & Williams, C. J. (1986). Attitude accessibility as a moderator of the attitude-perception and attitude–behaviour relations: An investigation of the 1984 presidential election. *Journal of Personality and Social Psychology, 51,* 505–514.

Fazio, R. H. & Zanna, M. P. (1978). On the predictive validity of attitudes: The roles of direct experience and confidence1. *Journal of Personality, 46,* 228–243.

Fazio, R. H. & Zanna, M. P. (1981). Direct experience and attitude-behaviour consistency. *Advances in Experimental Social Psychology, 14,* 161–202.

Fazio, R. H., Zanna, M. P. & Cooper, J. (1977). Dissonance and self-perception: An integrative view of each theory's proper domain of application. *Journal of Experimental Social Psychology, 13,* 464–479.

Feather, N. T. (ed.) (1982). *Expectations and Actions: Expectancy-Value Models in Psychology.* Hillsdale, NJ: Erlbaum.

Feinstein, J. S., Buzza, C., Hurlemann, R., Follmer, R. L., Dahdaleh, N. S., Coryell, W. H., Welsh, M. J., Tranel, D. & Wemmie, J. A. (2013). Fear and panic in humans with bilateral amygdala damage. *Nature Neuroscience, 16,* 270–272.

Ferguson, M. J. & Bargh, J. A. (2004). Liking is for doing: The effects of goal pursuit on automatic evaluation. *Journal of Personality and Social Psychology, 87,* 557–572.

Ferguson, M. & Porter, S. (2009). Goals and (implicit) attitudes. In G. Moskowitz & H. Grant (eds). *The Psychology of Goals* (pp. 447–479). New York: Guilford Press.

Festinger, L. (1954). A theory of social comparison processes. *Human Relations, 7,* 117–140.

Festinger, L. (1957). *A Theory of Cognitive Dissonance.* Stanford, CA: Stanford University Press.

Festinger, L. (1962). *A Theory of Cognitive Dissonance* (Vol. 2). Stanford, CA: Stanford University Press.

Festinger, L. (1964). *Conflict, Decision, and Dissonance.* Stanford, CA: Stanford University Press.

Festinger, L. & Carlsmith, J. M. (1959). Cognitive consequences of forced compliance. *Journal of Abnormal and Social Psychology, 58,* 203–210.

Festinger, L., Carlsmith, J. M. & Bem, D. J. (2007). Issue 4: Does cognitive dissonance explain why behavior can change attitudes? In J. Nier (ed.), *Taking Sides: Clashing Views in Social Psychology* (2nd edn; pp. 74–91). New York: McGraw-Hill.

Fiedler, K. & Bluemke, M. (2005). Faking the IAT: Aided and unaided response control on the Implicit Association Tests. *Basic and Applied Social Psychology, 27*(4), 307–316.

Fiedler, K., Kutzner, F. & Vogel, T. (2013). Pseudocontingencies: Logically unwarranted but smart inferences. *Current Directions in Psychological Science, 22*(4), 324–329.

Fiedler, K. & Unkelbach, C. (2011). Evaluative conditioning depends on higher order encoding processes. *Cognition and Emotion, 25,* 639–656.

Fincham, F. & Hewstone, M. (2001). Attribution theory and research: From basic to applied. In M. Hewstone & W. Stroebe (eds), *Introduction to Social Psychology* (3rd edn, pp. 197–238). Oxford: Blackwell.

Fishbein, M. & Ajzen, I. (1974). Attitudes toward objects as predictors of single and multiple behavioral criteria. *Psychological Review, 81,* 59–74.

Fishbein, M. & Ajzen, I. (1975). *Belief, Attitude, Intention, and Behavior.* Reading, MA: Addison-Wesley.

Fishbein, M. & Coombs, F. S. (1974). Basis for decision: An attitudinal analysis of voting behavior. *Journal of Applied Social Psychology, 4,* 95–124.

Fiske, S. T. & Morling, B. A. (1995). Schemas/schemata. In A. S. R. Manstead & M. Hewstone (eds), *The Blackwell Encyclopedia of Social Psychology* (pp. 489–494). Oxford: Blackwell.

Förderer, S. & Unkelbach, C. (2012). Hating the cute kitten or loving the aggressive pit-bull: EC effects depend on CS–us relations. *Cognition and Emotion, 26,* 534–540

Forgas, J. P. (ed.). (2006). *Affect in Social Thinking and Behaviour.* New York: Psychology Press.

Forgas, J. P. & Tehani, G. (2005). Affective influences on language use: Mood effects on performance feedback by experts and novices. *Journal of Language and Social Psychology, 24,* 269–284.

Förster, J. (1998). Der Einfluß motorischer Perzeptionen auf Sympathie-Urteile attraktiver und unattraktiver Portraits [The influence of motor perceptions on likeability judgments of attractive and unattractive portraits]. *Zeitschrift für Experimentelle Psychologie, 45,* 167–182.

Förster, J. (2004). How body feedback influences consumers' evaluation of products. *Journal of Consumer Psychology, 14,* 416–426.

Franco, F. M. & Maass, A. (1996). Implicit versus explicit strategies of out-group discrimination: The role of intentional control in biased language use and reward allocation. *Journal of Language and Social Psychology, 15,* 335–359.

Frey, D. & Rosch, M. (1984). Information seeking after decisions: The roles of novelty of information and decision reversibility. *Personality and Social Psychology Bulletin, 10,* 91–98.

Friese, M., Bluemke, M. & Wänke, M. (2007). Predicting voting behavior with implicit attitude measures. *Experimental Psychology (formerly Zeitschrift für Experimentelle Psychologie), 54*(4), 247–255.

Friese, M., Hofmann, W. & Schmitt, M. (2008). When and why do implicit measures predict behaviour? Empirical evidence for the moderating role of opportunity, motivation, and process reliance. *European Review of Social Psychology, 19,* 285–338.

Friese, M., Hofmann, W. & Wänke, M. (2008). When impulses take over: Moderated predictive validity of explicit and implicit attitude measures in predicting food choice and consumption behaviour. *British Journal of Social Psychology, 47,* 397–419.

Friese, M., Hofmann, W. & Wänke, M. (2009). The impulsive consumer: Predicting consumer behavior with implicit reaction time measures. In M. Wänke (ed.), *Social Psychology of Consumer Behavior* (pp. 335–364). New York: Psychology Press.

Friese, M., Wänke, M. & Plessner, H. (2006). Implicit consumer preferences and their influence on product choice. *Psychology & Marketing, 23,* 727–740.

Friestad, M. & Wright, P. (1994). The persuasion knowledge model: How people cope with persuasion attempts. *Journal of Consumer Research*, *21*, 1–31.

Frijda, N. H. (1988). The laws of emotion. *American Psychologist*, *43*, 349–358.

Froming, W. J., Walker, G. R. & Lopyan, K. J. (1982). Public and private self-awareness: When personal attitudes conflict with societal expectations. *Journal of Experimental Social Psychoogy*, *18*, 476–487.

Furnham, A. (1997). *The Psychology of Behavior at Work*. Hove: Taylor & Francis.

Gaertner, S. L. & Dovidio, J. F. (1986). The aversive form of racism. In J. F. Dovidio & S. L. Gaertner (eds), *Prejudice, Discrimination, and Racism* (pp. 61–89). Orlando, FL: Academic Press.

Gasper, K. & Clore, G. L. (2000). Do you have to pay attention to your feelings to be influenced by them?. *Personality and Social Psychology Bulletin*, *26*, 698–711.

Gawronski, B. & Bodenhausen, G. V. (2006). Associative and propositional processes in evaluation: An integrative review of implicit and explicit attitude change. *Psychological Bulletin*, *132*, 692–731.

Gawronski, B. & Bodenhausen, G. V. (2007). Unraveling the processes underlying evaluation: Attitudes from the perspective of the APE model. *Social Cognition*, *25*, 687–717.

Gawronski, B. & Bodenhausen, G. V. (2011). The associative-propositional evaluation model: Theory, evidence, and open questions. In J. M. Olson, M. P. Zanna (eds), *Advances in Experimental Social Psychology* (Vol. 44, pp. 59–127). San Diego, CA: Academic Press.

Gawronski, B., Deutsch, R., Mbirkou, S., Seibt, B. & Strack, F. (2008). When 'just say no' is not enough: Affirmation versus negation training and the reduction of automatic stereotype activation. *Journal of Experimental Social Psychology*, *44*, 370–377.

Gawronski, B., Galdi, S. & Arcuri, L. (2015). What can political psychology learn from implicit measures? Empirical evidence and new directions. *Political Psychology*, *36*(1), 1–17.

Gawronski, B., Hofmann, W. & Wilbur, C. J. (2006). Are 'implicit' attitudes unconscious?. *Consciousness and Cognition*, *15*(3), 485–499.

Gawronski, B. & Strack, F. (2004). On the propositional nature of cognitive consistency: Dissonance changes explicit, but not implicit attitudes. *Journal of Experimental Social Psychology*, *40*, 535–542.

Gawronski, B. & Strack, F. (2012). *Cognitive Consistency: A Fundamental Principle in Social Cognition*. New York: Guilford Press.

Gerbner, G. (1969). Toward 'cultural indicators': The analysis of mass mediated public message systems. *Educational Technology Research and Development*, *17*, 137–148.

Gerbner, G. & Gross, L. (1976). Living with television: The violence profile. *Journal of Communication*, *26*, 172–199.

Gerbner, G., Gross, L., Morgan, M. & Signorielli, N. (1986). Living with television: The dynamics of the cultivation process. In J. Bryant & D. Zillmann (eds), *Perspectives on Media Effects* (pp. 17–40), Hillsdale, NJ: Lawrence Erlbaum.

Gilovich, T. (1990). Differential construal and the false consensus effect. *Journal of Personality and Social Psychology, 59*, 623–634.

Giner-Sorolla, R. & Chaiken, S. (1994). The causes of hostile media judgments. *Journal of Experimental Social Psychology, 30*, 165–180.

Glasman, L. R. & Albarracín, D. (2006). Forming attitudes that predict future behavior: A meta-analysis of the attitude–behaviour relation. *Psychological Bulletin, 132*, 778–822.

Gollwitzer, P. M. (1999). Implementation intentions: Strong effects of simple plans. *American Psychologist, 54*(7), 493–503.

Gorn, G. J. (1982). The effects of music in advertising on choice behavior: A classical conditioning approach. *Journal of Marketing Research, 46*, 94–101.

Gosling, P., Denizeau, M. & Oberlé, D. (2006). Denial of responsibility: A new mode of dissonance reduction. *Journal of Personality and Social Psychology, 90*, 722–733.

Grabe, S., Ward, L. M. & Hyde, J. S. (2008). The role of the media in body image concerns among women: A meta-analysis of experimental and correlational studies. *Psychological Bulletin, 134*, 460–476.

Granberg, D. & Brent, E. (1983). When prophecy bends: The preference-expectation link in U.S. presidential elections, 1952–1980. *Journal of Personality and Social Psychology, 45*, 477–491.

Granberg, D. & Jenks, R. (1977). Assimilation and contrast effects in the 1972 election. *Human Relations, 30*, 623–640.

Green, A. (2005). 'Normalizing Torture on "24"', *The New York Times*, 22 May 2005 [online]. Available at: www.nytimes.com/2005/05/22/arts/television/22gree. html (accessed 4 January 2015).

Green, M. C. & Brock, T. C. (2000). The role of transportation in the persuasiveness of public narratives. *Journal of Personality and Social Psychology, 79*, 701–721.

Green, M. C. & Brock, T. C. (2002). In the mind's eye: Transportation-imagery model of narrative persuasion. In M. C. Green, J. J. Strange & T. C. Brock (eds), *Narrative Impact: Social and Cognitive Foundations* (pp. 315–341). Mahwah, NJ: Lawrence Erlbaum Associates.

Greenberg, J., Solomon, S. & Pyszczynski, T. (1997). Terror management theory of self-esteem and cultural worldviews: Empirical assessments and conceptual refinements. *Advances in Experimental Social Psychology, 29*, 61–139.

Greenwald, A. G. (1968). Cognitive learning, cognitive response to persuasion, and attitude change. In A. Greenwald, T. Brock & T. Ostrom (eds), *Psychological Foundations of Attitudes* (pp. 148–170). New York: Academic Press.

Greenwald, A. G. (1989). Why attitudes are important: Defining attitude and attitude theory 20 years later. In A. R. Pratkanis, S. J. Breckler & A. G. Greenwald (eds), *Attitude Structure and Function* (pp. 429–440). Hillsdale, NJ: Lawrence Erlbaum Associates.

Greenwald, A. G. & Banaji, M. R. (1995). Implicit social cognition: Attitudes, self-esteem, and stereotypes. *Psychological Review, 102*, 4–27.

Greenwald, A. G. & Nosek, B. A. (2001). Health of the Implicit Association Test at Age 3. *Zeitschrift für Experimentelle Psychologie, 48*, 85–93.

Greenwald, A. G. & Nosek, B. A. (2009).Attitudinal dissociation: What does it mean?. In R. E.Petty, R. H. Fazio & P. Briñol (eds), *Attitudes: Insights from the New Implicit Measures* (pp. 65–82). Hillsdale, NJ: Lawrence Erlbaum Associates.

Greenwald, A. G., McGhee, D. E. & Schwartz, J. L. K. (1998). Measuring individual differences in implicit cognition: The implicit association test. *Journal of Personality and Social Psychology, 74*, 1464–1480.

Greenwald, A. G., Poehlman, T. A., Uhlmann, E. L. & Banaji, M. R. (2009). Understanding and using the Implicit Association Test: III. Meta-analysis of predictive validity. *Journal of Personality and Social Psychology, 97*, 17–41.

Greenwald, A. G., Banaji, M. R., Rudman, L. A., Farnham, S. D., Nosek, B. A. & Mellott, D. S. (2002). A unified theory of implicit attitudes, stereotypes, self–esteem, and self–concept. *Psychological Review, 109*, 3–25.

Greifeneder, R., Bless, H. & Pham, M. T. (2011). When do people rely on affective and cognitive feelings in judgment? A review. *Personality and Social Psychology Review, 15*, 107–141.

Grice, H. P. (1978). Some further on logic and conversation. In P. Cole (ed.), *Syntax and Semantics, Vol. 9: Pragmatics* (pp. 113–128). New York: Academic Press.

Grohs, R., Wagner, U. & Steiner, R. (2012). An investigation of children's ability to identify sponsors and understand sponsorship intentions. *Psychology & Marketing, 29*, 907–917.

Gross, S. R., Holtz, R. & Miller, N. (1995). Attitude certainty. In R. E. Petty & J. A. Krosnick (eds), *Attitude Strength: Antecedents and Consequences* (pp. 215–245). Mahwah, NJ: Erlbaum.

Gunther, A. C. (1992). Biased press or biased public? Attitudes toward media coverage of social groups. *Public Opinion Quarterly, 56*, 147–167.

Haddock, G., Newson, M. & Haworth, J. (2011). Do memory-impaired individuals report stable attitudes?. *British Journal of Social Psychology, 50*, 234–245.

Hahn, A., Judd, C. M., Hirsh, H. K. & Blair, I. V. (2014). Awareness of implicit attitudes. *Journal of Experimental Psychology: General, 143*(3), 1369–1392.

Haire, M. (1950). Projective techniques in marketing research. *Journal of Marketing, 14*, 649–656.

Halberstadt, J. (2006). The generality and ultimate origins of the attractiveness of prototypes. *Personality and Social Psychology Review, 10*, 166–183.

Halberstadt, J. & Rhodes, G. (2003). It's not just average faces that are attractive: Computer-manipulated averageness makes birds, fish, and automobiles attractive. *Psychonomic Bulletin & Review, 10*(1), 149–56.

Hamilton, D. L. & Gifford, R. K. (1976). Illusory correlation in interpersonal perception: A cognitive basis of stereotypic judgments. *Journal of Experimental Social Psychology, 12,* 392–407.

Hammond, K. R. (1948). Measuring attitudes by error choice: An indirect method. *Journal of Abnormal and Social Psychology, 43,* 38–48.

Handley, I. M. & Lassiter, G. D. (2002). Mood and information processing: When happy and sad look the same. *Motivation and Emotion, 26,* 223–255.

Hansen, J. & Wänke, M. (2009). Liking what's familiar: The importance of unconscious familiarity in the mere-exposure effect. *Social Cognition, 27,* 161–182.

Hansen J. & Wänke M. (2010). Truth from language and truth from fit: The impact of linguistic concreteness and level of construal on subjective truth. *Personality and Social Psychological Bulletin, 36,* 1576–1588

Harber, K. D. (2005). Self-esteem and affect as information. *Personality and Social Psychology Bulletin, 31,* 276–288.

Harmon-Jones, E. & Harmon-Jones, C. (2007). Cognitive dissonance theory after 50 years of development. *Zeitschrift Für Sozialpsychologie, 38*(1), 7–16.

Harmon-Jones, E., Harmon-Jones, C., & Levy, N. (2015). An action-based model of cognitive-dissonance processes. *Current Directions in Psychological Science, 24*(3), 184–189.

Harris, G. T., Rice, M. E., Quinsey, V. L. & Chaplin, T. C. (1996). Viewing time as a measure of sexual interest among child molesters and normal heterosexual men. *Behaviour Research and Therapy, 34*(4), 389–394.

Hart, W., Albarracín, D., Eagly, A. H., Brechan, I., Lindberg, M. J. & Merrill, L. (2009). Feeling validated versus being correct: A meta-analysis of selective exposure to information. *Psychological Bulletin, 135,* 555–588.

Hastorf, A. H. & Cantril, H. (1954). They saw a game: A case study. *Journal of Abnormal and Social Psychology, 49,* 129–134.

Haugtvedt, C. P. & Petty, R. E. (1992). Personality and persuasion: Need for cognition moderates the persistence and resistance of attitude change. *Journal of Personality and Social Psychology, 63,* 308–319.

Haugtvedt, C. P., Petty, R. E. & Cacioppo, J. T. (1992). Need for cognition and advertising: Understanding the role of personality variables in consumer behavior moderates the persistence and resistance of attitude change. *Journal of Consumer Psychology, 1,* 239–260.

Haugtvedt, C. P. & Priester, J. R. (1997). Conceptual and methodological issues in advertising effectiveness: An attitude strength perspective. In W. D. Wells (ed.), *Measuring Advertising Effectiveness* (pp. 79–93). Mahwah, NJ: Lawrence Erlbaum Associates.

Haugtvedt, C. P., Schumann, D. W., Schneier, W. L., & Warren, W. L. (1994). Advertising repetition and variation strategies: Implications for under-standing attitude strength. *Journal of Consumer Research, 21,* 176–189.

Hausenblas, H. A., Carron, A. V. & Mack, D. E. (1997). Application of the theories of reasoned action and planned behavior to exercise behavior: A meta-analysis. *Journal of Sport & Exercise Psychology, 19,* 36–51.

Havas, D. A., Glenberg, A. M. & Rinck, M. (2007). Emotion simulation during language comprehension. *Psychonomic Bulletin & Review, 14,* 436–441.

Heider, F. (1946). Attitudes and cognitive organization. *Journal of Psychology, 21,* 107–112.

Heider, F. (1958). *The Psychology of Interpersonal Relations.* New York: Wiley.

Herring, D. R., White, K. R., Jabeen, L. N., Hinojos, M., Terrazas, G., Reyes, S. M., Taylor, J. H. & Crites, S. J. (2013). On the automatic activation of attitudes: A quarter century of evaluative priming research. *Psychological Bulletin, 139,* 1062–1089.

Higgins, E. T. (1997). Beyond pleasure and pain. *American Psychologist, 52,* 1280–1300.

Higgins, E. T. (2000). Making a good decision: Value from fit. *American Psychologist, 55,* 1217–1230.

Higgins, E. T. (2005). Value from regulatory fit. *Current Directions in Psychological Science, 14,* 209–213.

Higgins, E. T. (2012). Accessibility theory. In P. M. Van Lange, A. W. Kruglanski & E. T. Higgins (eds), *Handbook of Theories of Social Psychology* (Vol 1, pp. 75–96). Thousand Oaks, CA: Sage Publications.

Himmelfarb, S. (1993). The measurement of attitudes. In A. H. Eagly & S. Chaiken (eds), *The Psychology of Attitudes* (pp. 23–87). Fort Worth, TX: Harcourt Brace Jovanovich.

Hofmann, W., Gschwendner, T., Castelli, L. & Schmitt, M. (2008). Implicit and explicit attitudes and interracial interaction: The moderating role of situationally available control resources. *Group Processes & Intergroup Relations, 11,* 69–87.

Hofmann, W., De Houwer, J., Perugini, M., Baeyens, F. & Crombez, G. (2010). Evaluative conditioning in humans: A meta-analysis. *Psychological Bulletin, 136,* 390–421.

Hofmann, W. & Friese, M. (2008). Impulses got the better of me: Alcohol moderates the influence of implicit attitudes toward food cues on eating behavior. *Journal of Abnormal Psychology, 117,* 420–427.

Hofmann, W., Friese, M. & Strack, F. (2009). Impulse and self-control from a dual-systems perspective. *Perspectives on Psychological Science, 4*(2), 162–176.

Hofmann, W., Gawronski, B., Gschwendner, T., Le, H. & Schmitt, M. (2005). A meta-analysis on the correlation between the Implicit Association Test and explicit self-report measures. *Personality and Social Psychology Bulletin, 31*(10), 1369–1385.

Hoffmann, M., Lipka, J., Mothes-Lasch, M., Miltner, W. R. & Straube, T. (2012). Awareness modulates responses of the amygdala and the visual cortex to highly arousing visual threat. *Neuroimage, 62*(3), 1439–1444.

Hofmann, W., Rauch, W. & Gawronski, B. (2007). And deplete us not into temptation: Automatic attitudes, dietary restraint, and self-regulatory resources as determinants of eating behavior. *Journal of Experimental Social Psychology, 43,* 497–504.

Hofstede, G., Hofstede, G. J. & Minkov, M. (2010). *Cultures and Organizations: Software of the Mind* (3rd edn). New York: McGraw-Hill.

Holbrook, A. L., Berent, M. K., Krosnick, J. A., Visser, P. S. & Boninger, D. S. (2005). Attitude importance and the accumulation of attitude-relevant knowledge in memory. *Journal of Personality and Social Psychology, 88,* 749–769.

Holland, R. W., Verplanken, B. & van Knippenberg, A. (2003). From repetition to conviction: Attitude accessibility as a determinant of attitude certainty. *Journal of Experimental Social Psychology, 39,* 594–601.

Hollander, B. A. (2010). Persistence in the perception of Barack Obama as a Muslim in the 2008 presidential campaign. *Journal of Media and Religion, 9,* 55–66.

Holtz, R. & Miller, N. (2001). Intergroup competition, attitudinal projection, and opinion certainty: Capitalizing on conflict. *Group Processes & Intergroup Relations, 4,* 61–73.

Horcajo, J., Briñol, P. & Petty, R. E. (2010). Consumer persuasion: Indirect change and implicit balance. *Psychology & Marketing, 27,* 938–963.

Houston, D. A. & Fazio, R. H. (1989). Biased processing as a function of attitude accessibility: Making objective judgments subjectively. *Social Cognition, 7,* 51–66.

Hovland, C. I., Janis, I. L. & Kelley, J. J. (1953). *Communication and Persuasion.* New Haven, CT: Yale University Press.

Hovland, C. I. & Weiss, W. (1951). The influence of source credibility on communication effectiveness. *Public Opinion Quarterly, 15,* 635–650.

Hovland, C. I., Lumsdaine, A. A. & Sheffield, F. D. (1949). *Experiments on Mass Communication,* Vol. 3. Princeton, NJ: Princeton University Press.

Howard, D. J. (1997). Familiar phrases as peripheral persuasion cues. *Journal of Experimental Social Psychology, 33,* 231–243.

Hullett, C. R. (2005). The impact of mood on persuasion: A meta-analysis. *Communication Research, 32*(4), 423–442.

Hütter, M. & Sweldens, S. (2013). Implicit misattribution of evaluative responses: Contingency-unaware evaluative conditioning requires simultaneous stimulus presentations. *Journal of Experimental Psychology: General, 142,* 638–643.

Hütter, M., Sweldens, S., Stahl, C., Unkelbach, C. & Klauer, K. C. (2012). Dissociating contingency awareness and conditioned attitudes: Evidence of contingency-unaware evaluative conditioning. *Journal of Experimental Psychology: General, 141,* 539–557

Hymes, R. W. (1986). Political attitudes as social categories: A new look at selective memory. *Journal of Personality and Social Psychology, 51,* 233–241.

Ilies, R., Arvey, R. D. & Bouchard, T. J. (2006). Darwinism, behavioral genetics, and organizational behavior: A review and agenda for future research. *Journal of Organizational Behavior, 27,* 121–141.

Imhoff, R., Schmidt, A. F., Weiß, S., Young, A. W. & Banse, R. (2012). Vicarious viewing time: Prolonged response latencies for sexually attractive targets as a function of task- or stimulus-specific processing. *Archives of Sexual Behavior, 41*(6), 1389–1401.

Insko, C. A. (1965). Verbal reinforcement of attitude. *Journal of Personality and Social Psychology, 2*, 621–623.

Isen, A. M., Shalker, T. E., Clark, M. & Karp, L. (1978). Affect, accessibility of material in memory, and behavior: A cognitive loop? *Journal of Personality and Social Psychology, 36*, 1–12.

Isenberg, D. J. (1986). Group polarization: A critical review and meta-analysis. *Journal of Personality and Social Psychology, 50*, 1141–1151.

Ito, T. A. & Cacioppo, J. T. (2007). Attitudes as mental and neural states of readiness: Using physiological measures to study implicit attitudes. In B. Wittenbrink & N. Schwarz (eds), *Implicit Measures of Attitudes* (pp. 125–158). New York: Guildford.

Ito, T. A., Thompson, E. & Cacioppo, J. T. (2004). Tracking the timecourse of social perception: The effects of racial cues on event-related brain potentials. *Personality and Social Psychology Bulletin, 30*(10), 1267–1280.

Iyengar, S. & Kinder, D. R. (2010). *News That Matters: Television and American Opinion.* Chicago: University of Chicago Press.

Iyengar, S. S. & Lepper, M. R. (2000). When choice is demotivating: Can one desire too much of a good thing?. *Journal of Personality and Social Psychology, 79*, 995–1006.

Jaccard, J., Weber, J. & Lundmark, J. (1975). A multitrait-multimethod analysis of four attitude assessment procedures. *Journal of Experimental Social Psychology, 11*, 149–154.

Jacoby, L. L., Kelley, C. M., Brown, J. & Jasechko, J. (1989). Becoming famous overnight: Limits on the ability to avoid unconscious influences of the past. *Journal of Personality and Social Psychology, 56*, 326–338.

Janis, I. L. (1959). Motivational factors in the resolution of decisional conflicts. In M. R. Jones (ed.), *Nebraska Symposium on Motivation* (Vol. 7, pp. 198–231). Lincoln, NE: University of Nebraska Press.

Janis, I. L. & King, B. T. (1954). The influence of role-playing on opinion change. *Journal of Abnormal and Social Psychology, 49*, 211–218.

Janis, I. L. & Mann, L. (1965). Effectiveness of emotional role-playing in modifying smoking habits and attitudes. *Journal of Experimental Research in Personality, 1*, 84–90.

John, D. R. (1999). Consumer socialization of children: A retrospective look at twenty-five years of research. *Journal of Consumer Research, 26*(3), 183–213.

Johnson, B. T. & Eagly, A. H. (1989). Effects of involvement on persuasion: A meta-analysis. *Psychological Bulletin, 106*, 290–314.

Jonas, E., Fritsche, I. & Greenberg, J. (2005). Currencies as cultural symbols: An existential psychological perspective on reactions of Germans toward the Euro. *Journal of Economic Psychology, 26*(1), 129–146.

Jonas, K., Broemer, P. & Diehl, M. (2000). Experienced ambivalence as a moderator of the consistency between attitudes and behaviors. *Zeitschrift für Sozialpsychologie, 31*, 153–165.

Jones, C. R., Fazio, R. H. & Olson, M. A. (2009). Implicit misattribution as a mechanism underlying evaluative conditioning. *Journal of Personality and Social Psychology, 96*, 933–948.

Jones, E. E. & Sigall, H. (1971). The bogus pipeline: A new paradigm for measuring affect and attitude. *Psychological Bulletin, 76*, 349–364.

Jost, J. T., Banaji, M. R. & Nosek, B. A. (2004). A decade of system justification theory: Accumulated evidence of conscious and unconscious bolstering of the status quo. *Political Psychology, 25*(6), 881–919.

Judd, C. M. & Kulik, J. A. (1980). Schematic effects of social attitudes on information processing and recall. *Journal of Personality and Social Psychology, 38*, 569–578.

Julka, D. L. & Marsh, K. L. (2005). An attitude functions approach to increasing organ-donation participation 1. *Journal of Applied Social Psychology, 35*(4), 821–849.

Kaplan, K. J. (1972). On the ambivalence–indifference problem in attitude theory and measurement: A suggested modification of the semantic differential technique. *Psychological Bulletin, 77*, 361–372.

Karpinski, A. & Steinman, R. B. (2006). The single category implicit association test as a measure of implicit social cognition. *Journal of Personality and Social Psychology, 91*(1), 16–32.

Karpinski, A., Steinman, R. B. & Hilton, J. L. (2005). Attitude importance as a moderator of the relationship between implicit and explicit attitude measures. *Personality and Social Psychology Bulletin, 31*, 949–962.

Katona, G. (1975). *Psychological Economics*. New York: Elsevier.

Katz, D. (1960). The functional approach to the study of attitudes. *Public Opinion Quarterly, 24*, 163–204.

Kawakami, K. & Dovidio, J. F. (2001). The reliability of implicit stereotyping. *Personality and Social Psychology Bulletin, 27*, 212–225.

Keller, J., Bohner, G. & Erb, H.-P. (2000). Intuitive und heuristische Verarbeitung – verschiedene Prozesse? Präsentation einer deutschen Fassung des 'Rational-Experiential Inventory' sowie neuer Selbstberichtskalen zur Heuristiknutzung. *Zeitschrift für Sozialpsychologie, 31*, 87–101.

Keller, P. A. (2006). Regulatory focus and efficacy of health messages. *Journal of Consumer Research, 33*, 109–114.

Kelley, H. H. (1967). Attribution theory in social psychology. In D. Levine (ed.), *Nebraska Symposium on Motivation* (Vol. 15, pp. 192–238). Lincoln, NE: University of Nebraska Press.

Kelley, H. H. (1972). Causal schemata and the attribution process. In E. E. Jones, D. E. Kanouse, H. H. Kelley, R. E. Nisbett, S. Valins & B. Weiner (eds), *Attribution: Perceiving the Causes of Behavior* (pp. 151–174). Morristown, NJ: General Learning Press.

Kelly, C. & Breinlinger, S. (1995). Attitudes, intentions, and behavior: A study of women's participation in collective action. *Journal of Applied Social Psychology, 25*, 1430–1445

Kenrick, D. T., Gutierres, S. E. & Goldberg, L. L. (1989). Influence of popular erotica on judgments of strangers and mates. *Journal of Experimental Social Psychology, 25*, 159–167.

Kenworthy, J. B., Miller, N., Collins, B. E., Read, S. J. & Earleywine, M. (2011). A trans-paradigm theoretical synthesis of cognitive dissonance theory: Illuminating the nature of discomfort. *European Review of Social Psychology, 22*, 36–113.

Keren, G. & Schul, Y. (2009). Two is not always better than one: A critical evaluation of two-system theories. *Perspectives on Psychological Science, 4*, 533–550.

Kim, M. & Hunter, J. E. (1993). Attitude–behavior relations: A meta-analysis of attitudinal relevance and topic. *Journal of Communication, 43*, 101–142.

Kim, H., Rao, A. R. & Lee, A. Y. (2009). It's time to vote: The effect of matching message orientation and temporal frame on political persuasion. *Journal of Consumer Research, 35*, 877–889.

King, B. T. & Janis, I. L. (1956). Comparison of the effectiveness of improvised versus non-improvised role-playing in producing opinion change. *Human Relations, 9*, 177–186.

Kirmani, A. & Campbell, M. C. (2009). Taking the target's perspective: The Persuasion Knowledge Model. In M. Wänke (ed.), *Social Psychology of Consumer Behavior* (pp. 297–316). New York: Psychology Press.

Kiviniemi, M. T. & Rothman, A. J. (2006). Selective memory biases in individuals' memory for health-related information and behavior recommendations. *Psychology & Health, 21*, 247–272.

Klauer, K. C. & Mierke, J. (2005). Task-set inertia, attitude accessibility, and compatibility-order effects: New evidence for a task-set switching account of the Implicit Association Test effect. *Personality and Social Psychology Bulletin, 31*(2), 208–217.

Klauer, K. C., Schmitz, F., Teige-Mocigemba, S. & Voss, A. (2010). Understanding the role of executive control in the Implicit Association Test: Why flexible people have small IAT effects. *The Quarterly Journal of Experimental Psychology, 63*(3), 595–619.

Knobloch-Westerwick, S. & Meng, J. (2009). Looking the other way: Selective exposure to attitude-consistent and counterattitudinal political information. *Communication Research, 36*, 426–448.

Knowles, E. S. & Linn, J. A. (2004). Approach-avoidance model of persuasion: Alpha and omega strategies for change. In E. S. Knowles & J. A. Linn (eds), *Resistance and Persuasion* (pp. 117–148). Mahwah, NJ: Lawrence Erlbaum Associates.

Knowles, E. S. & Riner, D. D. (2007). Omega approaches to persuasion: Overcoming resistance. In A. R. Pratkanis (ed.), *The Science of Social Influence: Advances and Future Progress* (pp. 83–114). New York: Psychology Press.

Knutson, K. M., Mah, L., Manly, C. F. & Grafman, J. (2007). Neural correlates of automatic beliefs about gender and race. *Human Brain Mapping, 28*(10), 915–930.

Köcher, R. (2011). 'Eine atemberaubende Wende' ['A breath-taking turn'], *Frankfurter Allgemeine Zeitung*, 20 April.

Kothandapani, V. (1971). Validation of feeling, belief, and intention to act as three components of attitude and their contribution to prediction of contraceptive behavior. *Journal of Personality and Social Psychology, 19,* 321–333.

Kraus, S. (1995). Attitudes and the prediction of behavior: A meta-analysis of the empirical literature. *Personality and Social Psychology Bulletin, 21,* 58–75.

Krosnick, J. A. & Alwin, D. F. (1989). Aging and susceptibility to attitude change. *Journal of Personality and Social Psychology, 57,* 416–425.

Krosnick, J. A., Boninger, D. S., Chuang, Y. C., Berent, M. K. & Carnot, C. G. (1993). Attitude strength: One construct or many related constructs? *Journal of Personality and Social Psychology, 65,* 1132–1151.

Kruglanski, A. W. & Orehek, E. (2007). Partitioning the domain of social inference: Dual mode and systems models and their alternatives. *Annual Review of Psychology, 58,* 291–316.

Kruglanski, A. W. & Thompson, E. P. (1999). Persuasion by a single route: A view from the unimodel. *Psychological Inquiry, 10,* 83–109.

Kumkale, G. T. & Albarracín, D. (2004). The sleeper effect in persuasion: A meta-analytic review. *Psychological Bulletin, 130,* 143–172.

Kunda, Z. (1990). The case for motivated reasoning. *Psychological Bulletin, 108,* 480–498.

Kutzner, F., Vogel, T., Freytag, P. & Fiedler, K. (2011). A robust classic: Illusory correlations are maintained under extended operant learning. *Experimental Psychology, 58,* 443–453

Kuykendall, D. & Keating, J. P. (1990). Mood and persuasion: Evidence for the differential influence of positive and negative states. *Psychology & Marketing, 7,* 1–9.2

Laham, S. M., Kashima, Y., Dix, J., Wheeler, M. & Levis, B. (2014). Elaborated contextual framing is necessary for action-based attitude acquisition. *Cognition and Emotion, 28*(6), 1119–1126.

Laham, S. M., Koval, P. & Alter, A. L. (2012). The name-pronunciation effect: Why people like Mr. Smith more than Mr. Colquhoun. *Journal of Experimental Social Psychology, 48,* 752–756.

Laird, J. D. (1974). Self attribution of emotion: The effects of expressive behavior on the quality of emotional experience. *Journal of Personality and Social Psychology, 29,* 475–486.

Lamm, H. & Myers, D. G. (1978). Group-induced polarization of attitudes and behavior. *Advances in Experimental Social Psychology, 11,* 145–195.

Landwehr, J. R., Labroo, A. A. & Herrmann, A. (2011). Gut liking for the ordinary: Incorporating design fluency improves automobile sales forecasts. *Marketing Science, 30,* 416–429.

Lane, K. A., Banaji, M. R., Nosek, B. A. & Greenwald, A. G. (2007). Understanding and using the Implicit Association Test: IV: What we know (so far) about the method. In B. Wittenbrink & N. Schwarz (eds), *Implicit Measures of Attitudes* (pp. 59–102). New York: Guilford Press.

LaPiere, R. (1934). Attitudes versus actions. *Social Forces, 13*, 230–237.

Latané, B. (1981). The psychology of social impact. *American Psychologist, 36*, 343–356.

Lavine, H. & Snyder, M. (2000). Cognitive processes and the functional matching effect in persuasion: Studies of personality and political behavior. In G. R. Maio & J. M. Olson (eds), *Why We Evaluate: Functions of Attitudes* (pp. 97–131). Mahwah, NJ: Erlbaum.

Laws, D. R. & Gress, C. L. (2004). Seeing things differently: The viewing time alternative to penile plethysmography. *Legal and Criminological Psychology, 9*(2), 183–196.

Lazarsfeld, P. F. (1944). The controversy over detailed interviews—an offer for negotiation. *Public Opinion Quarterly, 8*, 38–60.

Lee, A. Y. & Aaker, J. L. (2004). Bringing the frame into focus: The influence of regulatory fit on processing fluency and persuasion. *Journal of Personality and Social Psychology, 86*(2), 205–218.

Leippe, M. R. & Elkin, R. A. (1987). When motives clash: Issue involvement and response involvement as determinants of persuasion. *Journal of Personality and Social Psychology, 52*, 269–278.

Lemon, N. (1973). *Attitudes and Their Measurement.* New York: Wiley.

Lerner, J. S., Small, D. A. & Loewenstein, G. (2004). Heart Strings and Purse Strings: Carryover effects of emotions on economic decisions. *Psychological Science, 15*, 337–341.

Levey, A. B. & Martin, I. (1975). Classical conditioning of human 'evaluative' responses. *Behaviour Research and Therapy, 13*, 221–226.

Levine, J. M. & Murphy, G. (1943). The learning and forgetting of controversial material. *Journal of Abnormal and Social Psychology, 38*, 507–517.

Lewin, K. (1935). *A Dynamic Theory of Personality.* New York: McGraw-Hill.

Lieberman, M. D., Ochsner, K. N., Gilbert, D. T. & Schacter, D. L. (2001). Do amnesics exhibit cognitive dissonance reduction? The role of explicit memory and attention in attitude change. *Psychological Science, 12*, 135–140.

Likert, R. (1932). A technique for the measurement of attitudes. *Archives of Psychology, 140*, 1–55.

Linder, D. E., Cooper, J. & Jones, E. E. (1967). Decision freedom as a determinant of the role of incentive magnitude in attitude change. *Journal of Personality and Social Psychology, 6*, 245–254.

Lord, C. G. & Lepper, M. R. (1999). Attitude Representation Theory. In M. P. Zanna (ed.), *Advances in Experimental Social Psychology* (Vol. 31, pp. 265–343). San Diego, CA: Academic Press.

Lord, C. G., Paulson, R. M., Sia, T. L., Thomas, J. C. & Lepper, M. R. (2004). Houses built on sand: Effects of exemplar stability on susceptibility to attitude change. *Journal of Personality and Social Psychology, 87*, 733–749.

Lord, C. G., Ross, L. & Lepper, M. R. (1979). Biased assimilation and attitude polarization: The effects of prior theories on subsequently considered evidence. *Journal of Personality and Social Psychology, 37,* 2098–2109.

Losch, M. E. & Cacioppo, J. T. (1990). Cognitive dissonance may enhance sympathetic tonus, but attitudes are changed to reduce negative affect rather than arousal. *Journal of Experimental Social Psychology, 26,* 289–304.

Lott, A. J. & Lott, B. E. (1972). The power of liking: Consequences of interpersonal attitudes derived from a liberalized view of secondary reinforcement. *Advances in Experimental Social Psychology, 6,* 109–148.

Lowe, R. H. & Steiner, I. D. (1968). Some effects of the reversibility and consequences of decisions on postdecision information preferences. *Journal of Personality and Social Psychology, 8,* 172–179.

Lumet, S. (Producer). (1957). *12 Angry Men* [Film]. Available from Orion Home Video, 1888 Century Park East, Los Angeles, CA 90067.

Maass, A., Ceccarelli, R. & Rudin, S. (1996). Linguistic intergroup bias: Evidence for in-group-protective motivation. *Journal of Personality and Social Psychology, 71,* 512–526.

McCann, C. D. & Higgins, T. E. (1992). Personal and contextual factors in communication: A review of the 'communication game'. In G. R. Semin & K. Fiedler (eds), *Language, Interaction and Social Cognition* (pp. 144–172). Thousand Oaks, CA: Sage Publications.

McConnell, A. R. & Leibold, J. M. (2001). Relations among the Implicit Association Test, discriminatory behavior, and explicit measures of racial attitudes. *Journal of Experimental Social Psychology, 37,* 435–442.

Macrae, C. N., Bodenhausen, G. V., Milne, A. B. & Jetten, J. (1994). Out of mind but back in sight: Stereotypes on the rebound. *Journal of Personality and Social Psychology, 67*(5), 808.

McCrea, S. M., Penningroth, S. L. & Radakovich, M. P. (2015). Implementation intentions forge a strong cue–response link and boost prospective memory performance. *Journal of Cognitive Psychology, 27*(1), 12–26.

McEachan, R. R. C., Conner, M., Taylor, N. J. & Lawton, R. J. (2011). Prospective prediction of health-related behaviours with the theory of planned behaviour: A meta-analysis. *Health Psychology Review, 5,* 97–144.

McGuire, W. J. (1961). Resistance to persuasion conferred by active and passive prior refutation of the same and alternative counterarguments. *The Journal of Abnormal and Social Psychology, 63,* 326–332.

McGuire, W. J. (1964). Inducing resistance to persuasion: Some contemporary approaches. *Advances in Experimental Social Psychology, 1,* 191–229.

McGuire, W. J. (1969). The nature of attitudes and attitude change. In G. Lindzey & E. Aronson (eds), *The Handbook of Social Psychology* (2nd edn, Vol. 3). Reading, MA: Addison-Wesley.

McGuire, W. J. (1973). The yin and yang of progress in social psychology: Seven koan. *Journal of Personality and Social Psychology, 26,* 446–456.

McGuire, W. J. (1985). Attitudes and attitude change. In G. Lindzey & E. Aronson (eds), *Handbook of Social Psychology* (3rd edn, Vol. 2). New York: Random House.

McGuire, W. J. & Papageorgis, D. (1961). The relative efficacy of various types of prior belief-defense in producing immunity against persuasion. *Journal of Abnormal and Social Psychology, 62*, 327–337.

McGuire, W. J. & Papageorgis, D. (1962). Effectiveness of forewarning in developing resistance to persuasion. *Public Opinion Quarterly, 26*, 24–34.

McHoskey, J. W. (1995). Case closed? On the John F. Kennedy assassination: Biased assimilation of evidence and attitude polarization. *Basic and Applied Social Psychology, 17*, 395–409.

Maheswaran, D. & Chaiken, S. (1991). Promoting systematic processing in low motivation settings: The effect of incongruent information on processing and judgment. *Journal of Personality and Social Psychology, 61*, 13–25.

Mahoney, M. J. (1977). Publication prejudices: An experimental study of confirmatory bias in the peer review system. *Cognitive Therapy and Research, 1*, 161–175.

Maio, G. R. & Olson, J. M. (2000). Emergent themes and potential approaches to attitude function: The function-structure model of attitudes. In G. R. Maio & J. M. Olson (eds), *Why We Evaluate: Functions of Attitudes* (pp. 417–442). Mahwah, NJ: Erlbaum.

Mann, L. & Janis, I. L. (1968). A follow-up study on the long-term effects of emotional role-playing. *Journal of Personality and Social Psychology, 8*, 339–342.

Manstead, A. S. R. & Parker, D. (1995). Evaluating and extending the theory of planned behaviour. *European Review of Social Psychology, 6*, 69–95.

Markus, H. R. & Kitayama, S. (1991). Culture and the self: Implications for cognition, emotion, and motivation. *Psychological Review, 98*, 224–253.

Martin, I. & Levey, A. B. (1994). The evaluative response: Primitive but necesssary. *Behaviour Research and Therapy, 32*, 301–305.

Martin, L. L., Abend, T., Sedikides, C. & Green, J. D. (1997). How would I feel if . . .? Mood as input to a role fulfillment evaluation process. *Journal of Personality and Social Psychology, 73*, 242–253.

Martin, R. & Hewstone, M. (2008). Majority versus minority influence, message processing and attitude change: The source-context-elaboration model. In M. P. Zanna (ed.), *Advances in Experimental Social Psychology* (Vol. 40, pp. 237–326). San Diego, CA: Elsevier Academic Press.

Martin, N. G., Eaves, L. J., Heath, A. R., Jardine, R., Feingold, L. M. & Eysenck, H. J. (1986). Transmission of social attitudes. *Proceedings of the National Academy of Science, 83*, 4364–4368.

Martin, R. & Hewstone, M. (2010). Introduction: Theory and research on minority influence. In R. Martin & M. Hewstone (eds), *Minority Influence and Persuasion: Antecedents, Processes and Consequences* (pp. 3–18). Hove, UK: Psychology Press.

Martin, R., Hewstone, M., Martin, P. & Gardikiotis, A. (2008). Persuasion from majority and minority groups. In W. D. Crano & R. Prislin (eds), *Attitutdes and Attitude Change* (pp. 361–384). New York: Psychology Press.

Marwell, G., Aiken, M. T. & Demerath, N. J. (1987). The persistence of political attitudes among 1960s civil rights activists. *Public Opinion Quarterly, 51*, 359–375.

Mazzocco, P. J., Green, M. C., Sasota, J. A. & Jones, N. W. (2010). This story is not for everyone: Transportability and narrative persuasion. *Social Psychological and Personality Science, 1*(4), 361–368.

Messner, C. & Vosgerau, J. (2010). Cognitive inertia and the implicit association test. *Journal of Marketing Research, 47*(2), 374–386.

Mierke, J. & Klauer, K. C. (2001). Implicit association measurement with the IAT: Evidence for effects of executive control porcesses. *Zeitschrift für Experimentelle Psychologie, 48*, 107–122.

Mierke, J. & Klauer, K. C. (2003). Method-specific variance in the implicit association test. *Journal of Personality and Social Psychology, 85*, 1180–1192.

Milgram, S., Mann, L. & Harter, S. (1965). The lost-letter technique: A tool of social research. *Public Opinion Quarterly, 29*, 437–438.

Millar, M. G. & Tesser, A. (1986). Effects of affective and cognitive focus on the attitude–behavior relation. *Journal of Personality and Social Psychology, 51*, 270–276.

Miller, A. G., McHoskey, J. W., Bane, C. M. & Dowd, T. G. (1993). The attitude polarization phenomenon: Role of response measure, attitude extremity, and behavioral consequences of reported attitude change. *Journal of Personality and Social Psychology, 64*, 561–574.

Mills, J. & Clark, M. S. (1982). Exchange and communal relationships. *Review of Personality and Social Psychology, 3*, 121–144.

Mitchell, C. J., De Houwer, J. & Lovibond, P. F. (2009). The propositional nature of human associative learning. *Behavioral and Brain Sciences, 32*, 183–198.

Moreland, R. L. & Beach, S. R. (1992). Exposure effects in the classroom: The development of affinity among students. *Journal of Experimental Social Psychology, 28*, 255–276.

Moscovici, S. (1980). Toward a theory of conversion behavior. In L. Berkowitz (ed.), *Advances in Experimental Social Psychology* (Vol. 13, pp. 209–239). New York: Academic Press.

Moscovici, S. (1985). Social influence and conformity. In G. Lindzey & E. Aronson (eds), *Handbook of Social Psychology* (Vol. 2, pp. 217–249). New York: Random House.

Moscovici, S. & Zavalloni, M. (1969). The group as a polarizer of attitudes. *Journal of Personality and Social Psychology, 12*, 125–135.

Moscovici, S., Lage, E. & Naffrechoux, M. (1969). Influence of a consistent minority on the responses of a majority in a color perception task. *Sociometry, 32*, 365–380.

Mugny, G. (1975). Negotiations, image of the other and the process of minority influence. *European Journal of Social Psychology, 5*, 209–228.

Mullainathan, S. & Shleifer, A. (2005). The market for news. *American Economic Review, 95,* 1031–1053.

Mullen, B. & Johnson, C. (1990). Distinctiveness-based illusory correlations and stereotyping: A meta-analytic integration. *British Journal of Social Psychology, 29,* 11–27.

Munro, G. D. & Ditto, P. H. (1997). Biased assimilation, attitude polarization, and affect in reactions to stereotyped-relevant scientific information. *Personality and Social Psychology Bulletin, 23,* 636–653.

Munro, G. D., Ditto, P. H., Lockhart, L. K., Fagerlin, A., Gready, M. & Peterson, E. (2002). Biased assimilation of sociopolitical arguments: Evaluating the 1996 U.S. presidential debate. *Basic and Applied Social Psychology, 24,* 15–26.

Murphy, M. C., Richeson, J. A., Shelton, J. N., Rheinschmidt, M. L. & Bergsieker, H. B. (2013). Cognitive costs of contemporary prejudice. *Group Processes & Intergroup Relations, 16,* 560–571.

Mussweiler, T. (2003). Comparison processes in social judgment: Mechanisms and consequences. *Psychological Review, 110,* 472–489.

Nabi, R. L. (2003). 'Feeling' resistance: Exploring the role of emotionally evocative visuals in inducing inoculation. *Media Psychology, 5,* 199–223.

Nemeth, C. J. (1995). Dissent as driving cognition, attitudes, and judgments. *Social Cognition, 13,* 273–291.

Nemeth, C. J. & Rogers, J. (1996). Dissent and the search for information. *British Journal of Social Psychology, 35,* 67–76.

Nevid, J. S. & McClelland, N. (2010). Measurement of implicit and explicit attitudes toward Barack Obama. *Psychology & Marketing, 27,* 989–1000.

Newby-Clark, I. R., McGregor, I. & Zanna, M. P. (2002). Thinking and caring about cognitive inconsistency: When and for whom does attitudinal ambivalence feel uncomfortable?. *Journal of Personality and Social Psychology, 82,* 157–166.

Newcomb, T. M. (1943). *Personality and Social Change: Attitude Formation in a Student Community.* New York: Dryden.

Newcomb, T. M. (1953). An approach to the study of communicative acts. *Psychological Review, 60,* 393–404

Newcomb, T. M. (1961). *The Acquaintance Process.* New York: Holt, Rinehart & Winston.

Newell, B. R. & Shanks, D. R. (2007). Recognising what you like: Examining the relation between the mere-exposure effect and recognition. *European Journal of Cognitive Psychology, 19*(1), 103–118.

Newton, N. & Newton, M. (1950). Relationship of ability to breast feed and maternal attitudes towards breast feeding. *Pediatrics, 11,* 869–879.

Niedenthal, P. (2007). Embodying emotion. *Science, 316*(5827), 1002–1005.

Nier, J. A. (2005). How dissociated are implicit and explicit racial attitudes? A bogus pipeline approach. *Group Processes & Intergroup Relations, 8,* 39–52.

Nijstad, B. A. (2009). *Group Performance*. New York: Psychology Press.

Nordgren, L. F., van Harreveld, F. & van der Pligt, J. (2006). Ambivalence, discomfort, and motivated information processing. *Journal of Experimental Social Psychology, 42,* 252–258.

Norman, R. (1975). Affective-cognitive consistency, attitudes, conformity, and behavior. *Journal of Personality and Social Psychology, 32,* 83–91.

Nosek, B. A., Greenwald, A. G. & Banaji, M. R. (2007). The Implicit Association Test at age 7: A methodological and conceptual review. In J.A. Bargh (ed.), *Social Psychology and the Unconscious: The Automaticity of Higher Mental Processes* (pp. 265–292). Hove, UK: Psychology Press.

Nosek, B. A., Hawkins, C. B. & Frazier, R. S. (2011). Implicit social cognition: from measures to mechanisms. *Trends in Cognitive Sciences, 15*(4), 152–159.

Nosek, B. A. & Smyth, F. L. (2007). A multitrait-multimethod validation of the Implicit Association Test: Implicit and explicit attitudes are related but distinct constructs. *Experimental Psychology, 54*(1), 14–29.

Nowak, A., Szamrej, J. & Latané, B. (1990). From private attitude to public opinion: A dynamic theory of social impact. *Psychological Review, 97,* 362–376.

Nuttin, J. M. (1985). Narcissism beyond Gestalt and awareness: The name letter effect. *European Journal of Social Psychology, 15,* 353–361.

O'Keefe, D. J. & Jackson, S. (1995). Argument quality and persuasive effects: A review of current approaches. In *Argumentation and Values: Proceedings of the Ninth Alta Conference on Argumentation* (pp. 88–92). Annandale, VA: Speech Communication Association.

Olson, M. A. & Fazio, R. H. (2003). Relations between implicit measures of prejudice: What are we measuring?. *Psychological Science, 14,* 636–639.

Olson, M. A. & Fazio, R. H. (2009). Implicit and explicit measures of attitudes: The perspective of the MODE model. In R. E. Petty, R. H. Fazio, P. Briñol (eds), *Attitudes: Insights from the New Implicit Measures* (pp. 19–63). New York: Psychology Press.

Olson, J. M., Vernon, P. A., Harris, J. A. & Jang, K. L. (2001). The heritability of attitudes: A study of twins. *Journal of Personality and Social Psychology, 80,* 845–860.

Orians, G. & Heerwagen, J. H. (1992). Evolved responses to landscapes. In J. H. Barkow, L. Cosmides & J. Tooby (eds), *The Adapted Mind: Evolutionary Psychology and the Generation of Culture* (pp. 555–580). New York: Oxford University Press.

Orne, M. T. (1962). On the social psychology of the psychological experiment: With particular reference to demand characteristics and their implications. *American Psychologist, 17,* 776–783.

Osgood, C. E., Suci, G. J. & Tannenbaum, P. H. (1957). *The Measurement of Meaning*. Urbana, IL: University of Illinois Press.

Osman, M. (2004). An evaluation of dual-process theories of reasoning. *Psychonomic Bulletin & Review, 11,* 988–1010.

Oswald, F. L., Mitchell, G., Blanton, H., Jaccard, J. & Tetlock, P. E. (2013). Predicting ethnic and racial discrimination: A meta-analysis of IAT criterion studies. *Journal of Personality and Social Psychology, 105,* 171–192.

Ottati, V. C. & Isbell, L. M. (1996). Effects on mood during exposure to target information on subsequently reported judgments: An on-line model of misattribution and correction. *Journal of Personality and Social Psychology, 71,* 39–53.

Ouellette, J. A. & Wood, W. (1998). Habit and intention in everyday life: The multiple processes by which past behavior predicts future behavior. *Psychological Bulletin, 124,* 54–74.

Owens, S. G., Bowman, C. G. & Dill, C. A. (2008). Overcoming procrastination: The effect of implementation intentions. *Journal of Applied Social Psychology, 38*(2), 366–384.

Paulhus, D. L. (1998). *Manual for the Balanced Inventory of Desirable Responding.* Toronto: Multi-Health Systems.

Paulhus, D. L. (2001). Normal narcissism: Two minimalist accounts. *Psychological Inquiry, 12*(4), 228–230.

Pavlov, I. P. (1927). *Conditioned Reflexes: An Investigation of the Physiological Activity of the Cerebral Cortex.* London: Oxford University Press.

Payne, B. K., Brown-Iannuzzi, J., Burkley, M., Arbuckle, N. L., Cooley, E., Cameron, C. D. & Lundberg, K. B. (2013). Intention invention and the affect misattribution procedure: Reply to Bar-Anan and Nosek (2012). *Personality and Social Psychology Bulletin, 39,* 375–386.

Payne, B. K., Burkley, M. A. & Stokes, M. B. (2008). Why do implicit and explicit attitude tests diverge? The role of structural fit. *Journal of Personality and Social Psychology, 94*(1), 16.

Payne, B. K., Cheng, C. M., Govorun, O. & Stewart, B. D. (2005). An inkblot for attitudes: Affect misattribution as implicit measurement. *Journal of Personality and Social Psychology, 89*(3), 277.

Payne, B. K. & Lundberg, K. (2014). The affect misattribution procedure: Ten years of evidence on reliability, validity, and mechanisms. *Social and Personality Psychology Compass, 8*(12), 672–686.

Pechmann, C. (1992). Predicting when two-sided ads will be more effective than one-sided ads: The role of correlational and correspondent inferences. *Journal of Marketing Research, 29,* 441–453.

Perloff, R. M. (1989). Ego-involvement and the third person effect of televised news coverage. *Communication Research, 16,* 236–262.

Perloff, R. M. (1999). The third-person effect: A critical review and synthesis. *Media Psychology, 1,* 353–378.

Perugini, M. (2005). Predictive models of implicit and explicit attitudes. *British Journal of Social Psychology, 44,* 29–45.

Perugini, M., Richetin, J. & Zogmaister, C. (2010). Prediction of behavior. In B. Gawronski & B. K. Payne (eds), *Handbook of Implicit Social Cognition: Measurement, Theory, and Applications* (pp. 255–277). New York: Guilford Press.

Peters, K. R. & Gawronski, B. (2011). Are we puppets on a string? Comparing the impact of contingency and validity on implicit and explicit evaluations. *Personality and Social Psychology Bulletin, 37*(4), 557–569.

Petrocelli, J. V., Tormala, Z. L. & Rucker, D. D. (2007). Unpacking attitude certainty: Attitude clarity and attitude correctness. *Journal of Personality and Social Psychology, 92*, 30–41.

Pettigrew, T. F. & Meertens, R. W. (1995). Subtle and blatant prejudice in Western Europe. *European Journal of Social Psychology, 25*, 57–75.

Petty, R. E. & Briñol, P. (2008). Persuasion: From single to multiple to metacognitive processes. *Perspectives on Psychological Science, 3*, 137–147.

Petty, R. E. & Briñol, P. (2010). Attitude change. In R. F. Baumeister & E. J. Finkel (eds), *Advanced Social Psychology: The State of the Science* (pp. 217–259). New York: Oxford University Press.

Petty, R. E. & Briñol, P. (2012). A multiprocess approach to social influence. In D. T. Kenrick, N. J. Goldstein & S. L. Braver (eds), *Six Degrees of Social Influence: Science, Application, and the Psychology of Robert Cialdini* (pp. 49–58). New York: Oxford University Press.

Petty, R. E., Briñol, P. & DeMarree, K. G. (2007). The meta-cognitive model (MCM) of attitudes: Implications for attitude measurement, change, and strength. *Social Cognition, 25*, 657–686.

Petty, R. E., Briñol, P., Loersch, C. & McCaslin, M. J. (2009). The need for cognition. In M. R. Leary & R. H. Hoyle (eds), *Handbook of Individual Differences in Social Behavior* (pp. 318–329). New York: Guilford Press.

Petty, R. E., Briñol, P. & Tormala, Z. L. (2002). Thought confidence as a determinant of persuasion: The self-validation hypothesis. *Journal of Personality and Social Psychology, 82*, 722–741.

Petty, R. E. & Cacioppo, J. T. (1977). Forewarning, cognitive responding, and resistance to persuasion. *Journal of Personality and Social Psychology, 35*, 645–655.

Petty, R. E. & Cacioppo, J. T. (1979). Issue involvement can increase or decrease persuasion by enhancing message-relevant cognitive responses. *Journal of Personality and Social Psychology, 37*, 1915–1926.

Petty, R. E. & Cacioppo, J. T. (1981). *Attitudes and Persuasion: Classic and Contemporary Approaches*. Dubuque, IA: Brown.

Petty, R. E. & Cacioppo, J. T. (1984). The effects of involvement on responses to argument quantity and quality: Central and peripheral routes to persuasion. *Journal of Personality and Social Psychology, 46*, 69–81.

Petty, R. E. & Cacioppo, J. T. (1986a). *Communication and Persuasion: Central and Peripheral Routes to Attitude Change*. New York: Springer.

Petty, R. E. & Cacioppo, J. T. (1986b). The elaboration likelihood model of persuasion. *Advances in Experimental Social Psychology, 19*, 124–203.

Petty, R. E., Cacioppo, J. T. & Goldman, R. (1981). Personal involvement as a determinant of argument-based persuasion. *Journal of Personality and Social Psychology, 41*, 847–855.

Petty, R. E., Cacioppo, J. T. & Schumann, D. (1983). Central and peripheral routes to advertising effectiveness: The moderating role of involvement. *Journal of Consumer Research, 10*, 134–148.

Petty, R. E. & Krosnick, J. A. (eds). (1995). *Attitude Strength: Antecedents and Consequences.* Mahwah, NJ: Erlbaum.

Petty, R. E., Ostrom, T. M. & Brock, T. C. (eds). (1981). *Cognitive Responses in Persuasion.* Hillsdale, NJ: Erlbaum.

Petty, R. E. & Wegener, D. T. (1998a). Matching versus mismatching attitude functions: Implications for scrutiny of persuasive messages. *Personality and Social Psychology Bulletin, 24*, 227–240.

Petty, R. E. & Wegener, D. T. (1998b). Attitude change: Multiple roles for persuasion variables. In D. Gilbert, S. T. Fiske & G. Lindzey (eds), *Handbook of Social Psychology* (4th edn, pp. 323–390). New York: McGraw-Hill.

Petty, R. E. & Wegener, D. T. (1999). The elaboration likelihood model: Current status and controversies. In S. Chaiken & Y. Trope (eds), *Dual Process Theories in Social Psychology* (pp. 41–72). New York: Guilford.

Petty, R. E., Wells, G. L. & Brock, T. C. (1976). Distraction can enhance or reduce yielding to propaganda: Thought disruption versus effort justification. *Journal of Personality and Social Psychology, 34*, 874–884.

Pfau, M., Ivanov, B., Houston, B., Haigh, M., Sims, J., Gilchrist, E., Russell, J, Wigley, S, Eckstein, J & Richert, N. (2005). Inoculation and mental processing: The instrumental role of associative networks in the process of resistance to counterattitudinal influence. *Communication Monographs, 72*, 414–441.

Pfau, M., Roskos-Ewoldsen, D., Wood, M., Yin, S., Cho, J., Lu, K. & Shen, L. (2003). Attitude accessibility as an alternative explanation for how inoculation confers resistance. *Communication Monographs, 70*, 39–51.

Pfau, M., Tusing, K. J., Koerner, A. F., Lee, W., Godbold, L. C., Penaloza, L. J., Shu-Huei, V. & Hong, Y. (1997). Enriching the inoculation construct: The role of critical components in the process of resistance. *Human Communication Research, 24*(2), 187–215.

Pham, M. T. (1998). Representativeness, relevance, and the use of feelings in decision making. *Journal of Consumer Research, 25*, 144–159.

Pham, M. T. (2008). The lexicon and grammar of affect-as-information: The GAIM. In M. Wänke (ed.), *Social Psychology of Consumer Behavior* (pp. 167–200). New York: Psychology Press.

Phelps, E. A. & LeDoux, J. E. (2005). Contributions of the amygdala to emotion processing: From animal models to human behavior. *Neuron, 48*(2), 175–187.

Phelps, E. A., O'Connor, K. J., Cunningham, W. A., Funayama, E. S., Gatenby, J. C., Gore, J. C. & Banaji, M. R. (2000). Performance on indirect measures of race evaluation predicts amygdala activation. *Journal of Cognitive Neuroscience, 12*, 729–738.

Pieters, R. & Zeelenberg, M. (2007). A theory of regret regulation 1.1. *Journal of Consumer Psychology, 17*, 29–35.

Pilkington, N. W. & Lydon, J. E. (1997). The relative effect of attitude similarity and attitude dissimilarity on interpersonal attraction: The moderating roles of prejudice and group membership. *Personality and Social Psychology Bulletin, 23*, 107–122.

Pleyers, G., Corneille, O., Luminet, O. & Yzerbyt, V. (2007). Aware and (dis)liking: Item-based analyses reveal that valence acquisition via evaluative conditioning emerges only when there is contingency awareness. *Journal of Experimental Psychology: Learning, Memory, and Cognition, 33*, 130–144.

Pomazal, R. J. & Jaccard, J. J. (1976). An informational approach to altruistic behavior. *Journal of Personality and Social Psychology, 33*, 317–326.

Pomerantz, E., Chaiken, S. & Tordesillas, R. S. (1995). Attitude strength and resistance processes. *Journal of Personality and Social Psychology, 69*, 408–419.

Powell, M. C. & Fazio, R. H. (1984). Attitude accessibility as a function of repeated attitudinal expression. *Personality and Social Psychology Bulletin, 10*, 139–148.

Pratkanis, A. R. (1988). The attitude heuristic and selective fact identification. *British Journal of Social Psychology, 27*, 257–263.

Pratkanis, A. R. (1989). The cognitive representation of attitudes. In A. R. Pratkanis, S. J. Breckler & A. G. Greenwald (eds), *Attitude Structure and Function* (pp. 71–98). Hillsdale, NJ: Erlbaum.

Prentice, D. A. & Carlsmith, K. M. (2000). Opinions and personality: On the psychological functions of attitudes and other valued possessions. In G. R. Maio & J. M. Olson (eds), *Why We Evaluate: Functions of Attitudes* (pp. 223–248). Mahwah, NJ: Lawrence Erlbaum Associates.

Prior, M. (2005). News vs. entertainment: How increasing media choice widens gaps in political knowledge and turnout. *American Journal of Political Science, 49*, 577–592.

Prohansky, H. M. (1943). A projective method for the study of attitudes. *Journal of Abnormal and Social Psychology, 38*, 393–395.

Putrevu, S. (2008). Consumer responses toward sexual and nonsexual appeals: The influence of involvement, need for cognition (NFC), and gender. *Journal of Advertising, 37*, 57–69.

Quigley, L., Nelson, A. L., Carriere, J., Smilek, D. & Purdon, C. (2012). The effects of trait and state anxiety on attention to emotional images: An eye-tracking study. *Cognition & Emotion, 26*(8), 1390–1411.

Raden, D. (1985). Strength-related attitude dimensions. *Social Psychology Quarterly, 48*, 312–330.

Reber, R., Schwarz, N. & Winkielman, P. (2004). Processing fluency and aesthetic pleasure: Is beauty in the perceiver's processing experience?. *Personality and Social Psychology Review, 8*, 364–382.

Redker, C. M. & Gibson, B. (2009). Music as an unconditioned stimulus: Positive and negative effects of country music on implicit attitudes, explicit attitudes, and brand choice. *Journal of Applied Social Psychology, 39*, 2689–2705.

Regan, D. T. & Fazio, R. H. (1977). On the consistency between attitudes and behavior: Look to the method of attitude formation. *Journal of Experimental Social Psychology*, *13*, 28–45.

Regan, D. T., Straus, E. & Fazio, R. H. (1974). Liking and the attribution process. *Journal of Experimental Social Psychology*, *10*, 385–397.

Reiter, H. L. (1980). The perils of partisan recall. *Public Opinion Quarterly*, *44*, 385–388.

Richard, R., de Vries, N. K. & van der Pligt, J. (1998). Anticipated regret and precautionary sexual behavior. *Journal of Applied Social Psychology*, *28*, 1411–1428.

Richeson, J. A. & Shelton, J. N. (2003). When prejudice does not pay Effects of interracial contact on executive function. *Psychological Science*, *14*, 287–290.

Rips, L. J. (1998). Reasoning and conversation. *Psychological Review*, *105*, 411–441.

Rivis, A. & Sheeran, P. (2003). Descriptive norms as an additional predictor in the theory of planned behaviour: A meta-analysis. *Current Psychology*, *22*(3), 218–233.

Robinson, R. J. & Friedman, R. A. (1995). Mistrust and misconstrual in union-management relationships: Causal accounts in adversarial contexts. *International Journal of Conflict Management*, *6*, 312–327.

Robinson, R. J., Keltner, D., Ward, A. & Ross, L. (1995). Actual versus assumed differences in construal: 'Naive realism' in intergroup perception and conflict. *Journal of Personality and Social Psychology*, *68*, 404–417.

Roese, N. J. & Jamieson, D. W. (1993). Twenty years of bogus pipeline research: A critical review and meta-analysis. *Psycologica Bulletin*, *114*, 363–375.

Rosenbaum, M. E. (1986). The repulsion hypothesis: On the nondevelopment of relationships. *Journal of Personality and Social Psychology*, *51*, 1156–1166.

Rosenberg, M. J. (1960). An analysis of affective-cognitive consistency. In M. J. Rosenberg, C. I. Hovland, W. J. McGuire, R. P. Abelson & J. W. Brehm (eds), *Attitude Organization and Change* (pp. 15–64). New Haven, CT: Yale University Press.

Rosenberg, M. J. (1965). When dissonance fails: On eliminating evaluation apprehension from attitude measurement. *Journal of Personality and Social Psychology*, *1*(1), 28–42.

Rosenberg, M. J. (1968). Hedonism, inauthenticity, and other goads toward expansion of a consistency theory. In R. P. Abelson, E. Aronson, W. J. McGuire, T. M. Newcomb, M. J. Rosenberg, & P. H. Tannenbaum (eds), *Theories of Cognitive Consistency: A Sourcebook* (pp. 73–111). Chicago, IL: Rand-McNally.

Rosenberg, M. J. & Hovland, C. I. (1960). Cognitive, affective, and behavioral components of attitude. In M. J. Rosenberg, C. I. Hovland, W. J. McGuire, R. P. Abelson & J. W. Brehm (eds), *Attitude Organization and Change* (pp. 1–14). New Haven, CT: Yale University Press.

Rosenthal, R. & Rosnow, R. L. (1991). *Essentials of Behavioral Research* (2nd edn). New York: McGraw-Hill.

Roskos-Ewoldsen, D. R. & Fazio, R. H. (1992). On the orienting value of attitudes: Attitude accessibility as a determinant of an object's attraction of visual attention. *Journal of Personality and Social Psychology, 63*, 198–211.

Roskos-Ewoldsen, D. R. & Fazio, R. H. (2008). On the orienting value of attitudes: Attitude accessibility as a determinant of an attraction of visual attention. In R. H. Fazio & R. E. Petty (eds), *Attitudes: Their Structure, Function, and Consequences* (pp. 357–378). New York: Psychology Press.

Ross, L., Greene, D. & House, P. (1977). The false consensus effect: An egocentric bias in social perception and attribution processes. *Journal of Experimental Social Psychology, 13*, 279–301.

Ross, M. (1989). Relation of implicit theories to the construction of personal histories. *Psychological Review, 96*, 341–357.

Ross, M., McFarland, C. & Fletcher, G. J. (1981). The effect of attitude on the recall of personal histories. *Journal of Personality and Social Psychology, 40*, 627–634.

Saegert, S. C., Swap, W. C. & Zajonc, R. B. (1973). Exposure, context, and interpersonal attraction. *Journal of Personality and Social Psychology, 25*, 234–242.

Sanbonmatsu, D. M. & Fazio, R. H. (1990). The role of attitudes in memory-based decision making. *Journal of Personality and Social Psychology, 59*, 614–622.

Sandberg, T. & Conner, M. (2008). Anticipated regret as an additional predictor in the theory of planned behaviour: A meta-analysis. *British Journal of Social Psychology, 47*, 589–606.

Saucier, D. A. & Miller, C. T. (2003). The persuasiveness of racial arguments as a subtle measure of racism. *Personality and Social Psychology Bulletin, 29*(10), 1303–1315.

Sayre, J. (1939). A comparison of three indices of attitude toward radio advertising. *Journal of Applied Psychology, 23*, 23–33.

Schachter, S. (1951). Deviation, rejection, and communication. *The Journal of Abnormal and Social Psychology, 46*, 190–207.

Schaller, M. (1992). In-group favoritism and statistical reasoning in social inference: Implications for formation and maintenance of group stereotypes. *Journal of Personality and Social Psychology, 63*, 61–74.

Schlosser, A. E. & Shavitt, S. (2009). The effect of perceived message choice on persuasion. *Journal of Consumer Psychology, 19*, 290–301.

Schmitz, F., Teige-Mocigemba, S., Voss, A. & Klauer, K. C. (2013). When scoring algorithms matter: Effects of working memory load on different IAT scores. *British Journal of Social Psychology, 52*, 103–121.

Schnabel, K. & Asendorpf, J. B. (2013). Free associations as a measure of stable implicit attitudes. *European Journal of Personality, 27*, 39–50.

Schuette, R. A. & Fazio, R. H. (1995). Attitude accessibility and motivation as determinants of biased processing: A test of the MODE model. *Personality and Social Psychology Bulletin, 21*, 704–710.

Schul, Y. & Schiff, M. (1993). Measuring satisfaction with organizations: Predictions from information accessibility. *Public Opinion Quarterly, 57,* 536–551.

Schultz, P. W., Nolan, J. M., Cialdini, R. B., Goldstein, N. J. & Griskevicius, V. (2007). The constructive, destructive, and reconstructive power of social norms. *Psychological Science, 18,* 429–434.

Schuman, H. & Converse, J. M. (1971). The effects of black and white interviewers on black responses in 1968. *Public Opinion Quarterly, 35,* 44–68.

Schuman, H. & Presser, S. (1981). *Questions and Answers in Attitude Surveys: Experiments on Question Form, Wording, and Context.* San Diego, CA: Academic Press.

Schwartz, S. H. (1978). Temporal instability as a moderator of the attitude–behavior relationship. *Journal of Personality and Social Psychology 36*(7), 715–724.

Schwarz, N. (1990). Feelings as information: Informational and motivational functions of affective states. In E. T. Higgins & R. Sorrentino (eds), *Handbook of Motivation and Cognition: Foundations of Social Behavior* (Vol. 2, pp. 527–561). New York: Guilford.

Schwarz, N. (2002). Feelings as information: Moods influence judgments and processing strategies. In T. Gilovich, D. Griffin & D. Kahneman (eds), *Heuristics and Biases: The Psychology of Intuitive Judgment* (pp. 534–547). New York: Cambridge University Press.

Schwarz, N. (2007). Attitude construction: Evaluation in context. *Social Cognition, 25,* 638–656.

Schwarz, N. & Bless, H. (1992). Constructing reality and its alternatives: An inclusion/exclusion model of assimilation and contrast effects in social judgment. In L. L. Martin & A. Tesser (eds), *The Construction of Social Judgment* (pp. 217–245). Hillsdale, NJ: Erlbaum.

Schwarz, N. & Bohner, G. (2001). The construction of attitudes. In A. Tesser & N. Schwarz (eds), *Blackwell Handbook of Social Psychology* (Vol. 1: Intraindividual processes, pp. 436–457). Oxford: Blackwell.

Schwarz, N. & Clore, G. L. (1983). Mood, misattribution and judgments of well-being: Informative and directive functions of affective states. *Journal of Personality and Social Psychology, 45,* 513–523.

Schwarz, N. & Clore, G. L. (2007). Feelings and phenomenal experiences. In. A. Kruglanski & E. T. Higgins (eds), *Social Psychology: Handbook of Basic Principles.* New York: Guilford Press.

Schwarz, N., Strack, F., Kommer, D. & Wagner, D. (1987). Soccer, rooms, and the quality of your life: Mood effects on judgments of satisfaction with life in general and with specific domains. *European Journal of Social Psychology, 17,* 69–79.

Schwarz, N. & Sudman, S. (eds). (1992). *Context Effects in Social and Psychological Research.* New York: Springer.

Sears, D. O. & Funk, C. L. (1990). The limited effect of economic self-interest on the political attitudes of the mass public. *Journal of Behavioral Economics, 19,* 247–271.

Sears, D. O. & Funk, C. L. (1999). Evidence of the long-term persistence of adults' political predispositions. *The Journal of Politics, 61*(1), 1–28.

Sechrist, G. B. & Stangor, C. (2001). Perceived consensus influences intergroup behavior and stereotype accessibility. *Journal of Personality and Social Psychology, 80,* 645–654.

Seibt, B., Häfner, M. & Deutsch, R. (2007). Prepared to eat: How immediate affective and motivational responses to food cues are influenced by food deprivation. *European Journal of Social Psychology, 37,* 359–379.

Semin, G. R. & Fiedler, K. (1988). The cognitive functions of linguistic categories in describing persons: Social cognition and language. *Journal of Personality and Social Psychology, 54*(4), 558.

Semin, G. R., Higgins, E. T., de Montes, L. G., Estourget, Y. & Valencia, J. F. (2005). Linguistic signatures of regulatory focus: How abstraction fits promotion more than prevention. *Journal of Personality and Social Psychology, 89,* 36–45.

Sharot, T., Fleming, S. M., Yu, X., Koster, R. & Dolan, R. J. (2012). Is choice-induced preference change long lasting?. *Psychological Science, 23,* 1123–1129.

Shavitt, S. (1989). Operationalizing functional theories of attitude. In A. R. Pratkanis, S. J. Breckler & A. G. (eds), *Attitude Structure and Function* (pp. 311–337). Hillsdale, NJ: Erlbaum.

Shavitt, S. (1990). The role of attitude objects in attitude functions. *Journal of Experimental Social Psychology, 26,* 124–148.

Shavitt, S. & Brock, T. C. (1986). Self-relevant responses in commercial persuasion: Field and experimental tests. In J. Olson & K. Sentis (eds), *Advertising and Consumer Psychology* (pp. 149–171). New York: Praeger.

Shavitt, S. & Fazio, R. H. (1991). Effects of attribute salience on the consistency between attitudes and behavior predictions. *Personality and Social Psychology Bulletin, 17,* 507–516.

Shavitt, S. & Nelson, M. (2002). The role of attitude functions in persuasion and social judgement. In J. P. Dillard & M. W. Pfau (eds), *The Persuasion Handbook: Developments in Theory and Practice* (pp. 137–153). Thousand Oaks, CA: Sage Publications.

Shavitt, S., Swan, S., Lowrey, T. M. & Wänke, M. (1994). The interaction of endorser attractiveness and involvement in persuasion depends on the goal that guides message processing. *Journal of Consumer Psychology, 3,* 137–162.

Shelton, J. N., Richeson, J. A. & Vorauer, J. D. (2006). Threatened identities and interethnic interactions. *European Review of Social Psychology, 17,* 321–358.

Sheppard, B. H., Hartwick, J. & Warshaw, P. R. (1988). The theory of reasoned action: A meta-analysis of past research with recommendations for modifications and future research. *Journal of Consumer Research, 15,* 325–343.

Sherif, M. & Hovland, C. I. (1961). *Social Judgment: Assimilation and Contrast Effects in Communication and Attitude Change.* New Haven, CT: Yale University Press.

Sherman, D. K. & Cohen, G. L. (2002). Accepting threatening information: Self-affirmation and the reduction of defensive biases. *Current Directions in Psychological Science, 11,* 119–123.

Sherman, D. K. & Cohen, G. L. (2006). The psychology of self-defense: Self-affirmation theory. In M. P. Zanna (ed.), *Advances in Experimental Social Psychology* (Vol. 38, pp. 183–242). San Diego, CA: Elsevier Academic Press.

Sia, T. L., Lord, C. G., Blessum, K. A., Ratcliff, C. D. & Lepper, M. R. (1997). Is a rose always a rose? The role of social category exemplar change in attitude stability and attitude–behavior consistency. *Journal of Personality and Social Psychology, 72,* 501–514.

Siemer, M. & Reisenzein, R. (1998). Effects of mood on evaluative judgements: Influence of reduced processing capacity and mood salience. *Cognition and Emotion, 12,* 783–805.

Silvia, P. J. (2006). Reactance and the dynamics of disagreement: Multiple paths from threatened freedom to resistance to persuasion. *European Journal of Social Psychology, 36*(5), 673–685.

Sivacek, J. & Crano, W. D. (1982). Vested interest as a moderator of attitude–behaviour consistency. *Journal of Personality and Social Psychology, 43,* 210–221.

Skinner, B. F. (1957). *Verbal Behavior.* New York: Appleton-Century-Crofts.

Slater, A., Quinn, P. C., Hayes, R. & Brown, E. (2000). The role of facial orientation in newborn infants' preference for attractive faces. *Developmental Science, 3*(2), 181–185.

Smetana, J. G. & Adler, N. E. (1980). Fishbein's valence x expectancy model: An examination of some assumptions. *Personality and Social Psychology Bulletin, 6,* 89–96.

Smith, B. L., Lasswell, H. D. & Casey, R. D. (1946). *Propaganda, Communication, and Public Opinion.* Princeton, NJ: Princeton University Press.

Smith, E. R., Fazio, R. H. & Cejka, M. A. (1996). Accessible attitudes influence categorization of multiply categorizable objects. *Journal of Personality and Social Psychology, 71,* 888–898.

Smith, E. R. & Zarate, M. A. (1992). Exemplar-based model of social judgment. *Psychological Review, 99,* 3–21.

Smith, G. H. (1947). Beliefs in statements labelled fact and rumor. *Journal of Abnormal and Social Psychology, 42,* 80–90.

Smith, M. B., Bruner, J. S. & White, R. W. (1956). *Opinions and Personality.* New York: Wiley.

Smith, N. K., Cacioppo, J. T., Larsen, J. T. & Chartrand, T. L. (2003). May I have your attention, please: Electrocortical responses to positive and negative stimuli. *Neuropsychologia, 41,* 171–183.

Smith, S., Fabrigar, L. & Norris, M. (2008). Reflecting on six decades of selective exposure research: Progress, challenges, and opportunities. *Social and Personality Psychology Compass, 2,* 464–493

Smith, S. M., Fabrigar, L. R., MacDougall, B. L. & Wiesenthal, N. L. (2008). The role of amount, cognitive elaboration, and structural consistency of attitude-relevant knowledge in the formation of attitude certainty. *European Journal of Social Psychology, 38,* 280–295.

Snyder, M. (1974). Self-monitoring of expressive behavior. *Journal of Personality and Social Psychology, 30,* 526–537.

Snyder, M. & DeBono, K. G. (1985). Appeals to images and claims about quality: Understanding the psychology of advertising. *Journal of Personality and Social Psychology, 49,* 586–597.

Snyder, M. & Kendzierski, D. (1982). Acting on one's attitudes: Procedures for linking attitude and behavior. *Journal of Experimental Social Psychology, 18,* 165–183.

Solomon, S., Greenberg, J. & Pyszczynski, T. (2004). The cultural animal: 20 years of terror management research. Greenberg, J., Koole, S. L. & Pyszczynski, T. (eds), *Handbook of Experimental Existential Psychology* (pp. 14–34). New York: Guilford.

Special Eurobarometer 385 (2012). *Publication of the Commission of the European Community.* Brussels.

Spruyt, A., Hermans, D., De Houwer, J., Vandromme, H. & Eelen, P. (2007). On the nature of the affective priming effect: Effects of stimulus onset asynchrony and congruency proportion in naming and evaluative categorization. *Memory & Cognition, 35*(1), 95–106.

Srull, T. K. (1984). Methodological techniques for the study of person memory and social cognition. In R. S. Wyer & T. K. Srull (eds), *Handbook of Social Cognition* (Vol. 2, pp. 1–72). Hillsdale, NJ: Erlbaum.

Staats, A. W. & Staats, C. K. (1958). Attitudes established by classical conditioning. *Journal of Abnormal and Social Psychology, 57,* 37–40.

Staats, C. K. & Staats, A. W. (1957). Meaning established by classical conditioning. *Journal of Experimental Psychology, 54,* 74–80.

Stahl, C., Unkelbach, C. & Corneille, O. (2009). On the respective contributions of awareness of unconditioned stimulus valence and unconditioned stimulus identity in attitude formation through evaluative conditioning. *Journal of Personality and Social Psychology, 97,* 404–420.

Stangor, C., Sechrist, G. B. & Jost, J. T. (2001). Changing racial beliefs by providing consensus information. *Personality and Social Psychology Bulletin, 27,* 486–496.

Stanley, D., Phelps, E. & Banaji, M. (2008). The neural basis of implicit attitudes. *Current Directions in Psychological Science, 17*(2), 164–170.

Steele, C. M. (1988). The psychology of self-affirmation: Sustaining the integrity of the self. *Advances in Experimental Social Psychology, 21,* 261–302.

Steele, C. M. & Liu, T. J. (1983). Dissonance processes as self-affirmation. *Journal of Personality and Social Psychology, 45,* 5–19.

Steffens, M.C. (2004). Is the Implicit Association Test immune to faking? *Experimental Psychology, 51,* 165–179.

Steffens, M. C. & Buchner, A. (2003). Implicit Association Test: Separating transsituationally stable and variable components of attitudes toward gay men. *Experimental Psychology, 50,* 33–48.

Stevens, S. S. (1946). On the theory of scales of measurement. *Science, 103,* 677–680.

Strack, F. (1992). The different routes to social judgments: Experiential versus informational strategies. In L. L. Martin & A. Tesser (eds), *The Construction of Social Judgments* (pp. 249–275). Hillsdale, NJ: Lawrence Erlbaum Associates.

Strack, F. & Deutsch, R. (2004). Reflective and impulsive determinants of social behavior. *Personality and Social Psychology Review, 8,* 220–247.

Strack, F. & Deutsch, R. (2014). The reflective—impulsive model. In J. W. Sherman, B. Gawronski & Y. Trope (eds), *Dual-process Theories of the Social Mind* (pp. 92–104). New York: Guilford Press.

Strack, F., Martin, L. L. & Stepper, S. (1988). Inhibiting and facilitating conditions of the human smile: A nonobtrusive test of the facial feedback hypothesis. *Journal of Personality and Social Psychology, 54,* 768–777.

Strack, F., Schwarz, N., Chassein, B., Kern, D. & Wagner, D. (1990). Salience of comparison standards and the activation of social norms: Consequences for judgements of happiness and their communication. *British Journal of Social Psychology, 29,* 303–314.

Strack, F., Schwarz, N. & Wänke, M. (1991). Semantic and pragmatic aspects of context effects in social and psychological research. *Social Cognition, 9,* 111–125.

Strack, F., Werth, L. & Deutsch, R. (2006). Reflective and impulsive determinants of consumer behavior. *Journal of Consumer Psychology, 16*(3), 205–216.

Sudman, S., Bradburn, N. M. & Schwarz, N. (1996). *Thinking About Answers: The Application of Cognitive Processes to Survey Methodology.* San Francisco, CA: Jossey-Bass.

Sutton, S. (1998). Predicting and explaining intentions and behavior: How well are we doing? *Journal of Applied Social Psychology, 28,* 1317–1338.

Sweeney, P. D. & Gruber, K. L. (1984). Selective exposure: Voter information preferences and the Watergate affair. *Journal of Personality and Social Psychology, 46,* 1208–1221.

Sweldens, S., Corneille, O. & Yzerbyt, V. (2014). The role of awareness in attitude formation through evaluative conditioning. *Personality and Social Psychology Review, 18,* 187–209.

Sweldens, S., Van Osselaer, S. J. & Janiszewski, C. (2010). Evaluative conditioning procedures and the resilience of conditioned brand attitudes. *Journal of Consumer Research, 37,* 473–489.

Taber, C. S. & Lodge, M. (2006). Motivated skepticism in the evaluation of political beliefs. *American Journal of Political Science, 50,* 755–769.

Tajfel, H. (1981). *Human Groups and Social Categories: Studies in Social Psychology.* Cambridge: Cambridge University Press.

Tajfel, H. & Turner, J. (1979). An integrative theory of intergroup conflict. In W. Austin & S. Worchel (eds), *The Social Psychology of Intergrouprelations* (pp. 33–47). Monterey, CA: Broks/Cole.

Tamir, M., Robinson, M. D., Clore, G. L., Martin, L. L. & Whitaker, D. J. (2004). Are we puppets on a string? The contextual meaning of unconscious expressive cues. *Personality and Social Psychology Bulletin, 30,* 237–249.

Teahan, J. E. (1975). A longitudinal study of attitude shifts among black and white police officers. *Journal of Social Issues, 31*(1), 47–56.

Tedeschi, J. T. (1981). *Impression Management.* New York: Academic Press.

Teige-Mocigemba, S., Klauer, K. C. & Sherman, J. W. (2010). Practical guide to Implicit Association Test and related tasks. In B. Gawronski & B. K. Payne (eds), *Handbook of Implicit Social Cognition: Measurement, Theory, and Applications* (pp. 117–139). New York: Guildford Press..

Tesser, A. (1978). Self-generated attitude change. *Advances in Experimental Social Psychology, 11,* 289–338.

Tesser, A. (1993). The importance of heritability in psychological research: The case of attitudes. *Psychological Review, 100,* 129–142.

Tesser, A. & Martin, L. L. (1996). The psychology of evaluation. In E. T. Higgins & A. W. Kruglanski (eds), *Social Psychology: Handbook of Basic Principles* (pp. 400–432). New York: Guilford.

Tesser, A. & Shaffer, D. R. (1990). Attitudes and attitude change. In M. R. Rosenzweig & L. W. Porter (eds), *Annual Review of Psychology* (Vol. 41, pp. 479–523). Palo Alto, CA: Annual Reviews.

Thistlethwaite, D. L. (1950). Attitude and structure as factors in the distortion of reasoning. *Journal of Abnormal and Social Psychology, 45,* 442–458.

Thompson, L. (1995). 'They saw a negotiation': Partisanship and involvement. *Journal of Personality and Social Psychology, 68,* 839–853.

Thurstone, L. L. (1931). The measurement of social attitudes. *The Journal of Abnormal and Social Psychology, 26,* 249–269.

Tooby, J. & Cosmides, L. (2005). Conceptual foundations of evolutionary psychology. In D. M. Buss (ed.), *The Handbook of Evolutionary Psychology* (pp. 5–67). Hoboken, NJ: Wiley.

Tormala, Z. L. & Petty, R. E. (2004). Resistance to persuasion and attitude certainty: The moderating role of elaboration. *Personality and Social Psychology Bulletin, 30,* 1446–1457.

Tormala, Z. L., Briñol, P. & Petty, R. E. (2006). When credibility attacks: The reverse impact of source credibility on persuasion. *Journal of Experimental Social Psychology, 42,* 684–691.

Tormala, Z. L., Briñol, P. & Petty, R. E. (2007). Multiple roles for source credibility under high elaboration: It's all in the timing. *Social Cognition, 25,* 536–552.

Tormala, Z. L., Clarkson, J. J. & Petty, R. E. (2006). Resisting persuasion by the skin of one's teeth: The hidden success of resisted persuasive messages. *Journal of Personality and Social Psychology, 91,* 423–435.

Tormala, Z. L. & Rucker, D. D. (2007). Attitude certainty: A review of past findings and emerging perspectives. *Social and Personality Psychology Compass, 1,* 469–492.

Tougas, F., Brown, R., Beaton, A. M. & Joly, S. (1995). Neosexism: Plus ça change, plus c'est pareil. *Personality and Social Psychology Bulletin, 21,* 842–849.

Tourangeau, R. & Rasinski, K. A. (1988). Cognitive processes underlying context effects in attitude measurement. *Psychological Bulletin, 103,* 299–314.

Tourangeau, R., Rasinski, K. A., Bradburn, N. M. & D'Andrade, R. (1989). Belief accessibility and context effects in attitude measurement. *Journal of Experimental Social Psychology, 25,* 401–421.

Triandis, H. C. (1980). Values, attitudes, and interpersonal behavior. In H. E. Howe, Jr & M. M. Page (eds), *Nebraska Symposium on Motivation 1979* (pp. 195–259). Lincoln, NE: University of Nebraska Press.

Triandis, H.C. (1994). *Culture and Social Behaviour.* New York: McGraw-Hill.

Triandis, H. C. & Suh, E. M. (2002). Cultural influences on personality. *Annual Review of Psychology, 53,* 133–160.

Trope, Y. & Liberman, N. (2000). Temporal construal and time-dependent changes in preference. *Journal of Personality and Social Psychology, 79,* 876–889.

Trope, Y. & Liberman, N. (2003). Temporal construal. *Psychological Review, 110,* 403–421.

Trope, Y. & Liberman, N. (2010). Construal-level theory of psychological distance. *Psychological Review, 117,* 440–463.

Unkelbach, C. & Greifender, R. (2013). *The Experience of Thinking: How the Fluency of Mental Processes Influences Cognition and Behaviour.* New York: Psychology Press.

Valins, S. (1966). Cognitive effects of false heart-rate feedback. *Journal of Personality and Social Psychology, 4,* 400–408.

Vallacher, R. R. (2015). From choice to gridlock: Dynamic bases of constructive versus dysfunctional political process. In J. P. Forgas, K. Fiedler, W. D. Crano, J. P. Forgas, K. Fiedler, W. D. Crano (Eds.), *Social psychology and politics* (pp. 209–226). New York: Psychology Press.

Vallacher, R. R. & Nowak, A. (2007). Dynamical social psychology: Finding order in the flow of human experience. In A. W. Kruglanski and E. T. Higgins (eds), *Social Psychology: Handbook of Basic Principles* (2nd edn; pp. 734–758). New York: Guilford Press.

Vallone, R. P., Ross, L. & Lepper, M. R. (1985). The hostile media phenomenon: Biased perception and perceptions of media bias in coverage of the Beirut massacre. *Journal of Personality and Social Psychology, 49,* 577–585.

Van Bavel, J. J., Xiao, Y. J. & Cunningham, W. A. (2012). Evaluation is a dynamic process: Moving beyond dual system models. *Social and Personality Psychology Compass, 6,* 438–454.

Van Boven, L. (2000). Pluralistic ignorance and political correctness: The case of affirmative action. *Political Psychology, 21,* 267–276.

Van den Bergh, O., Vrana, S. & Eelen, P. (1990). Letters from the heart: Affective categorization of letter combinations in typists and nontypists. *Journal of Experimental Psychology: Learning, Memory, and Cognition, 16,* 1153–1161.

Van Eerde, W. (2000). Procrastination: Self-regulation in initiating aversive goals. *Applied Psychology: An International Review, 49*(3), 372–389.

Van Harreveld, F., Rutjens, B. T., Rotteveel, M., Nordgren, L. F. & van der Pligt, J. (2009). Ambivalence and decisional conflict as a cause of psychological discomfort: Feeling tense before jumping off the fence. *Journal of Experimental Social Psychology*, 45, 167–173.

Van Veen, V., Krug, M. K., Schooler, J. W. & Carter, C. S. (2009). Neural activity predicts attitude change in cognitive dissonance. *Nature Neuroscience*, 12, 1469–1474.

Vargas, P. T., Sekaquaptewa, D. & von Hippel, W. (2004). It's not just what you think, it's also how you think: Prejudice as biased information processing. In J. D. Williams, W. Lee & C. P. Haugtvedt (eds), *Diversity in Advertising: Broadening the Scope of Research Directions* (pp. 93–119). Mahwah, NJ: Lawrence Erlbaum Associates.

Vargas, P. T., Sekaquaptewa, D. & von Hippel, W. (2007). Armed only with paper and pencil: 'Low-tech' measures of implicit attitudes. In B. Wittenbrink & N. Schwarz (eds), *Implicit Measures of Attitudes* (pp. 103–124). New York: Guilford Press.

Vargas, P. T., Von Hippel, W. & Petty, R. E. (2004). Using partially structured attitude measures to enhance the attitude–behaviour relationship. *Personality and Social Psychology Bulletin*, 30(2), 197–211.

Verhulst, B., Eaves, L. J. & Hatemi, P. K. (2012). Causation not correlation: The relationship between personality traits and political ideologies, *American Journal of Political Science*, 56, 34–51.

Verhulst, B., Hatemi, P. K. & Eaves, L. J. (2009). Personality traits and political ideologies. Paper presented at the 39th annual meeting of the Behavior Genetics Association, Minneapolis, MN, 17–20 June.

Verhulst, B., Hatemi, P. K. & Eaves, L. J. (2012). Disentangling the importance of psychological predispositions and social constructions in the organization of American political ideology. *Political Psychology*, 33(3), 375–393.

Verhulst, B., Hatemi, P. K. & Martin, N. G. (2010). The nature of the relationship between personality traits and political attitudes. *Personality and Individual Differences*, 49, 306–316.

Vinokur, A. & Burnstein, E. (1978). Novel argumentation and attitude change: The case of polarization following group discussion. *European Journal of Social Psychology*, 8(3), 335–348.

Vogel, T., Kutzner, F., Fiedler, K. & Freytag, P. (2010). Exploiting attractiveness in persuasion: Senders' implicit theories about receivers' processing motivation. *Personality and Social Psychology Bulletin*, 36, 830–842.

Vogel, T., Kutzner, F., Fiedler, K., & Freytag, P. (2013). How majorities become associated with rare attributes: Ecological correlations in stereotype formation. *Social Cognition*, 31, 427–442.

Vogel, T., Kutzner, F., Freytag, P. & Fiedler, K. (2014). Inferring correlations: From exemplars to categories. *Psychonomic Bulletin & Review*, 21, 1316–1322.

Von Hippel, W., Sekaquaptewa, D. & Vargas, P. (1997). The linguistic intergroup bias as an implicit indicator of prejudice. *Journal of Experimental Social Psychology*, 33(5), 490–509.

Wagner, B. C. & Petty, R. E. (2011). The elaboration likelihood model of persuasion: Thoughtful and non-thoughtful social influence. In D. Chadee (ed.), *Theories in Social Psychology* (pp. 96–116). Hoboken, NJ: Wiley-Blackwell.

Wallace, D. S., Paulson, R. M., Lord, C. G. & Bond, C. J. (2005). Which behaviors do attitudes predict? Meta-analyzing the effects of social pressure and perceived difficulty. *Review of General Psychology*, 9, 214–227.

Walther, E. (2002). Guilty by mere association: Evaluative conditioning and the spreading attitude effect. *Journal of Personality and Social Psychology*, 82, 919–934.

Walther, E., Gawronski, B., Blank, H. & Langer, T. (2009). Changing likes and dislikes through the back door: The US-revaluation effect. *Cognition and Emotion*, 23, 889–917.

Walther, E. & Nagengast, B. (2006). Evaluative conditioning and the awareness issue: Assessing contingency awareness with the Four-Picture Recognition Test. *Journal of Experimental Psychology: Animal Behavior Processes*, 32, 454–459.

Walther, E., Weil, R. & Langer, T. (2011). Why do we like the iPhone? The role of evaluative conditioning in attitude formation. *Social and Personality Psychology Compass*, 5, 473–486.

Wang, X. (2011). The role of anticipated guilt in intentions to register as organ donors and to discuss organ donation with family. *Health Communication*, 26(8), 683–690.

Wang, X. (2012). The role of attitude functions and self-monitoring in predicting intentions to register as organ donors and to discuss organ donation with family. *Communication Research*, 39, 26–47.

Wänke, M. (1997). Making context effects work for you: Suggestions for improving data quality from a construal perspective. *International Journal of Public Opinion Research*, 9, 266–276.

Wänke, M. (2007). What is said and what is meant: Conversational implicatures in natural conversations, research settings, media, and advertising. In K. Fiedler (ed.), *Social Communication* (pp. 223–255). New York: Psychology Press.

Wänke, M. (2013). Almost everything you always wanted to know about ease-of-retrieval effects. In C. Unkelbach & R. Greifender (eds), *The Experience of Thinking: How the Fluency of Mental Processes Influences Cognition and Behaviour* (pp. 151–169). New York: Psychology Press.

Wänke, M., Bless, H. & Igou, E. R. (2001). Next to a star: Paling, shining, or both? Turning interexemplar contrast into interexemplar assimilation. *Personality and Social Psychology Bulletin*, 27, 14–29.

Wänke, M., Bohner, G. & Jurkowitsch, A. (1997). There are many reasons to drive a BMW: Does imagined ease of argument generation influence attitudes? *Journal of Consumer Research*, 24, 170–177.

Wänke, M. & Hansen, J. (2015). Relative processing fluency. *Current Direction in Psychological Science*, 24(3), 195–199.

Wänke, M. & Reutner, L. (2010). Pragmatic Persuasion or the Persuasion Paradox. In J. Forgas, W. Crano & J. Cooper (eds), *The Psychology of Attittudes* and *Attitude Change* (pp. 183–198). New York: Psychology Press.

Wänke, M. & Schwarz, N. (1997). Reducing question order effects: The role of buffer items. In L. Lyberg, P. Biemer, M. Collins, E. DeLeeuw, C. Dippo & N. Schwarz (eds), *Survey Measurement and Process Quality* (pp. 115–140). Chichester, UK: Wiley.

Warner, S. L. (1965). Randomized response: A survey technique for eliminating evasive answer bias. *Journal of the American Statistical Association, 60*(309), 63–69.

Webb, E. J., Campbell, D. T., Schwartz, R. D., Sechrest, L. & Grove, J. B. (1981). *Nonreactive Measures in the Social Sciences* (2nd edn). Boston, MA: Houghton Mifflin.

Webb, T. L. & Sheeran, P. (2006). Does changing behavioral intentions engender behavior change? A meta-analysis of the experimental evidence. *Psychological Bulletin, 132*(2), 249.

Wegener, D. T. & Petty, R. E. (1997). The flexible correction model: The role of naive theories of bias in bias correction. *Advances in Experimental Social Psychology, 29*, 141–208.

Wegener, D. T., Petty, R. E. & Smith, S. M. (1995). Positive mood can increase or decrease message scrutiny: The hedonic contingency view of mood and message processing. *Journal of Personality and Social Psychology, 69*, 5–15.

Weigel, R. H. & Newman, L. S. (1976). Increasing attitude–behavior correspondence by broadening the scope of the behavioral measure. *Journal of Personality and Social Psychology, 33*, 793–802.

Wells, G. L. & Petty, R. E. (1980). The effects of overt head movements on persuasion: Compatibility and incompatibility of responses. *Basic and Applied Social Psychology, 1*, 219–230.

Wennekers, A. M., Holland, R. W., Wigboldus, D. J. & van Knippenberg, A. (2012). First see, then nod: The role of temporal contiguity in embodied evaluative conditioning of social attitudes. *Social Psychological and Personality Science, 3*, 455–461.

Werth, L. & Förster, J. (2007). How regulatory focus influences consumer behavior. *European Journal of Social Psychology, 37*(1), 33–51.

Wickens, D. D. (1959). Conditioning to complex stimuli. *American Psychologist, 14*, 180–188.

Wicker, A. W. (1969). Attitude versus action: The relationship of verbal and overt behavioral responses to attitude objects. *Journal of Social Issues, 25(4)*, 41–78.

Wiley, J. (2005). A fair and balanced look at the news: What affects memory for controversial arguments?. *Journal of Memory and Language, 53*, 95–109.

Wilson, D. T., Mathews, H. L. & Harvey, J. W. (1975). An empirical test of the Fishbein intention model. *Journal of Consumer Research, 1*, 39–48.

Wilson, T. D. & Dunn, D. S. (1986). Effects of introspection on attitude-behaviour consistency: Analyzing reasons versus focusing on feelings. *Journal of Experimental Social Psychology, 22*, 249–263.

Wilson, T. D., Dunn, D. S., Bybee, J. A., Hyman, D. B. & Rotondo, J. A. (1984). Effects of analyzing reasons on attitude–behavior consistency. *Journal of Personality and Social Psychology, 47*, 5–16.

Wilson, T. D., Dunn, D. S., Kraft, D. & Lisle, D. J. (1989). Introspection, attitude change, and attitude–behaviour consistency: The disruptive effects of explaining why we feel the way we do. *Advances in Experimental Social Psychology, 22*, 287–343.

Wilson, T. D. & Hodges, S. D. (1992). Attitudes as temporary constructions. In L. L. Martin & A. Tesser (eds), *The Construction of Social Judgments* (pp. 37–65). Hillsdale, NJ: Erlbaum.

Wilson, T. D., Lindsey, S. & Schooler, T. Y. (2000). A model of dual attitudes. *Psychological Review, 107*, 101–126.

Wilson, T. D., Lisle, D. J. & Kraft, D. (1990). Effects of self-reflection on attitudes and consumer decisions. *Advances in Consumer Research, 17*, 79–85.

Winkielman, P. & Cacioppo, J. T. (2001). Mind at ease puts a smile on the face: Psychophysiological evidence that processing facilitation elicits positive affect. *Journal of Personality and Social Psychology, 81*(6), 989–1000.

Winkielman, P., Halberstadt, J., Fazendeiro, T. & Catty, S. (2006). Prototypes are attractive because they are easy on the mind. *Psychological Science, 17*, 799–806.

Winston, S. (1932). Birth control and the sex-ratio at birth. *American Journal of Sociology, 38*, 225–231.

Wittenbrink, B., Judd, C. M. & Park, B. (2001). Spontaneous prejudice in context: Variability in automatically activated attitudes. *Journal of Personality and Social Psychology, 81*(5), 815–827.

Wolff, K., Nordin, K., Brun, W., Berglund, G. & Kvale, G. (2011). Affective and cognitive attitudes, uncertainty avoidance and intention to obtain genetic testing: An extension of the theory of planned behaviour. *Psychology & Health, 26*, 1143–1155.

Wood, M. M. (2007). Rethinking the inoculation analogy: Effects on subjects with differing preexisting attitudes. *Human Communication Research, 33*, 357–378.

Wood, W., Lundgren, S., Ouellette, J. A., Busceme, S. & Blackstone, T. (1994). Minority influence: A meta-analytic review of social influence processes. *Psychological Bulletin, 115*, 323–345.

Wood, W. & Quinn, J. M. (2003). Forewarned and forearmed? Two meta-analysis syntheses of forewarnings of influence appeals. *Psychological Bulletin, 129*(1), 119.

Worchel, S. & Arnold, S. E. (1973). The effects of censorship and attractiveness of the censor on attitude change. *Journal of Experimental Social Psychoogy, 9*, 365–377.

Worchel, S. & Brehm, J. W. (1971). Direct and implied social restoration of freedom. *Journal of Personality and Social Psychology, 18*, 294–304.

Worth, L. T. & Mackie, D. M. (1987). Cognitive mediation of positive affect in persuasion. *Social Cognition, 5*, 76–94.

Wright, P., Friestad, M. Boush, D. M. (2005). The development of marketplace persuasion knowledge in children, adolescents, and young adults. *Journal of Public Policy & Marketing, 24*(2), 222–233.

Wright, R. A. (1986). Attitude change as a function of threat to attitudinal freedom and extent of agreement with a communicator. *European Journal of Social Psychology, 16,* 43–50.

right, S., Manolis, C., Brown, D., Guo, X., Dinsmore, J., Chiu, C. P. & Kardes, F. R. (2012). Construal-level mind-sets and the perceived validity of marketing claims. *Marketing Letters, 23*(1), 253–261.

Wyer, R. S., Jr (2007). Principles of mental representation. In A. W. Kruglanski & E. T.Higgins (eds), *Social Psychology: Handbook of Basic Principles* (2nd edn, pp. 285–307). New York: Guilford Press

Wyer, R. J. & Srull, T. K. (1989). *Memory and Cognition in its Social Context.* Hillsdale, NJ: Erlbaum.

Yeung, C. M. & Wyer, R. J. (2004). Affect, appraisal, and consumer judgment. *Journal of Consumer Research, 31*(2), 412–424.

Young, A. I., Ratner, K. G. & Fazio, R. H. (2014). Political attitudes bias the mental representation of a presidential candidate's face. *Psychological Science, 25*(2), 503–510.

Zajonc, R. B. (1968). Attitudinal effects of mere exposure. *Journal of Personality and Social Psychology Monograph Supplement, 9* (2, Pt 2), 1–27.

Zajonc, R. B., Murphy, S. T. & Inglehart, M. (1989). Feeling and facial efference: Implications of the vascular theory of emotion. *Psychological Review, 96,* 395–416.

Zanna, M. P. & Cooper, J. (1974). Dissonance and the pill: An attribution approach to studying the arousal properties of dissonance. *Journal of Personality and Social Psychology, 29,* 703–709.

Zanna, M. P. & Fazio, R. H. (1982). The attitude–behaviour relation: Moving toward a third generation of research. In M. P. Zanna, E. T. Higgins & C. P. Herman (eds), *Consistency in Social Behavior: The Ontario Symposium* (Vol. 2, pp. 283–301). Hillsdale, NJ: Erlbaum.

Zanon, R., De Houwer, J., Gast, A. & Smith, C. T. (2014). When does relational information influence evaluative conditioning?. *The Quarterly Journal of Experimental Psychology, 67*(11), 2105–2122.

Zhong, S., Israel, S., Xue, H., Ebstein, R. P. & Chew, S. H. (2009). Monoamine oxidase A gene (MAOA) associated with attitude towards longshot risks. *PLoS One, 4,* e8516.

Zotev, V., Krueger, F., Phillips, R., Alvarez, R. P., Simmons, W. K., Bellgowan, P., Drevets, W. C. & Bodurka, J. (2011). Self-regulation of amygdala activation using real-time fMRI neurofeedback. *PLoS One, 6*(9), e24522.

Zyphur, M. J., Narayanan, J., Arvey, R. D. & Alexander, G. J. (2009). The genetics of economic risk preferences. *Journal of Behavioral Decision Making, 22,* 367–377.

Author index

Subject index